Centering on the examination of the social and legal context of adultery, homosexuality, impiety, and the public–private dichotomy in Athenian society, this book attempts to examine the problems of social control and the regulation of sexuality in a way that will be of interest to a broad readership. It uses a comparative approach to show how the examination of such issues can deepen our understanding of classical Athens, particularly in regard to the role of law in society. Further, it argues that this historical investigation can, in turn, enrich our general appreciation of the relation of social and legal norms, and the roles they play in regulating complex social practices, like those associated with sexuality, morals, and the family. In this regard, the argument aims at moving beyond a view of social control as implemented through a legal order which somehow 'imposes' its norms upon society, coercing individuals into patterns of deviance and conformity. Instead, it develops a view of classical Athenian society which emphasizes the study of social control as the dynamic interplay of legal and social norms *within* the context of ideology and practice.

This book will be of interest to a wide readership: classicists and ancient historians, lawyers, social theorists, historical sociologists, anthropologists, and cultural and social historians.

LAW, SEXUALITY, AND SOCIETY

LAW, SEXUALITY, AND SOCIETY

The enforcement of morals in classical Athens

DAVID COHEN

*Department of Rhetoric, University of California,
Berkeley*

CAMBRIDGE
UNIVERSITY PRESS

31697062

311-97

Published by the Press Syndicate of the University of Cambridge
The Pitt Building, Trumpington Street, Cambridge CB2 1RP
40 West 20th Street, New York, NY10011-4211, USA
10 Stamford Road, Oakleigh, Melbourne 3166, Australia

© Cambridge University Press 1991

First published 1991
Reprinted 1992
First paperback edition 1994
Reprinted 1994

Printed in Great Britain by Athenæum Press Ltd, Gateshead, Tyne & Wear

British Library cataloguing in publication data

Cohen, David
Law, sexuality, and society: The enforcement of morals in
classical Athens.
1. Greece. Athens. Law, ancient period
I. Title
343.85

Library of Congress cataloguing in publication data

Cohen, David, (David. J.)
Law, sexuality, and society: the enforcement of morals in
classical Athens/David Cohen.
p.   cm.
Includes bibliographical references and index.
ISBN 0 521 37447 2
1. Sexual ethics – Greece – Athens – History.   2. Sex and law –
Greece – Athens – History.   1. Title
HQ32.c64   1991
306.7'09495'12 – dc20   90-25932

ISBN 0 521 37447 2 hardback
ISBN 0 521 46642 3 paperback

UP

To D.D. and A.C.

Contents

Preface   *page* xi

1   Introduction   1
2   Models and methods I   14
3   Models and methods II   35
4   Public and private in classical Athens   70
5   The law of adultery   98
6   Adultery, women, and social control   133
7   Law, social control, and homosexuality in classical
    Athens   171
8   The prosecution of impiety in Athenian law   203
9   The enforcement of morals   218

Bibliography   241
Index   257

ix

Preface

This book represents an attempt to examine the problems of social control and the regulation of sexuality in an ancient society in a way that will be of interest to a broad audience. I have tried to show how a comparative approach to such issues can help to deepen our understanding of classical Athens, particularly in regard to the role of law in society. Further, I argue that this historical investigation can enrich our general appreciation of the relation of social and legal norms and the role they play in regulating complex social practices, like those associated with sexuality. In this regard, the argument aims at moving beyond a view of social control as implemented through a legal order which somehow imposes its norms upon society, coercing individuals into patterns of deviance and conformity. Instead, I develop an interpretation centered upon the study of social control as the dynamic interplay of legal and social norms *within* the context of ideology and practice.

In the past five years in which this study has emerged, friends and colleagues have contributed to its completion in a number of ways. Peter Garnsey, John Crook, Calum Carmichael, Tony Long, Felipe Gutterriez, and Stanley Brandes offered valuable comments on individual chapters. Herbert Morris, David Lieberman, Gregory Vlastos, Wolfgang Naucke, and Keith Hopkins have read significant parts of the manuscript and helped me to see it better as a whole. Further, Richard Saller was kind enough to read through the entire final version. Dieter Nörr and Dieter Simon provided me with the outstanding facilities of the Leopold Wenger Institut in Munich and the Max Planck Institut für Europäische Rechtsgeschichte in Frankfurt for eight months in 1987, during which the bulk of this study was written. Apart from their unfailing kindness and hospitality, both of these scholars also contributed significantly to my understanding of important issues. I also owe two further special debts of gratitude. The first is to David Daube for his continuing support, and patience with an unruly pupil. The second is to Moses Finley, who read early versions of several chapters before his death, and, as always, offered searching criticisms that were important in shaping my approach.

I am also grateful to the Alexander von Humbolt Stiftung and the American Bar Foundation for their generous support of my sabbatical research. John McVitty and Patricia Reilly provided invaluable help in proof-reading and checking references.

David Cohen
Berkeley

CHAPTER I

Introduction

As it is clear from Divine Scripture that our omnipotent God, detesting the sin of sodomy and wishing to demonstrate that fact, brought down his wrath upon the cities of Sodom and Gomorrah and soon thereafter flooded and destroyed the whole world for such horrible sins, our most honorable ancestors sought with their laws and efforts to liberate our city from such a dangerous divine judgment.

Sec. 8.1–212 (1981) Crimes against nature...If any person shall carnally know in any manner any brute animal, or carnally know any male or female person by the anus or by or with the mouth, or voluntarily submit to such carnal knowledge, he or she shall be guilty of a felony and shall be confined in the penitentiary not less than one year nor more than three years.

Sec. 16-6-2 (1984)...(a) A person commits the offense of sodomy when he performs or submits to any sexual act involving the sex organs of one person and the mouth or anus of another...(b) A person convicted of the offense of sodomy shall be punished by imprisonment for not less than one nor more than 20 years...

Unlike the first text, a Decree of the Council of Ten of Venice in 1458,[1] the latter two provisions are not quaint relics of medieval law, but sections from the current Criminal Codes of the states of Virginia and Georgia (26 States have such legislation). In 1986 the United States Supreme Court declared them constitutional exercises "of the legislative authority of the state."[2] The Court noted that law is

---

[1] Quoted in Ruggiero (1985: 109).

[2] *Bowers* v. *Hardwick* (1986: 2847), Burger C. J. concurring. *Bowers* upheld the Georgia statute, noting that, "The law...is constantly based on notions of morality, and if all laws representing essentially moral choices are to be invalidated under the Due Process Clause, the courts will be very busy indeed (2846)." The Court placed great weight upon the fact that 25 States had sodomy statutes similar to the one challenged in *Bowers*. The Virginia

I

"constantly based on notions of morality,"[3] indicating that in contemporary America the question of whether or not "the states have an interest in regulating private morality sufficient to override a right to privacy"[4] still plays a central role in determining the limits of individual liberty. Conceptions of justice which can tolerate such legislation are not confined to American jurisprudence. In Britain, recent decisions have asserted a traditional power of the courts to regulate immorality even in the absence of legislation or judicial rulings defining the conduct in question as illegal. As Lord Morris of Borth-y-Gest put it in upholding the conviction of a man who published a directory of London prostitutes,

> ...the law is not impotent to convict those who conspire to corrupt public morals...There are certain manifestations of conduct which are an affront to and an attack upon recognised public standards of morals and decency, and which all well-disposed persons would stigmatise and condemn as deserving of punishment.[5]

Such decisions threaten to dissolve the distinction between public and private spheres, which, in the western tradition since Kant, has defined the limits of permissible state intervention into the lives of citizens. More specifically, these cases pose the question of the justification of punishing immorality as such, of imprisoning citizens for consensual, non-violent, but unorthodox, sexual acts or other kinds of purported immorality. By what right can a secular state use the coercive force of the criminal law to regulate such behavior? Does it follow that, because "all well-disposed persons" would condemn an immoral act, or find it offensive, that it ought to be punished?[6] To what extent is it proper for a community or state to establish standards of orthodoxy for moral conduct? What realms of

---

statute was summarily affirmed by the Supreme Court in 1976 in *Doe* v. *Commonwealth's Attorney*, 425 U.S. 901. For an analysis of these cases see Fuller (1985); also Note, *Miami Law Review* (1985).   [3] *Bowers* (1986: 2846).

[4] Note, *Miami Law Review* (1986: 637). Since the landmark case of *Griswold* v. *Connecticut* in 1965, the issues of a right to privacy and the valid scope of state power to regulate private morality have been among the most controversial and dynamic in American constitutional law and jurisprudence. Chapters 4 and 8 will briefly take up *Griswold* and its aftermath.

[5] *Shaw* v. *Director of Public Prosecutions*, House of Lords (1961) A.C. 220. The principle of Shaw was affirmed in *Knuller* v. *Director of Public Prosecutions* (1973). There is, of course, extensive jurisprudential commentary on *Shaw*, e.g. Hart (1963), Devlin (1965).

[6] As the dissenting opinion of Blackmun J. in *Bowers* puts it, "'...mere public intolerance or animosity cannot constitutionally justify the deprivation of a person's liberty'" (quoting *O'Connor* v. *Donaldson*, 422 U.S. 563, 575). As in *Shaw*, the *Bowers* majority apparently did not find such arguments persuasive.

behavior, if any, should remain immune in principle from regulation, and why should they enjoy such immunity? Such questions lie at the heart of the problem of the enforcement of morals.

In the Anglo-American world, discussion of such issues has taken place within a framework largely defined by the liberal tradition. Since the classic nineteenth-century debate between J. S. Mill and J. F. Stephen, philosophers and jurists have debated the legitimacy of imposing punishment on individuals who engage in "immoral" conduct such as prostitution, homosexuality, sodomy, fornication, or adultery. From the historical perspective, this process represents the attempts of an increasingly secular society to decide what classes of activities condemned by ecclesiastical authority were also to be regulated by the state. This ecclesiastical heritage, as the French philosopher and legal historian Pierre Legendre has shown, attempted to construct juristically an ideal morality, avowedly divorced from the social facts of actual human relations, and impose it as a system through instruments like ecclesiastical law and the confessional. It is largely this legal and theological historical experience which causes us to think of the "enforcement of morals" as an imposition of moral principles through the coercive power of the law.

Because this intellectual heritage has formed our very way of defining what the issues are, it has, for the most part, gone unchallenged. Both sides of the debate about enforcing morals accept that the law *can* impose a morality on a given society, even when that morality bears little relation to actual social practices. Further, both sides evince little interest in the empirical realities of moral values or behavior as expressed in the social practices of the society in question. Instead, one typically makes assumptions based upon vague generalizations about "community standards," "the average citizen," "all decent persons," or "the legislator as representative of the community." In Britain, Lord Devlin and Lord Morris could assert with assurance that all decent persons despised prostitution or homosexuality as immoral, yet both were surely aware that they themselves were members of a social class which, in its behavior, condones the discreet exercise of these practices. Likewise, the massive failure of American attempts to regulate or eradicate prostitution, homosexuality, or the use of marijuana or cocaine through the criminal law, bears witness to the necessity for rethinking such assumptions.

This study departs from traditional treatments in suggesting that law cannot "enforce" morality. In fact, the more the moral standards embodied in the law diverge from social practice the less influence law is likely to have. The law can imprison a few prostitutes but it cannot eradicate prostitution in a society which supports it. The law can impose suffering upon a few individuals, but it cannot change or "preserve" the moral order of a society. The "morality" the law "enforces" is only one part of the normative order of the society as embodied in its practices and its understanding of itself. In America these clearly tolerate discreet forms of prostitution, drug use, homosexuality, and other acts outlawed by American sodomy statutes,[7] in complicated and contradictory patterns that only a more differentiated methodology can adequately describe. Similarly, to explain the way an ancient society evaluated, regulated, or censured immoral activities, the historian must look beyond the proscriptions embodied in legal statutes.

This book does not propose yet another abstract jurisprudential definition of privacy or of the legitimate limits of state enforcement of morality. Nor does it explore the philosophical basis of claims about rights to sexual autonomy and privacy.[8] Instead, I shall argue that the kinds of questions enumerated above should not and cannot be answered in a purely juristic framework. Thus I shall attempt to analyze the concrete ways in which Athenian society actually defined and "enforced" norms relating to unorthodox sexual and religious behavior. In examining the interplay of systems of social and legal norms, and their relationship to political ideology in a particular historical setting, I aim at contributing to our understanding of how the moral structures of a society are actually reproduced.[9] Further, studying the way in which a culture defines what is deviant or abnormal reveals the conceptions of normalcy which underlie such definitions. But this study is not designed either

---

[7] Since Kinsey, the discrepancy in America between "official" views of immorality and moral standards as reflected in actual sexual practices has been clear.

[8] It is beyond the scope of this book to attempt to advance the vast philosophical discussion on privacy. Scholars like David Richards have done much to clarify the complicated issues in this area, and the brief discussion of these philosophical questions in Chapter 4 relies upon their efforts. This study can only contribute to the philosophical discussion by pointing to certain dimensions of social life which philosophers sometimes ignore. For a recent survey of the literature see Parent (1983a).

[9] The word "reproduction" is preferable to "enforcement" because "enforcement" tends to imply a model of externally imposed order. The shortcomings of such an approach are set out in Chapter 2, which also explains what it means to "reproduce" a system of norms.

as a "historical survey" of legal or philosophical ideas about the enforcement of morals, or as an antiquarian description of "how the Greeks did it." Rather, it is an exercise in historical legal sociology. It aims at explaining why Athenian law and society marked certain forms of sexual and religious behavior as deviant, how this deviance was regulated and/or punished, and how this process, taken as a whole, relates to the democratic ideology which dominated Athens during most of the classical period. It shows how modern theory can help illuminate the past, and, in turn, how this understanding of another culture can enrich our theoretical perspective.

Although western societies provide the examples mentioned above,[10] the issue of the legal enforcement of morality arises wherever there is a formal institutionalized differentiation[11] of legal norms. That is, the content of the valid legal norms and the patterns of their enforcement represent a conscious or unconscious decision as to which areas of social and moral life the law will regulate. Nearly all legal cultures punish certain categories of violent moral wrongdoing like murder, assault, robbery, rape, or arson. As Demosthenes explained to an Athenian jury, such acts, because of their inherent violence, represent offenses against the whole community.[12] Very few societies apply sanctions to immoral conduct like lying (outside of certain categories of economic relations), betrayal of friendship, non-physical cruelty, and so on. Sexuality, on the other hand, is perhaps the area where one finds the greatest cross-cultural divergence in patterns of legal enforcement of societal norms.[13] In the ancient world, for example, most Near Eastern legal codes prohibit a wide range of sexual activities (e.g. incest, bestiality,

---

[10] For the different way in which, for example, German legal scholars approach issues of law and morals, see the excellent survey by Geddert (1984), and the collection of essays edited by Drier (1983).

[11] See Luhmann (1972: 217ff.) on "Ausdifferenzierung."

[12] Demosthenes 21.44–5. Of course in some societies one or another of these offenses is not treated as a public offense. In Hittite law, murder is not directly punished as a crime, and in Athens, its traditional formal status is that of a private lawsuit, though by the fourth century its "public" nature was apparent. Homicide is so treated by Plato in his proposed revision of Athenian law in *Laws* 871. On Plato's treatment of homicide see Gernet (1976: cxcvff.).

[13] Different cultures generate widely divergent arguments for or against the legal regulation of sexuality: the autonomy of the individual, the autonomy of the family, "rights" to privacy or sexual self-expression, theological doctrines such as pollution or sin, etc. The standard view is that Athenian society had no conception of a "private sphere beyond the reach of the state" (Finley, 1985b: 116). The argument in Chapter 9 seeks to challenge and modify this position.

and homosexuality) which Athenian law leaves unpunished.[14] Yet within Greece, as Plato reminds us, there were also considerable differences: some cities prohibited homosexuality, some permitted it, and in others the situation was ambiguous.[15] Because *within* particular cultures it frequently gives rise to controversy over the propriety of regulation, sexuality can serve as a useful focal point for the investigation of a particular society through a comparative methodology.[16]

In societies where legal norms, procedures, and punishments do not constitute a normative coercive mechanism separate from other means of social control, the problem of the legitimate scope of the *legal* enforcement of morality cannot, of course, arise. But, on the other hand, the fact that in a developed legal culture legal norms do incorporate moral standards does not imply that they, so to speak, pre-empt the field of social control. This may seem obvious, yet juristic discussions of law and morality often ignore its implications. The law embodies only one mode of social regulation, and one cannot discuss the problem of law and morals as if it existed in a vacuum, independent of politics, ideology, or, as Weber put it, of economy and society.[17] One might, of course, argue that this narrow focus is legitimate if one proposes to analyze only the specific relation of *law* to morality. Nonetheless, such a claim *assumes* the relative autonomy of the legal sphere: that is, that one can meaningfully consider the legal enforcement of morality apart from the more general social processes of which the moral practices of a society and their relations to patterns of legal enforcement are but a part. It is one of the central arguments of this book that this is not feasible. Legal norms[18] do not exist in a state of autonomy vis-à-vis social

---

[14] For Biblical Law see Leviticus 20:9ff. For the Hittite Code see Neufeld (1951: 53–7, secs. 187–200). For the Middle Assyrian Code, see Driver and Miles (1975: 70–1, 391, sec. 20). For Babylonian law, see Driver and Miles (1952: 318ff., sec. 154–8). The Athenian sources will be set out in subsequent chapters.   [15] *Symposium* 182.

[16] Most modern treatments of the enforcement of morals through the criminal law likewise focus upon sexual offenses, particularly homosexuality and prostitution. See e.g. Hart (1963), Devlin (1965). Because sexual offenses like homosexuality, adultery, and prostitution involve consensual relations between adults they most clearly pose the antinomy of privacy/autonomy v. regulation. The present study includes the regulation of religious belief through the prosecution of impiety so as not to skew the analysis through a too exclusive concentration on sexuality.

[17] See Weber (1968: 311–19, 325–32, 753–900), and the lengthy discussion of legal and ethical norms in the *Critique of Stammler* (1977).

[18] I speak here of the legal norms of the criminal law which pertain to actual wrongdoing. The question of the autonomy of purely regulative offenses and the like is another matter.

norms and the coercive and non-coercive processes through which they are articulated into the social practices and principles according to which individuals orient their conduct.[19] This study describes in a concrete historical context the way in which normative structures are reproduced, and the dynamic inter-relationship of legal and social norms as one aspect of this complex process.

From this perspective, the crucial question is thus not how the law was used to enforce morality in classical Athens, but rather how Athenian citizens oriented their behavior and expectations towards norms, how they reacted towards and characterized those who violated such normative expectations, and the role which the law played in that process. Of course, the practices and institutions which contribute in one way or another to the reproduction of the normative aspects of a social system are too many and too complex to receive comprehensive treatment here. For example, there will be some discussion of education (particularly Plato's insistence on its importance), though other aspects of socialization will scarcely receive mention. Instead, the principal focus centers upon the system of social and legal norms relating to adultery, incest, homosexuality and homosexual prostitution, and impiety, the ways in which these norms influence social behavior, and the larger patterns of social practices in which the norms and behavior are embedded.[20] Consideration of each of these areas gives rise to a series of questions which guides the subsequent analysis: what legal norms regulated (for example) homosexual behavior? In what way were these norms interpreted and enforced? What were the normative expectations of the community, or different parts of the community, in regard to homosexuality? How were they translated into patterns of social control and definitions of deviance and normality? How did the ideologies, values and social norms upon which such expectations rest diverge from one another, and what contradictions, conflicts, ambiguities, or ambivalences did they embody? How do these systems of legal and social norms relate to one another, and what is their relative importance in societal processes of normalization and

---

[19] Watson makes the case for autonomy in his three books on the civil law tradition (1981, 1984, 1985).

[20] In Goffman's or Giddens' terms, social control should be viewed from the perspective of interaction, not of behavior *determined* by institutional or other mechanisms (Goffman and Giddens will be discussed at length in Chapter 2). When I speak of social control it is in this voluntaristic interactional sense of normative expectations, behavior purposively oriented towards these expectations, and responses to such behavior.

social control? A broad definition of the problem of the enforcement
of morals can thus raise important questions which an approach
focusing solely upon law or solely upon society could address only
incompletely. It can serve as a sort of analytical wedge for
illuminating broader aspects of social order in Athens.

How does one go about answering such questions for an ancient
society like classical Athens? The existing secondary literature
provides little help, for classical scholars have almost entirely
neglected such issues.[21] As always in the ancient world, the amount
and types of extant evidence strongly influence the approach, but in
regard to Athens we are fortunate to have some knowledge not only
of the substantive law and social practices relating to these areas, but
also of what some members at least of that society thought about
such problems.[22] Their testimony helps to reassure us that this
question of the enforcement of morals is not merely a modern
preoccupation which we impose upon the ancient sources, but rather
one to which the Athenians themselves attached considerable
significance (even if they might have formulated it somewhat
differently).[23] This fact makes classical Athens particularly interesting for comparative investigation, for, as will be seen, here one finds

[21] Dover (1974) surveys popular morality; see also Ferguson (1958). Adkins also discusses
some aspects of Greek morality in *Merit and Responsibility* (1960) and *Moral Values and
Political Behaviour in Ancient Greece* (1972), but none of these books concerns itself with the
relation of law and morals or with mechanisms of social control. Morality is largely treated
as an abstract system of concepts rather than sociologically. Dover's *Greek Homosexuality*
(1978) is the most interesting attempt to show how law and morality interacted in a
particular area of Greek life, but this is a secondary focus of his study (see also his "Eros
and Nomos," 1964). There are, of course, extensive discussions of Aristotle and Plato's
treatment of morality, but only Hamburger (1971) discusses law and morality at any length
(see e.g. Part III), and his treatment far from exhausts the field. The only recent work to
frame the general problem of law and morals (but which then dismisses it as outside its
scope) is Finley's *Democracy Ancient and Modern* (1985b: Chapters 4 and 5).

[22] For other Greek cities we are almost utterly ignorant as to all three of these aspects. Of
course there are a few individual statutes from one city or another, but the preservation of
isolated provisions is of no real use; it is the *system* that matters. For Sparta there is more
evidence (see e.g. Cartledge 1981a and b), but I believe that we have no way of
disentangling myth, propaganda, ideology, idealizations, and social reality in a discussion
of, say, homoeroticism in Sparta. Moreover, the crucial dimension provided in Athens by
members of the culture discussing and criticizing its practices is entirely absent from
classical Sparta. It is for these reasons that the study is confined to classical Athens. (See
for example Cartledge's [1986] criticisms of MacDowell's [1986] inadequate attempts to
reconstruct Spartan law, and Cohen [1989].) This position also rests upon the
presupposition that one can only speak of the law of each individual Greek *polis*, not of *Greek
law per se*. For a review of the literature on this matter see Cohen (1983: Chapter 4).

[23] Chapter 9 discusses this problem through an examination of the conflict between the
ideology of Athenian radical democracy and theories of the state and society which demand
greater control over the lives of families and individuals (e.g. Plato, Aristotle, Isocrates).

a society which explicitly perceived conflict over the propriety of state regulation of sexuality and the family as a political issue inextricably connected to its conception of democracy. Plato and Aristotle discussed the enforcement of morals as a question of political theory and practical politics, not of jurisprudence or analytic philosophy. It played a central role in their critique of Athenian democracy, and to resolve the problems it posed they each called for a radical reorganization of the means of state control over the individual and the family.[24]

The method which I propose for exploring the issues sketched above is comparative in its approach. What does this mean? In the most general sense, it draws upon evidence from other societies and other legal systems wherever this may serve to explain or clarify a particular point. As Weber argued throughout his mature work, only through comparisons with other cultures can one come to understand the reasons why a particular society developed in the way it did.[25] Some classicists arrive, for example, at particularistic explanations for what they regard as unique or bizarre features of Athenian society like the "seclusion"[26] of women, or the marriage of heiresses to the nearest male relative of their deceased father. Comparative analysis, however, reveals that such institutions are typical products of certain forms of social organization, and helps us to understand their nature and role in the social system. This is not to suggest that the separation of male and female spheres in classical Athens is the same as in contemporary Saudi Arabia or Turkey. All three share important features and also differ widely. The point is that awareness of the similarities and recurrent features (both at the level of ideology and social practice) leads to an understanding of the differences, and this in turn assists in analyzing the way in which a particular society works.

Further, this study employs a comparative methodology in a more specific sense. Specifically, it builds upon the application of a comparative model drawn from social anthropological investigations of contemporary Mediterranean societies. This model, developed at

[24] These issues will be discussed at greater length in Chapter 9.
[25] This is one of the major methodological premises of *Economy and Society* (1968); again, Weber makes the point succinctly in the Introduction to the *Protestant Ethic* (1958: 27). For an illuminating discussion of the differences between evolutionist and comparativist theories of historical explanation see Schluchter (1985) 1–12. See K. Thomas (1963) on the value of comparative anthropological evidence in historical investigation.
[26] See Chapter 6.

length in Chapter 3, provides an analytical tool for describing the
objective and subjective facets of normative order and some of the
central social processes which maintain it. Such a method possesses
greater explanatory power than conventional methods of description
used in Greek historiography and has several further advantages.
First, no historical account proceeds without theoretical presuppositions.[27] An articulated model, however, provides a basis for
criticism, discussion, and modification, whereas implicit postulates
do not. The potential gain here involves greater theoretical rigor and
insight. Second, using a comparative model broadens the focus on
the social processes of ancient Greek society, placing them in the
context of the experience of other cultures. Given that the
investigation of any topic in Greek social history resembles trying to
put together a jigsaw puzzle when half the pieces are missing and
without the convenient picture on the cover of the box, such a
comparative context can assist the historian in providing possible
"pictures." That is, by studying similar social practices in other
cultures, one can generate hypotheses for Athenian society on the
basis of the typical patterns of social organization to which such
practices relate. The wealth of documentary evidence which social
anthropological studies generate, when applied systematically
through a well-constructed model, can thus be used to suggest how
the isolated bits and pieces of Athenian material might fit together.

The depiction of Athenian society which such a procedure
produces is not the only possible interpretation. The nature of the
ancient evidence (and of historical evidence in general) is such as to
permit a discrete series of inferences in any given case. All may be
logically possible, and there exists no means of "proving" that only
one is "correct."[28] My interpretation of Athenian society can
therefore only aim at presenting an alternative perspective, a

[27] See Abrams (1982: 300): "As the acknowledged masterpieces of the discipline of history
become increasingly theoretically explicit, and as the unity of theoretical method between
history and sociology becomes thereby steadily more obvious, the continued insistence of a
rump of professional historians that theory is not part of their trade becomes steadily less
firmly the effective basis of the 'institution' of history and steadily more plainly an
ineffectual nostalgia." See also Giddens (1986: 355–64), and Thomas (1963). On the
general nature and role of presuppositions see Alexander (1983: vol. 1).

[28] See Schluchter (1985: 146) on the fallacy that when engaging in causal explanation the
historian is somehow "recreating" something with an ontological status independent of his
implicit or explicit interpretative categories: "But we must be aware that through this
procedure we achieve only a mental reconstruction of our subject and not a portrayal of the
actual course of events." For a brilliant application of a similar methodological approach
to Roman law and intellectual history, see Nörr (1986).

perspective which I believe accounts for the evidence better than most traditional interpretations. Social history advances not by collectively aiming at an orthodox reconstruction of historical "truth," but by generating and comparing a rich variety of competing explanations and theoretical approaches.[29]

This study applies a comparative method to the analysis of the normative structures which inform aspects of sexuality and religion at Athens. This leaves unanswered what kind of theoretical framework can provide an adequate basis for such an inquiry. Sexuality and religion are, from the standpoint of theory, particularly appropriate subjects since they offer (and demand) an approach which can do justice to both subjective and objective perspectives on order. This point frames one of the central arguments of this book, namely that only such a theory of social order can aptly describe the process by which morals are "enforced" in Athenian or any other society. Chapter 2 explores these theoretical issues and sketches a theory of social order and action which provides the basis for the detailed model of communal norms and social control set out in Chapter 3. The ensuing chapters (4–9) apply the model to central areas of Athenian sexuality and to impiety. Chapter 4 sets the stage by examining the conceptions of public and private in Athenian ideology and social practice. Chapters 5 and 6 take up the legal and social contexts of adultery and suggest a number of ways in which such an examination can contribute to current discussions of the status of women at Athens. Chapter 7 considers the important topics of attitudes towards, and regulation of, homosexuality and homosexual prostitution.[30] Next, Chapter 8 shifts the focus to the subject of norms regarding religious belief through an investigation of the prosecution of impiety. Finally, Chapter 9 attempts to draw the strands of the argument together in a general assessment of the

---

[29] To some readers this point may sound elementary, but it surely goes against the implicit assumptions of most standard accounts of Greek history.

[30] Chapter 9 contains the discussion of incest, for which the evidence is too scanty to require chapter length treatment. The analysis limits itself to these four topics (homosexuality, homosexual prostitution, incest and adultery) because they are the areas where conflict and ambiguity within and between the legal and moral realms are richest. I have excluded rape (except for a brief consideration of homosexual rape and *hubris*) for two reasons. First, it is a crime of violence and thus involves an entirely different set of issues than for example adultery. As in most ancient or modern legal systems, rape is not problematic from the standpoint of the enforcement of morals. Second, the evidence for the actual prosecution of rape is so sparse, even by Athenian standards, that there is little that can be said about the social context of the law.

ideology and practice of the enforcement of morals at Athens, questioning the standard view that classical Athens knows of no "private sphere" free from state regulation.

For the sake of clarity, it may be helpful to summarize the main strands of argument alluded to above as a set of theses which provide the underpinnings of the following chapters:

1 In classical Athens the community judged individuals who engaged in homosexual relations, homosexual prostitution, or adultery in accordance with a matrix of legal rules and social norms, expectations, and values which was characterized by contradiction, ambivalence, and ambiguity. Investigation of these complex patterns of legal, social, and political regulation of illicit sexuality in Athens can shed new light on Athenian society in particular, as well as on general approaches to social control and the enforcement of morals.

2 Traditional juristic approaches to the enforcement of morals are unsuited for such an investigation because they focus too one-sidedly on law as the embodiment of societal morality and the coercive means for its preservation. Social historical analysis can help disclose the nature of these shortcomings.

3 An adequate methodology must be able to take into account the full range of social practices through which a society exercises social control, and, in the process, reproduces its normative structures. Such an approach must relate legal regulation to this larger context of which it is a part.

4 All social practices are normatively structured. This structure is embodied in the expectations, values, rules, and beliefs by which individuals assess one another in social interaction. In a given historical context, examination of the patterns of practices can lead to the reconstruction of such normative contexts. More specifically, by examining the social contexts of behavior relating to homoerotic courtship or adultery one can draw inferences about the norms, expectations, and values towards which individuals orient such conduct.

5 In order to permit such inferences, a certain type of theoretical orientation must inform the description of such social practices. That is, one must adequately portray the subjective dimension of social action, the way in which individuals orient their behavior

to norms and expectations, and in doing so interpret and manipulate them to influence anticipated judgments.

6 Because of the nature of the evidence for Athenian society, a comparative social anthropological approach offers the most fruitful means of pursuing the historical investigation suggested by (1) above. In exploring the relation between law and social practices as forms of social control, such an approach leads to a new interpretation of privacy, democratic ideology, and the enforcement of morals at Athens. The theoretical provisos set out in (2–5) provide guidelines for the content of this approach.

CHAPTER 2

Models and methods I

In classical Athens the law punished intentional homicide with death or perpetual exile. In addition, statutes clearly distinguished various forms of voluntary and involuntary homicide, as well as killings in self-defense, and described the various courts which tried such cases. In a number of its central features such a statutory scheme differs little from the treatment of homicide in most Western legal systems up to the contemporary period. Classical scholars and historians of Greek law have sometimes argued, however, that these provisions were "primitive," in important respects.[1] They point out, for example, that Athenian offenses fell into two procedural categories: the *dike*, or private suit, prosecutable by only the injured party, and the *graphe*, or public indictment, prosecutable by any citizen.[2] The action for homicide belonged to the former. This categorization, they argue, shows that Athenian homicide law had not yet fully evolved out of the more "primitive" stage of self-help.[3] Homicide, it is often concluded, was not of central concern to the state, but rather primarily involved the family.[4]

Such explanations rely upon questionable assumptions involving evolutionary models of societal and institutional development.[5] More generally, they also reveal the weakness of an unexamined positivist approach to legal institutions which asks only what the

[1] See e.g. MacDowell (1978: 109–10, 114–15), who contrasts "primitive" or "crude" aspects, with others which represent "progress," and, at length, Paoli (1959: passim).

[2] On the scholarly dogmas associated with this classification, see Hansen (1981: 12–13).

[3] MacDowell (1963: 17ff.) discusses the way modern scholarship (e.g. Hansen [1981]) has assumed that *only* the family could prosecute for homicide. For this evolutionary perspective see Latte (1968b: 288ff.), Bonner and Smith (1938: Chapter 8), and Paoli (1959).

[4] My point here has nothing to do with the familiar distinction between crime and delict. Instead it concerns drawing conclusions from the statutory form of regulations, as opposed to looking at them in their concrete social historical context.

[5] For a fuller discussion of the problems of such evolutionary models in Greek law, see Cohen (1989), and, more generally, Radcliffe-Brown (1965: 50).

relevant statutes provide. Athenian homicide law no doubt developed the way it did for reasons in fact associated with family solidarity, self-help, and so on (though the real nature of such developments is irretrievably lost to us).[6] Why it *remained* the same through a period of several centuries which saw the development of an elaborate judicial and administrative governmental apparatus, a clear conceptualization of the notion of violent crime as a public offense, and a concomitant decline in the political significance of family solidarity,[7] is another question. In fact, the "public" nature of homicide was clear enough in the fourth century, whatever technical label attached to the action. There was no need to alter its statutory procedural status because to Athenians it was inconceivable that homicide would go unprosecuted. Not to prosecute the murder of a family member constituted, as Plato's *Euthyphro* unequivocally demonstrates, a violation of the most weighty religious and ethical duties and was regarded as one of the worst forms of impiety. In a largely endogamous community,[8] which widely practiced adoption in the absence of male heirs, there was little danger that no kin would be available. And, if they hesitated, they faced severe social censure and disgrace, as well as possible legal prosecution for impiety.[9] My concern here is not the Athenian law of homicide itself, but rather the more general issue of placing law in a broader social and normative context. The positivist account of "the law" as nothing more than the relevant valid statutes blinds us to the normative structures of the community of which the law is but a part and which gives it its social meaning.

[6] Despite the hopes of the historical reconstructionists who want to "read backwards" from fifth- and fourth-century institutions to earlier periods. See Wolff (1946: 74) and MacDowell (1963: 7) on the impossibility of generalizing about the early history of Athenian homicide law. As Radcliffe-Brown (1965: 50) succinctly puts the case against such reconstructions "My objection to conjectural history is not that it is historical, but that it is conjectural. History shows us how certain events or changes in the past have led to certain other events or conditions... But it can only do this when there is direct evidence for both the preceding and the succeeding events or conditions and also some actual evidence of their interconnection. In conjectural history we have direct knowledge about a state of affairs existing at a certain time and place, without any adequate knowledge about preceding conditions and events, about which we are therefore reduced to making conjectures. To establish any probability for such conjectures we should have to have a knowledge of laws of social development which we certainly do not possess and to which I do not think we shall ever attain."   [7] See G. Herman (1987).

[8] An endogamy enforced by the law of citizenship.

[9] See Chapter 8 on the purview of the impiety legislation.

What kind of theory of law and society can encompass the richness
of phenomena as complex as Athenian homoeroticism, which, as
Plato says, legal and social norms neither clearly prohibit nor clearly
condemn?[10] This chapter offers an alternative to the legal positivist
and instrumentalist perspectives. Its account of social order provides
the general theoretical framework for the model of norms and social
regulation set out in the next chapter and subsequently applied to
classical Athens. This interpretation develops the argument that the
law does not "enforce" the normative "structures" embodied in
legal "codes," but rather that the social practices of knowledgeable
agents reproduce the normative structuring properties[11] constitutive
of social systems: "the rules and resources drawn upon in the
production of social action are at the same time the means of system
reproduction."[12] This thesis forms the core of the theory of social
order called for in propositions 3 and 5 at the end of Chapter 1. Only
an approach based upon such theoretical premises can encompass
the various aspects of the demarcation and regulation of illicit
sexuality at Athens.

Since much of the subsequent argument takes off from this
premise, it may be helpful to "flesh it out" a bit straightaway rather
than waiting for the theoretical elaboration later in this chapter. To
use an illustration, the basic idea is that when an Athenian man
courts a boy he does so according to the normative expectations of
the boy, his family, and the community of which he is a part (all
social interaction, including courtship, is normatively structured by
such expectations, though these expectations may conflict or reflect
moral ambivalences about the conduct). Yet the norms reflected in
such expectations do not simply *determine* his behavior. He possesses
the knowledgeability that almost all individuals have about the
norms, values, beliefs, and practical expectations of the society in
which they live. This knowledgeability enables individuals to
influence evaluations of their behavior by interpreting and manipulating their words and deeds and the normative categories by which
they are judged. Thus the courting man, in anticipation of such
expectations, will manage appearances to convey, say, the impression to the boy's family and other observers that his intentions

---

[10] *Symposium* 183.
[11] When I refer to structure below it is in this sense and not in the sense of "external"
structures. The meaning of such terms and distinctions will be set out in section II of
Chapter 3.   [12] Giddens (1986: 19).

are honorable, that he is anxious not to endanger the boy's reputation by being seen with him at inappropriate times or places, that his friendship is a great benefit to the boy, and so on. At the same time, in justifying his attempts to seduce the boy he will manipulate the relevant normative criteria, arguing, for example, that intercourse is only illicit if the man doesn't truly care for the welfare of the boy, or if the boy agrees to intercourse for material gain, etc.[13] All of this strategic behavior is oriented towards the normative structures reflected in the values and expectations of the community. This orientation of behavior according to norms, even when expressed in strategies of avoidance or justification for violation, reaffirms the validity of the underlying normative structures. In this way, behavior oriented towards norms provides the means for their reproduction, that is, for the maintenance of their validity over time. In the same way, when I speak English according to rules of grammar and syntax, I both manipulate those rules according to my communicative needs and contribute to the reproduction of the English language.[14] This simple, yet fundamental, insight provides the basis for a more complex understanding of normativity and social control than traditional juristic accounts can provide. The following presentation begins with an analysis of the shortcomings of such traditional legal accounts of order (Section I) and then moves to a description of a theory of social order which provides a more satisfactory basis for the ensuing historical investigation (Section II).[15]

[13] The first two speeches in Plato's *Phaedrus* provide a perfect example of the way in which individuals manipulate norms, values, and expectations according to their particular purposes. In arguing opposing views of the question of whether a boy should rather submit to a lover than a non-lover, both speeches appropriate the culturally common repertoire of normative expectations concerning homoerotic behavior.

[14] This is Giddens' example, explained and elaborated at (1986: 21).

[15] At the risk of laboring the point, one of the central aims of this study is to demonstrate the value of conceptual models and comparative evidence from other disciplines. Without an adequate theoretical basis, how can one justify the categories for selection, organization, and interpretation of evidence which one inevitably employs, whether explicitly or implicitly? As a leading sociologist, Anthony Giddens, puts the case from the other perspective: "Those who have wanted to model sociology upon natural science, hoping to discover universal laws of social conduct, have tended to sever sociology from history. In breaking with such views, we have to go further than simply asserting that sociology and history – or, more accurately, the social sciences and history – are indistinguishable, provocative though such a claim may appear to be."

I

Talcot Parsons, one of the founders of modern social theory, argues
in his seminal work, *The Structure of Social Action*, that to explain
constraint and obedience to rules the sociologist must pose the
following question. Preliminarily, he must ascertain what the rules
are, and then ask "what then is their source and what is the nature
of the force that constrains?"[16] The implicit answer to these
questions, which informs most jurisprudential discussions of the
enforcement of morals, is relatively straightforward: the relevant
rules are those defined by statutory law, and the force that constrains
is the coercive power of the legislator. If one would inquire further
as to what theory of social order is implicit within such a view, the
answer seems likewise clear that the approach to law is positivistic,
the conception of social order is instrumental and utilitarian. Order
depends upon the calculating response of individuals to the external
compulsion embodied in legal sanctions. Within such a framework,
with its purely external conceptualization of order, the only question
that can arise about law and morals is "Should the criminal law be
used to regulate immorality?" Yet defining the problem in this way
assumes that the law is or can be the principal instrument by which
moral rules are "enforced," when that should, in fact, be one of the
main questions under discussion.

As a way of moving towards a more general level of theoretical
discussion of the defects of such views, one might identify four
common threads of argument implicit in much of the jurisprudential
literature on law and morals. No one text may display an attachment to all four tenets, and individuals on different sides of
the debate often share some of the central presuppositions they
represent:

1 The law is the central pillar of social order. Through its coercive
   force it can preserve the moral structure of society.

2 Obedience to the law is based upon the rational, self-interested
   calculations of individuals in the face of the threat of punishment.

[16] Parsons (1968: 381).

3 Individuals (legislators, magistrates, etc.) can change or defend the moral order of a society through the law, and immoral individuals, or offensive ones, can endanger it.[17]

4 Society has one morality. It is embodied in legal statutes and in the reflections of judges and legislators about community standards of right and wrong.

The first three propositions indicate that instrumentalism defines the theoretical framework of such discussions of law and morality. The fourth proposition rests upon an inadequate conceptualization of morality and social normativity. The task of this section is to provide a critique of instrumentalism and a more adequate account of morality and norms. This forms the basis for the constructive theoretical analysis in Section II.

Roberto Unger and Jeffrey Alexander, in their respective critiques of modern social theory, have exposed the shortcomings of instrumentalist theories.[18] Unger, for example, identifies a central division in social theory involving two approaches to the problem of order, one oriented towards instrumentalism, the other towards legitimacy and consensus.[19]

Instrumentalism may be characterized by its attachment to a certain conception of the social bond and to a particular view of the nature of the rules on which organized social life depends. It holds that men are governed by self-interest and guided by judgments about the most efficient means to achieve their privately chosen aims... This theory places the immediate determinant of conduct within the individual rather than in the groups to which he belongs.

Instrumental rules are treated by the individual as one more factor to be taken into account in his calculus of efficiencies. This means that he will comply with the rules only to the extent his own goals are better served by compliance than by disobedience. The fear of the sanction operates to

---

[17] This formulation is based upon the opposing accounts of Hart and Devlin. Whereas Devlin (1965: Chapter 1) argues that the law must prohibit and punish immorality if society is to survive, Hart (1963: passim) attempts to distance himself from such an approach by articulating a standard of offensiveness.

[18] Unger (1975: 152–4); Alexander (1983: vols 2–3).

[19] On Unger's view, proposition (3) is characteristic of both modes of political thought: "Modern social thought was born proclaiming that society is made and imagined, that it is a human artefact rather than the expression of an underlying order" (1987: vol. 1, 1). Unger's argument has its roots in Hegel's discussion of constitutional tradition and legislation (1981: 286–7). Hayek has most forcefully expounded this element of the critique of instrumentalism (1977: vol. 1, 8–34; 1978: 3–34).

internalize the requirements of social order in individuals' reasoning about the most effective means to attain personal ends. Consequently the sanction becomes the crucial part of the rule.[20]

Unger, like Alexander, focuses upon the internal contradictions of such a position, arguing that it cannot account for either social continuity or cohesion.[21] The instrumentalist interpretation of rules cannot explain the actual existence of non-instrumental rules that ought to be obeyed, and in fact tend to be obeyed, independently of the individual's calculus of means and ends.[22] As Alexander puts it in his critique of Weber, legal rules function instrumentally, "as a purely external form of collective order. The law's normative impact is achieved more through its enforceability than through belief in the legitimacy of its normative meaning."[23] On such a view, modern legal order is based simply upon "external political coercion."[24] This kind of instrumental approach, which conceives of order as based upon external coercion through the law, gives rise to the idea that "enforcement" plays the central role in the relation of law and morals: "External compliance is all that matters."[25] Indeed, it is within such an instrumentalist framework that the debate about law and morals has largely been carried out.

The conception of morality implied in proposition (4) (above) is likewise one-sided. It cannot account for the richness, diversity, ambiguity, stratification, and contradictions that are characteristic of moral life and of morality's relation to the law.[26] Nor does it relate the existence of moral rules to the conduct of moral agents, that is to the actual social practices for which they provide orientation and which in turn reproduce them. The view of morality as a univocal system of ethical principles is a necessary corollary to the belief that morality is something that the law can "enforce."[27] Yet one cannot

---

[20] Unger (1976: 24–6). Alexander's critique of instrumentalism is a major theme throughout the four volumes of *Theoretical Logic in Sociology*.   [21] Unger (1976: 27).

[22] Unger (1976: 29).   [23] Alexander (1983: vol. 3, 115).

[24] Alexander (1983: vol. 3, 81).   [25] Alexander (1983: vol. 3, 82).

[26] Here I mean law not in the positivist sense of "valid statutes," but rather in the sociological sense of institutions, legal relations, patterns of interpretation, enforcement and resistance, etc.

[27] To admit that the moral conceptions embedded in the law may only represent the morality of a segment of the society, or derive from the dominant religious institutions, or represent a particular ideology of how society ought to be, would give away the case. The fiction of "society's" moral standards enshrined in the law finds recurrent expression in judges' and jurists' references to "all well-disposed persons," "recognized public standards," "the man in the Clapham omnibus" (Devlin, 1965: 15), or "community standards of decency." As

assume a congruence between the moral norms expressed through the criminal law and the morality of society as a whole. There is no one morality of a complex culture. Classical historians sometimes fall into this trap when they write as if there was only one Athenian attitude towards homosexuality or adultery. To say that homosexuality was tolerated at Athens is just as misleading as to say that it was condemned, for in this area Athenian culture was not only stratified, but also fraught with ambivalence, ambiguity, and conflict. To sidestep the matter by referring to the "dominant morality" only exacerbates the problem. E. P. Thompson's discussion of popular attitudes towards the law nicely illustrates this point:

...we must realize that there have always persisted popular attitudes towards crime amounting at times to an unwritten code, quite distinct from the laws of the land. Certain crimes were outlawed by both codes: a wife- or child-murderer would be pelted and execrated on the way to Tyburn...But other crimes were actively condoned by whole communities – coining, poaching...[28]

Legal historians have usually dismissed such phenomena as unworthy of serious attention. Likewise, many historians have regarded investigations of "popular morality" as perhaps entertaining, but of little real significance. For too many scholars in these disciplines, law consists simply of statutes, cases, and treatises, the morality of Christian ethics and the ideal values of the upper strata. Yet recent social historical scholarship on law, sexuality, morals, and religion has shown how much actual practices and attitudes at the local level might vary from the official norms promulgated at the national level, and how wide the gap between the elite and the vast majority of the population might be.[29] Official definitions of marriage, for example, had little to do with the

cases like *Shaw* reveal, such statements are often empirically meaningless and are merely reflections of certain political ideologies.

[28] (1966: 59ff.), and cf. 583ff.) for a description of conflict between law and what Thompson calls the "moral economy." On the general question of popular attitudes and resistance towards the law, see Sharpe (1983, 1986); Cockburn (1977); Brewer and Styles (1980); Macfarlane (1981); Hay (1975); Marchant (1969); Houlbrooke (1979).

[29] On religious heterodoxy and its suppression see Ginzburg (1982); Le Roy Ladurie (1982); Marchant (1969); Febvre (1982); Houlbrooke (1979); Hill (1975, 1985); Morton (1979); Thomas (1973); Nalle (1987); O'Neil (1987); Martin (1987); DeDieu (1987); Kamen (1985). For sexuality and morality see Stone (1977); Flandrin (1979); Quaife (1979); Menefee (1981); Ariès (1985); Ruggiero (1985); Emmison (1973); Foucault (1980, 1982); Thompson (1971, 1974); Davis (1975); Rossiaud (1978).

common understanding that a promise to wed and sexual intercourse made a couple man and wife.[30] The conflict between such time-honored local norms and official legislation necessarily made the attempts of ecclesiastical or secular legislation against fornication largely futile.[31] Should one characterize the activities of the Church Courts in seventeenth-century England as the "enforcement of morals" and leave the matter at that, when the statistics concerning the effectiveness of excommunication rather forcefully indicate that compliance was largely a matter of voluntary submission?[32] Investigation of such questions is indispensable for a fuller understanding of normative order in a particular period.

If many lawyers and historians have ignored such problems, traditional sociological accounts of the relation between social norms and morality have not often been much more illuminating. The distinguished German sociologist R. König, for example, gives one of the common sociological interpretations of society's normative structure:

Social norms are not in the first instance the obligatory norms of ethics which have an existence independent of whether or not anyone complies with them. Much more they are based upon [how much?] what in the rule actually happens or at least can happen in a given community. Social norms are in reality no more than expectations which individual groups or whole societies have of one another under particular conditions.[33]

Such a view, however, is misleading, for it merely restates the dichotomy, going back at least to Tönnies, of *Sitte* and *Sittlichkeit* (moral practice v. ideal ethical standards), not taking into account their dynamic interdependence.[34] Both these ethical norms, which supposedly have independent existence, and the norms revealed through behavior, serve as inter-related elements of the patterns of practices that constitute a social system.[35] They play different, but inter-connected roles in the repertoire of normative strategies and

---

[30] Quaife (1979: 44ff.).
[31] Within individual communities one also finds conflict over the validity and interpretation of norms, competing values, patterns of resistance at official and popular levels, etc. See Sharpe (1986: 73–93, 143–67); Quaife (1979: 38–58, 89–210).
[32] See Marchant (1969); Houlbrooke (1979).   [33] König (1982: 186).
[34] Tönnies (1909: 42ff.). Moral philosophers like Herbert Morris have offered far more satisfactory accounts of moral interaction and agency, though traditional sociological accounts do not seem to have profited from them. See Morris (1985). Goffman's model of interaction corresponds in striking ways to Morris' views. See e.g. "On Face-Work," Goffman (1967).
[35] I use the term "social system" in Giddens' sense (1986: 162ff.), discussed below.

practices that sociologists like Pierre Bourdieu and Erving Goffman have described.[36] The ideal norms of ethics, even when violated, serve as points of orientation for behavior and explanation. Having to take into account the norm or normative expectations in formulating a strategy of, or excuse for, deviance shows the strength of the normative structure.[37] As the distinguished social theorist Niklas Luhmann puts it, "The fact of the orientation of conduct to a norm, not compliance with a norm, is decisive for ascertaining its validity."[38] An adequate account of the norms governing activities like homosexuality, prostitution, or adultery must relate the codes of law and ethics to the social practices of knowledgeable actors who define, manipulate, interpret, ignore, violate, and, ultimately, reproduce them.[39]

To sum up, in the analysis of law and morals a broader perspective, focusing on both the subjective and objective dimensions of social order, can correct the instrumentalist portrayal of law as merely domination.[40] In particular, this perspective requires "the continuous relation of law to broader normative order" and produces "a very different understanding of legal relations themselves."[41] Unless one maintains that the normative order of a culture has an existence independent of the conduct and consciousness of individuals over time, it follows that neither law nor morality can be understood apart from the social practices through which they interact in a concrete social context. In setting out such a multi-dimensional theory of social practices, Bourdieu has emphasized just

[36] See pp. 28–34.

[37] Goffman (1971: 98–121); and see Canguilhem (1978: 145ff.).

[38] Luhmann (1972: 124).

[39] In another kind of approach, Luhmann defines the moral order of a social system as built around the "orientation towards the conditions for respect and disgrace" (1984: 122). Through the process of interpenetration the respect of others becomes a pillar for the demands of social order, and the demands of social order vary according to what is signalled as the conditions for respect or the loss thereof (320). Luhmann's account of morality is Durkheimian in its orientation: "all moral facts consist in a rule of sanctioned conduct" (Durkheim, 1964: 425). More specifically, social order is based upon rules "which cannot be violated without the offender incurring blame from public opinion which can range from utter disgrace to simple disapproval, passing through all the shades of reproach" (Durkheim, 1964: 427). Unlike Durkheim, however, Luhmann denies the cohesive force of morality in highly complex societies, and accentuates its potential for producing conflict and disintegration (1984: 318 ff.).

[40] Dissatisfaction with instrumentalism's impoverished description of social order does not imply that the legitimacy or consensus theory ought to be adopted in its stead (Giddens 1987: 214, Alexander 1983, vol. 2: 292–6, Unger 1976: 31–7).

[41] Alexander (1983: 117). This insight provides the basis for Alexander's critique of Weber's theory of legal domination.

this inseparability, arguing that one cannot ignore "the dialectical relationship between the objective structures and the cognitive and motivating structures which they produce and which tend to reproduce them," nor the fact that "these objective structures are themselves products of historical practices and are constantly reproduced and transformed by historical practices whose productive principle is itself the product of these structures."[42] To apprehend complex Athenian social phenomena like homosexuality requires that one uncover this dialectic by dissecting the interplay of the rules, discourse, and practices which embodies it.

II

What would constitute such an account of social order, capable of illuminating Athenian social and legal relations? Before proposing an actual theory, it may prove helpful to set out a concrete example of the way in which historical investigation can profit through employing such a perspective. This brief detour can assist in clarifying the requirements that a satisfactory theory must meet if it is to describe complex social processes of normalization.[43]

In his investigation of the social transformations that by the nineteenth century had produced a "new" working class in England, E. P. Thompson provides a brilliant example of the power of a multi-dimensional analysis to describe a complex process of historical change, and of the importance that historical studies can have for social theory and vice versa.[44] *The Making of the English Working Class* offers a vivid demonstration of Unger's claim that "At a minimum, history can draw attention to alternatives the existing theoretical vocabulary either disregards or confuses."[45]

Most relevant here is Thompson's portrayal of the long process by which a new work ethic was infused in the emergent working class, a new inner discipline adequate to the demands of the Industrial Revolution. Whether one agrees or not with Thompson's conclusions, he clearly demonstrates the indispensability of going beyond

---

[42] Bourdieu (1977: 83, and see also 164).

[43] Weber's (1958) *Protestant Ethic and the Spirit of Capitalism* is perhaps the master example of such an inquiry; one could also use Bourdieu (1977), or Foucault (1979, 1980).

[44] A great deal of controversy has surrounded Thompson's work. The best recent account of the problems relevant here (including Thompson's conflict with Perry Anderson) is Giddens (1987: Chapter 9). [45] Unger (1975: 147).

an instrumental understanding of the way in which a normative order is created or "enforced." For example, in demonstrating his thesis that "Methodism was the desolate inner landscape of Utilitarianism in an era of transition to the work discipline of industrial capitalism,"[46] Thompson deploys a view of social action predicated upon external conditions and internal normative order, an order which can be influenced by institutions capable of manipulating ideology and beliefs. He describes the struggle for the creation of a new moral order in terms of the re-socialization of the lower classes through the internalization of middle-class values.[47]

In effect, Thompson's analysis focuses on the enforcement of morality through a variety of social institutions (factories, churches, schools, law and magistrates, the military, societies for the enforcement of orderly moral conduct, etc.) which used discipline[48] to create a new collective morality, a new social order. He concludes that, although it is difficult to generalize, "it is clear that between 1780 and 1830 important changes took place. The 'average' English working man became more disciplined, more subject to the productive tempo of 'the clock', more reserved and methodical, less violent and less spontaneous."[49] *The Making of the English Working Class* succeeds in demonstrating the true complexity of the process of enforcing a new morality, and of the "texture and variety of human agency" over time.[50] Significantly, in this process the law plays an important, but by no means a dominant or even leading, role. As Weber saw, the problem in creating the work discipline necessary for industrial capitalism was not that of imposing external constraints, bur rather of producing an internalized compulsion for disciplined work, turning the worker "into his own slave driver."[51]

From Thompson's discussion emerge two basic requirements for a theory of society adequate to an historical sociological investigation of the enforcement of morals. Firstly, it must offer an account of the subjective aspects of the problem of order, going beyond the instrumental view of order as based upon the coercive power of the law. Secondly, the description of the subjective pole of normative

---

[46] Thompson (1966: 365, and cf. 369–78).
[47] See Thompson (1966: Chapter 12).
[48] I use discipline in the sense developed by Weber (1968: vol. 2, 1146–58) and Foucault (1979: 135–228).　　[49] *Ibid.* 409–10.　　[50] Giddens (1986: 217).
[51] Weber, quoted by Thompson (1966: 357). The modern economic order, however, is characterized by the *external* compulsion of impersonal economic forces; Weber (1958: 181–3).

order, agency, must be rich enough to account for the strategic complexity of such social practices.[52] Anthony Giddens has advanced such a theory of society which emphasizes precisely this relation between agency, practices, and institutions. Giddens' theory of "structuration," along with Bourdieu's "theory of practice," meets the two requirements set out above. Together they provide the theoretical foundation for an examination of the interplay of rules, discourse, and practices governing illicit sexuality at Athens. Further, they can provide substantiation for the claims advanced above (in propositions (3)–(5)) concerning the normative structure of all social interaction, the possibility of illuminating that structure by examining the patterns of such interaction, and so on. In what follows, Giddens' theory provides a general theoretical framework for understanding social order, while Bourdieu's discussion of the interrelation of different levels of normative order (e.g. law, ideal norms, norms of practice) in concrete contexts of social practices demonstrates how a historian might profitably apply such a theoretical approach.

The starting point for the theory of structuration is that

The basic domain of study of the social sciences is neither the experience of the individual actor, nor the existence of any form of societal totality, but social practices ordered across space and time. Human social activities, like some self-reproducing items in nature, are recursive. That is to say, they are not brought into being by social actors but continually recreated by them via the very means whereby they express themselves as actors. In and through their activities agents reproduce the conditions that make these activities possible.[53]

This "recursive ordering"[54] of social practices is expressed in a conception of agency built upon the notion of "reflexivity," a term derived from what Giddens sees as the "reflexive" nature of the "knowledgeability" of human agents.

[52] Not every subjective theory of order can do this. As Giddens points out, for example, Parsons' reconciliation of voluntarism and order, expressed in the view "that actors internalize, as motives, the shared values upon which social cohesion depends," leaves little room for "the knowledgeability of social actors as constitutive in part of social practices" (Giddens 1986: xxxvii).

[53] Giddens (1986: 2), and see (1987: 135–6), and (1986: 35): "It would not be true, however,... to say that the routines of daily life are the 'foundation' upon which the institutional forms of societal organization are built in time-space. Rather, each enters into the constitution of the other, as they both do into the constitution of the acting self."

[54] Giddens (1986: 3).

"Reflexivity" hence should be understood not merely as self-consciousness but the monitored character of the ongoing flow of social life. To be a human being is to be a purposive agent, who has both reasons for his or her activities and is able, if asked, to elaborate discursively upon those reasons (including lying about them)...Human action occurs as durée, a continuous flow of conduct...Purposive action is not composed of an aggregate or series of separate intentions, reasons and motives. Thus it is useful to speak of reflexivity as grounded in the continuous monitoring of actions which human beings display and expect others to display.[55]

Such a portrayal of agency provides the basis for rejecting the view of rules and norms as determinative of action. The Athenian man courting the adolescent object of his desire recognizes both the limitations and possibilities (including the ambiguities, contradictions, and ambivalences) implied by the repertoire of rules, values, and beliefs of the community of which he is a part. He strategically orients his conduct towards the expectations and expected reactions of the boy, his family, and others so as to arrive at his erotic goal with a minimum of interference and danger. The "reflexive" nature of agency provides the basis for illuminating the normative structures that inform such interaction.

This perspective on agency transforms the rigid notion of structure as something external to, and determinative of, conduct into a concept capable of expressing a broader view of order: "Understood as rules and resources implicated in the 'form' of collectivities of social systems, reproduced across space and time, structure is the very medium of the 'human' element of agency. At the same time, agency is the medium of structure, which individuals routinely reproduce in the course of their activities."[56] Thus "social systems" are organized as the reproduction of social practices as sustained in the encounters of human beings over time.[57] Such a perspective on social action enables one to move beyond the view that society enforces morality by determining behavior by the coercive force of the threats embodied in the law. Individuals do not mechanically respond to societal norms either through calculative reactions to

---

[55] Giddens (1986: 3).
[56] Giddens (1987: 220–1), and cf. 61: "Structure is both the medium and the outcome of the human activities which it recursively organizes. Institutions, or large-scale societies, have structural properties in virtue of the continuity of the actions of their component members. But those members of society are only able to carry out their day-to-day activities in virtue of their capability of instantiating those structural properties."
[57] Giddens (1986: 83). This account of agency enables Giddens to give a far more satisfactory account of values than a functionalist account can. See e.g. Parsons (1964: 194–6).

threats or through the internalization of norms as motives that determine action.[58] In pursuing their goals (e.g. homoerotic or adulterous seduction) by structuring their interactions according to mutual expectations, individuals reproduce the normative resources of their culture out of which such expectations arise. In seeking to recover the norms, values, and beliefs of an ancient society, the historian must look beyond the rules reflected in the law and other official ideologies to the social practices which instantiate and reproduce them. Normative "structures" exist nowhere else than in such practices considered over time.

In elaborating his views on structure and agency Giddens draws heavily upon several strands in Goffman's classic studies of social interaction. These ideas form the foundation for the claims made in propositions (3)–(5) at the end of Chapter 1. The first of these involves the notion that in all social interaction (verbal or non-verbal) individuals "monitor" their behavior in regard to the anticipated and actual reactions of the others involved. Judgments about deviance, normality, reliability, and so on, are largely based upon one's ability to participate in such mutual monitoring. Take, for example, a person sitting alone and in disarray in a waiting room, who does not compose his features and posture in an appropriate manner when others enter and look at him. Goffman shows the way in which such behavior violates the "situational proprieties" of this kind of encounter, giving rise to judgments based upon the normative expectations underlying such "proprieties." This extreme example involves one of the most serious breaches, that of not engaging in mutual monitoring at all. Such behavior commonly leads observers to conclude that the individual is "disturbed," "abnormal," and so on. Further, mutual monitoring arises out of the "practical knowledgeability" that individuals possess concerning the expectations (reflected in rules, exceptions, recognized excuses and justifications for deviation, etc.) associated with any social situation, even those as ephemeral as two persons passing in a corridor.[59] These

---

[58] These are the two perspectives on action offered by most varieties of utilitarianism and by Parsons. See n. 47 above.

[59] "Awareness of social rules, expressed first and foremost in practical consciousness, is at the very core" of this knowledgeability; Giddens (1986a: 22–3). Here Giddens is drawing heavily on Goffman (1961, 1963a, 1967), who (1963: 140ff.) also discusses the way in which the law is only a small part of the normative system regulating public behavior; and cf. Goffman (1971: 98). Insisting that abstract rules, like those of the law, are not necessarily the most influential in the structuring of social activity, Giddens argues that "the

two observations provide the basis for the final strand of argument, which concerns the normative character of all the routine encounters which are constitutive, for Goffman and Giddens, of social practices.[60] Examples like those given above may appear trivial in themselves, but they underscore this important point that normative structures inform all social interaction:

All competent members of society are vastly skilled in the practical accomplishments of social activities and are expert 'sociologists'. The knowledge they possess is not incidental to the persistent patterning of social life but is integral to it... *Structure has no existence independent of the knowledge that agents have about what they do in their day-to-day activities.*[61]

Examination of such day-to-day activities can serve as the first step in uncovering the normative structures they embody.

As anthropological studies suggest, norms figure as "factual boundaries of social life, to which a variety of manipulative attitudes are possible." Norms are thus not "external" principles,[62] internalized as a "programmer" or determinant of social conduct, but "always enabling as well as constraining,"[63] they are part of the rules and resources that make up the practical consciousness of knowledgeable agents monitoring their interaction with one another.[64] In viewing normative structures and institutions as constituted by the social practices which reproduce them over time,[65] Giddens provides a theoretical justification for examining social practices to discern the normative properties on which public order is based.[66] The goal is to understand the dynamic relationship connecting the different levels of normative order in the repertoire of

---

structuring quality of rules can be studied in respect of... the forming, sustaining, termination, and reforming of encounters... the prescriptions invoked in the structuring of daily interaction are much more fixed and constraining than might appear from the ease with which they are ordinarily followed" (Giddens 1986: 21–2; and see Garfinkel 1984: 35–75). [60] Giddens (1987: 14).

[61] Giddens (1986: 26). My emphasis.

[62] On this see also Canguilhem (1978: 54–77, 146–7). See especially the discussion on 65ff., taking off from the point that "The normal... is not a judgement of reality but rather a judgement of value..." See also the discussion on 145ff. of the conceptual distinction between "norm" and "normal." [63] Giddens (1986: 26).

[64] Giddens (1986: 25, 30); Goffman (1963a, 1967, 1971: passim). See also Comaroff and Roberts (1981).

[65] "The structural properties of social systems are both medium and outcome of the practices they recursively organize..." (Giddens, 1986: 26).

[66] See Goffman (1967: 1–10, 22ff., 35ff., 139ff.). Giddens explicitly sets himself this task in *Social Theory and Modern Sociology* in the chapter "Erving Goffman as a Systematic Social Theorist"; see also Giddens (1986: 68–73). Cf. Garfinkel (1984: 35ff.).

"rules and resources" in relation to which actors expect one another to orient their conduct. To describe, then, the norms embodied in social practices associated with, for example, Athenian homosexual courtship, one must identify such rules and resources and trace the ways individuals manipulate them in their mutual interaction.

The conclusion to one of Goffman's classic discussions of public encounters aptly sums up much of the argument thus far:

Since the domain of situational proprieties is wholly made up of what individuals can experience of one another while mutually present, and since channels of experience can be interfered with in so many ways, we deal not so much with a network of rules that must be followed as with rules that must be taken into consideration, whether as something to follow or carefully to circumvent...

Situational requirements are of a moral character: the individual is obliged to maintain them; he is expected to desire to do so, and if he fails, some kind of public cognizance is taken of his failure. But once this character of situational obligation is granted...We may expect to find many different motives for complying with them, many different reasons for breaking them, many different ways of concealing or excusing infractions, many different ways of dealing with offenders....One theme of this study, then, is that a moral rule is not something that can be used as a means of dichotomizing the world into upholders and offenders.[67]

Subsequent chapters will apply Goffman's analysis to phenomena like Athenian homosexual courtship or the behavior of women in public. As Goffman shows, all such behavior is regulated by a normative order which is neither necessarily rational nor contradiction-free, but nonetheless serves to orient mutual expectations and to distinguish "proper" and "improper" conduct.[68] Analysis of normative judgments in regard to such practices can reveal societal conceptions of deviance and, hence, of the "normal."[69]

In his classic work of anthropological theory, *Outline of a Theory of Practice*, Bourdieu develops a theory of social practices that can

---

[67] Goffman (1963a: 240–1), and cf. (1971: 108–41), and (1967: 1–45, 97–112, 137–48). See Canguilhem's similar analysis of medical judgments of insanity (1978: 64).

[68] See Canguilhem (1978: 145ff.). For a discussion of the seeming arbitrariness of some normative categories see Goffman (1963a: 56–9; e.g. it is proper to walk on the street but not to stand on it). Not complying with such norms is one of the principal bases for judgments of sickness, abnormality, etc. See also Bourdieu (1977: 109–14).

[69] I use "the normal" here in Canguilhem's sense: "The normal is then at once the extension and the exhibition of the norm...A norm draws its meaning, function, and value from the fact of the existence, outside itself, of what does not meet the requirement it serves. The normal is not a static or peaceful, but a dynamic and polemical concept" (1978: 146, and cf. 65).

provide invaluable assistance in understanding the manipulable nature of norms. He shows, for example, that kinship does not consist, as some anthropologists have supposed, of objectively given, inflexible rules that are mechanically applied. Instead, individuals draw upon their culture's complex, ambiguous, and sometimes contradictory understanding of kinship relations to further their purposes in particular circumstances. Thus a certain degree of kinship can be "close" or "distant" depending on whether an individual wishes to emphasize or disavow the relation in a certain context.[70] Through such analyses Bourdieu does much to clarify the nature of contradiction, ambiguity, and conflict in normative systems and social practices, illustrating the point made above that social morality does not consist of one rational, internally consistent code of ethical principles. Indeed, a basic theme that runs through the ensuing investigation of classical Athens is that contradiction, conflict, and ambivalence are fundamental characteristics of normative systems and the social practices in which they are instantiated. Failure to appreciate this can have unfortunate consequences: for example, when evidence that contradicts a particular view of *the* Athenian attitude towards, say, women or homosexuals, is dismissed as "misleading," "unrepresentative," and so on, when it in fact represents genuine conflict within the culture. The maxim to be followed here is, "Don't look for the functions social practices fulfill, look for the contradictions they embody."[71]

In making the case for the necessity of a theory of *practice*, Bourdieu, like Giddens, starts by rejecting the view that the observer can "explain" social action as determined by rules.[72] Accordingly, he argues that one must move from "the mechanics of the model to the dialectic of strategies," for otherwise one inevitably falls into the trap of viewing the normative structures of a society as objectively given, as purely external to the social agents.[73] In other words, he adopts a multi-dimensional approach to social action and order, substituting "strategy for the rule."[74]

[70] J. Davis (1973: 62–6), and see also Leach (1954, 1961), who offers an illuminating discussion of the manipulable nature of kinship relations.
[71] Giddens (1979: 130).
[72] Bourdieu (1977: 2). This methodological error Bourdieu labels "objectivism"; see the discussion on 3ff., and in Bourdieu (1980: 51–70, 333ff.).
[73] Bourdieu (1977: 3ff.).
[74] Bourdieu (1977: 9). Bourdieu explores this theme again, showing the incapability of the juridical viewpoint to apprehend the complexity of the social world in "La Terre et les Stratégies Matrimoniales" (1980: 249–70). There, he demonstrates the way in which laws

In adopting a strategic interpretation of the interplay of conduct and normative structures over time, Bourdieu shows that, as part of the learned repertoire of behavior with which agents confront the ordinary and extraordinary situations of their lives, they manipulate the normative categories of their culture to achieve particular effects in particular situations.[75] Often, for example, they maintain the appearance that they have not in fact violated the norm by manipulating the description of the action, of the norm, and/or the action itself.[76] This repertoire has its source in the process of socialization which produces what Bourdieu calls the "habitus": "systems of durable, transposable dispositions,...structuring structures, that is...principles of the generation and structuring of practices and representations..."[77]

The operation of the habitus over time reproduces the social system which provides the framework guiding both actions and the perceptions of them and reactions to them, and within which they have a normative and cultural meaning. In applying such a perspective to social interaction in Athenian society – to adultery, homosexuality, privacy, and so on – one must apprehend action as practice, as the strategically informed response of knowledgeable agents, and not as determined by norms which are simply given. It is this latter view, however, which implicitly informs most historical accounts, which typically describe behavior either as norm-conforming or norm-violating, with the norms as an objective category that somehow exists apart from the realm in which the actors find themselves.

Bourdieu provides an example of the explanatory power of such a theory of practice in his analysis of anthropological debates about kinship. He shows the way that, in arguing about whether parallel-cousin marriage forms the exception that proves the "rule" of

---

of inheritance are manipulated as part of larger familial strategies of inheritance and marriage.   [75] Bourdieu (1977: 8).

[76] See e.g. Bourdieu (1977: 8–15, 19–22). Comaroff and Roberts explore the role of the "normative repertoire" of a culture in regard to the outcome of disputes. Their analysis emphasizes that this repertoire does not determine outcomes, but rather is "strategically appropriated and manipulated by individuals in the cause of their competing constructions of reality." Further, "It is not...merely within the context of confrontation that interaction is seen indigenously to be rule-governed and yet negotiable, normatively constrained and yet pragmatically individualistic. For Tswana, the dispute process represents everyday life in a microcosm" (240). The interactionist model they construct on these principles serves as the basis for a powerful critique of the "rule-centered" paradigm in legal anthropology.

[77] Bourdieu (1977: 72), and see also the discussion at (1980: 87–109).

exogamy, anthropologists commonly reduce kinship to an "objective," contradiction-free system, ignoring the strategic "meaning" which kinship has within the context of social practices where actors rank and organize it to suit the needs of the particular occasion. An understanding of the modes of manipulation of such norms provides the basis for questioning the very "notion of rules and rule-governed behavior in the twofold sense of behavior conforming objectively to rules and determined by obedience to rules."[78] Applied to classical Athens, his description of the manipulation of categories of kinship according to strategies of obedience and avoidance oriented towards the "rule" can help, for example, to explain the otherwise puzzling central argument of an oration of Isaeus, where the speaker argues that claims of kinship are far more problematic than claims to inherit under a will, because it is so difficult to evaluate the competing and contradictory assertions of those who claim to be the nearest of kin.[79] He enumerates a variety of claimants who came forward in this case, all asserting that they were the nearest kin to the deceased, but the speaker's own argument is no less a rhetorical strategy oriented towards what sorts of claims concerning kinship the judges are likely to find probable.

Bourdieu penetratingly describes the dynamics of such manipulations among the Kabyle:

The ambiguity of the strategies into which it enters is such as to lead us to ask whether parallel-cousin marriage should be seen as the ideal, hardly ever achieved in practice, of accomplished marriage; or as an ethical norm (a duty of honor) which bears on every marriageable person but which can conceivably be broken (when circumstances make it impossible); or simply as a "move" recommended in certain situations. It is because it is all these things at once that it is a favored object of manipulation. In this case the second order strategies, aimed at disguising the first order strategies and the interests they pursue, under the appearance of obedience to the rule, arise from the ambiguity of a practice that is objectively amenable to a twofold reading, the genealogical reading, which everything encourages, and the economic and political reading, which would presuppose access to complete information on the exchanges between the groups in question. But the ideological trap works both ways: too much faith in the native accounts can lead one to present a mere ideological screen as the norm of practice; too much distrust of them may cause one to neglect the social function of a lie

---

[78] Bourdieu (1977: 31). Davis (1973: 62–6) analyzes the way such patterns operate in an Italian community.

socially devised and encouraged, one of the means agents have of correcting the symbolic effects of strategies imposed by other necessities.[80]

Lying, as will appear in the next chapter, is an important mechanism of manipulation,[81] but a very complex one in which, for example, certain kinds of lies are known to be so by kin who nonetheless support the actor in his re-construction of the event so that it fits in with accepted normative categories. Such strategic reconstructions, indeed any manipulations, presuppose that the community which judges such conduct does so according to normative structures of which they are all aware. In "face-to-face" societies a common stock of moral and social knowledge fulfills this function. Such manipulation can only occur within a framework in which normative judgments may be anticipated and influenced. As Goffman emphasizes, it is not the categories of obedience and disobedience which are particularly significant, but rather the modes of orientation toward the norm. Having now clarified the nature of normative structures and the way in which social action is oriented towards them, the next chapter examines, in the context of modern Mediterranean communities, the social practices embodying these structures and the modalities of social control and manipulation to which they give rise.

---

[80] Bourdieu (1977: 43). He takes up this theme again in *Le Sens Pratique* (1980: 271–331). The significance of the lie and its relation to gossip and reputation will be explored at greater length in the next chapter.   [81] See du Boulay (1976).

CHAPTER 3

Models and methods II

I

If privacy occupies a central place in contemporary discussions of the enforcement of morals, its role in the Athenian context was no less important. Plato, for example, clearly realized that if a state was to carry out a program of moral education privacy was one of the most significant barriers that would have to be overcome.[1] Analyzing the conceptions of privacy in the context of political ideology at Athens is a relatively straightforward matter, for which Aristotle, Plato, and the Athenian orators provide a great deal of interesting evidence. The foregoing chapter has suggested, however, that while political ideology may be important, it is far from the whole picture, representing only one aspect of the social system that a full presentation must take into account. Here the question presents itself: how, for an ancient society, can the historian reconstruct the rich texture of social practice? In my view, comparative evidence from contemporary social anthropology can play a crucial role in such an undertaking. This chapter illustrates the use to which anthropological models may be put in sorting out the historian's "jigsaw puzzle" alluded to above.[2] To put it another way, though ancient historians commonly label communities like classical Athens

[1] See the discussion of *The Laws* in Chapter 9.
[2] As Keith Thomas (1963: 12) argues in his classic statement of the case, "One great incentive for historians to read anthropology is that the anthropologist can offer detailed analyses of phenomena roughly comparable to those which historians are endeavouring to reconstruct with a good deal less evidence." Further, the "test" of the "validity" of a model is not the demonstration of its "truth," but rather an assessment of its capability to explain more of the available evidence than any other model. The following chapters argue that the model presented here can render a more meaningful account of the evidence in regard to homosexuality, adultery, the social regulation of women, and privacy, than those currently accepted. As for the impossibility of doing purely "objective" historical work, "untainted" by models and theory, see Finley (1985a: 47–66).

35

"face-to-face" societies, they rarely (if ever) provide a detailed account of the structures and practices which define such social systems. The richness of the anthropological record describing contemporary Mediterranean "face-to-face" communities vastly exceeds that available for any ancient society. This chapter starts with such communities in an attempt to define more precisely just what this "face-to-faceness" implies.[3]

The model which I propose here is drawn from the social anthropology of contemporary Mediterranean societies. It is worth repeating that I do not view this as the only valid model, but rather as one that is capable of producing interesting and fruitful comparative analyses. The basic idea is that an adequate model must be capable of accounting for central structural aspects of the social practices constituting the social system under discussion. In these terms, the ensuing discussion will describe certain structural principles of the social systems characteristic of traditional Mediterranean cultures.[4] Subsequent chapters show the way in which we may fruitfully apply these principles to the study of ancient Athens. The ancient historian can learn a great deal from both the differences and similarities such a comparative analysis identifies, but such a comparison must be systematic. For this reason, the present chapter develops a model of spatial and gender differentiation, privacy, and social control in some detail. Ensuing treatments of topics like public and private, assessment of reputation, or regulation of illicit sexuality can then build upon this treatment without first rehearsing the full anthropological context.

The relevant structural principles may be described in terms of three foci of patterns of social practices:

(1) The politics of reputation, including, but not limited to, the complementary opposition of honor and shame.
(2) The politics of gender, encompassing the complementary opposition of male and female in regard to division of labor, social roles, the family, sexual roles, etc.

---

[3] See Brandes (1987: 131) on characteristics of "face-to-face" societies.
[4] "All structural properties of social systems...are the medium and the outcome of the contingently accomplished activities of situated actors" (Giddens 1986: 191; and see the general discussion of structure at 162–93).

(3) The politics of spatial differentiation, including privacy, intimacy, and the complementary opposition of public and private.[5]

These three structural properties appear here in abstract form, and the bulk of this chapter will be devoted to fleshing out the Mediterranean context of the social practices which they serve to orient, and which, in turn, reproduce them. I have stated them in the form of "the politics of..." so as to avoid the too rigid dichotomization which might have been implied by formulating them more conveniently in terms of the antinomies of honor–shame, public–private, and male–female. Apart from seeking to avoid the "Mediterranean reductionism" which may result from comparisons based upon treating such antinomies as fixed "codes" of conduct, this formulation also has an additional advantage. Casting structural principles in terms of political relations (in the broadest sense) underscores the way in which knowledgeable agents, in orienting their behavior toward the normative categories embodied in the principles, manipulate those categories according to strategies of avoidance, apparent conformity, consensus, excuse, and so on.[6] Before proceeding to the discussion of these structural principles in the Mediterranean context, however, it is first necessary to consider some general objections to such an enterprise. These will be taken up in Section II. Section III will examine the differentiation of public and private, and IV will turn to the politics of reputation. While both of these sections deal with some of its other aspects, I defer discussion of the ideological components of the "politics of gender" to subsequent chapters on adultery and homosexuality in classical Athens.

---

[5] Herzfeld (1986: 215) sets out the reason for using the cumbersome phrase "complementary opposition," as will be discussed below. I also use terms like "dichotomy" or "antinomy" for the sake of variation, but they are meant in this sense.

[6] To take one example, Goffman's analysis in *Behavior in Public Places* emphasizes the disjunction between public and private behavior, and the way in which public behavior is, at every level (appearance, non-verbal communication, actual encounters), institutionalized and normatively regulated. This does not imply, however, that patterns of interaction are "determined" by an external structure. Rather, Goffman (1963a: 42) argues that "we deal not so much with a network of rules that must be followed, as with rules that must be taken into consideration, whether as something to follow or carefully to circumvent."

II

There is a variety of objections which might arise to the employment
of a Mediterranean model for purposes of comparative historical
analysis, but most of them fall into one of two categories. The first of
these concerns the justification for using a Mediterranean model as
the basis for comparisons with ancient societies. The second objection
focuses upon the problem of over-generalization and reductionism,
that is, upon the anthropological validity of the model itself. These
will now be considered in turn.

One possible objection holds that comparison between the ancient
and modern Mediterranean is based upon an unjustified assumption
of historical continuity. Despite the value of comparative historical
studies like those of Walcot, Baroja, or Levy and Friedl one cannot
simply assume historical continuity.[7] This comparative study,
however, in no way rests upon such historical claims. In the absence
of proof of the historical persistence of cultural patterns one must
treat a Mediterranean model like any other model: it possesses no
special evidentiary advantages and its success or failure depends
upon its internal coherence, anthropological accuracy, and explanatory power – not upon historical continuity.

Why then the Mediterranean? The main reason is that I know of
no other group of similarly well-documented societies which manifest
the same patterns of social practices. To be sure, there are many
other societies where similar patterns occur. For example, Gregor's
study of the South American Mehinaku reveals many interesting
parallels in regard to the social division of public and private space,
the sexual division of labor, and so on.[8] On the other hand, other
structural principles (for example in regard to male–female
sexuality) differ so radically that no general model based upon the
Mehinaku could adequately explain the practices associated with
adultery or homosexuality in classical Athens. A further possibility
would be to resort to historical studies of the family and sexuality.
Historians like Stone, Foucault, Donzelot, and Flandrin have

---

[7] Walcot (1973), Baroja (1958), Levy and Friedl (1958). See Herzfeld's criticisms (1980:
passim). Walcot's book is invaluable for its detailed comparisons with the Homeric world,
but he rarely draws upon evidence from the classical period. See Davis' (1977) excellent
discussion of the problem in the final chapter of the most ambitious comparative study of
Mediterranean societies.

[8] Gregor (1985), Godelier (1987), and Herdt (1982, 1984) also provide interesting
comparative evidence from societies outside the Mediterranean.

constructed models of the family or sexuality, but they are explicitly designed to explain specific developments in early modern Europe and hence are of doubtful applicability.[9] Comparative evidence from medieval or early modern Europe can be provocative, as well as helpful for clarifying particular points, but it cannot serve as the basis for an adequate comparative model.[10]

The second type of objection mentioned above questions the validity of generalizations about modern Mediterranean societies. In the 1960s a growing body of ethnographic studies of individual Mediterranean communities gave rise to various attempts toward a comparative, synthetic account of "Mediterranean" society. The collections edited by Pitt-Rivers and Peristiany on topics like honor and shame, or Mediterranean family structures are the best known examples of this.[11] While these comparative assessments were firmly rooted in detailed ethnographic accounts of particular communities, later synthetic efforts sometimes attempted to move to a much higher level of generalization.[12] The most penetrating critique of such overly general abstractions about "Mediterranean society" has been made by the anthropologist Michael Herzfeld.[13] In a series of articles over the last seven years he has argued that much of this subsequent work has taken complementary oppositions like "honor and shame" out of their social contexts and reduced them to abstract formal equations, a process which "fed a growing tendency to homogenize 'Mediterranean society.'"[14] In this process, these antinomies "sacrificed 'complementarity' to 'opposition' and so lost their significance as essentially manipulable and rhetorically subtle symbols."[15]

[9] Stone (1977), Foucault (1980), Donzelot (1979), Flandrin (1979); and see also Goody (1983) and Ozment (1983).
[10] The historical evidence from other periods suffers from some of the same shortcomings as is the case for antiquity. For example, there is relatively little qualitative evidence for peasant families in early modern England, and Stone's (1977) failure to deal with this problem is, as critics have pointed out, one of the major shortcomings of the model he proposes. It is for precisely such reasons that Keith Thomas argues for the usefulness of anthropological evidence (see n. 2 above).
[11] Pitt-Rivers (1958), Peristiany (1963, 1966b, 1976).
[12] E.g. Davis (1977), J. Schneider (1971). See, most recently, Gilmore (1987a).
[13] See also Silverman (1970: 211), who did much to discredit Banfield's theory of amoral familism as a general feature of Mediterranean social organization. While recognizing the Mediterranean as "a meaningful unit of cultural taxonomy," Silverman warns against overemphasis on cultural uniformity.
[14] Herzfeld (1986: 215) and also (1980, 1983, 1984, 1987).
[15] *Ibid.* For the best, and most recent, answers to Herzfeld's reservations by a group of anthropologists nonetheless also committed to moving away from over-generalized

Herzfeld's criticisms are not leveled at all comparative Mediterranean studies.[16] He specifically praises the synthetic work of Pitt-Rivers on honor and shame because of the richness of its ethnographic account and attention to linguistic and social variation. It is rather the reductionist tendency to speak of "Mediterranean society" and of fixed abstract dichotomies apart from detailed examination of the ethnographic context, that he with justification rejects. Outstanding recent work on honor and shame, for example, studiously avoids such reductionism.[17] Likewise, this study does not argue for a *homo mediterraneus* whose characteristics may be expressed in a few simple formulae. The argument is rather that, despite many differences, there are typical patterns of social practices that characterize a wide range of Mediterranean communities. These patterns may vary considerably from place to place, but there is also considerable similarity in the underlying normative structures. Indeed, the very rhetorical fluidity of the complementary oppositions of honor–shame, male–female, and public–private that Herzfeld notes, constitutes one of the central features of the model that I propose. For this reason I have not focused on just one society, nor do I rely upon general comparative surveys. The ensuing discussion rather builds upon an analysis of individual anthropological studies of communities in Portugal, Spain, Italy, Greece, Turkey, Lebanon, Cyprus, Egypt, Algeria, Malta, and Morocco. By surveying a large geographical area, which, as Braudel has shown, at least for some purposes must be considered as a whole, one avoids the objections of anecdotal use of evidence, and also of basing a model upon an atypical, and hence too narrow, basis.[18]

Focusing in a detailed way upon a larger group of communities adds richness to the account and gives one a sense both of the possibilities for variation and of the central recurring features. One can, for example, point to the great variety of courtship practices found in Mediterranean communities. They range, for example, from the open, but strictly regulated courtship of Andalusia, to

---

dichotomies, see the essays by Brandes, Gilmore, Giovannini, and Delaney, in Gilmore (1987a).

[16] Although his most recent statement goes farther in this direction than his earlier statements; see Herzfeld (1987).

[17] See e.g. Brandes (1981) and the recent collection of papers on honor and shame published as a special issue of the *American Anthropologist: Honor and Shame: the Unity of the Mediterranean* (Gilmore 1987a).

[18] Braudel (1972); this is one of the major themes that runs through the entire study.

Greek or North African communities where there is no licit public courtship at all and a girl who returns the greeting of a young man in the street may be assumed to have an illicit relation with him. But, within this variety of permissible courtship practices one finds the notions of strict limits, enforced by the families involved and by the community, of socially delineated categories of permissible and impermissible public and private behavior, and of differentiated roles and expectations for men and women. The limits may vary, but the fact that the community assesses the reputation of the girl and her family according to the orientation of behavior to these norms is the same. For the girl, chastity is always the *official* expectation; only the behavior which is thought to impugn chastity changes. Behavior judged by the community to impugn chastity damages the reputation of the girl and her family, though various manipulative responses, again differing from one place to another, are possible to redeem or partially redeem what has been soiled.[19] It is from an assessment of such patterns, and of the social practices of which they are a part, that we can reach an understanding of the underlying normative structures and the way they are reproduced.

III

The politics of spatial differentiation

A commonplace of contemporary scholarship holds that a gender-related dichotomization of public and private spheres characterizes Mediterranean communities, both ancient and modern.[20] While speaking of a public–private dichotomy may prove useful, it should not lead to formulaic rigidity and over-generalization. For example, taking this dichotomy over-literally as an absolute opposition has led many classical scholars to misapprehend the social role of women by assuming that they were virtual prisoners in their houses (see Chapter 6).[21] Here Herzfeld's term "complementary opposition"

---

[19] See Handman (1983: 79–216), Antoun (1968: 678–87), du Boulay (1974: 120–41), Pitt-Rivers (1971: 84–97). One could multiply the examples. The same is true, for example, of the various practices relating to the behavior of betrothed couples.

[20] I do not mean to imply that this pattern is uniquely Mediterranean. Such a dichotomy is widespread, including in societies with very different forms of social organization. See e.g. Gregor (1985: 22–51).

[21] See Delaney's (1987: 42) illuminating comments on the way that sexual dichotomization and female modesty do not produce isolation but rather a full social life for women in a Turkish village.

helps to make the interconnectedness of the categories of public and private clearer. At the level of social practice the public–private antinomy exists in a dynamic relation with intersecting oppositions associated with reputation and gender. I treat them separately so as to avoid the danger of conflation: for example, treating spatial differentiation as solely an aspect of gender differentiation, when in fact it is far more. As will become apparent, however, discussion of one category immediately raises issues related to the others, and rightly so, for in social life they function as different aspects of a complex normative system, in terms of which actors orient their conduct according to the anticipated expectations of public and private audiences. The fundamental normativity of such structural properties, serving as essential elements in the social control implicit in the reproduction of social systems, figures as one of the central theses of the following exposition.

The piazza and the café

In purely spatial terms, the simplest way of conceptualizing public and private spheres distinguishes the house from everything outside of its walls, that is, according to the antinomy inside–outside.[22] When one moves beyond a purely spatial description, however, the matter becomes more complicated. Although this antinomy expresses important aspects of the family's relation to the community,[23] one cannot simply reduce "public life" to "everything that transpires outside the house." A purely spatial account cannot adequately describe the public sphere, and for this reason anthropologists tend to introduce other criteria, usually economic, political, and sexual:

The opposition between the inside and the outside, a form of the opposition between the sacred of the left hand and the sacred of the right hand, is

---

[22] See Dubisch (1986: 197). Dubisch emphasizes the association of women with the inside, on which, see also Brandes' (1975: 113) account of Andalusia: "Nowhere is this role better encapsulated than in the village census, where invariably a married woman's occupation is listed either as 'domicilio' – 'house', or, even more telling, 'su sexo' – 'her sex'." Cf. Lloyd and Fallers (1976: 246ff.), Friedl (1967: 98–9), Antoun (1968), du Boulay (1974: 17ff.), Bourdieu (1977: 89ff., 1979: 133–53), Gilmore (1987a: 1–3).

[23] "The house as a physical structure is deeply linked with the identity of the family…" Further, "it is one of the characteristics of the society that the solidarity of the house rests not so much on everyone within it behaving well to each other, as the united front they all present to the outside world" (du Boulay 1974: 17, 19). See also Bourdieu (1966: 233), Tentori (1976: 284), Friedl (1962: 14–18). The solidarity of feuding societies is particularly strong, showing the range of variation; see e.g. Campbell (1979), Chelhod (1971), and Boehm (1984).

concretely expressed between the feminine area, the house and its garden... an enclosed space, secret, and protected, sheltered from intrusion and from the gaze of others, and the masculine area, the 'thajmaath,' the place of assembly, the mosque, the café, the fields, or the market place. The opposition is between the secrecy of intimate life, entirely veiled in modesty, and the open area of social relationships, of religious and political life... In the Kabyle village the two areas are distinctly separate; the path that leads to the fountain avoids the domain of men.[24]

Bourdieu's description of public and private in Kabylia (Algeria) is both rich and particularistic, expressing an opposition abstractly in terms of the secrecy of intimate life, focused on the house, and the "open area" of social relations, politics, and religion. Most analyses of the public sphere are less complex and evocative. Maraspini, for example, simply describes public life in the Italian village of Calimera as a male domain centering around the piazza with its cafés and nearby business establishments. In Calimera, "women do not go to the café, except on very rare occasions..."[25] Similarly, Photiadis, in his study of the café in Greek villages, argues that men's groups center around the coffee house, and though women also belong to groups they are excluded from the public space preempted by the men.[26] Likewise, in Malta, Boissevain describes public space as essentially that of the men:

The areas of the village around the parish church and the small square... are the territory of the men... Here are located the clubs and wine shops which are their particular preserve... The center of the village, the *pjaza*, is, thus, a male area. In fact, women and girls, when they have to pass through this area in the late afternoon or evening... do so rapidly and often in two's. They don't linger there. Their area is located away from the center, on their doorsteps, or in their houses and in the numerous little grocery and notion shops run, for the most part, by women; there, they meet with relatives and friends... This important line of social cleavage runs through all aspects of Maltese social organization. It is a basic structural principle.[27]

[24] Bourdieu (1966: 221) and cf. (1979: 133–53). As will appear in subsequent chapters, many elements of this description are strikingly similar to classical Athens.

[25] Maraspini (1968: 184, and cf. 61ff.). The occasions he enumerates when women do appear are also the typical occasions when women in classical Athens participate in public life. Note, however, that among the semi-nomadic Sarakatsani (Campbell 1979) the occasions for such participation are more restricted than in many other areas of Greece, e.g., Ambeli (du Boulay, 1974), Vasilika (Friedl, 1962), or Pouri (Handman, 1983).

[26] Photiadis (1965: 46–50), and cf. Sanders (1962: 205–17).

[27] Boissevain (1969: 42), and see Brandes (1975: 112ff., 140ff.; 1981: 218), Cutileiro (1971: 107), Kenny (1962: 55f.), and Mernissi (1975: 51ff.).

Boissevain's further description reveals that in the Maltese community he studied, women also engaged in economic and social relations, which are spatially "outside" when compared to the "inside" domain within the walls of the house. Such relations are not peculiar to Malta, but are just as "typical" of Mediterranean towns and villages as the association of men with the cafés and piazzas. Are these public relations? Are the porches, fountains, or shops where women gather for talk public areas? What differentiates them from the piazza and the café? Treatments which reduce the public–private opposition to the male space of the café or piazza and the female spaces of the house provide little help in answering such questions. Instead, one must turn from the piazza to the house, from the house to the neighborhood of which it is a part, and then, finally, back to the community.

The house

In what sense is the house the domain of women and not of men? In purely spatial terms the opposition inside–outside, as was seen above, does not exactly match the oppositions male–female, public–private. As Bourdieu argues in his famous description of the Kabyle house, such categories are relative and not absolute:

... the same thing may, in different universes of practice, have different things as its complement and may, therefore, receive different, even opposed properties, according to the universe. The house, for example, is globally defined as female, damp, etc., when considered from the outside, from the male point of view, i.e. in opposition to the external world, but it can be divided into a male-female part and a female-female part, when it ceases to be seen by reference to a universe of practice coextensive with *the* universe, and is treated instead as a universe (of practice and discourse) in its own right, which for the women it indeed is, especially in winter [because in winter men spend much more time inside the house].[28]

Nor are economic criteria absolute. In the Portuguese community of Vila Velha a traditional saying goes, "A mulher em casa, o homem na praça ('the woman at home, the man in the square'). The square immediately evokes cafés, taverns... business transactions, working agreements – the whole world with which a man

[28] Bourdieu (1977: 110).

must come into contact."[29] Yet women (not from wealthy families, of course) often work outside the house: as servants, in agricultural labor, in shops, etc.[30] What, then, does Dubisch's statement mean that in all parts of Greece "The house is the special responsibility of the woman, and she is functionally and symbolically associated with it"?[31] Some symbolic associations of women with the house were suggested by Bourdieu, above. Functionally, the woman is associated with the house in that the house is the domain of the family, and in the sexual division of labor the family is largely the sphere of the woman. While this functional identification is valid, it is also true that the house is also identified with the family as a whole, and in certain aspects particularly with men:

The house as a physical structure is deeply linked with the identity of the family, for as the family is the principal and irreducible group of this society, so the house in which the family lives is the chief stronghold of those values which are basic to the society.[32]

In this sense men are also intimately associated with the family and the house, for it is their role to protect the house, to shield the sphere of intimacy it represents.[33] For this reason the reputation of men is closely associated with the family, with the house, and particularly the women who dwell within it.[34]

Thus one cannot base the opposition of the female domestic sphere to the male public sphere upon any absolute spatial, economic, or social criteria. Women move, work, and see friends outside the house; men are, in important ways, associated with the house and the family (as will be seen more fully below). I do not mean to question the accuracy of the generalization associating men with public life and women with domestic life in traditional Mediterranean communities.[35] The purpose is rather to emphasize two points: first of all the danger of conceptual incoherence and circularity in defining social spatial differentiation in terms of rigid dichotomies expressed primarily by means of examples (men in the

---

[29] Cutileiro (1971: 107). On Moroccan markets see Hoffman (1967: 79–84).
[30] See e.g. Bell (1979: 122ff.).
[31] Dubisch (1986: 197). See also Maher (1974: 129–31), Pitt-Rivers (1971: 84ff.), du Boulay (1974: 63–4, 130ff.), Dimen (1986: passim), Pavlides and Hesser (1986: passim), Bell (1979: 123).
[32] Du Boulay (1974: 17).   [33] Bourdieu (1977: 123ff.).
[34] Pitt-Rivers (1966: 51), Bell (1979: 2–3, 105), Peristiany (1966: 182–3), Zeid (1966: 252ff.).   [35] Gilmore (1987b: 14).

café, women in the home); secondly, the fact that such gender-related spatial differentiation is fundamentally related to social expectations; that is, they are normatively structured. Sayings like "A mulher em casa, o homem na praça," or "The man is a guest in the house" are not objective observers' *descriptions* of how all men and women in fact act. Rather, as traditional sayings or maxims they reflect at the ideological level expectations of how men and women, ideally, *ought* to act. Such sayings constitute part of the normative repertoire of the community, and, as such, are subject to rhetorical manipulation, strategically defined exceptions, and so on. Women ought to work in the house, but under the appropriate circumstances, as judged by public opinion, working in the fields may entail no loss of reputation.[36] Thus statements associating men with the piazza and women with the home are at once prescriptive and, as ideologically tinted generalizations, descriptive. This normative content is brought out by informants' statements, like that of the men of San Blas, who say "The home is for eating and sleeping; otherwise a man belongs with his friends."[37]

Husbands and wives are thus judged by each other, and by the community, according to the way they maintain a proper relation to the house – a pattern no less true for classical Athens. Men who spend too much time around the house endanger their reputation – they are likely to be thought odd or womanly.[38] For, as du Boulay notes in her classic study of a Greek village, the role of the man necessarily takes him out of the house into the public sphere. Hence the saying, "The man is a guest in the house," or as one woman informant put it, "Anyway, what has a man to do in the house?"[39] On the other hand, the social expectations concerning the female role center on the home, and reputation is largely based upon criteria that follow from this:

---

[36] See Herzfeld (1980: 342): "In Vergadi (Peloponnese) ... a family's *filotimo* [roughly, honor in the sense of conformity to positive community expectations] is not diminished if the female members work in the fields 'when public opinion recognizes the need for it'." See also Friedl (1962: 22–3), Williams (1968: 67ff.), Sweet (1967: 175ff.), Pitt-Rivers (1971: 86–7), Aswad (1967: 142–9), Bell (1979: 122), Davis (1980: 92–4), Kenny (1962: 6off.), Gilmore (1987b: 1–3), and the excellent discussion of Maher (1974: 113ff., 150ff.).

[37] Brandes (1981: 218) and cf. the many such sayings reported by Pitt-Rivers (1966), and Bourdieu (1966, 1979). Kenny (1962: 57) describes the contrast between the ideal "home-bound" role of women and the fact of the "active life outside the home she creates and the small community circle of which it forms a part."

[38] Stirling (1966: 101), Maher (1974: 112), Bourdieu (1979: 141), Brandes (1981: 218), Gilmore (1987b: 14), Loizos (1975: 92).   [39] Du Boulay (1974: 129).

...absence from the home or irregularities in customary activities which cannot be minutely and indisputably accounted for in society, will almost inevitably be taken as evidence of surreptitious liaisons...Evidence of infidelity is direct proof of a woman's worthlessness in all other fields, and, conversely, careless behavior about the house and neglect of household duties are referred back to the basis of a woman's honor and cause aspersions to be cast on her chastity. A woman's place, in fact, is in the home, and any prolonged absence from it except for matters directly related to the welfare of the family is disliked by the husband and aversely noted by the community. 'Do you know', said one woman to me, 'how a man rejoices and how he loves his wife when he finds her always in the house?'[40]

The patterns of social practices associated with the house and the areas outside its walls express the central normative aspects of spatial differentiation. Further, the expectations of the community constitute a central structuring principle of those practices. The next section takes up the physical and social setting which expresses and reproduces such expectations. I defer the full discussion of the normative content of these expectations until the consideration of the politics of reputation in Section IV.

The neighborhood

If the public areas with which men are normatively associated are represented by the piazza and the café, the public space which women legitimately (i.e. in the eyes of the community) occupy is focused on the fountain and the neighborhood. Freeman has emphasized the structuring role, in Mediterranean communities, of recurrent "patterns of housing and water use [which] serve to maintain physical proximity and tight controls on a population which is bound by deeper imperatives to perpetuate such patterns."[41]

[40] Du Boulay (1974: 131). See also Dubisch (1986: 200): "Ideally a woman should be confined to the house, leaving its boundaries only as necessity demands and never for idle or frivolous reasons...Of course, this does not mean that a woman never leaves the house, for there is a wide range of legitimate duties that takes her outside." Antoun, in his survey of the "modesty" of women in the Middle East (1968: 675ff.), makes much the same argument. See also Maher (1974: 61), Williams (1968: 76ff.), Aswad (1967: 142–9), Lloyd and Fallers (1976: 260), Cutileiro (1971: 106ff.), Brandes (1975: 112ff., 140ff.), Bourdieu (1977: 160ff.). The parallels with classical Athens are explored at some length in Chapter 6.

[41] Freeman (1970: 90). For similarities in patterns of residence in Morocco, see Hoffman (1967: 64–78).

For women, in many Mediterranean towns and villages, the neighborhood constitutes a focus of normative structuring principles which serve to orient major aspects of social life.[42] In the Greek community studied by Kennedy, for example,

It is not considered correct social behavior to be outside one's neighborhood for a purpose not recognized by mainstream culture, and visiting a woman friend is not supported by the dominant culture. This proscription means that visiting often must occur in relative secrecy, either in someone's kitchen while men are in the fields or at places like the village springs while women are performing laundry tasks.[43]

The normative structuring of neighborhood life is not imposed upon women from without, but is rather reproduced by them as they carry on their social relations in conscious and unconscious orientation towards its standards. Goffman has demonstrated the essentially normative character of most forms of social interaction in public,[44] and this thesis seems no less true for many Mediterranean communities. As Cutileiro says of Vila Velha (Portugal),

Since women remain in the villages most of the time, whereas men go to work outside, neighborly relations are basically feminine relations. Supervising children's play, borrowing cooking utensils or provisions ... are some of the favors exchanged among poor neighbors, but the exchange of favors does not exhaust the features of the neighborhood relationship. Neighbors are basically watchers of their neighbors' behavior.[45]

In order to understand better why the neighborhood, as the "most important extra-kinship source of social integration,"[46] forms a recurring structuring feature of social life one need only call to mind the pervasive influence of those physical factors of which Freeman speaks. As in ancient Athens, where historians have emphasized that "narrowness of space" is a central component of political life,[47] many Mediterranean villages and towns are characterized by relatively great housing density: "Houses in the street are

---

[42] The house is clearly also central but, as will appear, from at least one perspective it cannot be strictly separated from the neighborhood. The church is yet another such focus. See Brandes' excellent discussion of women and the neighborhood in Becedas, Andalusia (1975: 145–57), and cf. Handman (1983: 115ff.), Fernea (1969: 70–82, 126–35, 179–87: 1980: 61–128), Altorki (1986: 51–121).   [43] Kennedy (1986: 129).

[44] See Chapter 2, and Goffman (1963a, 1971).

[45] Cutileiro (1971: 137), and see also Handman (1983: 115ff.), Brandes (1975: 145ff.) du Boulay (1974: 169–229).   [46] Brandes (1975: 145).

[47] Finley (1985b: 50), and cf. Pitt-Rivers (1971: 168).

tightly packed and separated by narrow streets. Village life is very much public since much of it is led outdoors. From her doorstep a woman can hear what is said at five or six other doorsteps and see what goes on in front of an even larger number of houses."[48] Physical proximity, coupled with unrelenting observation and the quick flow of information into gossip and information networks, are constants from which few villagers outside of the wealthier classes can escape.[49] As in classical Athens, where Wilamowitz spoke of the "neighbors who know everything,"[50] "There is a fund of common knowledge about all community members." Further, this knowledge serves as the basis of reputation and social control.[51] As Freeman argues in her study of Valdemoro (Spain),

It is a cultural fact that life in the village binds its members in certain ways and patterns in their relationships to one another...Alternatives to some of these patterns are generally recognized, but the patterns are nonetheless perpetuated and manipulated only within limits. For example, the physical arrangement of the pueblo is such that even houses...at the edges of the nucleus are still within hearing distance, and there is no house which is not in sight of at least two others. There is some tendency to insulate houses by building the stables or a storage room on one side, so that the living quarters are not adjacent, and the main common walls are very thick. However, houses open directly onto streets, as do their windows, and there is no such thing as a wall or fence shielding houses from the street.[52]

In the Italian town of Pisticci neighborhoods may vary in size, some people may live on main routes, others in more isolated areas, but the neighborhood (*vicinato*) is a group "which has daily, in most cases hourly, contact."[53]

Pisticcese houses often have no windows, so doors are left open to let in light: people can see in and out easily enough. In summer a large part of family life goes on outside the front door...Who passes by, who buys what

---

[48] Cutileiro (1971: 137), and see Pitt-Rivers (1971: 1–33), Maraspini (1968: 136ff.), and Brandes (1975: 30), who describes the houses of Becedas as "cluttered closely together in long narrow streets." The pictures of Moroccan villages and hamlets in Hoffman (1967: plates 1–4) make this point with particular force. See also Hoffman's description of great housing density (72ff.).

[49] See Brandes (1975: 6), Maraspini (1968: 145), and for the wealthy see Pitt-Rivers (1966: passim), Maher (1974: 61, 150ff.).   [50] Quoted by Finley (1952: 27).

[51] Brandes (1975: 6), and see Kenny (1962: 76).   [52] Freeman (1970: 86–7).

[53] Davis (1973: 66) reports that an artisan living on a busy street knew everyone in the quarter. Davis' neighbors knew everyone in the hundred or so nearest houses (the size of a small village). In communities where houses are less closely packed, comings and goings are no less sharply observed; see Campbell (1979: 313), Handman (1983: 105–26, 164ff.).

food, who changes his or her clothes how many times a day, is all observed and commented on. When there are quarrels within the family, when a child is beaten or a woman weeps, the neighbors know immediately...People should mind their own business, they say; but there is a premium on doing some things in public: justifying one's behavior, for example; or publicizing good actions.[54]

Such are the physical aspects of community life which make possible the exchange of information required for what Herzfeld aptly terms moral taxonomies, "systems...for the ranking of one's fellow-citizens according to a set of ethical criteria" based upon "public evaluation of behavior" and "degrees of conformity to a social code."[55] Now, since in an important sense "the neighborhood is a community of women,"[56] and since the reputation of a family rests in significant measure upon the public evaluation of the behavior of its women,[57] that evaluation largely arises from information networks based upon the neighborhood. "It is the women who do the gossiping who observe and comment, *triticano*. The men are not there; and they rely for their information on their wives."[58] Careful attention to the lives of others, and the rapid flow of information so gathered forms the basis of these moral taxonomies of public evaluation. "Inter-linked groups of mothers, daughters, and neighbors secure the gossip coverage of the village, and the washing places and shops are the local exchange markets for dealing in such currency."[59] Often, as in Valdemoro, the washing place (*lavadero*) "functions as an observation center, and the women function as a clearing house for general and public...gossip. The *lavadero* is the setting for that kind of gossip which serves to keep people within bounds..."[60]

---

[54] Davis (1973: 66–7). Brandes develops the idea of necessary publicity, involving the requirements that villagers stay in public view lest they be regarded as abnormal or dangerous. "In Becedas only the woman who lets her neighbor know about her activities is trustworthy. Conversely, a woman who wishes to be trusted will be sure to stay in the public eye" (1975: 153). Freeman, in discussing information networks, refers to neighbors as "an ever present constabulary" (1970: 86). See also du Boulay (1974: 182–223), Handman (1983: 161ff.), and Campbell (1979: 192ff., 210ff.) on the connection between observation, gossip, and social control.　　[55] Herzfeld (1980: 340–1).

[56] Davis (1973: 71).　　　　　[57] Zeid (1966: 253), Peristiany (1966: 182–5).

[58] Davis (1973: 71–2).

[59] Cutileiro (1971: 138–9); his discussion also emphasizes the speed of information flow (137). See also Campbell (1979: 313).

[60] Freeman (1970: 88). Du Boulay (1974: 209) notes that the change in patterns of women's associations due to technological changes in agricultural methods influences the opportunities for information exchange.

Gossip, as Cutileiro notes, serves as a particularly effective form of social control since it is impossible to locate its exact source and eliminate it. "The most minute details of appearance and behavior have to be carefully watched, since comments will always be made and unfavorable comment will spread through the whole village."[61] Since "The prestige of an individual, or a family, is constantly being evaluated and re-evaluated in the community through gossip...,"[62] actors must constantly remain aware of the inferences which others might draw from their actions. As in many other communities, the Sarakatsani may regard a girl who goes to the well too often, or takes too long to return from the pastures, as having had an illicit assignation.[63] "Everyone must weigh their actions precisely on account of the interpretation, correct or false, which will be attached to them." As one young woman in a Greek village put it, "In the village everything is given a bad interpretation. Therefore one has no choice but to lie. If you don't you can't manage."[64]

The spatial category of the neighborhood thus connects women to the spheres of social, moral, and, hence, public relations. The normative basis of spatial categories, as they operate in patterns of social practices, links them intimately to categories of gender, reputation, and power. If the neighborhood forms one of the major public domains in which women play a prominent part,[65] men's associations appear far less limited, but rather drawn from the whole community.[66] How are these two spheres related to one another? How do the normative properties of neighborhood life fit in with the larger normative structures of the community? How do those of the community relate to larger political entities like the state? To these large and complicated questions I can offer only a few tentative remarks. In the analysis of the particular context of classical Athenian society I will address them in somewhat greater depth.

---

[61] Cutileiro (1971: 140). As will be seen below, this may have tragic consequences. See also du Boulay (1974: 207ff.), Maraspini (1968: 62).

[62] Campbell (1979: 312).

[63] Campbell (1979: 86, 277).

[64] Du Boulay (1974: 93).

[65] Others, like religious activities, agricultural work, and so on, vary according to the setting (rural, urban, etc.) and the different forms of social organization and stratification.

[66] See e.g. Photiadis (1965: passim).

The community

In their respective studies of Spanish and Greek communities, Freeman and Photiadis argue that social control operates largely through informal channels. Freeman focused upon the neighborhood and concluded that the official political and judicial machineries of control "are in reality only secondary forces in village life."[67] "A person's freedom to create and manipulate his own image is hampered by his omnipresent neighbors, by their tendency to commit him to an image supported by accumulated public information about him and their power as a group to make of him an outcast."[68] Photiadis, on the other hand, studied the political role of the café in Greek villages, and assigned to it a central function in regard to social control:

The male adult demands that his family members behave in line with the expectations of the coffee house... Mothers often reprimand their daughters who have been out late by saying, "How is your father going to face the coffee house after this?"... "The coffee house will laugh at you" is a strong threat and warning for members of these... groups who have deviated or contemplate deviation. So this system of controls is built on interaction and decisively controls the behavior of the villagers.[69]

Freeman and Photiadis have both identified important moments in the normative structuring of social practices in their communities. However, they also seem to have taken the trees for the forest in reaching their rather reductionist conclusions. Taken together these passages help to illustrate the dynamic relationship existing between the café/piazza and the neighborhood, as well as the intimate link between male and female contributions to the public presentations and evaluations of conduct through which the community maintains social order. Though the house, the neighborhood, and the piazza play the dominant role in the politics of reputation which produce the "moral taxonomies" of public evaluation of behavior, they are hardly the *sole* forces of social control. They do, however, represent a major force in village communities. For example, Cutileiro reports of Vila Velha that "Local men will not, as a rule, attempt any violence against local women. I know of no case of rape."[70] This is surely not due simply to the official legal sanctions but rather to the dynamics of social control in a small "face-to-face" community

---

[67] Freeman (1970: 83).   [68] Freeman (1970: 89).
[69] Photiadis (1965: 50).   [70] Cutileiro (1971: 101).

where rape would be practically impossible to conceal.[71] Lison-Tolosana's account of an unsuccessful attempt in Belmonte under-scores this point.[72] Moreover, such communities expect unofficial sanctions for such behavior. For example, in Vila Velha brothers bear much of the responsibility for the sexual purity of their sisters. In an extreme case, one brother was murdered with his sister because he had taken no action after learning of her marital infidelity. "Public opinion, though not the law, was with him."[73] Indeed, there can be considerable disjunction between the normative expectations of the community and the requirements of the national legal system.[74] Pitt-Rivers has described the way in which state and community institutions can exist side-by-side, sometimes in opposition, sometimes overlapping.[75] Theft is, of course, illegal, but is almost never reported to the police if the suspect is a member of the community. If, however, the wrongdoer is either a stranger or one of the "shameless" (*sin verguenza*), a moral outcast, the police are notified.[76] On the other hand, though the police are quite unlikely to enforce existing laws concerning adultery, villagers sometimes resort to the *vito* (a kind of *charivari*), "an outburst of aggressive ridicule on the part of the anonymous pueblo against one who transgresses, an outburst provoked, it might be said, by a manifestation of anti-social sex."[77] Yet the *vito* is itself illegal, and the Guardia Civil may step "in to protect the adulterer against the sanctions of the pueblo, [or] the thief against the *sabia* [a wise-woman/sorceress] who would find him out."[78] At other times officials may close their eyes and allow communal action to take its course.[79]

While unofficial mechanisms of sanctions and control may be very strong in small communities, even there the requirements of vengeance and the like, which are ideally demanded by community

[71] I exclude cases of rape that occur outside the physical boundaries of the village, e.g. in distant pastures. These constitute a separate category in many legal systems because the required cry for help of the woman cannot be heard. See Chelhod (1971: 244ff), Deuteronomy 22:27, and Driver and Miles (1975: 40–1, 55–9) for Babylonian and Assyrian law.   [72] Lison-Tolosana (1966: 326).
[73] Lison-Tolosana (1966: 326), and cf. Campbell (1979: 193).
[74] See Campbell's discussion (1979: 193ff.) of homicide and revenge among the Sarakatsani, where there is a clear conflict between the norms with which the community identifies and the national legal culture which is officially sovereign. Cf. Pitt-Rivers (1977: 9) and Chelhod (1971).   [75] 1971: 160–202.
[76] Pitt-Rivers (1971: 178ff.). Sharpe reports a similar pattern in prosecutions of strangers in seventeenth-century England.   [77] Pitt-Rivers (1971: 174).
[78] Pitt-Rivers (1971: 179).   [79] Pitt-Rivers (1971: 174).

norms, may be greatly moderated by concern for the legal consequences.[80] At the same time the existence of legal sanctions, the possibility of resort to official intervention, and so on, figure as elements in agents' strategies in their competition for prestige, economic advantage, etc. Official and unofficial normative systems interconnect and together contribute to the maintenance of public order.[81] Even in the analysis of small villages, focusing exclusively upon either law and official political institutions or informal social mechanism of control is inadequate. The historical investigation of classical Athens must seek to penetrate the relations of conflict and reinforcement between the various normative systems.

The foregoing analysis has revealed some of the complexity of the politics of differentiation of space in Mediterranean communities. The ways in which the concepts discussed are differentially applied and manipulated "by the different status groups defined by age, sex, class," and occupation have barely been touched upon in this necessarily summary account, though they will come up again. The discussion has emphasized both the complex implications of the normative conceptualization of space and the corollary need to avoid rigid dichotomization. Finally, the discussion has underscored the way in which social practices cannot adequately be explained in terms of a "system" of rules which govern (in the strong sense of determine) the conduct of individuals and groups.

IV

The politics of reputation

The argument of this section explores some of the typical features of the normative structures and social practices through which judgments are expressed in many Mediterranean communities. The

---

[80] See Bourdieu (1977: 40ff., 93ff.) and the classic study of Black-Michaud (1975), criticized and developed by Boehm (1984). Chapters 5 and 6 discuss law, ideology and practice in regard to the killing of adulterers in classical Athens.

[81] Pitt-Rivers (1971: 161). "The legal and moral sanctions of this society each prescribe a code of behavior, but the two codes are far from being identical...Clearly, there is a large field of conduct which both the law and moral values prohibit, but there is also a large part of the Penal Code to which the pueblo is morally indifferent, while much that is regarded as wrong is free of legal injunction...But there is a sphere, finally, where the two sets of sanctions, instead of reinforcing one another, come into conflict...To co-operate with the government by denouncing to the inspector is an act of treason against the community" (178). See also Maraspini (1968: 95).

values usually translated, for the sake of convenience, as honor and shame occupy a central place in the analysis. I attempt, however, to avoid conflating terms like *filotimo*, *honore*, *nif*, *dropi*, *verguenza*, *vergogna*, and *ha'ram* into a homogeneous Mediterranean "code" of honor and shame, and focus instead on the various criteria and processes by which reputation is assessed in different communities. The aim is to identify similarities in the underlying structural properties that link reputation, gossip, secrecy, and public opinion with such values in a complex of social practices that contributes significantly to the reproduction of the social system.[82]

Black-Michaud, in his classic comparative study of honor and the feud, defends his methodology against possible objections that comparative analysis is unwise because honor can be used in many senses, rendering generalization impossible. He answers these charges in two ways. The first is by claiming that despite outward appearances the inner dynamic is constant, for all conflicts over honor may "be attributed to the same desire to acquire and demonstrate the possession of prestige..." Secondly, he argues that the fluid and manipulable nature of concepts like honor renders comparative analysis both possible and fruitful:

... the very versatility of the notion of honor is intrinsic to its function, which is to provide a zone of ambiguity creating room for political manoeuvre. In feuding societies there are few hard and fast rules as to which actions are honorable and which are not. Individuals interpret the notion very much as they please and as circumstances permit, manipulating it in furtherance of their own political ends.[83]

In regard to the politics of reputation the manipulation of normative categories like honor functions rhetorically. That is, it occurs as part of a dynamic relationship to an audience, or audiences. To use the language of Goffman and Bourdieu, it is inter-actional and strategic, and thus not limited by what "they please," as Black-Michaud has it, but rather by what sorts of interpretation the community will accept under the particular circumstances.

[82] Brandes (1987: 121) gives the best recent summary of "a specifically Mediterranean variety of the honor-and-shame syndrome, a substratum of beliefs that many peoples in this small, but highly diverse, part of the world share. For one thing, honor – which might best be translated as esteem, respect, prestige, or some combination of these attributes, depending on local usages – is treated throughout this area as a sort of limited good...Wherever we look, Mediterranean honor appears to be related to control over scarce resources, including, of course, land and property, political power, and, perhaps most notably, female sexuality with its procreative potential."

[83] Black-Michaud (1975: 179).

In the Portuguese and Spanish communities studied by Pitt-Rivers, Cutileiro, Brandes, Freeman, and Lison-Tolosana, the reputation of a family "is related to its material position and to the moral behavior of its members."[84] Through the operation of the principle of solidarity the reputation of individual members is largely determined by the reputation of their family. On the one hand, "Social status is inherited primarily from the father whose patrilineal surname a son inherits and will transmit to his descendants."[85] Likewise the damage to the reputation of the family due to the transgression of one of its members (particularly the women) is also inherited. On the other hand, "The economic status of the family depends upon the father's ability to maintain or improve its wealth."[86] Economic factors can influence a man's reputation in a variety of ways.[87] Great wealth (relatively speaking) can remove one from the corporate body of village men: "The pueblo is envisaged as a community of equals amongst whom economic differences do not amount to differences of social class, even though they are considerable... From this community the *senoritos* are excluded; they are accorded, as a title of respect, the prefix *Don*..."[88]

Further, within the community a man's reputation depends in part on his ability to provide adequately for his family, as a woman's is connected to her management of the affairs of the house.[89] Conformance to community norms of proper objects for expenditure also affects reputation. "Spending money, even to excess, is more important than possessing it, provided the money is spent on objects the community regards as appropriate."[90] Competition in spending offers a way of enhancing reputation, for example in buying drinks at the café, or contributing to public projects. Even those who are not wealthy put away money "to be used on public occasions, to make a show."[91] In this agonistic setting, competition, whether over

---

[84] Cutileiro (1971: 140), Pitt-Rivers (1966: passim), Brandes (1975: 75ff.).

[85] Pitt-Rivers (1977: 29).   [86] Pitt-Rivers (1977: 29).

[87] See Gilmore's excellent analysis of this perspective on reputation and honor (1987b: 90–102).

[88] Pitt-Rivers (1977: 30), and cf. Brandes (1980: 63–4). There has been much debate among Mediterranean anthropologists about rural egalitarianism. The most recent and thorough treatments are O'Neill's *Social Inequality in a Portuguese Hamlet* (1987), and Gilmore's *Aggression and Community* (1987b).   [89] Gilmore (1987b: 90–102).

[90] Lison-Tolosana (1966: 323). See also Schneider (1969: 147ff.), du Boulay (1974: 110ff.).

[91] Lison-Tolosana (1966: 323–4) examines the way in which poorer men who cannot compete with money compete through demonstrating other forms of prowess. See du Boulay's description of competition for reputation (1976: 391ff.).

expenditure or some other form of prowess, aims at proving "through concrete manifestations...manliness, [and] personal worth."[92] Yet "Reputation is not only a matter of pride, but also of practical utility. Where free association of a contractual kind governs the forms of cooperation and enterprise, a good name is the most valuable of assets."[93] As Davis reports of Pisticci,

The connection between domestic reputation and the wider societal honor in a society such as Pisticci appears to be that where rules of behavior are sanctioned informally, political activity and patron-client relationships depend upon trust: a man must have a reputation, and he must have something at stake when he enters the political arena.
...How a man behaves in his family is, therefore, the guide to his probable behavior in the less closely controlled and supervised political and economic spheres...[94]

If reputation is connected to social and economic status, these are by no means its only determinants. Among the Sarakatsani, other aspects of reputation include *timi* (honor), leadership, hospitality, lineage, marriage alliances, and the effective display of pride. Such attributes are interconnected, for "Without the imputation of honor and the quality of being honorable, wealth and numbers only represent a prestige which is, at best, equivocal. And weakness, or poverty, draws in its train doubts about the honor of a family, however socially conformist it may be."[95] Reputation is thus a judgment which exists in the consciousness of the community, based upon "expectations of how unique individuals and their equals ought to behave."[96] Further, because of the character of public life centered in the neighborhood, "Reputation is formed in the neighborhood...If a man...wants to impress people he says 'Go to my neighbours; they will tell you what sort of man I am.'"[97]

If a reputation arises from community judgments concerning the "quality of conformance to positive social expectations,"[98] those expectations vary according to gender, age, and social and economic

---

[92] Lison-Tolosana (1966: 324).
[93] Pitt-Rivers (1977: 18). See Davis (1973: 71): "Reputation is the basis of forming alliances for all purposes – mutual aid, politics, marriage, farming...," and also Black-Michaud (1975: 172ff.), P. Schneider (1969: passim), du Boulay (1976: 391).
[94] Davis (1973: 22–4).   [95] Campbell (1979: 306), Lison-Tolosana (1966: 315ff.).
[96] Davis (1973: 71). See Herzfeld (1980: 340–1), Aswad (1967: 142–9), Sweet (1967: 175ff.), Cutileiro (1971: 105–8), Lison-Tolosana (1966: 186ff.). For examples of similar patterns in seventeenth-century Spain see Weisser (1976: 78ff.).
[97] Davis (1973: 71). See also Kenny (1962: 76ff.).   [98] Herzfeld (1980: 348).

status.[99] Norms are thus not homogeneous and embodied in an abstract code rigidly applied, but are differentiated and manipulable. For example, although most Mediterranean communities in principle expect women to focus their activities upon the house, in Vergadi (Peloponnese), again, a family's *filotimo* is not diminished if its female members work in the field "when public opinion recognizes the necessity for it."[100] At the same time, women both orient their behavior according to these norms and manipulate them so as to influence judgments. In the Lebanese village of Harouch, where not working outside the house is a great mark of economic and social status for women, female informants *not* from well-to-do families all claimed that they *only* worked at home.[101]

From the standpoint of moral psychology, the examples given above reflect a culture whose values closely involve shame. The moral perspective of shame involves evaluating oneself in significant measure according to the way in which one is seen by others. Guilt, however, arises more from an internal recognition, before oneself, of wrongdoing, and is expressed through remorse, repentance, and a desire to restore a damaged relationship. Shame, on the other hand, connects to perceptions of having fallen short in the eyes of others (though these expectations may also be internalized), and expresses, through feelings of humiliation, defilement, exposure, unworthiness to withstand the gaze of others, the need to "cover" or hide oneself, or defeat others in competition.[102] Concepts like *verguenza*, *vergogna*, *dropi*, and *ha'ram* play a prominent role in the normative structures of many Mediterranean communities, and although there are, of course, variations, I would suggest that they all incorporate a core idea of judging oneself and others not according to inner moral

---

[99] For a discussion of variation according to class see Pitt-Rivers (1977: 62), who concludes "The moral sanctions of the pueblo have only a limited importance for the middle classes and none for the upper... their reputation looks to their equals for validation, not to their inferiors." Cf. Campbell (1979: 297ff.).

[100] Herzfeld (1980: 342–3); as he puts it later, "*Filotimo* is demonstrated through the adequate recognition of social obligation." Cf. Kennedy (1986: 138) and P. Schneider (1969: 145).

[101] Williams (1968: 67, 79). See also Pitt-Rivers (1971: 62ff.), Bourdieu (1966: 222), Cutileiro (1971: 104ff.), Maher (1974: 113), and cf. O'Neill (1987: 127) and Behar (1986: 15–16).

[102] The best philosophical discussion of the moral psychology of shame and guilt is Morris (1976). See also Piers and Singer (1963), Pitt-Rivers (1977: 21ff.), Black-Michaud (1975: 223ff.), Campbell (1979: 310–12), du Boulay (1974: 104–17, 130–6). Antoun's detailed discussion (1968: passim) of the idiom of modesty makes the connection clear, as in sayings like "The woman is born clean... She is like the mirror. The slightest breath clouds it. She is like glass; once it is broken it cannot be repaired." Cf. Bourdieu's (1966: 210ff.; 1977: 44ff.) account of Kabyle proverbs, like "Shame is the maiden," or the son-in-law as the "veil cast over shame."

states, but according to public judgments of success in conforming one's external behavior to expected normative standards.[103] Du Boulay's discussion of the politics of reputation in the Greek village of Ambeli makes this point nicely:

... the villager's honor is, broadly speaking, something which is granted him by public opinion and which may not be possessed in defiance of it. A man who is denied a reputation for honor has... no honor. Avoidance of social condemnation therefore equals retention of honor rather than avoidance of doing wrong. Thus it comes to be that there is a very significant sense in which it is considered more important to be seen to be honorable than it is actually to be so...

It is as a direct result of this state of affairs that the villager is on the whole concerned only with sanctions imposed upon him by others as a result of his doing wrong, and only very marginally, if at all, with the damage he may have inflicted on himself by the act.[104]

Similarly, Bourdieu's discussion of *nif* (honor) among the Kabyle brings out the way in which this concept is based upon the community's assessment of one's worth as a person: "The sentiment of honor is lived out openly before other people. *Nif* is above all in the action of defending, cost what it may, a certain public image of oneself."[105]

It is characteristic of dishonor that once public, it is irreversible. Hence the politics of reputation require that one pay scrupulous attention to the way one's words and deeds will be interpreted by others:

[103] Brandes notes that in Becedas villagers "generally do not choose between alternative courses of action on the basis of what is morally right or wrong, but rather on the basis of what will *appear* acceptable to the community" (1975: 149). He, du Boulay (1974), and Pitt-Rivers (1966, 1971) have most explicitly emphasized the significance of shame orientation. See also Kenny (1962: 79ff.) on *verguenza*.

[104] Du Boulay (1974: 82–3). She argues that villagers are not concerned about the effect of wrongdoing upon their own conception of themselves as a person, but are rather ashamed "at the slur on [their]...integrity which would follow if the community were to find out about it." See also Kennedy's discussion (1986: 138) of the term *philotimos* as concern about maintaining the *appearance* of honor. This is much the same in classical Athens, where reputation is a category for the moral evaluation of oneself and others. The role of shame in such discussions finds vivid expression in Plato's well-known debate between Callicles and Socrates over the nature of the good life. There, the terms of the debate centrally involve the category of what kinds of lives and pleasures will be envied or despised by others.

[105] Bourdieu (1966: 208); here again the language is that of shame: "The point of honor is the basis of the moral code of an individual who sees himself always through the eyes of others... Hence it is that the dynamics of exchanges of honor are based essentially upon the pressure of public opinion" (210–12). See also Campbell (1979: 268ff.), P. Schneider (1969: 148), Black-Michaud (1975: 178ff.), du Boulay (1976: 391), Zeid (1966: passim), Pitt-Rivers (1977: Chapter 2).

honor...is only irrevocably committed by attitudes expressed in the presence of witnesses, the representatives of public opinion... Public opinion forms therefore a tribunal before which claims to honor are brought, "the court of reputation" as it has been called, and against its judgments there is no redress. For this reason it is said that public ridicule kills...[106]

In Andalusia, *verguenza* thus has two sides. On the one hand it is the sentiment which "makes a person sensitive to the pressure exerted by public opinion," but it is also "the reputation earned in consequence."[107] A man who violates these expectations is said to be *sin verguenza*, shameless, without shame.[108] Likewise, in Ambeli, the person who ignores public evaluation, who doesn't act with reference to the norms of the community as enshrined in public opinion, is *atimos* (without honor, dishonored) or *chamenos* (lost). Those seen to deviate from these norms are ridiculed and mocked, giving rise to feelings of *dropi* (shame). Fear of mockery leads villagers to refrain from actions which they think will meet with this reaction, and they nearly always express this by saying that *dropi* prevents them from so acting.[109] If in this sense shame, with honor, forms the basis of reputation,[110] it is, at the same time, radically differentiated according to gender:

...the conduct which establishes repute depends upon the status of the person referred to. This is particularly evident in the differentiation of the sexes. The honor of a man and of a woman therefore implies quite different modes of conduct. This is so in any society. A woman is dishonored, loses her verguenza, with the tainting of her sexual purity, but a man does not.[111]

An understanding of the politics of reputation requires a detailed exploration of this differentiation, and to this task the discussion now turns.

Among the Greek Sarakatsani, honor, *timi*, is fundamental to reputation, and "expresses the idea...of social worth evaluated in a complex of competing groups and individuals."[112] *Timi* is related to two "sex-linked qualities that distinguish the ideal moral character

---

[106] Pitt-Rivers (1977: 6–7). On ridicule and its relation to shame see Brandes (1975: 115) and Pitt-Rivers (1971: 160–77).   [107] Pitt-Rivers (1977: 20).

[108] Pitt-Rivers (1977), Cutileiro (1971: 140ff.), Kenny (1962: 80), Gilmore (1987b: 95), Brandes (1980: 48).

[109] Du Boulay (1974: 108ff.). Cf. Brandes (1975: 115ff.; 1980 passim).

[110] Pitt-Rivers (1977: 20). He notes that as a moral sentiment, *verguenza* has other meanings not associated with honor "such as shyness, blushing, and the restraint which derives from emotional inhibitions, the fear of exposing oneself to criticism."

[111] Pitt-Rivers (1977: 20).   [112] Campbell (1979: 28).

of men and women": manliness (*andrismos*) for men, *dropi* (shame, sexual modesty) for women.[113] According to the principle of the solidarity of the family (as viewed by the community), it follows from these two underlying principles of *timi* that the reputation of a man is inextricably connected to the sexual modesty, or adequate display of the sense of shame (*dropi*) of his mother, wife, daughter, or sister.[114] From this fundamental feature of the politics of reputation across the Mediterranean flow far-reaching consequences.

For men, apart from the economic and social factors described above, a quality like that which the Sarakatsani refer to as *andrismo*, or the Andalusians as *hombria* (maleness, manliness), commonly constitutes a major element of reputation. On the one hand, manliness is meant quite literally as the physical embodiment of sexual potency.[115] As Pitt-Rivers reports of Andalusia, "The ideal of the honorable man is expressed by the word *hombria*, manliness…" Manliness is embodied in the "physical quintessence of the male (*cojones*) [testicles]."[116] The adjective *manso*, which means both tame and also castrated, conveys the contrary sense.[117] Likewise, in regard to *andrismo* among the Sarakatsani, "The physical characteristics of manliness are important. A man must be *barbatos*, that is, well-endowed with testicles and the strength that is drawn from them."[118] In the Italian village of Calimera, "Lack of manliness vitiates the possession of any of the other [desirable qualities]. And manliness is understood primarily in its physical and sexual aspect."[119] Sexual boasting, and "admiration felt for the recognized Don Juans of the village, are all further examples of a man's potency. The worst insult to a young boy is to call him '*fiminuccia*,' little female."[120]

[113] Campbell (1979: 269). See Antoun (1968: 68off.) and Bourdieu (1966: 223–4) for the shame-oriented vocabulary of the sexual modesty of women. Protecting the modesty of a woman is to "cover," "clothe," or "veil" her. Failure to do so "exposes" her, and likewise "exposes" the man's honor.

[114] Pitt-Rivers (1977: 29) summarizes the pattern, arguing that the greatest dishonor for a man follows from the sexual impurity of his mother, and after that, his wife. Since the impurity of his mother calls into question his own status and patrimony this is often the worst possible insult. See also Maraspini (1968: 151, 180), and Antoun (1968: 671–2).

[115] Gilmore (1987b: 96).

[116] Pitt-Rivers (1977: 22), Maraspini (1968: 115), Kenny (1962: 81).

[117] Pitt-Rivers (1977: 22), and see Maraspini (1968: 115).

[118] Campbell (1979: 269–70). On the basis of manliness in physical potency see also Maraspini (1968: 149–50), Brandes (1981: 124–6), P. Schneider (1969: 148), Handman (1983: 87). [119] Maraspini (1968: 151ff.).

[120] Maraspini (1968: 152). See P. Schneider (1969: 148), where the man without honor is "una fimmina" (a woman), or "un saccu vacanti" (an empty sack); Gilmore (1987: 10–11); and Kenny (1962: 66).

The latter point introduces a complication into the moral division of labor, for, if women must manifest sexual modesty and shame (*dropi, verguenza, vergogna, ha'ram*) and men are admired for being predatory Don Juans, then conflict seems inevitable.[121] In fact, success in protecting the sexual integrity of the women of one's house against incursions by other men ("covering their shame" in Kabylia) forms another major component of manliness and reputation.[122] Thus the Garrese of Sicily say "If a man cannot keep his house in order, he is not much good for anything else,"[123] an expression that nicely encompasses all symbolic and other connotations of the house. As du Boulay summarizes the case, honor as the basis of a man's reputation is embodied not only in characteristics like courage, quick temper, and sexual potency, but also in those "qualities which make a responsible and authoritative husband and father, a good provider for the household."[124] One also finds these two poles of reputation in many communities in Spain, Portugal, Italy, Turkey, Lebanon, Algeria, Morocco, Cyprus, and Malta, where as with "both...the Sarakatsani and the people of Ambeli, the values of manliness have the same orientation – to guard the virtue of the women and the honor of the house in both economic and moral terms."[125] This duality constitutes a pervasive structural property of social practices in many Mediterranean societies.

If the community expects men to preserve their reputation through guarding the sexual integrity of their women (with exceptions that will be discussed below), it ridicules those who fail in this endeavour. "Among Arabs the man who does not do so is termed 'cuckold' (*dayyuth*) a term that in a religious context confers the strongest opprobrium in meaning 'reviled one.' In one of its popular meanings *dayyuth* refers to an animal that stands by and

---

[121] Maraspini (1968: 155) notes the conflict; see also Pitt-Rivers (1977: 23).

[122] Bourdieu (1966: 221–5). Cutileiro (1971: 98–9) says of Vila Velha that the wife's ability to control her *vicio* forms the moral foundation of the family; see also Antoun (1968: 638), Campbell (1979: 287), Herzfeld (1986: 219), and Stirling (1966: 113ff., 211ff.). Stirling's well-known study, *Turkish Village*, was criticized for neglecting honor and shame (see Yalman 1966). Stirling (1966) later stated that the society he had depicted bore striking similarities to those described by Pitt-Rivers, Bourdieu, and Campbell.

[123] Giovannini (1986: 104–5). [124] Du Boulay (1974: 109).

[125] Du Boulay (1974: 110). Pitt-Rivers (1977: 29) concludes "A conflict of values is therefore implicit between the male pride which expresses itself in gallantry towards the female sex, and that which reposes upon a firm attachment to the duties of the family man." See also Stirling (1966: 36, 118ff., 211ff.), Delaney (1987: 41–2), Maraspini (1968: 150ff., 175ff.), Gilmore (1987b: 90–102); and the excellent discussion of the various meanings of *honra, honradez, honrado*, and *verguenza* in Lison-Tolosana (1966: 315ff.).

watches while other males make sexual connection with his mate."[126] This also forms the core idea of the cuckold in many other Mediterranean communities (*cabrão, corno, cabron, cornuto*), the man who wears the horns of the goat. The literature on this topic is vast, but it suffices to note the double connotation of this attribution. The goat is both an animal widely identified with the woman and also an animal that watches as its mate has intercourse with others.[127] Cutileiro summarizes what he regards as the typical pattern of Portuguese villages,

The bride's virginity and the wife's fidelity are the basic moral assumptions on which the family is built.... When a man becomes a husband...he becomes for the first time the full trustee of a woman's honor, and her behavior is intimately tied up with his reputation and the fate of their family. The risk of his wife's adultery...is the risk of perpetual dishonor: if it happens he will forever be a *cabrão* or *corno* (cuckold).[128]

Thus masculine and feminine honor and shame exist in a complementary relationship which constitutes another structural principle of the politics of reputation.[129] The reputation of a woman depends upon her fulfillment of community expectations of chastity. Giovannini's comparative study of female chastity in the Mediterranean argues for a pervasive pattern of chastity as the basis for judgments of social worth.[130] On the other hand men assert their manliness and enhance their reputation by demonstrating their potency. In Spain, Portugal, and Italy this widespread pattern particularly emphasizes the manliness of the predatory male whom women must resist: "the social pressure or *vigencia* which compels a young man to be, or at least attempt to be, a Don Juan...is only possible in a society in which the supreme feminine *vigencia*...is virginity or chastity. The Don Juan cannot exist without this *vigencia* and vice-versa..."[131] If a man succeeds in this endeavor and this

[126] Antoun (1968: 680).
[127] See Kenny (1962: 83), Blok (1981: passim), and Brandes' extensive discussion (1981: passim). On women and goats see also Campbell (1979: 31). As P. Schneider (1969: 148) puts it, the cuckold is "not just a man without honor but dishonored and no longer a man." Cf. Maraspini (1968: 180).
[128] Cutileiro (1971: 99, 102), Lison-Tolosana (1966: 323–5), Delaney (1987: 41–2).
[129] See Campbell (1979: 271), Pitt-Rivers (1977: 21–3), Stirling (1966: 118ff., 211ff.), Antoun (1968: passim).   [130] Giovannini (1987: 61–74).
[131] Cf. Mernissi's (1975: 83) description of a similar dynamic in Morocco: "In a country like Morocco, heterosexual encounter is the focus of so much restriction, and consequently attention, that seduction becomes a structural component of the culture." Chapter 6 discusses the way this dynamic operated in classical Athens.

becomes known, the woman loses her honor (as do her husband, brothers, and father), but *his* reputation grows.[132] The contingency, "if it becomes known," deserves emphasis, for, as Campbell demonstrates in his discussion of the *dropi* (sexual shame) expected of women, "honor is something imputed by others. In these matters the individual woman can never retreat within her own conscience. Her honor depends upon the reputation the community is willing to concede, not upon the evidence of facts in any case difficult to determine."[133]

As one would expect in a culture oriented toward shame, it follows from this sexual dynamic that reputation depends largely upon the *appearance* of honor as judged by others rather than the inner reality. For this reason a complex of practices associated with secrecy, gossip, and the lie intimately connects with the politics of reputation. Du Boulay's classic account of reputation, gossip, lying, and mockery in Ambeli sets out the link:

The public element in the organization of village life has an important bearing on the way in which the quality of sexual shame is lived out, for since honor is given to the individual by the community, and since feminine honor depends on the possession of shame, it is vital for the possessor of shame that this fact should be demonstrated to the community. It is in fact as important to be seen to be chaste as it is to be chaste.

In practical and personal terms the logic behind this...is one which depends upon the theory that it is safe always to assume the worst of women. This is because a woman, however genuine her sense of shame, is thought to be in danger of losing her honor since men are insistent and she is by nature frail...And since it is assumed in this way that she will inevitably fall if she puts herself into temptation, it becomes her business as an honorable woman not to put herself into temptation at all. If, therefore, she is seen in a compromising situation, she will inevitably be assumed to have been compromised, whether or not this is actually so...[134]

To be the object of gossip and speculation may be in itself compromising. As Thucydides has Pericles say in the Funeral

---

[132] Lison-Tolosana (1966: 335), Maraspini (1968: 150ff., 175ff.). On the other hand, the same cultures emphasize the insatiability and sexual danger of women, whose ravenous desires lead men to destruction (see e.g. Brandes, 1981). Chapter 6 takes up this implicit contradiction in the ideological conceptualization of women.

[133] Campbell (1979: 270).

[134] Du Boulay (1974: 112). Cf. Cutileiro (1971: 99ff.) and Maraspini (1968: 180) on the appearance of honor. Freeman (1970: 140) notes the importance of inferences from appearances, e.g. spending too much money on oneself or the household is considered "a bad sign" for a woman. Inferences from public aspects of behavior also play an important role in Athenian sexual politics, as will appear in Chapters 4–7.

Oration, "The greatest glory of woman is to be least talked about by men, whether they are praising you or blaming you."[135] Gossip can destroy a woman's reputation irreparably, though based merely upon inference. Lison-Tolosana relates that in Belmonte,

One girl was ill in bed and people began to whisper that she had attempted to bring about a miscarriage. The sensational story spread like wildfire and soon reached the ears of the family concerned. ... They rushed to the priest, the mayor, the civil guard. The priest, speaking in church, attacked the unknown slanderers, the mayor summoned the young men one by one to the Town Hall and attempted to find out who had started the rumour; the civil guard did exactly the same in their barracks but without success. The girl in question left the pueblo.[136]

Thus concludes Maraspini, in his description of Calimera,

It is not enough for a girl to remain chaste, or for a married woman to be a faithful wife: she must, in addition, appear chaste. If her behavior is too lively; if she makes too easy friendships with men; if she behaves too independently; if she smokes or wears trousers, or is seen to perform some activity reserved to the male; no matter how innocent of any factual fault she may be, the very failure to keep up the appearance of respectability is enough to compromise her beyond repair.[137]

The connection between the behavior and the inference appears to be primarily one of convention rather than logic. Failure to maintain these conventions can damage one's reputation not simply because it follows that a woman who wears trousers will also have illicit relations, but also because the disposition underlying the lack of compliance is in itself threatening. Evasion arouses far less hostility than open defiance and the questioning of community values that it implies.[138] As Goffman argues of social interaction in general, orientation towards norms, even when expressed in strategies of avoidance, constitutes the decisive token of commitment to membership in the moral community.[139]

Since neighbors are inquisitive and physical proximity often great (III above), the house, and the potentially damaging information it

---

[135] 2.45. For Roman versions see Seneca, *De Cons. H.* 19.6., Elder Seneca, *Controversiae* 1.2.10.
[136] Lison-Tolosana (1966: 333), see Maraspini (1968: 180), du Boulay (1974: 168–229), Antoun (1968: passim).
[137] Maraspini (1968: 180); cf. P. Schneider (1969: 149), Pitt-Rivers (1971: 208).
[138] See Pitt-Rivers (1971: 174ff.).
[139] See also Bourdieu's (1977: 196) incisive discussion of "the social conditions of the cross-censorship to which each agent submits with impatience but which he imposes on all others."

encloses must be protected from gossip and disguised through the lie.[140] The physical and moral conditions of village life make privacy a difficult commodity to obtain, especially since it is in itself damaging to awaken the impression that one has something to hide. The house as a physical and moral presence embodies the notion of a sphere more protected than any other from intrusion. As such, the protected spatial category of "inside" can be taken quite literally: "Within the house secrets are kept... I was entrusted, by the young widow in whose house I was living, with a secret which she would not tell her brother or father because they were 'in another house.'"[141] As an instrument of maintaining secrecy the lie thus "serves a vital function in reconciling the need for individual families... to lead a private life, with the sanctions (curiosity leading to mockery) which must operate if the moral code is to have force."[142]

The way in which the community assesses reputation according to relative conformance to normative expectations has now been described in some detail. I have avoided the use of terms like "moral code" because such normative expectations are not embodied in a homogeneous, contradiction-free system of abstract principles, but rather in complex patterns of social practices in which norms present themselves as fluid categories invoked and articulated in a manipulative and rhetorical manner. The remainder of this section will take up the issues of homogeneity and manipulation in a more explicit fashion.[143]

For both men and women, the specific content of standards for the assessment of reputation may vary considerably between communities or social groupings. But, though the criteria for evaluation of manliness, for example, may differ, the underlying link of manliness to reputation remains constant, both within communities and, generally speaking, regionally. In some societies where physical strength and courage are a necessity (e.g. the Sarakatsani, Bedouin, Kabyle),[144] competitive and assertive aspects of manliness are given emphasis as preserving the honor of the family. In more peaceful and less harsh economic settings the more "domestic" side of being a good provider often receives greater emphasis (e.g. Ambeli, Vila

[140] Two classic studies of the lie are du Boulay (1974, 1976) and Handman (1983).
[141] Du Boulay (1974: 22).
[142] Du Boulay (1974: 200, and 197ff.), and see also Bourdieu (1966: 223).
[143] The topic of contradiction plays an important role in the ensuing analysis of Athenian society, so discussion of it is deferred to Chapters 6, 7, and 9.
[144] See Bourdieu (1966), Pitt-Rivers (1966), Zeid (1966), Black-Michaud (1975: 178ff.).

Velha, Belmonte, or Calimera).[145] Yet within individual communities both orientations are often present. As du Boulay argues,

Thus two standards exist, one which accords with the image of the householder as a diligent and sober provider, whose reputation depends increasingly on his intrinsic merit as regards his opportunities and what he does with them, and only secondarily on direct confrontation with others; the other which accords with the image of the volatile defender of family interests against the depredations of others, and is primarily concerned with demonstrating his comparative merit over that of his neighbors.[146]

Likewise the standards of reputation for women, based upon qualities like *dropi, verguenza,* and so on, are not homogeneous, though here too the underlying idea of conforming to community expectations of sexual and moral behavior remain the same. In Vila Velha, for example, the "official," ideal standards provide that the adultery of the wife indelibly stains the honor of the family.[147] Yet long term adulterous relationships between wealthy men and women from poor families do exist and are unofficially tolerated. Such relationships, about which the husbands pretend not to know, are viewed as examples of "the moral handicaps of poverty."[148]

If the relative dishonor of the cuckold can vary within and across societies, the same holds true for the reputation of the adulterer. As noted above, the pressure towards *Donjuanismo* appears particularly pronounced in some Spanish and Italian communities, though here too there may be considerable variation according to age and class.[149] Yet almost everywhere (including, as will be seen, classical Athens), in greater or lesser degree, a certain ambiguity attaches to the adulterer. On the one hand, the adulterer affirms his manliness through the seduction of the women of others, and affirmation of manliness is positively valued. On the other hand, he is the destroyer of reputations and families, and, hence, a source of disorder in the community.[150] In Ambeli, for example, men who have adulterous

---

[145] See du Boulay (1974), Cutileiro (1971), Lison-Tolosana (1966), Maraspini (1968).

[146] Du Boulay (1974: 111). Cf. P. Schneider (1969: 148ff.).

[147] Cutileiro (1971: 140–1).

[148] Cutileiro (1971: 145–6). Of course, one can argue that here too the husband who knows of his wife's adultery and draws economic advantages from it still controls her sexuality. Other forms of institutionalized deviation from ideal standards are described by Maraspini (sexual relations between cousins, 1968: 182) and Handman (courtship, 1983: 147ff.).

[149] Pitt-Rivers (1977: 10). Kenny (1962: 66) reports the popular verse: "La vida del mozo es saltar tapias y corrales/Dormir en camas ajenas y morir en los hospitales." (The life of a young man is to jump over walls and fences/To sleep in the beds of others and die in the poorhouse.)

[150] This duality is brought out in the figure of Don Juan, and clearly underlies Mozart/Da Ponte's portrayal of Don Giovanni.

affairs are often disapproved of, not for infidelity, but because "such affairs lead to gossip and possibly quarrels which harm the family."[151] As Handman recounts of Pouri, men boast of their sexual exploits in the café, but when those who listen and joke about them return home, they are obliged to condemn them when they tell their wives. Adultery is seen as bringing disorder even as it serves as proof of virility. On the one hand it is condemned, but on the other hand, "continually to prove their virility...is one of the means by which men justify and preserve the superiority which is conferred upon them by the fact of being male."[152]

As Black-Michaud points out, the fluid, differentiated quality of the norms relating to reputation is precisely what makes them particularly manipulable.[153] The structural contradictions of normative systems, regarded by Giddens as one of the "constitutive features of human societies,"[154] fuels the rhetorical and strategic potential of social interaction. The existence of a complex repertoire of complementary and contradictory ideologies and practices makes possible the subtlety and richness of the social settings I have just sketched. No one has explored these issues with greater subtlety than Bourdieu in *Outline of a Theory of Practice*, "The Sentiment of Honor in Kabyle Society," and "The Kabyle House or the World Reversed." A major aspect of his argument shows the way in which reputation and honor are not *determined* by objectively given "structures" or "codes," but rather how actors strategically manipulate norms and community expectations in a complex "rhetoric of honor."

From one perspective, according to Bourdieu, the game of honor constituted by insult, challenge, and riposte, can be seen as subject to certain principles. From the basic principle of equality in honor follow three corollaries: a challenge involves the recognition of honor; to issue a challenge to one incapable of riposte is to dishonor oneself; only a challenge from one's equal in honor deserves to be taken up – one who responds to an inferior dishonors himself.[155] In his initial account of this "game of honor," Bourdieu argued that these principles "presuppose the choice of playing a set game in

---

[151] Du Boulay (1974: 125).

[152] Handman (1983: 87). P. Schneider (1969: 149) points out that the evaluation of *prepotente* behavior as either the epitome of honor or the parody of it depends on who is making the judgment. One might add, making the judgment for what particular reasons, in what particular rhetorical/strategic situation.

[153] Black-Michaud (1975: 179).   [154] Giddens (1986: 193).

[155] Bourdieu (1966: 206), Pitt-Rivers (1977: 10).

conformity with certain rules."[156] He noted, however, that all players of this game are "rhetoricians of honor," who "play on the ambiguities and equivocalities of conduct." In *Outline of a Theory of Practice*, however, he re-analyzed the same material in light of the general theory of social practices he develops there, rejecting the notion of an abstract set of rules as misleading:

The driving force of the whole mechanism is not some principle (... equality in honor) still less the set of *rules* which can be derived from it. Rather, it is "the sense of honor," a disposition inculcated in the earliest years of life and constantly reinforced ... inscribed in the body schema and in the schemes of thought, which enables each agent to engender all the practices consistent with the logic of challenge and riposte ... by means of countless inventions, which the stereotyped unfolding of a ritual would in no way demand ... The mastery which defines excellence finds expression in the play made with time which transforms ritualized exchange into a confrontation of strategies. The skilled strategist can turn a capital of provocations received or conflicts suspended, with the potential ripostes, vengeances, or conflicts it contains, into an instrument of power, by reserving the capacity to reopen or cease hostilities in his own good time.[157]

Similarly, Bourdieu describes the way in which actors manipulate the collective definition of a situation (for example, an insult to a woman by someone from another group) either so as to mobilize support by bringing it within the category of legitimate public interests requiring a collective response, or, on the other hand, to pursue the strategy of reducing it "to a merely private affair."[158] The point here is that reputation is not "determined" by the mechanical application of "rules" imposed upon individuals from without. It exists only in the minds of the members of the community, and, as such, changes according to the patterns of social practices constituted by observation, gossip, inference, interpretation, secrecy, lying, mockery, and the rhetoric of honor: that is, through the manipulation of public opinion and "collective definitions" by knowledgeable actors pursuing their particular strategies. The orientation of such practices around the normative expectations of the community contributes to the reproduction of the social system in which they are embedded. The politics of reputation, operating through the normalizing force of social pressure and public opinion, thus constitute a structuring principle for the maintenance of the social order.

[156] Bourdieu (1966: 204). [157] Bourdieu (1977: 14–15).
[158] Bourdieu (1977: 40ff.).

CHAPTER 4

Public and private in classical Athens

Although the notion of "privacy" might appear more immediately relevant to a discussion of social control and the enforcement of morals, for a number of reasons this chapter initially focuses instead upon the complementary opposition of "public and private." First, the contemporary definition of the problem in terms of the nature and boundaries of "rights to privacy" or "individual autonomy" reflects preoccupations characteristic of modern liberalism, whereas ancient societies are commonly held not to have possessed concepts of rights and individual autonomy.[1] Further, when we examine the recent judicial cases and the legal and philosophical secondary literature, we find a marked inability to agree about the nature and status of privacy or rights to privacy. Thus a prominent scholar in this area, in writing about this definitional confusion, identifies five major categories of definitions of privacy, all of which, he argues, are completely misguided. By proposing yet another he is not likely to have resolved the underlying difficulties.[2]

For these reasons, rather than taking an abstract definition of privacy as a starting point, I will begin instead with a dichotomy conceptually prior to privacy: the contrast of the public and private spheres. Here we run little risk of entirely imposing modern categories upon the ancient evidence, for we find the antithesis of the private (*idios*) and the public (*demosios*) everywhere in classical Greek literature from Homer onwards. An analysis of the terms of this antithesis can illuminate the way in which concerns about privacy in fact arise in Athenian society, and in political and legal thought.

---

[1] This view may be wrong, but *starting* the inquiry from the perspective of privacy would nonetheless leave important methodological objections unanswered. The most provocative recent treatment of privacy as a cultural category is found in Barrington Moore's *Privacy* (1984), which includes an important chapter on classical Athens.

[2] Parent (1983a: 341–6).

Further reflection will show that the form that these concerns take devolves from the political context in which they are formulated. Thus Chapter 9 considers the relation of notions of autonomy of a private sphere to the conflict of political ideologies at Athens.

I

Public and private

In ways reminiscent of the modern Mediterranean communities discussed above, Athenian sources express a gender-oriented distinction between public and private both in terms of persons, places, and, more abstractly, spheres of life. Thus, Aristotle in the *Politics* (1277a) contrasts a man's political role with being a private citizen. Likewise, Xenophon comments that the wrongs of private citizens are less important than those of political leaders because they cause little harm (*Ag.*11.5–6). The identification of private and public with different social roles serves as a commonplace in the Athenian orators, where speakers contrast the greater glory and risks of being a rhetor with the quiet security of the private citizen (Hyperides 4.9). Further, a passage in Demosthenes' attack on his enemy, Meidias, shows the manipulability of these labels which individuals attached to roles that could be assumed and discarded, determining the interests which came into play. Thus Demosthenes argues that Meidias' assault upon him while he was producing a chorus in a festival was an attack upon the whole city. Attacking a man as a private citizen differs fundamentally, he says, from attacking him as a judge or magistrate. The former is a private matter to be settled by the individual through a lawsuit (note that he says either a public or private lawsuit), the latter an offense against an inviolable official, and hence against the city itself, not to be settled by private vengeance but by disenfranchisement (Dem. 21.31–5). Despite the exaggeration, this passage shows the way in which Athenians conceived of individuals as having both private and public roles. Further, it also demonstrates the manipulability of these categories according to various rhetorical strategies.[3]

[3] See Bourdieu (1977: 40) and the discussion below. See Foley (1981a: 148ff.) for a discussion of the public/private dichotomy in Athens, though her discussion focuses much more closely on its sexual aspects.

Thus Athenians not only made a distinction between "private citizens" and "political leaders," but also between the different roles which any man might assume in the course of his activities. In another speech Demosthenes comments that the Council (*Boule*) is the master of its own secrets and no private citizen may enter (25.23). This differentiation is perhaps not particularly surprising in the Athenian context, but anthropological evidence shows it is by no means universal. The persistent employment of such a distinction speaks for a highly developed sense of "the public" as a category in Athenian thought.[4]

The second area of distinction between public and private is spatial. Here Athenian patterns closely follow those discussed in Chapter 3. Athenians identified the private, in the first instance, with the physical boundaries of the home, the threshold and door embodying the separation of the two spheres.[5] They thought of public space in terms of places where *men* gathered: the agora, the Assembly, the courts, the baths, athletic grounds, and so on. As I will comment upon in some detail later, private space in this narrow sense is largely female space, enclosed, hidden, guarded, dark. Public space, on the other hand, is associated with men and with the public activities through which men pursue reputation and honor.

A number of legal categories manifest the cultural significance of these spatial distinctions. First of all, some crimes seem to stand in the most serious category of offenses in Athenian criminal law not because of the magnitude of the immediate damage they cause, but rather because they typically take place in public places and hence threaten the social order.[6] For this reason cloak-snatching (*lopodusia*), for example, receives a far more severe penalty than ordinary theft.[7] More significant is the legal category of exclusion from public places. In Athens, a wide variety of offenses brought some degree or another of loss of civic rights (*atimia*, literally: the state of being without

---

[4] Some social theorists (e.g. Roberto Unger) have emphasized that differentiation of social roles is essential to that dichotomization of public and private life which they see as arising with and characteristic of "modernism." The foregoing should indicate that such a differentiation is not an exclusively "modernist" phenomenon. Its origins are necessarily unclear, but Chapter 9 will suggest that the particularly strong expression of this dichotomy found in classical Athens may be related to the development there of a certain form of democratic ideology.   [5] See e.g. Euripides, *Trojan Women*, 645ff.

[6] I.e. the law punishing *kakourgoi*. The treatment of adulterers under this law will be discussed in Chapter 5.

[7] It is punished by death, as is aggravated, or "manifest," theft, which also represents a severe threat to the social order (see Cohen, 1983: Chapter 3).

honor). In Athens, then, as in many modern Mediterranean communities, to be shut out of the public space where men gather, whether by force of law or of public opinion, eliminates the possibility of maintaining one's standing in the eyes of the community, and marks one with dishonor. In both of these social worlds men must continuously inhabit the appropriate public places to preserve or enhance their reputations. Thus Athenian men who have prostituted themselves may not address the Assembly or enter the temples (Aeschines 1.46, Dem. 22.30–2). Homicides, and those accused of homicide, are barred from the agora, temples, and other public places (Antiphon 5.9, 6.4–5, 35–6). Similarly, Andocides reports a decree that excluded those convicted of impiety from the temples and the agora (1.71–2). Another law barred women taken in adultery from temples and religious festivals ([Dem.] 59.85–7), the public areas appropriate to them. Finally, Lycurgus expresses the moral sentiment underlying such provisions when he says that it is shameful that a wrongdoer like Leocrates should be allowed to enter the agora or participate in public rites (1.5–7,142).[8]

Athenians conceived of their city in terms of articulated public and private space around which the citizen's life was organized and given meaning. Thus the rhetor Andocides is said to have gone into exile because of the decree barring those guilty of impiety from entering the agora or other such public places. Whether or not this actually occurred, the story bears witness to the perceived force of these spatial categories and their linkage to reputation and prestige. In modern Mediterranean societies *legal* sanctions do not debar citizens from public space, but the force of shame and public opinion may. In either world, the man who cannot face his fellow citizens in places like the café, the market, the assembly, the temples, or the piazza bears a mark of Cain. He is paradigmatically a man without honor. The decree against Andocides also demonstrates the awareness among Athenians of the political and social significance of such spatial categories, and the way the community might employ them to express public condemnation. Shut out from the public realm, a man was thrown back upon private space and classified with those who inhabited it – women, children, and slaves. In Athens, as Plato says, men make women guardians of the house

---

[8] And cf. Aeschines 1.28–30, on those who dishonor their parents or throw away their shields in battle.

(*Laws* 805e),[9] and, as in the modern Mediterranean, a man who spent too much time in private space therefore ran the risk of dishonor. The politics of reputation required a man to lead a public life.[10]

More abstractly, Athenians also distinguished public and private as characterizing antithetical spheres of life. Such a distinction is a commonplace in the orators, and is usually expressed in phrases like "both in public and in private" (*idiai kai demosiai*). Although scholars acknowledge the existence of such a dichotomization, they have paid rather less attention to its meaning. Typically, they portray public and private in binary opposites, the public sphere encompassing everything which is not private (or vice versa). Thus, if the house embodies the private sphere, then everything outside the house is public. I would suggest, however, that public and private are relational concepts standing in a "complementary opposition" to one another. As Weinstein argues in his critique of contemporary philosophers who employ public and private as paired opposites, "the two notions are probably best conceived as layers of onion skin, any given layer potentially counting as private in relation to one or more layers."[11] Bourdieu argues for a similar conceptualization of spatial relations in his classic description of the Kabyle house. He demonstrates that spatial categorizations, for example, shift with the seasons because men spend much more time in the house during the winter than during the rest of the year. Likewise, in Athens a symposium taking place within the house is seen as private in relation to conversation in the agora or baths, for example, but public in relation to the free women in the house.

Having said this, the task remains to identify the center of the onion. The modern discussion of privacy and the private realm, associated as it is with the liberal tradition, focuses primarily upon the autonomy and conscience of the individual. Some philosophers have even suggested that a right of privacy exists independent of cultural contingency and have sought to justify this claim by

---

[9] See also Arendt (1958: Chapters 4–9), who recognizes the association of dishonor with confinement to the private sphere, but draws the untenable conclusion that Athenians primarily identified freedom with participation in public life and thus had no notion of privacy comparable to ours. Her interpretation addresses only one of the two major areas in which freedom was felt to be important, as will appear below.

[10] Xenophon, *Oeconomicus* 7.30–1, Maher (1974: 112), and see Gregor (1985: 23) for the same patterns among the Mehinaku; cf. Godelier (1987: 10–11) for Melanesia.

[11] (1971: 34). This view is quite similar to that taken by Bourdieu (1977).

grounding this right in the conception of what it is to be a person.[12]
If the modern conception of the private focuses in the first instance
upon the individual, the Athenian conception centers upon the
house, the *oikos*. Thus, the modern liberal view sees the determination
of the marriage-partner by the family as a violation of the privacy or
autonomy of the individual. From this perspective the decision of the
family is a "public" decision,[13] but from the Athenian perspective it
is a private matter, and, indeed, a private matter where the public
may not intrude. Plato, in the *Laws* and the *Republic*, argues for the
desirability of state regulation of the family, but expects great
resistance to interference in this area. Similarly, in the *Politics*
Aristotle sharply criticizes the contemporary Athenian practice of
non-regulation.[14]

In Athens, then, the private sphere begins with the house. At its
very core are the marital relation and, spatially speaking, the
women's quarters. Accordingly, intrusion into this space represents
the most serious, and most socially reprehensible, violation of the
private sphere.[15] Accordingly, numerous passages in the Athenian
orators implicitly identify the house as the primary locus of the
private. Isocrates (*Antidosis* 282,285), for example, treats the
household as synonymous with the private sphere. In another vein,
Demosthenes argues that in the previous century Athenians built
lavishly for the state, "but in their private lives (*idia*) they were
modest, building ordinary houses" (Dem. 3.25–6, 23.206–8). In
another oration, he quotes a poem of Solon which says that when the
state is in disarray the public curse enters the private sphere, and the
courtyard and gate of the house no longer offer protection (Dem. 19,
255). These physical boundaries of the house represent, at least in
times of civic peace, a kind of liminal area marking the *political*
transition from public to private. Demosthenes elsewhere provides
an example of the "public curse" that violates this boundary, in a
speech against Timocrates (24.197). There he calls for the
prosecution of public officials who violate the private sphere of

---

[12] Benn (1971: 3). Such claims may well appear puzzling, since the concept of what it is to
be a person, as Barrington Mcore (1984) has shown, is itself necessarily culturally
contingent.   [13] Weinstein (1971: 42).

[14] In Rome, Augustan legislation regulating marriage, divorce, and reproduction produced
considerable resistance for its perceived invasion of the sphere of familial autonomy. See
Nörr (1977).

[15] Cf. Demosthenes 37.45–6, Lysias 3.23, and other passages cited below. Roman law
embodies similar values in the law of *iniuria*.

citizens by breaking down doors and invading the house (and cf. Dem. 25.52 and Lysias 12.30–1). Spatial categories could thus connect to intangible claims against interference by the state or its officials.

In Greek the word *oikos* refers both to the house and the persons who inhabit it. The notion of a private sphere associated with the physical dwelling extends to the family which occupies it. At the abstract level, Aristotle conceptualizes familial relations according to a structurally parallel antithesis. He argues that the family constitutes a separate sphere of relations, outside the realm of social justice.[16] In the *Nicomachean Ethics* he similarly concludes that domestic justice (*to oikonomikon dikaion*) between husband and wife likewise constitutes a separate sphere from political justice (1134b15). This does not imply, however, that the household is entirely free or anarchic. For Aristotle, at least, it possesses its own natural normative order and thus constitutes an independent sphere (*Metaphysics* 1075a18–23). In these passages, then, Aristotle expresses in a synthetic way the notion, common to Mediterranean or other communities with a strong sense of family solidarity, that family relations constitute a law unto themselves. All radical political reformers, from Plato to the contemporary period, have had to confront this basic social fact. We must view Plato's elimination of the traditional family in the *Republic*, and his less radical limitations on it in the *Laws*, from this perspective.

While many passages testify to the house as the central locus of the private sphere, it in fact extends far beyond. Viewing "the private" as a manipulable, relational category best explains the great variety of (implicit) definitions found in Athenian sources: classification of things as "public" or "private" in a particular instance depends on the comparative context and rhetorical motivation of the description. Thus the broadest, and one of the most frequent, usages regards everything outside of the realm of political action as "private life."[17] Isocrates, for example, speaks of returning to "private life" after holding public office for one year (3.17). In this narrowest conceptualization of the public sphere, everything apart from

---

[16] Between father and son, master and slave, justice does not apply. The relation between man and wife, on the other hand, is characterized by something similar to social justice, yet different (*Magna Moralia* 1194b5–24).

[17] Euripides, *Ion* 598–601; Demosthenes 19.103–4; Hyperides 4.9; Xenophon, *Mem.* 3.4.12, 3.11.16; Isocrates, *Areop.* 72–3, *Against the Sophists* 14, *Antidosis* 99, 201.

engaging in political leadership in the affairs of the city qualifies as private life. Indeed, it is this formulation which underlies the famous doctrine of different lives, found in Isocrates, Aristotle and Plato, and widely debated in fourth-century Athens. This doctrine, inquiring whether the life of contemplation, the life of pleasure, or the life of political leadership is best, builds upon a radical dichotomization of life in terms of public (politics) and private realms (philosophy, pleasure).[18] An oration of Isocrates provides one of the most telling formulations of this conceptual division: after reviewing Alcibiades' political career, Isocrates refers to all of his other activities as "the other life" (*ton allon bion*),[19] a phrase also used by the rhetor Lycurgus when he says he has conducted his case properly in not slandering "the other life," i.e. the non-political activities, of his opponent.[20] While in some contexts orators and philosophers find this formulation useful, other passages frequently offer a broader view of the public sphere.

Thus, whereas the narrow view holds that public life centers upon political leadership (in the sense described by Callicles in Plato's *Gorgias*, and ordinarily applied to those who aspire to be public figures like Demosthenes, Pericles, or Cleon), the broader view conceives of public life in terms of the obligations of the citizen to the city. The orator Isaeus, for example, attacks an opponent by listing all of the public obligations of a wealthy man which he did not fulfill (trierarchies, choruses, embassies, benefactions, etc., 5.36–46). Frequently in the orators, a speaker either demonstrates that he is a good citizen by listing all of the public services which he has performed (including military service, public prosecutions, participating in debates in Assembly, carrying out assigned public offices, etc.), or asserts that his opponent is a bad citizen because he has not done so.[21] A reading of such passages, however, shows how fluid some of these categories could be, for speakers sometimes consider an activity as private which they later label as public.[22] It is the relational quality of the public–private dichotomy which accounts for this fluidity and makes it so easy for a speaker to manipulate these categories for his particular rhetorical purposes. Sometimes the public nature of the wrong is emphasized so as to arouse the court

---

[18] Aristotle, *N.E.* 1095b23; and see the well-known discussions in Plato's *Apology* and *Gorgias*.
[19] *Team of Horses* 22.   [20] *Against Leocrates.* 1.149.
[21] Lycurgus 1.139–40; Xenophon, *Mem.* 4.4.1–2, 4.6.14; Lysias 16.11ff.; Aristotle, *N.E.* 1123a.   [22] See e.g. Isocrates, *Team of Horses.*

against the accused as a public wrongdoer (e.g. Demosthenes 21, Lysias 1), sometimes the private nature of the act is underscored so as to place them outside the scope of the law (e.g. Demosthenes 18.111–12). In a modern context, Bourdieu demonstrates precisely the same kind of strategic manipulation of normative categories among the Kabyle.[23] There, as in Athens, in exploiting this manipulability the politics of reputation are largely played out in relation to these classifications of things as "public" and "private." Indeed, the frequency and vehemence with which Athenian orators employ such arguments testify to their potential social force. As in the communities studied by the social anthropologists discussed in Chapter 3, a man's reputation affects the way people judge him in all arenas of life.

If the public sphere is larger than politics, so the private sphere is more extensive than the household. Economic activities are normally considered private,[24] as are various kinds of social relations. For example, the speaker in an oration of Lysias (16.9–12) gives the court an account of what he terms his "private life," stating that he inherited a little property, married off his two sisters with a respectable dowry, shared his patrimony with his brother, and comported himself reputably in his financial and social dealings. His public life he characterizes as including military service, civic duties, decorous behavior in public (no gambling or dissipation) and no involvement in lawsuits. We must remember, however, that such an account is an exercise in persuasion, tailored to a particular public situation. Accordingly, given the fluid nature of these categories we cannot rigidly delineate the kinds of social relations which fall into one category or another. The wedding feast, for instance, that one gives for one's deme is usually characterized as a public obligation, the one which one gives for friends and relations as a private one. However, we can easily imagine circumstances under which such classifications might shift. Indeed, discussions of friendship (*philia*) readily furnish examples of just such variation.

A few passages treat friendship as a sort of third category, not part of public life, but not part of private life in the narrow sense either. We can, then, contrast friendship with the private sphere represented

---

[23] Discussed above in Chapter 3.
[24] Xenophon, *Mem.* 3.4.12, 2.4.6; Isocrates, *Antidosis* 276–7, 282, 285.

by the family.[25] Most treatments, however, represent friends as belonging to the private sphere. Aristotle, for example, says that just conduct towards friends is a *private* matter of concern to them alone, and constitutes a sphere beyond the law.[26] Further, intimate friends belong, for some purposes, to the most private sphere represented by the house. Indeed, linguistic usage testifies to this relation, for intimate friends are said to be like part of the household.[27] From this it follows that examining friendship can help illuminate the nature and limits of the privacy attaching to the household, a subject which the following section takes up.

Before turning to the problem of claims about privacy, however, certain features of the public–private dichotomy merit more detailed consideration. The main issue concerns the relation of the public and private to the politics of reputation and, more specifically, the group of norms associated with the values of honor and shame.[28] The categories of public and private, in all three senses developed above (civic role, spatial, and spheres of life), closely connect to normative ascriptions of honor and excellence, disgrace and shame. To begin with, political life affords the greatest opportunities to enhance one's reputation in the polis, and, concomitantly, the greatest risks of disgrace. The community judges men who run this risk by different and harsher standards than those that apply to men in private life, but also grants them far greater glory upon success (Dem. 19.103–4, 24.192–4). Moreover, those who do not participate in public life to the level expected on account of their wealth or aptitudes suffer in their honor (Aristotle, *N.E.* 1163b5ff.).

Thus Aristotle defines honor in terms of such participation, measured by performing sacrifices, benefactions to the state, receiving public maintenance or a public funeral, and so on (*Rhetoric* 1361a). Applying the same criteria, in the Funeral Oration,

---

[25] See Isocrates, *Aegineticus* 10–11, but the long description of the intimacy of friends seems to indicate that it is in fact part of, or at least closely related to, the narrowest conceptualization of the private sphere.

[26] Recalling his similar characterization of the family as a separate sphere of justice, as discussed above. See *E.E.* 1235a6, *N.E.* 1162a16–b36, 1113b22, *Rhetoric* 1374a, and Demosthenes 18.121–2.

[27] *Oikeios chreisthai*, Isaeus 2.3, 3.19, 9.10–11; or the phrase *panu oikeios*; see generally Isocrates, *Antidosis* 99, *Areop.* 31; Isaeus 2.3, 3.19, 9.10–11; Dem. 53.4, 58.40; Aristotle, *N.E.* 1137a5, *Magna Moralia* 1188b17.

[28] The general relevance of values of honor and shame to Athenian society is widely recognized. See e.g. Latte (1920–1), Adkins (1960: Chapters 1–10), Dodds (1971: Chapters 1 and 2), Dover (1974: 226–36), (1978: 81–109). Chapters 6 and 7 will take up the relation of honor and shame to sexuality and gender in greater depth.

Thucydides has Pericles say "This is a peculiarity of ours, we do not say that a man who takes no interest in politics minds his private business, we say that he has no business here at all" (2.40). Similarly, in Plato's *Gorgias* Callicles criticizes Socrates' life as shameful and a disgrace because he has not participated in political activity. Plato represents this opinion as one that most Athenians would share (as in the *Apology*), and extant Athenian political and judicial orations abound with variations on the same theme. Indeed, the sentiment goes back to Homer and the assembly of heroes "where men win renown." As in the Mediterranean communities described in Chapter 3, men make and maintain their reputation in public activity. In Athens the agora, the Assembly, the baths, and other such places served as the equivalent of the piazza, the village assembly, and the café in more modern settings. Men who avoided such places risked censure and marginalization.

The same normative criteria apply to men in their private roles. Aristotle, for example, describes private morality as a kind of unwritten law attended by praise and blame, honor and dishonor (*Rhetoric* 1374a). The man who confines his activities to the private sphere in the narrowest sense, the house, loses his honor, for such self-confinement is woman-like. Indeed, one can go further, and describe the house as a central nexus of the oppositions honor/shame and public/private. In a striking formulation of this thesis, Bourdieu, in his study of the Kabyle, relates the house to these other categories in the following way: house – inside – private – concealment – secret – dark – shame – female:male – honor – light – open – outside – public.[29] To win honor, then, a man must live his life in public. Honor exists only in the evaluation of the community and requires openness and publicity. The "common fund of knowledge" and shared values characteristic of "face-to-face" communities serves as the basis for reputation and judgment.

Accordingly, a common topos in Athenian orations, like the similar saying widely found in today's Mediterranean, holds that the honorable man can say that his life is open and known to all through his reputation.[30] Thus, in one trial Hyperides maintains that no one can deceive the community in which he lives, and further argues that the verdict should be based upon an assessment of the accused's whole life (1.14). Again, Demosthenes replies to accusations about

[29] Bourdieu (1977: 140–57).   [30] See Chapter 3.

his private life by reminding the judges that he has always lived in their midst, and asks them to judge him by his reputation and the common knowledge of his private life.[31] According to such valuations, only the dishonorable want to hide their wrongdoing or shame, and for this concealment they employ secrecy and the lie. Thus, says Xenophon, men seek to keep shameful illicit homosexual love secret, but honorable chaste love is public and not hidden; many know of it including the family of the boy.[32]

As du Boulay suggests for modern Greek communities, individuals constantly manipulate these categories, for it is more important to be thought honorable by the community than to be honorable before one's conscience. Based upon such implicit values, Isocrates gives the advice that one should sacrifice conspicuously in public so as to gain the reputation of being pious and law-abiding.[33] Such behavior, as was seen above, typifies societies sensitive to the values associated with shame. Hence, the man of honor must pay scrupulous attention to appearances (as must the modest woman), for it is from public acts that the community draws inferences about what it does not actually see.

In his description of the life of the Spartan king Agesilaus, Xenophon provides a striking example of the way in which reputation and honor depend upon such inferences from public behavior. Agesilaus, he says, always lodged in a public place like a temple, so that no one could slander him with engaging in homosexual activities. No one, Xenophon claims, would believe such stories about Agesilaus, because all knew that he spent his time in such places where this sort of clandestine behavior was impossible.[34] Conversely, the boy seen alone with a man after dark or in a hidden place will suffer accordingly in his reputation. Similarly, observers will assume that the modern Greek girls who make too many trips to the spring, or spend too long in returning from the pastures, are engaged in an illicit sexual liaison.[35] Explicitly applying such standards, Aeschines says that in secret, in private houses and lonely places, men hide their vice from public scrutiny (1.90, cf. 75). Only the man without honor, then, who is literally shame-less, has no

---

[31] 18.10, and cf. 18.8, 268, and Lysias 21.18; Aeschines 2.144–5, 3.78.
[32] *Symposium* 8.8–24, and see Hyperides 1.14; Lysias 21.18; Dem. 18.8; Aeschines 1.75–6; Xenophon, *Ag.* 5.6–7.   [33] *Demonicus* 13.43, and cf. Isaeus 1.39, 2.36.
[34] 5.6–7; see also Andocides 1.130–1; Aeschines 1.75.
[35] See Chapter 3, pp. 63–5, and Chapter 6, pp. 161–6.

concern for how he appears to others (Dem. 25.25, 51.15). The community thus assesses reputation according to success in managing appearances. Because certain kinds of behavior by convention give rise to certain inferences of illicit activity, individuals can manipulate assessments by "monitoring" their behavior. If du Boulay's Ambeliot informant can claim that villagers read one another's lives as hunters read tracks, it is also true that, like all good hunters, they know the appropriate techniques for covering those tracks. Xenophon's Agesilaus provides the classic example of such behavior.

If honor is won in public it may also be lost in private: a man unable to protect his private sphere incurs dishonor. Thus some men whose wives have dishonored them prefer to hide their shame in silence;[36] or a man marrying an illegitimate daughter conceals it and does not go through a public ritual (Isaeus 8.20). As in modern Greece, Morocco, Turkey, or Andalusia, in general, failure to preserve the sexual purity of one's wife, daughter, or sister brings dishonor. Indeed, the adulterer is seen as an offender who enters the house and violates its most private core, the women that it encloses and protects. Thus entering the house by force or stealth, and particularly penetrating into the presence of the free women within, is an act of hubris (Lysias 1.4, 25, 36, Dem. 18.132), an offense which intimately links sexuality and honor and which was punishable with death at Athens.[37]

Upon such injury, the only way to restore injured honor is revenge,[38] but this can pose grave threats to public order. For this reason, Isocrates classifies hubris as a matter of public concern, commenting that from acts of hubris arise feuds, death, exile, and even greater misfortunes. Such hubris, he concludes, has destroyed many households and depopulated many cities (*Lochites* 2.8–9). Similarly, Demosthenes argues that private wrongs differ from public offenses, for the violence that characterizes the latter is a wrong also against those who were not directly involved. For this reason, he continues, all citizens may prosecute an act of hubris, even if the victim is a slave (21.48). The perceived gravity of offenses

---

[36] Aeschines 1.107; and cf. Aristotle, *Rhetoric* 1373a.

[37] See the similar valuation of such conduct in the Roman law of *iniuria* (D. 47.10). Hasluck's (1954: 198) description of the severity of Albanian customary law's treatment of theft that involves housebreaking makes this connection succinctly: "Because human life had been endangered and the house's honor tarnished, housebreaking always implied that the men in the house were weak and the womenfolk light." See also Boehm (1984) for Montenegro.

[38] Lysias 1, passim.

like hubris testifies eloquently to the importance attached to protection of the public sphere, and to its intimate connection with honor and reputation.

II

Privacy

The foregoing discussion of the relation of honor and shame to the public–private opposition has indicated the way in which concerns about privacy were considered important in at least two senses that are not unrelated to modern discussions of the subject. The first concerns intrusion into private space in a physical sense, the second has to do with control of information about what goes on in one's private life. Indeed, the politics of reputation placed great emphasis on protection against either kind of intrusion. Because in such a social system reputation is so important, private matters that could damage reputation must remain secret. As Aristotle says, hubris against the women of the family or its sons (here hubris has strong sexual connotations) are wrongs that a man would be ashamed to disclose (*Rhetoric* 1373a). Therefore, shameful aspects of private life must not become common knowledge through gossip or slander (see e.g. Lysias 7.18–19). Hence, the house is seen as sheltering the private sphere, including the sexual purity and reputation of the women on whom the honor of a family in significant part depends. Community opinion sanctions this protection, for reputation and shame require vengeance for injuries done to a sister, her children, or one's wife.[39] The law provides further reinforcement by allowing the adulterer or thief to be killed with impunity if caught within the house, and by making offenses against personal autonomy and honor a major public offense.[40]

These observations suggest two dimensions in which we might fruitfully explore the idea of privacy in Athenian society. The first illuminates the nature of Athenian conceptions of privacy by examining the social norms and practices which regulate access and intrusion into the private sphere in all its various senses: house, financial affairs, sexuality, family relations, and so on. I have already touched upon several of these. The second dimension concerns law

[39] Demosthenes 59.12; Hyperides, *Lycophron* 6.
[40] Athenian law made *hubris* a major offense, and also punished calumny; see Lysias 10.8–9.

and political ideology. It focuses on the way in which they define and protect the private sphere on the one hand, and the extent to which they limit it and intrude on the other. The rest of this section will deal with the first of these two dimensions. After the examination of adultery, homosexuality, and impiety in Chapters 5–8, Chapter 9 takes up the relation of law and political ideology to the enforcement of morals.

As noted above, the house represents a physical embodiment of claims of privacy associated with the family. Indeed, some scholars have gone so far as to see the house as a sort of absolute barrier of privacy. On this view, women are not permitted to go beyond the threshold, and when any men who are not close relatives are in the house the women confine themselves to the inner recesses. I, however, do not believe that Athenian conceptions of privacy were as narrow as this. First of all, the restrictions on the movement of women outside the house have often been greatly exaggerated.[41] This misapprehension arises in part because of bias towards the lives of the elite, and in part because many scholars have not sufficiently distinguished between ideology and cultural ideals on the one hand and actual social practice on the other. Secondly, the private sphere as represented by the family and house, though a significant barrier, was far from impenetrable.

Indeed, if the family must protect the house from physical intrusion which may bring dishonor (thieves, adulterers, or other *hubristai*), and from abstract intrusion in the sense of knowledge of shameful things which transpire within, friendship (*philia*) serves as the exception which proves the rule. For it is a constitutive feature of close friendship that one becomes an intimate of the family, sharing its secrets and being accepted into the house, including into the presence of its women. These ties of friendship could sometimes even be portrayed as competing with familial connections. Thus, in an inheritance case, Isaeus reports that some testators prefer their friends over even their nearest kin and bequeath their estates to them (4.18–19).[42] Significantly, in classical Greek the word *philoi* (literally: "dear ones") can refer either to friends, or relations, or both.

Friendship thus represents a major axis of permissible intrusion

---

[41] See Chapter 6 below.
[42] Of course, Isaeus' point may involve rhetorical exaggeration, or manipulation of the categories of friend and family in regard to this particular case. On the other hand, the basic argument must have possessed a measure of credibility to the audience.

into the private sphere. *Philia* embodies an idea of friendship where privacy barriers are relaxed, tempering the antagonistic social relations associated with honor and shame (a social ethic expressed in the proverbial formula "honor" involves helping one's friends and harming one's enemies). The inter-marriage of houses/lineages (*oikoi*) represents a further axis of permissible intrusion, of relaxation of barriers. Marriage involved a strategic decision made by the family for the furtherance of its interests, among which the alliance with other (worthy) families was a significant one. The orations of Isaeus, written for inheritance cases, bear eloquent testimony to the fact that, although men became related through marriage (*oikeioi*), this did not necessarily mean that their substantive relationship was one of *philia*.[43] Indeed, agonistic relations among relatives mark these orations, reflecting the competition for inheritances upon which they are based. As one plea puts it,

We made...this present...as a proof that we have more regard for our relatives, even though they be wretches, than for money...He, on the other hand...robbed us of all he could...as though we were his enemies and not his relatives. (5.30)

If Isaeus could plausibly claim that men, in their wills, sometimes preferred their friends to their nearest kin, it is because they were often not on good terms with the latter.[44]

As in the communities of the modern Mediterranean described above, in classical Athens friends and neighbors represented a resource in distress. Likewise, at Athens the "price" of this asset involved opening the familial realm to non-kin. In Lysias' oration *Against Eratosthenes*, a cuckolded husband reports that he went to his friends to plan his revenge on the adulterer. They, he reveals, assisted him in planning his revenge and surprising the man in the act of adultery, after which he put him to death. This account is significant not only because the husband could count on his friends' assistance, but also because this request meant sharing his shame and his revenge with them. Moreover, this act involved entrusting them not only with the restoration of his honor (if he had not apprehended the man he would have had to count on their discretion to keep his

---

[43] Isaeus 5.30; and see 34, where a brother-in-law can be expected to take the part of his relative.

[44] For the general intimacy of true friendship see the extensive discussion in Aristotle's *Nicomachean Ethics*, Books 8 and 9.

shame secret), but also with his very life. Their testimony would have played a crucial role in his defense against the charge of homicide.[45]

In another oration of Lysias (3), neighbors hear, and help to expel, a nocturnal intruder (3.7), and a fragment of Aristotle reports a case where neighbors play a similar role in the apprehension of a nocturnal thief (Fr. 84). Similarly, Isaeus recounts that families commonly summon intimate friends to serve as witnesses of important family transactions: "You all know that when we are proceeding to a deliberate act which requires the presence of witnesses, we habitually take with us our closest acquaintances and most intimate friends..." (3.19 and 9.10–11). As in the homicide trial in Lysias' *On the Murder of Eratosthenes*, the implicit assumption was that one could count upon such solidarity. In fact, Isaeus frequently relies upon the argument that if friends and neighbors did not know of a certain transaction or family event it could not have taken place. In one case, for example, neighbors testify that the woman whom one party alleges to be a man's wife could only have been an hetaira because of the debauchery and serenading that went on whenever she was in the house (Isaeus 3.13–14). Neighbors, then, represented a resource in time of need, but also a focal point of observation, gossip, and social control. In classical Athens the neighborhood also served as a fundamental axis for privacy, social control, and the politics of reputation.

Aristotle's discussion of friendship lends support to this view. Thus he repeatedly emphasizes that friends share all things – possessions, joys, and sorrows. For him the mark of true friendship is passing one's life together, living together, for close friends belong to the realm of greatest intimacy (1166a30ff., 1171a–1172a). Various passages in the orators make Aristotle's general description concrete. In the portrayal of social interaction described in the texts, friends participate in the major events of family life: family festivals, wedding celebrations, sacrifices, and funerals.[46] During these they are almost certainly in the presence of the women of the family, a clear mark of intimacy. Further, Plato, in the *Laws*, explicitly links friendship and limitations on privacy. Portraying friendship as a

---

[45] This is one of the typical reasons that neighbors are called as witnesses in the apprehension of a wrongdoer. The functioning of this widespread institution depends upon the absolute trustworthiness of one's friends and neighbors.

[46] Demosthenes 58.40; Isaeus 2.3, 8.18; Aristophanes, *Acharnians* 1056, 1067–8, and cf. 253.

kind of threshold linking the private sphere of the family to the community, he argues that the state should encourage friendship and group associations because it is through friendship that the politically detrimental aspects of privacy are overcome. For, he argues, friends bring out into the light of day private affairs and aspects of one's character that would otherwise remain secret.[47] Thus the private sphere extends beyond the house and its inhabitants, beyond kinship. Though traditional interpretations regard the house, and the women and secrets it contains, as closed off from intrusion by the community, as one would expect from the Mediterranean communities described above, examination of social practices and beliefs related to friendship reveals the limitations of this view. The social functions of friends and neighbors made the Athenian *oikos* far less private than some scholars have imagined.[48]

Plato's accounts of male gatherings from which modesty required free women to absent themselves have served as a cornerstone of such interpretations. Indeed, although the model of upper class entertainment one sees in Plato is exclusively male,[49] one finds considerable evidence indicating that many men not only frequented one another's houses but were also well acquainted with the wives and children of their close friends. One of Antiphon's orations, for example, describes a man who lives outside of Athens but has a room in his friend's house where he stays whenever he is in town (1.14). Similarly, the cuckolded husband in Lysias' *Against Eratosthenes* has a close friend over to dinner alone in a way which suggests it was a regular occurrence. It is unlikely that those many Athenian families of low or modest social circumstances could rely on servants to serve such guests while the wife and her daughters demurely hid in the innermost rooms until the friend had left.[50]

Despite the widespread view of Athenian women physically

---

[47] 738d-e. Note that he is talking about the attributes which friendship and group association actually have, and the way in which these attributes could be exploited in a near ideal political organization. The passage thus cannot be dismissed as part of his utopian legislation.

[48] For the modern Mediterranean, see particularly du Boulay (1974); Kennedy (1986); Dubisch (1986).   [49] More precisely, free women of good repute are absent.

[50] Comparative evidence from societies with similar values concerning feminine modesty suggests that, apart from the wealthy, the women of the families served and attended the meals, though they themselves ate afterwards in the kitchen. When intimate friends were present they would join in the conversation after the meal. See the references in the preceding footnote. These issues concerning the sexual division of space and labor are taken up in greater detail in Chapter 6.

cloistered in their houses, close friendships and social interaction
were not exclusively male prerogatives. In a pattern reminiscent of
that described by Brandes, du Boulay, Bourdieu and others as
characteristic of Mediterranean communities, women both in rural
and urban areas formed intimate friendships with their neighbors,
constantly visiting one another for a variety of purposes, not least
simple companionship.[51] An oration of Demosthenes expresses this
succinctly when the speaker says "my mother and their mother were
intimate friends, and used to visit one another, as was fitting, since
they both lived in the country and were neighbors." Archaeological
evidence indicates that houses in Athens, as in modern Mediterranean communities, were cramped closely together. As one would
expect given these physical conditions operating in a "face-to-face"
society, the extant evidence suggests that neighboring families were
often intimate with one another. Although the primary attachments
were male–male, female–female, one also finds the high degree of
inter-family intimacy characteristic of many Mediterranean communities which also share the public–private, male–female pattern
of social organization.

This model of social interaction best explains the extant evidence
for Athenian society in the classical period. In an oration of
Demosthenes (53) a man describes in some detail his intimate
friendship with a neighbor. He reports that whenever he went away
on public or private business he left both his house and his financial
affairs completely in the hands of his friend. Clearly, this close
"house-friend" (*panu oikeios*, 4) had access to the house and must
have been well acquainted with his friend's wife.[52] Such situations
occurred often enough to give rise to the sentiment reported by
Aristotle that it is particularly easy to have an adulterous relation
with the wife of a friend or neighbor.[53] What made it particularly
easy was that close friends had ready access to the house and were
already acquainted with their friend's wife. Thus a character in
Euripides' *Electra* speaks of such an event as a commonplace: "When
an adulterer corrupts his neighbor's wife and is forced to marry

---

[51] Demosthenes 55.23–4; Aristophanes, *Lysistrata* 300. See Demosthenes 53.4 for the intimacy
of neighbors. Chapter 6 will take up the question of the role of women in some detail. See
the discussion of friendship among women in Chapter 3.
[52] See e.g. Demosthenes 47.53, 57, where the wife is not exactly flustered in the presence of
men and negotiates with them like an astute businesswoman; and cf. 79, and 81 in the same
oration.   [53] *N.E.* 1137a5, *Magna Moralia* 1188b17.

her..."[54] In a similar vein, Demosthenes comments that the law permits men to kill even their friends if they commit hubris against or seduce the women of the family.[55] The argument based upon such examples may seem perfectly obvious in light of the experience of later historical periods. Ruggiero, for example, in his brilliant study of crime and sexuality in Renaissance Venice, concludes that "Neighborhood, occupation, and friendship provided the context for adultery, especially at the lower social levels, demonstrating that the noble ideal of isolating married women was unattainable for the more humble."[56] For Athens, however, given the widespread opinion that Athenian women resided behind the walls of the house in splendid isolation, one must make the argument in detail (see Chapter 6). Friends thus represented a category of non-kin, who, for good or for ill, might be admitted to the innermost core of privacy that the house protected.

This intimacy of neighbors thus involves both positive and negative aspects.[57] On the one hand, friends and neighbors were an important source of support as lenders, guardians during absence, witnesses of important transactions or of wrongdoing being done to one, and even as co-defenders of the house.[58] On the other hand, the knowledge that one had of one's neighbors' lives could be used against them, or intimacy might be otherwise abused. Another oration of Lysias (7) provides a striking articulation of these attitudes when the defendant argues that he could not have removed the stump of a sacred olive (a capital offense) without his friends and neighbors knowing about it. Neighbors, he says, know everything about their neighbors' affairs and nothing one does in the light of day would escape their notice. He goes on to say that he is close friends with some of his neighbors, but with others he is feuding. They, he argues further, would have certainly borne witness against him if he had removed the stump since he could not have hidden such an open action from them. Neighbors have knowledge of all things,

---

[54] *Electra* 920ff. This passage is, of course, a literary invention. The remark is not, however, part of the dramatic action, but rather in the nature of a commonplace. Given the similar evidence cited, one may, with caution, view it as supporting the pattern suggested. Chapter 6 will argue for the importance of such "bits and pieces" of evidence for reconstructing the practices and attitudes of everyday life.

[55] 23.53–6. He is referring to the law of justifiable homicide.

[56] Ruggiero (1985: 60).

[57] As neighbors could be friends and allies, so also could neighborly relations produce hostility and feud, as in Lysias 7 and Demosthenes 55.

[58] Aristotle, *N.E.* 1159b30, 1165a30; Demosthenes 53; Lysias 1.8–23, 3.6.

he concludes, even those shameful ones that we try to hide from everyone. Even taking rhetorical exaggeration into account, this argument, to be at all plausible, must have reflected the way in which the ordinary citizens who made up an Athenian court would perceive social reality. The speaker may manipulate these categories in his favor, but his rhetorical strategy reveals the underlying normative structures. In many modern Mediterranean communities neighbors serve as the primary source of the information necessary for the politics of reputation, and a considerable body of evidence from drama and the orators corroborates my suggestion that this pattern applies to ancient Athens as well. The neighborhood helps to gather and focus the common knowledge that makes social control effective.

This common store of knowledge which the politics of reputation require and produce helps to explain the nature of Athenian social relations.[59] From this perspective, we might well reflect on the implications of one of the orations of Isaeus discussed above, where neighbors testify that they inferred from the fact that the alleged wife of a man accompanied him to banquets, dined with strangers, and was serenaded at her house, that she must be an hetaira and not his legal wife (3.13–14). Pericles, as appropriate in the rhetorical context of a funeral oration, expresses as ideology the positive interpretation of these fundamental facts of a "face-to-face" society: "We do not get into a state with our next door neighbor if he enjoys himself in his own way…" (Thuc. 2.37). As opposed to this idealized vision of tolerance and social harmony, Isaeus characterizes neighbors as reporting quarrels, love affairs, and immorality (3.13), and Aeschines reports that men hate neighbors who too closely describe their shameful deeds.[60] These descriptions move us from the permissible intrusion of friends into the private sphere to the realm of impermissible intrusions upon privacy: from the friend as an intimate of the house and family, to the realm of secrecy, shame, gossip, and the slanderers who are often described as the "destroyers of friendship."[61]

Thus far, the discussion has addressed many of the passages relevant to privacy as a desire to limit intrusion, observation, or

---

[59] Finley and Wilamowitz both comment briefly on the Athenian "neighbors who know everything."   [60] 3.174 and cf. [Dem.] 25.88–90 and Lysias 7.

[61] Xenophon, *Ag.* 11.5–6; Aristotle, *N.E.* 1157a23, 1158b10. See especially Gilmore's (1987b) extensive discussion of this point.

gossip that could damage one's reputation. Next, it must address the
framework which can incorporate this evidence into a larger social
pattern in which privacy plays a significant role. Towards this end
comparative anthropological work on privacy may prove helpful.
There are relatively few anthropological studies of privacy, but, in
one of the most important, "Publicity, Privacy, and Mehinaku
Marriage," Gregor develops an interpretation which provides an
illuminating contrast with classical Athens.[62] Gregor tries to relate
the problems of privacy among the Mehinaku (an Amazonian
Indian tribe) to the physical conditions of public and private life.
The small size of the community, the closeness of the houses and their
extreme physical flimsiness (as well as other factors) make physical
privacy in the modern sense almost unknown, though Mehinaku
culture displays considerable sensitivity to the categories of public
and private. Gregor concludes that "the delicate interplay of
privacy and publicity that emerges from social conduct" may be
unique to such societies where physical privacy before the observing
community is almost impossible.[63] I believe that Gregor overstates
the case here. The ensuing argument suggests that, despite important
differences, similar patterns of social control, and of interplay
between public and private, emerge from the social practices of both
classical Athens and some modern Greek rural communities. In both
instances, however, a far higher degree of *physical* privacy is possible
than among the Mehinaku. In this case, both the differences and the
similarities can prove instructive.

Gregor argues that "Ordinarily Mehinaku couples act their roles
in conformity with community expectations. The daily exposure of
their relationships to the critical surveillance of their fellow men
places them under considerable obligation at least to honor the
publicly visible obligations owed their spouses."[64] Here the central
feature involves compulsion towards conformity with socially
accepted norms of behavior due to the openness of one's life to the
observation of the community. This normative structuring of social
interaction through observation and opinion strongly resembles the
Mediterranean communities described in Chapter 3. The Mehinaku

---

[62] The most important comparative and historical sociological treatment of privacy is
provided by Barrington Moore's excellent study, *Privacy*. R. Firth's classic *Symbols: Public
and Private* also takes up some of these issues.

[63] Gregor (1974: 348), and see generally his later study of sexuality among the Mehinaku,
Anxious Pleasures (1985).   [64] 1974: 342.

also know the common fund of knowledge and values which form the life-blood of social control in "face-to-face" societies. Gregor describes in some detail the various activities through which the watchful community evaluates the state of marital relations of other couples.[65] As in Athens and the Mediterranean world, in the main they draw inferences from observed public behavior, which behavior also clearly involves a communicative strategy directed towards the community (a fact which Gregor perhaps does not emphasize enough). For example, the arrangement and closeness of a couple's hammocks, whether they bathe together or separately in the river, whether the husband conspicuously gives (or appears to give) his whole catch to his wife immediately upon returning to the village, form the basis for community assessments of the "state of a marriage." Naturally, couples often manipulate these "signs" as a way of influencing the community's judgment.

As Gregor puts it, "Significantly, the most enduring Mehinaku marriages appear to be between husbands and wives who... are most skillful at the management of information which would compromise their relationship."[66] Secrecy, lying, discretion, and willful in-attention are means of achieving privacy, means which serve, following Simmel,[67] to bind and reinforce relations.

The simplest method of maintaining the appearance of marital peace is discretion. The visibility of everyday conduct within the community makes it inevitable that spouses will be exposed to information that would compromise their relationships. In this setting a husband and wife must make an active effort to remain ignorant of each other's conduct.[68]

At Athens, of course, expectations of sexual fidelity were quite different, and were largely determined by the politics of reputation and values of honor and shame. Sexual jealousy was certainly not unknown, however, and went in both directions. Men drew inferences from the outward behavior of their wives, but clearly the opportunities for infidelity were much more unequal as was the need for discretion.[69] However, the idea of discretion, or selective

---

[65] It should be noted that, in sharp contrast to Mediterranean communities, among the Mehinaku both men and women regularly engage in extra-marital sexual relations. This fact is universally acknowledged, but both parties expect discretion from their partners. The wife is generally expected to be particularly discreet, and sexual jealousy is common among both men and women. See Gregor (1985: 22–68).   [66] 1974: 345.

[67] Simmel (1950: 330–8).   [68] Gregor (1974: 345).

[69] These issues concerning jealousy, inferences from public behavior, and the like, are treated in detail in Chapter 6.

inattention, could function in the family as a whole, and in social relations in general, tempering the burden that the politics of reputation might represent. Consider the following passage from Demosthenes' oration, *Against Aristogeiton*, worth quoting at length. Athenians, Demosthenes claims, live together according to the same principles

as families in their private homes. How then do such families live? Where there is a father and grown up sons and possibly also grandchildren, there are bound to be divergent wishes; for youth and age do not act in the same way. Nevertheless whatever the young men do, if they are modest, they do it in such a way as to avoid notice; or if this is impossible, at any rate, they make it clear that such was their intention. The elders in their turn, if they see any lack of moderation in spending or drinking or amusement, manage to see it without showing that they have seen it...And that is just how you...live in this community on humane and brotherly principles, some seeing the actions of those who have failed or met with misfortune, as the saying goes, "Seeing they see not, hearing they hear not." While the others do what they do cautiously, without concealment, and in accord with their sense of shame. (88–90)

Demosthenes further argues that this pattern characterizes not only the family, but social relations in general, producing civic harmony. Pericles represents the same view in the famous passage of the Funeral Oration (quoted above) which speaks of tolerance for the conduct of one's neighbors. This is, however, a highly rhetorical interpretation; not false, but only one part of the picture. As the speaker in Lysias' oration *On the Olive Stump* says, he is friends with some of his neighbors and lives in a state of feud with the others. The kinds of social relations described by Demosthenes were, in the ideal case, true of the family and friendship, but they did not govern all of social life, which in Athens was often far from harmonious. If such an ethic of discretion and deliberate inattention functioned among family and friends so as to ease the tension of life under "face-to-faceness," in regard to others, secrecy and privacy served as barriers for the protection of reputation. This is no less true among the Mehinaku, for there the mutual intentional ignorance which Gregor describes between husband and wife does not characterize their relationship to the community. Indeed, the community attempts to acquire as much information as possible, and, as in the Greek communities described by Handman, du Boulay, and Campbell, gossip about the marital affairs of others forms a major social pastime.[70]

Because of the very low degree of *physical* privacy, the Mehinaku have a relatively easy time obtaining information about their neighbors. Of course, norms limit the legitimate modes of observation, but the community has ample observational criteria open before it (hammock placement, etc.). Privacy is only made possible through secrecy: the use of secret trails for clandestine visits, secret bathing places, secret distribution of part of the catch to one's mistress. Couples have to work hard together to create privacy if they do not want their problems to be the subject of community gossip. They may go to their garden outside the village together (an institutionalized method), but the most secure way in which they can achieve privacy is leaving the community by taking a trip together.[71]

Most Athenians could more easily obtain greater physical privacy within the home. On the other hand, some illicit homoerotic activities appear to have required the secrecy of hidden or lonely places outside the house (Aeschines 1.82–4, 90). As was seen above, it was difficult to hide shameful activities from one's neighbors. Further, even though the walls of one's house might hide the shameful act itself from public view, reputation was based upon inferences from the *public* aspects or consequences of the act that were impossible to hide completely. In an oration of Aeschines, for example, homoerotic conduct is inferred from a young man entering the house of strangers, or from being seen in lonely places with older men, or at night, etc.[72] Thus, the politics of reputation, and the social control it involves, feed on conventional inferences from objectively innocuous public behavior. Arranging one's public behavior in the light of such conventions is a socially acceptable way to cover illicit activity in private. For in orienting one's behavior towards such conventions one reaffirms (and reproduces) the underlying norms which structure such expectations.[73] The physical environment of

---

[70] As it does in many other Mediterranean (and non-Mediterranean) communities. See Chapter 3 for references.

[71] It is striking that whereas in many societies, as in Athens, "inside" is the domain of privacy, to some extent this is not the case among the Mehinaku. They have so little privacy inside that their life there is largely incorporated into the public realm. To achieve true privacy they must go outside the house and the village.

[72] Chapter 7 considers these issues at length.

[73] Hence the ritualized nature of homoerotic courtship. As long as one maintains the conventions (that is, the appearances they require), the community will judge the relation

the Athenian family offered far greater privacy than was possible among the Mehinaku, but something much like that "delicate interplay of public and private" which Gregor construed as unique to groups like the Mehinaku appears in Athens as well. Privacy requires not only the managing of appearances, but also secrecy; that is, the preservation of certain activities as truly "private." The studies of modern Greek communities referred to in Chapter 3 can help to clarify the similar social practices that operated in Athens.

Du Boulay's classic study of a Greek village provides one of the best accounts of gossip, mockery, lying, and secrecy, as they apply to the categories of public and private. As among the Mehinaku, or in classical Athens,

Since everyone automatically suspects everyone else of concealing faults or of trying to deceive them in some way, it is the business of everyone to find out as much as they can about others by whatever means are available. Eaves-dropping, questioning and checking the answers given by some with those given by others... are all common means in this battle for knowledge that is never ceasing... In such a community, discretion in general obviously becomes a paramount virtue, and discretion as regards the family, vital. (188)

As among the Mehinaku and in Athens, reputation is based upon inferences from public behavior.[74] Preservation of secrets, and reputation, requires that villagers guard their actions, for

the public nature of village life makes it such that villagers read the lives of others from signs and indications much as a hunter tracks an animal by its prints... a girl away with her goats for longer than the customary time means an illicit rendezvous in the forest.[75]

According to the same principles of inference, a widespread custom ordains that display of a bloodstained sheet "proves" that the bride was a virgin. As in Athens, where it is a commonplace in judicial orations that appearances are taken to indicate reality, "excessive care must be taken not to give the wrong indications even though the action behind these indications may be perfectly innocent." Since the judgment of the community depends upon inferences from public behavior, for reputation the appearance of honor is more

as licit. Failure to comply with normative expectations results in condemnation, not just because the inferences point to illicit conduct, but because of the very challenge contained in the failure to keep up appearances. These issues will be taken up at greater length in the treatment of homosexuality in Chapter 7.
[74] Similar patterns prevail, of course, in many other Mediterranean communities. See Chapter 3 on the politics of reputation. [75] Du Boulay (1976: 399).

important than the reality. As noted above, this sentiment was widespread at Athens and coincides with Glaucon's conclusion in Plato's *Republic* (361e) that the happiest man is the unjust man with a reputation for justice, or, as Isocrates puts it in his advice to Demonicus (17), "Guard against slander even if it is false, for the many are ignorant of the truth and only look to reputation." Thus, says Aeschines, "reputation makes private deeds public knowledge," and in Athens the community bases judgments about reputation upon just such inferences from public behavior as those du Boulay describes.[76]

What follows, since human beings are fallible, is that if reputation is to be preserved, then shameful acts must be hidden from the watchful, judgmental community. In the Greek villages studied by Campbell and du Boulay, lying thus necessarily becomes one of the most common strategies to preserve privacy. "Lying is thus a phenomenon built into the structure of social relations, and is a vital safety-valve for the tensions that would otherwise accumulate under the pressure of an ideal code and the eagle eyes of an inquisitive community."[77] Lying also serves a vital function "in reconciling the need for individual families to lead a private life, with the sanctions... which must operate if the moral code is to have force."[78]

For Athens we do not have the kind of evidence needed to demonstrate that lying fulfilled such a function. However, one does find the other elements of this pattern of the politics of reputation involving protecting privacy through secrecy and the management of appearances. The passages already cited from Lysias, Isocrates, Xenophon, Aristotle, and Demosthenes show the way in which slander was perceived as a significant threat to honor, reputation, and friendship. One could not afford to ignore such attacks, first because this would lead to the conclusion that they were true, secondly because failure to take vengeance for the damage to one's honor was itself shameful (Lysias 10.2–4). As was typical elsewhere in the Mediterranean, such slander could take the form of attacks on the sexual reputation of women, since this was also an attack upon the honor of the men to whom they were related. Theophrastus gives as an example of slander (*kakologia*) sexual aspersions about mothers or wives. Such aspersions serve as a common tactic in Athenian orations for undermining the credibility of one's opponent, for in this

---

[76] Aeschines 1.127–30, 153–5, 3.162.   [77] Du Boulay (1974: 193).
[78] Du Boulay (1974: 200).

society a man's reputation might be as important as the facts of the case.[79] Indeed, a striking passage from Plato's *Symposium* shows how children were socialized to think in such categories. Plato has Pausanias, in his discussion of Athenian attitudes towards homo-eroticism, comment that if a boy's playmates see an older man courting him, "You may be sure that they will call him names, while their elders will neither stop their being rude nor tell them they are talking nonsense."[80]

In such a society, public opinion, operating through the politics of reputation as based upon values like honor and shame, served as a powerful coercive force. Isaeus says that the compulsion (*ananke*) of public opinion would force men to marry the daughters of a deceased relative (1.39) or to provide a dowry for their sisters.[81] Men judged others, and expected to be judged, by reputation. As a speaker in another oration of Demosthenes says, "You know that my father loved honor too much to do something shameful."[82] Significantly, Athenians saw such questions of reputation and honor as linked to forms of political organization. Demosthenes, for example, argues that shame operates with particular compulsive force in a democracy because the truth cannot be hidden: "Of all forms of government, the most antagonistic to men of shameful habits is that in which it is possible for anyone to make known their shame. And what form of government is that? Democracy."[83] This connection of privacy, honor and shame to political ideology brings us to the political aspect of privacy. Chapter 9 will address this topic, arguing that conceptualizations of privacy, and the autonomy of the private sphere, formed one of the crucial differences between democratic and anti-democratic ideology at Athens. The notion of a private sphere, protected in important respects from intrusion by the state, served as one of the central tenets of Athenian democratic theory. Intervening chapters, focusing on the prosecution of religious and sexual offenses at Athens, will provide the material for this argument.

---

[79] See e.g. Demosthenes 18.123, 129–31, 21.79, 22.61; Aeschines 1. 127–31, 153–4.
[80] 183c–d. Cf. Aeschines 1.48.   [81] Isaeus 1.39, 2.37, 42–3; Demosthenes 4.10.
[82] Demosthenes 52.29, and cf. 1–2 in the same oration.
[83] Demosthenes 22.31, 60.26; cf. Hyperides, *Lycophron* 14. Whether one views Demosthenes 60 as genuine or not, the same sentiment finds expression in other genuine Demosthenic speeches, and other contemporary Athenian sources.

CHAPTER 5

The law of adultery

Different legal systems address the social problem of adultery in a variety of ways. Some only prohibit men from engaging in intercourse with the wives of others, some punish all extra-marital intercourse, others ignore adultery altogether. Within these parameters, different societies may punish adultery as a public offense or a religious transgression, or treat it as a purely private wrong (or some combination of these). In the ancient world, for example, one finds all of these possibilities embodied in Assyrian, Babylonian, Biblical, Greek and Roman legislation permitting the summary execution of adulterers or imposing other legal penalties.[1] Because of this diversity of possibilities, an examination of adultery may reveal much about general attitudes and patterns of regulation concerning sexuality and the family, as well as illuminating the relation of such regulation to conceptions of public and private. According to the multi-dimensional perspective set out in earlier chapters, such an analysis should encompass both legal and extra-legal forms of sanctions and control, and seek to uncover their interrelation.

Because considerable confusion has clouded previous discussions of the Athenian law of adultery, this chapter addresses the preliminary task of establishing what the relevant statutes provided, and then sets out what little we know about how the law was actually applied. The next chapter builds upon this discussion in attempting to place the practice of adultery within a broad context of social norms and practices. I argue that an understanding of this broader context necessitates a re-assessment of both the role of women in

---

[1] For Biblical Law see Deuteronomy 22, Carmichael (1974: 39, 51–2, 166–70), and Daube (1978); for Roman Law see D. 48.5.21ff., and Daube (1972), Goria (1975), and Gardner (1986). For the Babylonian and Assyrian codes, see Driver and Miles (1975: 37–50) and Roth (1988); for Hittite Law see sections 197–8 of the Hittite Code, in Neufeld (1951: 56–7).

public and private spheres, as well as of the way in which one conceptualizes the Athenian ideology of gender. Adultery, then, provides an entering wedge for identifying and discussing central aspects of law, society, and sexuality at Athens.

I

Although we do not possess a text of the actual statute(s), since the nineteenth century unusual unanimity has reigned among scholars about the main features of the treatment of adultery in Athenian law.[2] The great nineteenth-century scholar Justus Herrman Lipsius, author of what remains the standard reference work on Athenian law, seems to have felt somewhat uneasy about what one might regard as certain anomalies in the definition of adultery. If he did, he nonetheless passed them over with the explanation that over time practice must have altered the original meaning of the statutory language (a process for which no evidence exists).[3] Modern treatments, however, seem to regard the topic as essentially unproblematic.[4] Though the current orthodoxy portrays a law of adultery unique among other ancient legal systems for which evidence exists, no one has re-examined the question of how adultery was defined. In what follows, I suggest that the generally accepted interpretation rests upon certain premises which are fundamentally untenable. As an alternative, I propose a reconstruction of the statute which, in my opinion, governed the offense of adultery in classical Athens. Since the way in which one regards the Athenian legal regulation of sexuality would differ radically according to which version of the law of adultery one accepts, the ensuing analysis necessarily involves a close examination of the relevant texts.

In classical Greek the word *moicheia* denotes the kind of illicit sexual intercourse which the standard dictionaries render as "adultery." The word *moichos* refers to a man who engages in *moicheia*, but there is no classical Greek term which corresponds to "adulteress." A woman serves as the object of *moicheia*, never the active agent. Accordingly, Athenians employed such circumlo-

---

[2] Lipsius (1984: 429–35); Thonissen (1875: 312–19). Beauchet (1897: 233–44) does not consider the issue of definition and treats *moicheia* simply as the equivalent of adultery.

[3] Lipsius (1984: 429).

[4] See e.g. MacDowell (1978: 124), Cantarella (1976: 131), Paoli (1976: 254), Lacey (1968: 114), Dover (1974: 209), Wolff (1968: 642).

cutions as "The woman with whom the adulterer was apprehended..." What classes of women does *moicheia* encompass and to
what kinds of illicit sexual activity does it refer? In most legal
systems, ancient or modern, "primitive" or "advanced," adultery
centrally involves a voluntary violation of the marital bond. Indeed,
precisely this attribute distinguishes adultery from other kinds of
illicit sexual relations like seduction and rape.[5] Since scholars of
Greek law generally agree that such was not the case at Athens, I
will first examine the evidence which leads to such a startling
conclusion.

In his oration *Against Aristocrates*, Demosthenes reviews all of the
Athenian legislation concerning homicide. One of the statutes he
quotes provides the basis for all modern discussions of the scope and
meaning of the words *moicheia* and *moichos* in Athenian law:

If a man kills another unintentionally in an athletic contest, or overcoming
him in a fight on the highway, or unwittingly in battle, or in intercourse
with his wife, or mother, or sister, or daughter, or concubine kept for
procreation of legitimate children, he shall not go into exile as a manslayer
on that account.[6]

Some scholars refer to this text as the Athenian adultery statute.[7]
Others, however, note that it is a law concerning justifiable homicide,
but nonetheless view it as providing the legislative definitional basis
of the law of adultery. Thus Sir Kenneth Dover, in a representative
formulation, argues that

It was *moicheia*, 'adultery', to seduce the wife, widowed mother, unmarried
daughter, sister, or niece of a citizen; that much is made clear from the law
cited by Demosthenes 23.53–5. The adulterer could be killed, if caught in
the act, by the offended head of the household; or he could agree to pay
compensation; or he could be prosecuted or maltreated or injured...[8]

This interpretation represents the core of the generally accepted
view, adhered to by virtually all scholars who have written about
moicheia, including Wolff, Latte, Harrison, Paoli, Cantarella, Lacey,

---

[5] The element of voluntariness distinguishes it from rape. All ancient legal systems
distinguish rape and adultery according to the woman's consent and the man's use of force.
See for example the Middle Assyrian Laws, sections 12–16 (Driver and Miles, 1975:
387–9, 423); for Biblical Law, Deuteronomy 22–7; and the Hittite Code sections 197–8
(Neufeld 1951: 56–7). They also distinguish seduction and adultery by reserving the
former for unmarried women (or, sometimes, more specifically, virgins); see n. 16, below.

[6] Demosthenes 23.53.   [7] Lacey (1968: 114), Wolff (1968: 642).

[8] Dover (1974: 209).

Erdmann, and MacDowell. Their respective accounts vary as to many of the details of the law, but not as to the extension of *moicheia* beyond the marital relationship.[9] Before discussing the fundamental inadequacy of this position, I will first attempt to make as strong a case for it as possible, so as to articulate clearly the elements of the argument which implicitly or explicitly supports it. Because most scholars since Lipsius have simply assumed this to be the only possible interpretation of the statutory definition of *moicheia*, they usually confine themselves to sketching, or merely referring to, the orthodox position, rather than arguing for it. For this reason, rather than attacking the case as presented by any particular scholar, I prefer to begin by presenting all the available evidence in its most favorable light, constructing the strongest argument which one *could* build upon it.[10]

One begins, of course, with the homicide statute quoted above, which the greatest twentieth-century scholar of Greek law, Hans Julius Wolff, refers to as "the Athenian adultery statute."[11] One next demonstrates this statute's application in an actual case by referring to the argument in Lysias' oration, *On the Murder of Eratosthenes*. In that prosecution for *homicide*, against a husband (Euphiletus) who had killed a man he found in the act of adultery with his wife, the husband has the statute read to the jury as part of his defense that the killing was justified.[12] Although the oration does not actually quote the statute, the speaker uses the words "with his wife," and also refers to its extension to concubines. This identical wording, one argues further, confirms that it is the same statute cited by Demosthenes. A passage in Aristotle's *History of the Athenian Constitution* provides further confirmation that this statute does, in fact, apply to adultery. Aristotle summarizes the law of justifiable homicide as applying to cases where "someone admits homicide but declares it to have been legal (for instance when he has killed a man taken in adultery), or who in war has killed a fellow citizen in ignorance, or in an athletic contest..."[13] Finally, one can point to

---

[9] Latte, *RE* 2446–9; Harrison (1968: 33–6), Paoli (1976: 252–307), Cantarella (1976: 131–59), Erdmann (1979: 286ff.), MacDowell (1978: 124–5).

[10] Since most scholars, perhaps because they simply followed Lipsius, have not argued through the definitional issue, it would be easy enough to point out the inadequacies of their treatment of the meaning of *moicheia*. Since the real issue concerns adultery, and not a particular scholarly presentation of it, I make here a, to my mind, stronger case for the orthodox view than any existing publication of which I am aware.

[11] Wolff (1968: 642).   [12] Lysias 1.30–1.   [13] Aristotle, *Ath. Pol.* 57.3.

the Demosthenic oration *Against Neaera*, which provides an example
of an allegation of adultery based upon intercourse with an
unmarried woman. These four passages constitute the only extant
evidence for the traditional view. Taken together, one might
conclude, they show that, in Athens, *moicheia* did, in fact, mean "to
seduce the wife, widowed mother, unmarried daughter, sister, or
niece of a citizen..."[14]

What objections might one raise against such an argument? To
begin with, comparative evidence suggests caution in accepting this
conclusion. Such a statutory scheme would render Athens unique
among ancient, medieval, and modern Western legal systems.
Whether in the ancient Near Eastern or Biblical Codes, in Byzantine,
Roman, or Canon Law, in the Laws of Manu, in the statutes of all
early modern European states, or, for that matter, in the customary
law of groups as diverse as the Nuer, the Trobrianders, the Bedouin,
or the Sarakatsani nomads of modern Greece, virginity and the
marital relation both represent distinct categories of sexual prohibition.[15] This is not to say that all societies have legislated against
illegitimate sexual intercourse on the part of women. Rather, when
such legislation exists, it typically distinguishes the categories of
intercourse with unmarried virgins from intercourse with married
women.

Not only do such statutory schemes characteristically define the
contours of adultery and seduction quite differently, but one often
finds wide divergences in the severity of the penalties attached to
them.[16] This is not surprising, for the interests at stake differ
fundamentally in each case: the father desires to maintain the
qualifications of his daughter for marriage; the husband, among

---

[14] Dover (1974: 209).

[15] For Biblical Law see Deuteronomy 22:22, Leviticus 20.10, Carmichael (1974: 39ff.,
166ff.), Daube (1978: 177–97), and Patai (1959); for other Near Eastern systems, see the
Middle Assyrian Laws sec. 12–16, in Driver and Miles (1975: 36ff., 387ff.); for neo-
Babylonian law see Roth (1988); for Roman and Byzantine law see Daube (1972:
373–80), Mommsen (1965: 694ff.), Goria (1975), and Burgmann (1983: 234–7); for the
Nuer, Evans-Pritchard (1951: 41–2, 120–2); for the Sarakatsani, see Campbell (1979:
193–200); for the Baruya, Godelier (1987: 62); for the Mehinaku, see Gregor (1985:
10–68); for the Bedouin, Chelhod (1971: 244ff.). For an acute analysis of the
anthropological dimensions of these phenomena, see also Pitt-Rivers (1977), particularly
Chapters 2, 4, and 7. For the early modern period, see Stone (1977: Chapters 10–12),
Ruggiero (1985: 16–69) and Quaife (1979: 89–142).

[16] Compare for example, in Assyrian law, the relatively small monetary penalty for seduction
of a virgin (section 56), and death for seduction of a married woman (sections 13–15);
Driver and Miles (1975: 387–9, 423).

other things, wants to ensure that his children are, in fact, his own.[17] In addition, pagan, Jewish, and Christian cultures invest the marital and/or the virginal state with particular religious, ritual, or symbolic significance. Thus some societies (the Trobrianders, for example) regard pre-marital intercourse as a bagatelle, but take adultery much more seriously. In others (the Bedouin or Sarakatsani, or in Roman or Biblical law), the pre-marital loss of virginity represents a very serious transgression, as does the adultery of a married woman.[18] The examples of various legal arrangements could be multiplied, but they all share the common feature of clearly distinguishing between the illicit sexual activities of unmarried girls and of married women.

Athenian society also took the preservation of virginity as a pre-condition for honorable marriage very seriously, and attached great weight too to the sexual fidelity of wives and the legitimacy of children.[19] One would expect legal and social norms to reflect the social categories which distinguish these two areas of concern. Though this brief reference to comparative evidence points up the fundamental importance of these two sexual/legal categories, this does not establish that Athenian law did not differ from most other legal systems. It simply suggests that one ought to inquire closely before concluding that, for legal purposes, acts of intercourse with a "wife, widowed mother, unmarried daughter, sister, or niece"[20] were all the same, were all covered by the term *moicheia*, and were all punished by death.

More specifically, a closer reading of this justifiable homicide statute calls into question the very premises on which the traditional interpretation rests. The most basic of these centers on the assumption that this statute defines *moicheia*. Beyond the fact (normally not mentioned) that the words *moichos* and *moicheia* nowhere appear in the statute, there are further substantive arguments which weigh against such an assumption.

To begin with, the statute represents a part of the law of justifiable homicide. Demosthenes refers to it in a discussion of Athenian legislation on homicide, not adultery or sexual offenses, and Aristotle

---

[17] Lysias 1.33–5; for the early modern period, see for example Johnson's repeated assertion of the traditional doctrine that all property depends upon the chastity of women. If a wife is adulterous, then one's property will end up in the hands of another man's offspring. Boswell (1906: vol. I, 347–8, 623–4, vol. II, 287–8).

[18] See the references in n. 15 above. [19] See Cantarella (1986: 40–51).

[20] Dover (1974: 209).

also brings it under this same rubric. Like other such statutes in ancient or modern codes, it does not define *offenses*, but rather sets out exculpatory or justificatory *conditions* – exceptions to the general prohibition against homicide. In most ancient and modern legal systems, including classical Athens, most criminal statutes define offenses and specify appropriate penalties. Such statutes articulate categories of prohibitory norms: theft, rape, homicide, arson, assault, adultery, etc. Other statutes specify conditions under which individuals who commit such acts, particularly homicide, may not be punished. Indeed, the most common variety of such statutes enumerates the categories of circumstances under which a killing may not result in conviction for homicide.[21] Such statutes thus define cases where the defendant admits killing, but claims that his conduct falls within one of the classes of excusable or justifiable killings specified or implied by the statute.[22] This distinction between prohibitory norms and conditions of excuse or justification is fundamental to understanding the legal meaning of the Athenian law which provided that individuals who killed in war, the games, or upon finding a man engaged in sexual intercourse with their wives, ought to suffer no legal penalty.

In fact, this statute neither prohibits nor defines adultery. Indeed, it does not prohibit anything, but rather enumerates exculpatory or justificatory conditions relating to the law of homicide. Thus the statute quoted by Demosthenes no more proves that adultery was an offense punishable by death, than it proves that participating in athletic contests, or fighting in a war also constituted capital offenses. Yet logic would require one to adopt such a conclusion if one overlooks this distinction and views the statute as defining offenses and establishing penalties. Therefore, the statute quoted by Demosthenes cannot contain Wolff's "Ehebruchsgesetz" (adultery statute).[23]

---

[21] See Fletcher (1978: 552–77, 759–817) for the best discussion of these categories in American, English, French, German, and Russian law. For an exploration of the difficult theoretical problems involved in distinguishing justification and excuse, see Eser and Fletcher (1987–8), particularly the essays by Eser, Greenawalt, and Hassemer. For ancient systems see Daube (1969: Chapter 3).

[22] This is not a description based upon modern categories. Aristotle refers to the Athenian statute in just these terms (*Ath. Pol.* 57.3). Whether the individual categories specified by the statute are to be understood as conditions of excuse or of justification is irrelevant here.

[23] Unless one believes that *moicheia* was not an offense at all at Athens, but was only subject to extra-judicial self-help. There can be no question of this for we know of too much other legislation on the subject, as the ensuing discussion will show.

An examination of the actual wording of the statute reinforces this conceptual objection to the standard interpretation. This clarification of the nature of the provision also explains why one finds no reference whatsoever to *moicheia* either in the text itself or in Demosthenes' lengthy discussion of it. The statute, in fact, refers to *any* act of sexual intercourse which leads to the killing of the male participant. This fact cannot be emphasized enough. It exculpates the perpetrator who stands within a certain degree of relation to the female participant, and therefore applies with equal force to rape, adultery, and seduction. Indeed, Demosthenes discusses it in just such terms: he specifically refers to rape (23.56) and seduction (54–5), but neither mentions, nor refers to, *moicheia*. This, of course, makes perfect sense. From the standpoint of the law of homicide it makes no difference whether the offender is a seducer, a rapist, or an adulterer; all may be killed with impunity if caught in the act by certain male members of the family.[24] The purpose of the statute is not to prohibit certain conduct (illicit intercourse, athletic competition, warfare), but rather to prevent the prosecution of those who justifiably or excusably kill someone in connection with one of these activities. It is for *this* reason, so as to include the killing of rapists, seducers, *and* adulterers within its general exculpatory provisions, that the statute enumerates the wife, the mother, the daughter, and so on.

Lysias' own presentation of the law of rape, in *On the Murder of Eratosthenes*, reinforces this interpretation. In that oration, the accused husband, Euphiletus, cites the law of rape as defining the women protected within its purview as "those for whom it is permitted to kill" (32).[25] This shows that the justifiable homicide statute, to which he is clearly referring, did not cover simply adultery, but also rape. Thus the statute merely includes adulterers as one of the types of sexual offenders whom, along with rapists and seducers, the laws of homicide do not protect. Its (narrow) purpose

---

[24] A passage in Plato's *Laws* supports this interpretation. Plato's law of justifiable homicide explicitly limits the right to kill to cases of rape (874c): "If a husband discovers his wedded wife being raped and kills the attackers, let him be innocent under the law." Plato seems to have recognized the ambiguity in Draco's formulation and eliminated it, since under his legislation adultery was no longer a serious offense. A comparison of the wording of the two statutes reveals how striking is the absence in Draco's formulation of any noun or verb describing the nature of the offense or offender.

[25] The existing Greek forensic orations were delivered by the prosecutor or defendant, but written by an orator hired for that purpose (except, of course, in the case of orations where the orator himself is a party to the litigation).

is to define precisely the degree of kinship relation to which the exculpatory protection applies. The statute does not show that the man who has intercourse with the unmarried sister or daughter, or the widowed mother of another, is a *moichos*. Rather, it demonstrates that such offenders, whether they raped a woman or seduced a virgin, could be killed with impunity, as could the *moichoi* who engaged in consensual intercourse with married women. Neither the language nor the context of the statute (nor ordinary language, for that matter) provides a basis for concluding that what is meant in each case is *moicheia*.[26]

As a possible objection to my account, one might point out that Euphiletus, in *On the Murder of Eratosthenes*, has this statute read to the judges (30). Yet this hardly advances the traditional view. The statute is, indeed, relevant here, but no more so than in a case where a man had killed a rapist and claimed that it was justifiable homicide because of his relation to the woman. More significant, however, is the way in which Lysias describes the statute, for careful attention to his actual words reveals that he portrays *moicheia* as an offense which, by its very nature, involves the marital bond. After the justifiable homicide statute has been read, Euphiletus offers his interpretation to the judges: "You hear how ... [the lawgiver] explicitly states that a man who takes this vengeance on an adulterer whom he takes with his wife shall not be convicted of murder" (30–1). The emphasis upon *moicheia* as an offense specifically associated with marriage receives more explicit emphasis in the next sentence, which claims that the lawgiver considered this protection of the marital relationship of such importance that he even extended it to cover concubines. He makes no reference to its extension to other women (mothers, sisters, or daughters), although it would fit his rhetorical purposes well to do so here. Instead, the whole discussion presupposes that *moicheia*, like adultery in other legal systems, essentially involves a violation of the marital relation.[27]

---

[26] Nor does the formulation of the statute in *Ath. Pol.* 57.3. Aristotle is not quoting, but referring in a shorthand manner to the provisions regarding justifiable homicide. Accordingly, he reverses the order and leaves out the central case of self-defense. The case of the adulterer would, in all likelihood, be by far the most common (seduction of widows was probably not such a problem) and Aristotle avoids the cumbersome formulation of the homicide statute by using the normal statutory formulation referring to the taking of the adulterer in the act – the standard case.

[27] It is interesting to note that, though Roman legal texts sometimes use *stuprum* and *adulterium* interchangeably, the *lex Julia* and subsequent legislation focus on the criminality of violating the marital relationship. The husband, in later texts, becomes the "avenger of

In a similar vein, explanation of why the justifiable homicide statute extends its coverage to a certain class of concubinage provides further support for this interpretation. The reason emerges in an ensuing passage, where Euphiletus appeals to the alleged purpose behind the legislation (33–4). Adulterers are worse than rapists, he insists, because they cause wives to be more attached to them than to their husbands. Moreover, he continues, they cause uncertainty as to the paternity of children. This, of course, represents the classic ground, in Athens and far beyond, for antipathy towards adultery: a cuckolded husband never knows whether the children who stand to inherit his property are indeed his own. But all this only makes sense if *moicheia* is, in its very conception, an offense against marital procreative relations. It is for this reason that Euphiletus includes the concubine kept for the purpose of having free children in his argument. His point would be unintelligible if *moicheia* could be any act of illegitimate intercourse with any close female relative.

Lysias' view of *moicheia* in this oration is not idiosyncratic. A variety of other classical Athenian sources confirms its validity. Most accounts of Athenian adultery have ignored this testimony because they assume without question that the justifiable homicide statute read by Demosthenes sets out the legal definition of adultery. Xenophon, for example, explains that most states allow adulterers to be put to death with impunity because *moicheia* is an offense which destroys the *philia*, the relationship of love, friendship, and trust, between husband and wife (*Hiero* 3.3). This coincides precisely with Lysias' interpretation of Athenian legislation, discussed above. Furthermore, a law quoted in the oration *Against Neaera* provides that the man who catches the adulterer in the act must divorce his wife (87). As the speaker puts it, she becomes an outcast from the home of her husband.[28] This law does represent actual Athenian legislation regulating *moicheia*, and its terms clearly presuppose a definition of that offense as involving only a married woman.

Apart from the evidence of forensic orations, Aristotle describes the *moichos* as one who has intercourse with married women (*E.E.* 1221b). Likewise, in a number of other passages he presents *moicheia*

---

the marriage-bed," *Cod. Th.* 9.7.2. For recent discussions of the Roman treatment of adultery, see Rousselle (1988: 78–92), Gardner (1986), and Cantarella (1972).

[28] One also finds such legislation in Rome and the ancient Near East. These laws, among other things, aim at preventing collusive allegations of adultery by requiring divorce. See the references in n. 15 above.

as an offense by definition directed against marriage.[29] These quasi-definitional references by Aristotle confirm the presentation of *moicheia* in Lysias, and find further support in that genre of classical Greek literature in which references to adultery occur most frequently – Aristophanic comedy.

Although many scholars hold that the range of the word *moichos* in ordinary language is quite wide, and that it is often used as a general term of derogation, a careful study of all usages of the word in extant classical Athenian authors reveals that one must not overstate such a claim.[30] In Aristophanes, for example, the use of *moicheia* and *moichos* is generally confined to accusations or descriptions of intercourse with a married woman. Indeed, the Aristophanic comedies consistently present the *moichos* as the sexual rival of the husband. A passage in *Lysistrata* perhaps puts this most neatly, when the women who have barricaded themselves in the Acropolis swear an oath to have intercourse with "Neither husband nor *moichos*" (212; and cf. 107). Similarly, in *Thesmophoriazusae* a character claims that the plays of Euripides have caused husbands to shut up their wives to keep them from their *moichoi*, a theme to which the play often returns (410ff., and cf. 339–45, 397ff., 478–519). Of course these passages are all comic, but the humor depends upon a shared perception of the triadic relation of husband, wife, and *moichos*. The fictional settings and comic exaggeration in no way detract from the point that the *moichos* consistently appears as the rival of the husband, as the lover of a married woman. Similarly, Aristophanes does not refer to the lovers of unmarried girls as *moichoi*.[31]

In fact, the only seemingly unequivocal reference to an unmarried woman as a party to *moicheia* occurs in that puzzling exemplar of Athenian forensic oratory, *Against Neaera*. However, given the context of the accusation (part of a plot of fraud and extortion), and the general nature of that oration, I believe that there are sufficient

---

[29] See *N.E.* 1134a19, and 1138a25, which will be discussed below, and cf. *Rhetoric* 1375a, which must refer to adultery with "violation of marital bonds of trust."

[30] The words *moichos* and *moicheia* occur frequently in Aristophanes, Plato, Aristotle, Xenophon and the Athenian orators. They hardly occur at all in tragedy or Thucydides. The overwhelming majority of occurrences refer implicitly or explicitly to intercourse with the wife of another. There are, of course, some passages where the context does not permit identification of the implied significance. No passage in these authors, however, refers explicitly to the seduction of a virgin as *moicheia*, or to the seducer as a *moichos*. The case of [Dem.] *Against Neaera* is discussed immediately below.

[31] See e.g. *Ecclesiazusae* 224ff., 519ff., and 912ff.

grounds for not taking that particular usage too seriously.[32]
Moreover, the application of the term *moicheia* to the "seduction" of
the divorced daughter of Neaera, occurs in the context where she
pretends to be married so as to entrap men in a fraudulent charge of
this offense. Indeed, both the weight of general usage and, more
importantly, the rationale which consistently underlies the antipathy
towards the *moichos*, point towards a conceptualization of *moicheia* as
adultery; that is, Athenian linguistic usage, social norms, and legal
culture reflect an understanding of *moicheia* as an offense against the
marital relation. This premise provides one explanation of the
seriousness with which adultery was taken at Athens, as in other
ancient legal systems, and the ensuing chapter will explore several
others.

The foregoing analysis, then, has undermined the accepted view
that the law of justifiable homicide embodied the legal relations
which defined *moicheia*. Further, it identified a core notion of
adultery as the violation of marital *philia*, or, to put it more cynically,
of the husband's claim to exclusive sexual access to his wife. Having
rejected the traditional account of the Athenian law of adultery it
remains to provide an alternative, to see to what extent Athenian
law reflected the conceptualization which, I have argued, defines
moicheia. Beyond providing immunity from punishment for those
who killed rapists, seducers, *or* adulterers, through what kinds of
statutory provisions did Athenian law define, regulate and punish
the activities of the men and women who disobeyed its prohibitions?

---

[32] There are fundamental problems with the narrative of the events described in this oration.
It is implausible that Neaera's daughter could have been married, divorced with attendant
public scandal, a party to another very public scandal concerning the status of her
children, then a party to a lawsuit concerning a fraudulent accusation of adultery, and,
after all this, be foisted off on an unsuspecting man from a good family who had no idea
of her background and believed that she was an Athenian citizen. Secondly, there is the
particular problem of the accusation of adultery against Epaenetus, where Epaenetus
claims that she is not Stephanus's daughter, but Neaera's (66ff.). This supplies the basis
for the claim that intercourse with an unmarried woman can be considered *moicheia*.
Epaenetus, of course, had been tricked into being taken as an "adulterer." Of crucial
importance for understanding these allegations is that this accusation of fraud and
extortion against Neaera and Stephanus is simply a repetition of another accusation earlier
in the oration. There, Neaera *herself* posed as a respectable woman living with her
husband. Stephanus pretended to discover her adultery, and they blackmailed the unlucky
victim (41ff.). The accusation against Neaera's daughter is a repetition of this scheme.

II

Strangely enough, though we know that an adultery statute(s) existed apart from the exculpatory provisions of the law of homicide, scholars have paid little attention to its nature or scope. *Against Neaera*, for example, refers at length to a law which provides that the husband who takes his wife in adultery must divorce her.[33] Yet the citation of the statute seems incomplete, for it mentions only the provisions that apply to the husband and wife (mandatory divorce and exclusion of the wife from public religious life), but leaves out the treatment of the adulterer. Such an omission need not surprise one, since in that particular rhetorical context the treatment of the adulterer is irrelevant. Further, the wording of the portion quoted indicates that a preceding section had, in fact, dealt with the taking of the adulterer: "When he has taken the adulterer, it shall not be permitted for the man who has taken him to co-habit with his wife. If he does co-habit, he shall lose his civic rights" (87).[34] What, then, did the missing part(s) of the law provide, and how did these provisions relate to the law of justifiable homicide? For an answer to these questions one must turn again to the narrative of avenged adultery in Lysias' *On the Murder of Eratosthenes*.

As mentioned above, Euphiletus, the avenging husband on trial for homicide, invokes in his defense an Athenian statute pertaining to justifiable homicide. As was seen, this invocation fuels the traditional interpretation. Significantly, however, all discussions of the law of adultery overlook that Euphiletus, *before* referring to the homicide statute, first asks that another statute be read to the judges. Only *after* this does he call for the next statute, presumably the law of justifiable homicide. Significantly, Euphiletus introduces this *first* statute as the law which he claims commanded him to kill the adulterer: "It is not I who am going to kill you, but the law of the city..." (26, and repeated later). Unfortunately, the text of the oration includes a quotation of neither statute.[35] One must, then,

---

[33] Demosthenes 59.85–8, and cf. Aeschines 1.183, discussing the same provision. On the similar requirement of Augustan legislation in Roman law, see Crook (1984: 106).

[34] For Roman law see D.48.5.30.

[35] In Athenian practice the party did not himself read the text of the law, but rather indicated when the selected text was to be read to the court. In some orations later editors supplied the text of the laws, sometimes correctly, sometimes not. This is not the case with *Against Eratosthenes*, however, so one can only infer what statute is meant. In the case of the statute of justifiable homicide this is relatively straightforward, for Euphiletus himself

first identify the first statute and then inquire further why Euphiletus
had two statutes read concerning the killing of the adulterer.

To answer these questions it is necessary to examine closely the
precise words used after the reading of the law. Earlier, Euphiletus
had explained how he and his friends had surprised the adulterer,
and bound him, naked, to exact their vengeance. Then he asks for
the first statute to be read. Immediately thereafter he comments
"He did not deny (ἠμφισβήτει) (his guilt)...but admitted (ὡμολόγει)
doing wrong..."[36] This, of course, closely parallels Euphiletus'
previous description of his confrontation of the adulterer, where he
used much the same words: "This man acknowledged (ὡμολόγει)
doing wrong, and he entreated and supplicated me not to kill him
but to accept payment." It is striking that Euphiletus appears so
anxious to show that the adulterer did not dispute the charge, but
admitted his wrongdoing. Why does he bring up the matter at all,
since the only witnesses were Euphiletus and his allies?[37]

The answer to this question has to do with the way Athenian law
treated a particular statutory class of offenders: the *kakourgoi*, or,
literally, "evil-doers." These *kakourgoi* included thieves, robbers,
murderers, burglars, and adulterers.[38] Athenian law subjected
persons apprehended in the act of committing these crimes to various
procedures of summary arrest and/or execution. Euphiletus' words,
I will argue, clearly echo the law governing the treatment of these
wrongdoers, indicating that consideration of adulterers as subject to
the law of *kakourgoi* may help to illuminate the questions raised
above.[39]

The definitive modern study of *kakourgoi* includes adulterers as one
of the classes of offenders governed by this legislation.[40] A passage in
an oration of Aeschines specifically lists adulterers as falling under
this law, and no textual or contextual grounds appear for doubting
the accuracy of his account: "For what cloak-snatcher or thief or

---

paraphrases part of the law in the text. Since Demosthenes preserves the text, the
identification is fairly unproblematic.   [36] 29.

[37] Under Athenian law they would likely have been prosecutable through complicity and,
presumably, would likewise tailor their testimony, like Euphiletus, to remove any possible
hint that their conduct did not satisfy what the law required.

[38] See Hansen (1976: 44).

[39] No previous treatment has explored the relation of the law of adultery to the law of
kakourgoi. Cantarella has now accepted this interpretation, though with some reservations
concerning the scope of the law (Cantarella, 1991).

[40] Hansen (1976: 44–5). Earlier accounts of *kakourgoi* had not included adulterers, but had
limited the category to offenses against property.

adulterer doing such an act secretly will be punished? For whereas those who are caught in the act are instantly put to death if they acknowledge (ὁμολογῶσι) their crime, those who have done the act secretly and deny their guilt are tried in the courts..." (1.91). Aristotle's *History of the Athenian Constitution* describes in similar terms the procedure by which the responsible magistrates (The Eleven) decided whether summary execution or trial was appropriate: "If they acknowledge (ὁμολογῶσι) their guilt they are put to death, but if they deny (ἀμφισβητῶσιν) it they are brought to trial" (*Ath. Pol.* 52.1).[41] Close examination of Euphiletus' words reveals that he was probably paraphrasing this same statute, for when he says that the adulterer did not deny (ἠμφισβήτει), but admitted (ὡμολόγει) his guilt, he uses the same linguistic formulation as both Aeschines and Aristotle.

In sum, adulterers fell within the provisions of the law of *kakourgoi* and the summary procedures which it established. This helps to explain why Euphiletus goes to some lengths to emphasize the way in which he apprehended the adulterer and his wife in the act of intercourse (23–8). As in Roman law, and most other ancient legal systems, the law provided that the adulterer, like the thief or burglar, was only subject to summary arrest or execution if actually taken in the very act (ἐπ'αὐτοφώρῳ).[42] Indeed, one of the chief purposes of the law of *kakourgoi* was to define and delimit those dangerous situations where the law must tolerate self-help. This danger did not arise from a perception of such offenses as inherently violent. Rather, the Greeks considered burglary, theft, and adultery crimes of stealth.[43] But, because (in the Greek view) these offenses typically involve a penetration of the house,[44] they inherently risk a violent con-

---

[41] The meaning of this rather puzzling provision will be described below in Section III.ii.

[42] Euphiletus tells his slave-turned-informer that he *must* apprehend the adulterer in the very act. The discussion in Digest 48.5.23–4 also lays great weight upon this fact, citing Athenian law as requiring apprehension "in the act." Summary execution is only permitted if it immediately follows apprehension. Indeed, Ulpian maintains that the *paterfamilias* can only kill his daughter if he finds her in the house in which he or his son-in-law is actually living. If he finds her in a house which he owns, but does not dwell in, he cannot kill her. Ulpian's explanation of these requirements, however, is not particularly convincing. On thieves and adulterers and the reason for treating them in similar ways, see Hasluck (1954: 198), and Cohen (1983: Chapter 3).

[43] On theft, see e.g. Aristotle, *Topica* 126a33 and 149b28, where theft is defined as λάθρᾳ ἀλλότρια κλέπτειν.

[44] Roman law similarly focuses upon the house. See e.g. Ulpian's and Papinian's discussions of the meaning of this requirement at D.48.5.23–4. For the use of the house as a classificatory category in Assyrian law, see Driver and Miles (1975: sections 12–16).

frontation between the intruder and the men whose duty requires them to protect the family, the house, and the honor associated with them. Hasluck, commenting on the treatment of thieves in Albanian customary law, explains that housebreaking, "because human life had been endangered and the house's honor tarnished,...always implied that the men in the house were weak or the womenfolk light."[45] As in Roman, Biblical, and Near Eastern provisions, the chief restrictive element on the permitted violent response to intrusion arose from the requirement that the wrongdoer be caught red-handed.[46] The adulterer or thief who escaped detection remained legally immune from summary procedures.[47]

An aggrieved husband, who wished to avoid the danger of a prosecution for homicide like the one brought against Euphiletus, could take the freshly caught adulterer to the responsible magistrates (Athenian law referred to this procedure as *apagoge*, "leading away"). If he acknowledged his guilt they had him put to death immediately. If, however, he denied his culpability, he received a trial, and the law provided the death penalty upon conviction.[48] The husband who insisted on exacting vengeance himself could only plead that in so doing he carried out the mandate of the law. Euphiletus makes precisely this argument (25–6). The fact that after he orders the reading of the first statute his next words directly paraphrase the law of *kakourgoi* (as we know it from Aristotle), justifies the inference that this was the statute which he first adduced as the law governing the case.

Given this hypothesis that the law subjected adulterers to the capital penalty and summary procedures which applied to *kakourgoi*, why did Euphiletus have a second statute read to the court? One possibility is that the second statute is not the law of justifiable

---

[45] 1954: 198. This association of theft, adultery, and dishonor is widespread, as is neatly brought out in the seventeenth-century English tract, *A Plaine and Familiar Exposition of the Ten Commandments* (J. Dodd and R. Cleaver, London 1610): "the adulterer is a thief, by intruding his child into another man's possession." Dr Johnson expressed the same sentiment, when he says that the thief merely makes off with the sheep, but the adulterer gets the sheep and the farm as well (quoted in Stone 1977: 637).

[46] D.48.5.23ff.; Deuteronomy 22.22 ("is discovered"); Middle Assyrian Code section 15 (Driver and Miles 1975: 389). For the similar pattern prevalent among peoples with very different forms of social and political organization, see e.g. Evans-Pritchard (1951: 120).

[47] It is common in ancient legal systems that capital penalties for certain offenses could only be imposed if the wrongdoer was apprehended in the act. "Flagrance," to use Gernet's term, was constitutive of the offense: see Gernet (1976a: 267–8, 320–1); and Cohen (1983: Chapter 3). For Roman and Biblical law see Daube (1947: 201ff.) and Jackson (1972: 156). [48] Cf. Lysias 13.68. See Paoli (1976: 312ff.).

homicide by Demosthenes, as scholars have always assumed. This seems unlikely, but no evidence indicates that there was not a new statute specifically relating to adulterers. This would explain discrepancies between the wording of the statute quoted by Demosthenes, and the summary of the statute referred to by Lysias. Euphiletus says that the law *explicitly* provides immunity for "the man who takes an adulterer (*moichos*) with his wife" (30–1). The text quoted by Demosthenes, on the other hand, contains no explicit reference to the wrongdoer.[49] More probably, however, Lysias did refer to the law of justifiable homicide cited by Demosthenes. If so, one wonders why Lysias included it after having already presented a law which specifically applied to adultery and provided for summary redress. It may be that he invoked the law of homicide simply as further supporting evidence that he had killed justifiably. On the other hand, his strategy would also make sense if, for example, the law of *kakourgoi* limited, in some way, the husband's right to kill the adulterer. If this were so, then Lysias sought to buttress Euphiletus' case by appealing to the older, more general homicide statute with its unqualified right to kill certain sexual offenders taken in the act.[50] The existing evidence does not permit a definitive choice between these possibilities.

If the law of adultery did limit the right of the husband to kill the adulterer taken in the act, this would represent a restriction on the broad range of self-help permitted under the law of justifiable homicide.[51] The law of theft (also within the framework of the regulation of *kakourgoi*) includes a similar restriction. This statute permits a person to kill only the *nocturnal* thief caught in the act. A thief apprehended during the day must be taken to the magistrates for summary execution, or, if he denies the charge, trial (where the penalty is also death). The nocturnal thief operates under

---

[49] Plato, in the *Laws*, revises the Athenian scheme, distinguishing clearly between involuntary and justifiable homicide (865, 874). He seems to eliminate the ambiguity in Draco's statute by explicitly confining it to rape (874c). Under his legislation the penalties for adultery are minor, so the husband can no longer kill the adulterer with impunity.

[50] Conflict between legislation passed at different periods was not unknown at Athens. Both Aristotle and Demosthenes refer to the confusion which the duplication of statutes could cause. The law reform of 403/2 aimed, in part, at systematizing Athenian law by removing such ambiguities and contradictions.

[51] In Roman law the *lex Julia de adulteriis* seems to have limited the right of the husband to kill the adulterer and adulteress taken in the act. The *paterfamilias*, instead, enjoys this right, subject to certain restrictions; see D.48.5.23–30. The right of the husband to take immediate vengeance was restored by Justinian, in *Nov.* 117.15.

circumstances both more clearly incriminating, and far more threatening than his diurnal counterpart.[52] Most likely, the statute defining a thief as a *kakourgos* limited a prior, broader right of self-help (*Hausgewalt*), where any thief taken in the act might be killed. One wonders if the law of adultery underwent a similar development. The extant evidence indicates that it did, though due to its paucity any interpretation necessarily remains tentative.

One can begin with the language with which Lysias describes the statute concerning treatment of the adulterer. In his concluding remarks he says that the laws command that "If someone takes an adulterer in the act, let him do with him whatever he pleases…"[53] These words seem to paraphrase closely the actual statutory language. The law of which they form a part, and to which Lysias refers, must be the first law which he cited as regulating adultery (28–9).[54] This rather general formulation raises the question of whether or not the statute presupposed, or articulated, some limits on the husband's treatment of the adulterer. Relevant here, perhaps, is the adultery provision cited in the oration *Against Neaera* (66–7), which concerns the action which one may bring on behalf of a man wrongly held for ransom as an adulterer. This law belongs to the category of public prosecutions (*graphai*) whereby any citizen can initiate the suit, and aims at providing a measure of control over those men who apprehend adulterers and choose not to turn them over to the magistrates for execution or trial. The law provides that if the judges find a man guilty of adultery in the trial to which this procedure gives rise, the magistrates turn him back over to the husband, who, in the presence of the court, and without a blade, may do whatever he pleases to him (66–7).[55] Returning the adulterer to the husband operates to re-establish the *status quo ante*. The husband had to relinquish for trial the adulterer on whose behalf the action had been brought. After the court had found that the husband had lawfully apprehended the adulterer, it again placed him in the aggrieved man's power, subject, however, to the proviso

---

[52] Cohen (1983: Chapter 3).   [53] 49.

[54] Note the phrase (μοιχὸν λαβών) in Aristotle, *Ath. Pol.* 57.3; Lysias 1.30, 14.68; Isaeus 8.44.

[55] Note also the provision in regard to the adulteress who attends religious festivals, who may be mistreated but not killed (86–7). The statute uses a similar formulation, holding that someone may do whatever he pleases, except killing. The purpose of the condition that the husband not use an instrument is obscure. It may have to do with preventing the shedding of blood before the court, or it may just mean "any abuse short of death," as for the adulteress.

that any mistreatment must take place before the court and without a blade.[56]

The central issue here concerns whether this phrase, "without a blade," means that the husband could not put the adulterer to death. Further, if that is the case, does it also imply that the law of *kakourgoi* also limited the right of the husband to put to death the adulterer taken in the act? At least three possibilities suggest themselves:

(1) The law of *kakourgoi* did permit the husband to put the adulterer taken in the act to death. On the other hand, the law restricted the husband's right to kill the adulterer after the trial vindicating the original act of self-help because, for example, the moment of "flagrance," to use Gernet's term, had passed.[57] On this view, the right to exercise this most extreme form of self-help depends upon the unique qualities of that moment when the husband captures the adulterer, in his house, in the very act of intercourse.[58] That constellation of hubris, honor, vengeance, and *Hausgewalt*, accounts for the state's relaxation of its monopoly over the right to execute wrongdoers.[59] When the scene shifts to the court of law, the husband may humiliate and abuse the adulterer, but he may not shed his blood.

(2) The statute governing *kakourgoi* partially, or totally, limited the husband's conduct; if he wanted the adulterer put to death he would have had to take him (by *apagoge*) to the Eleven for summary execution. Thus the phrase "let him do whatever he pleases" must have also contained an implicit or explicit qualification, as in the other statute governing the return of the adulterer to the husband after trial (i.e. "let him do whatever he pleases without a blade"). This would explain why Euphiletus

---

[56] Some scholars have argued that the adulterer was customarily subjected to certain forms of sexual abuse, abuse which would have humiliated him and symbolically reduced him to the status of a woman or slave. (See e.g. Dover, 1968: 227; MacDowell, 1978: 124, and Latte, *RE* 2446–9.) Such forms of abuse are not uncommon in such contexts, whether in Athens or elsewhere. See, for Roman law, Ulpian's comments in Digest 48.5.23. For a discussion of the problems in generalizing about Athenian legal practice in this matter, see Cohen (1985: 385–7).   [57] Gernet (1976a: 267–8, 320–3).

[58] Hasluck describes how Albanian customary law required the husband who suspected his wife of adultery to wait until the opportunity to take them in the act (1954: 213). If no such opportunity arises, the only recourse is divorce. This, of course, recalls Euphiletus' behavior in *Against Eratosthenes*. For other examples of this widespread pattern see Evans-Pritchard (1951: 120ff.) and Chelhod (1971: 121ff.).

[59] See Latte (1968b: 252–94).

would omit reference to this clause, and, glossing over its provisions, immediately move to the second statute concerning justifiable homicide – a provision originating from the period when the law of *kakourgoi* had not yet limited the right of self-help.[60] The husband who did not want to turn the adulterer over to the authorities could hold him for ransom, but not indefinitely. The prosecution against the husband holding an adulterer had the effect, even when it vindicated the husband's summary self-help arrest, of forcing the husband to take a limited vengeance before the court. Presumably, he then had to release the adulterer, for otherwise the provision about exacting vengeance in the presence of the judges would make little sense. Just as the threat of a prosecution for homicide limited the actions of a husband like Euphiletus, so the prosecution against the husband holding the adulterer limited the possibilities for mistreatment, virtual enslavement, ransom, and feud.

(3) Finally, ambiguity and confusion may have characterized the state of Athenian law on these matters. In a legal system with no jurists, precedent, or other mechanisms for applying an authoritative interpretation of statutory language to particular cases, the meaning of phrases like "let him do whatever he pleases" or "without a blade" could remain unclear. Each case was decided according to the collective unstated opinion of the several hundred lay judges who, on any particular day, were assigned to decide such a case without discussion. The way such ambiguity could influence a case like that described by Lysias appears from considerable evidence which indicates that it was not customary to kill the adulterer.[61] If most husbands preferred either to abuse and ransom the adulterer, or, perhaps, to turn him over to the appropriate magistrates, the Athenian lay judges most likely would have interpreted vague statutory language in the light of these practices. Such circumstances would explain the desperation with which Euphiletus argues that the *law* mandated that he put the adulterer to death. In pleading for his life he needs to establish that adultery must be

---

[60] For examples of systems of customary law that develop mechanisms to cope with the problem of self-help in case of adultery leading to blood-feud, see Hasluck (1954: 212ff.), Campbell (1979: 185ff.), Chelhod (1971: 121ff.) and Black-Michaud (1975: 223ff.).

[61] This evidence will be discussed below. See e.g. Xenophon, *Memorabilia* 2.1.5; Isaeus 8.44; and Aristophanes, who always refers to mistreatment rather than death.

punished by death; this is his rhetorical position. For this reason, he repeatedly claims that the laws commanded him to kill the adulterer, which they certainly did not – they merely held him guiltless if he did so.[62]

To summarize, the statutory language treating the adulterer as a *kakourgos* probably included the provision that the husband, if he took the adulterer in the act, could do with him what he pleased, or take him to the Eleven. It remains unclear whether this clause also provided that the husband could only do as he pleased short of inflicting death. In any event, whether due to such a specific explicit limitation, or to uncertainty as to the scope of the words on account of the fact that, according to custom, aggrieved husbands normally abused and ransomed adulterers but did not kill them, there does seem to have been some conflict between the newer law of *kakourgoi* and the older statute concerning justifiable homicide. Such conflict was not unusual at Athens, and the law of theft provides just such an example.

Demosthenes, in the oration *Against Aristocrates* (60–1), quotes a law of justifiable homicide that affords an unrestricted right to kill thieves and robbers. On the other hand, the provisions of the law of *kakourgoi* only permit one to kill a thief, taken in the act, at night (Dem. 24.113). One can imagine a case where a man who killed a daytime thief making off with his property would appeal to the older law in just the way Euphiletus does, claiming that it required him to act as he did. Given the nature of the Athenian legal system such a situation must not have been uncommon. Indeed, Aristotle, in the *Rhetoric* (1375b), considers the kinds of arguments that can be made in such cases of statutory conflict where one law has become obsolete. There are no criteria for deciding which one of the possibilities enumerated above is "correct," but some such problem underlies Lysias' citation of the two laws. The desperation with which Euphiletus pleads that he did not kill Eratosthenes, but rather the laws did, perhaps bears witness to this uncertainty. One also wonders why, despite the minutely detailed description of the events leading up to the apprehension of Eratosthenes, Lysias refrains from

---

[62] See Jackson's insistence on this same distinction as regards the right to kill the thief in early Biblical law (1972: 154–5). For this same rhetorical reason Euphiletus resorts to the specious argument about rape being a lesser offense. He is comparing two things which are not comparable since they reflect different legal categories – justifiable homicide as opposed to a penalty in a lawsuit.

describing the actual killing. It is striking that he does not even allude to the manner of its accomplishment. Whether this omission relates to the explicit limitation expressed in the other adultery statute, "let him do as he pleases *without a blade*," must remain a matter for speculation.

A further source of limitations on the right to kill the adulterer arises from a peculiarity of the law of *kakourgoi*. As appeared above, when an adulterer is brought before the Eleven, they ask him if he denies committing the act which gave rise to the summary arrest (*apagoge*).[63] If he acknowledges his guilt he faces immediate execution, if he denies the accusation he receives a trial.[64] The crucial issue that arises here concerns when, and by whom, the adulterer must be asked if he denies the charge. In other words, did the adultery statute provide that the husband (probably in the presence of witnesses) could ask the question and put the adulterer to death if he acknowledged his guilt?[65] Or did the law rather ordain that only the Eleven could do so?[66] In this latter case, it would seem that the husband could mistreat and ransom the adulterer, but not kill him; the Eleven alone could apply the death sentence. The laws of theft show that either arrangement was possible. The thief taken at night could either be killed on the spot or taken off to the Eleven, but the diurnal thief could not be summarily executed by the injured party, but had to be brought before the Eleven.[67]

A striking, yet heretofore unnoticed, feature of *On the Murder of Eratosthenes* is that Lysias devotes considerable energy to establishing that Euphiletus asked the proper questions. As noted above, he twice has Euphiletus describe his actions with an apparent paraphrase of the statutory language (i.e. "He did not deny, but openly acknowledged his guilt"). What remains unclear is whether he immediately thereafter appeals to the law of justifiable homicide

[63] See Paoli (1976: 312).

[64] The whole point of arrest based upon apprehension in the very act in the presence of multiple witnesses is that it is very difficult to deny one's manifest guilt. Clearly, the accused must present some sort of plausible excuse of the kind envisioned by Aristotle in the *Rhetoric* (e.g. ignorance that the woman was married).

[65] A natural reaction to this is to wonder who would ever acknowledge their guilt if it meant immediate death. The point of the requirement of "flagrance" is that when one has just been surprised, naked, in the act of intercourse, by an enraged husband accompanied by many witnesses, the overwhelming nature of the circumstances make it rather difficult for all but the most cool-headed not to do just what Euphiletus claims the adulterer did: admit one's guilt and plead for mercy.

[66] As Aristotle, *Ath. Pol.* 52.1, perhaps implies. On the Eleven, see Paoli (1976: 221–33).

[67] Demosthenes 23.113–14.

because *the Eleven* should have put the question, not Euphiletus, or
whether the statute, in fact, allowed the husband to act as summary
executioner in the Eleven's place. In other words, does Lysias
emphasize this aspect to show that Euphiletus fulfilled a statutory
requirement for summary execution by the husband, or to show that
although he acted in place of the Eleven, he nonetheless gave
Eratosthenes the same opportunity to deny his guilt as they would
have? Although the relation of the law of *kakourgoi* to adultery seems
certain, the extant evidence does not permit a definitive resolution of
this particular detail. Tantalizingly suggestive is a passage from
Aristophanes' comedy, *Clouds*, where the personification of sophistry,
the Unjust Argument, asks: "If you chance to be taken as an
adulterer, what will you say (in your defense) to him (πρὸς αὐτόν)?"
(1079–80). "Him" is clearly the husband, and the passage thus
agrees with Lysias' presentation of the husband giving the adulterer
an opportunity to deny his guilt. Comedy, however, hardly furnishes
sound evidence for details of legal practice. In summary, it seems
clear that some technical legal difficulty motivates Lysias' treatment
of the two laws he cites, and the arguments he develops on the basis
of them. Which of the issues discussed above forms the basis of that
difficulty, though, must remain an open question.

Though some details remain unclear, nonetheless it now seems
possible to formulate a hypothetical reconstruction of the main
provisions of the law of adultery. I believe that all the major elements
of this law are quoted or closely paraphrased in the various orations
of Lysias, Demosthenes and Aeschines examined above. One may
bring them together, using the theft provisions of the law of *kakourgoi*
as a model. I do not claim that the result is a word-for-word replica
of the actual statute. Rather, I advance it as a summary of the
argument to this point, based upon an approximation of the main
constitutive elements of the law as reflected in the evidence – a sort
of patchwork of the extant fragments.

The phrase quoted by Lysias in his summary at the end of *Against
Eratosthenes* provides a logical starting point: "If someone takes an
adulterer let him do whatever he pleases" (49; ἐάν τις μοιχὸν
λάβη...). To this, following the language of the statute cited by
Demosthenes (24.113–14), which provides for the treatment of
thieves as *kakourgoi*, one may add the phrase, "or lead him off by
summary arrest to the Eleven" (ἢ ἀπαγαγεῖν τοῖς ἕνδεκα). An
alternative reading, based upon the possible limitations on the

husband's right to kill the adulterer, would require the addition of the phrase "without a blade."[68] This qualification yields: "If someone takes an adulterer, without a blade let him do whatever he pleases, or lead him off by summary arrest to the Eleven." Given the fact that *immediately* after the reading of the first statute Euphiletus comments "he did not deny...but admitted doing wrong," it is likely that the statute incorporated this phrase as well.[69] As seen above, however, it is not clear precisely under which circumstances the law afforded an opportunity to deny the charges. Though one can imagine other logically permissible permutations, the analysis suggests two main possible readings for the first part of the statute. *Against Neaera* furnishes the text of the (presumed) second part:

If someone takes an adulterer, (without a blade) let him do whatever he pleases or take him to the Eleven. If he admits his guilt death is the penalty, but if he denies it let him be brought into court...

If someone takes an adulterer, if he admits his guilt let him do with him what he pleases, but if he denies it let him be led off to the Eleven...

...When he has caught the adulterer, it shall not be lawful for the one who has caught him to continue living with his wife, and if he does so he shall lose his civic rights; and it shall not be lawful for the woman who is taken in adultery to attend public sacrifices; and if she does attend them, let her suffer whatever may be inflicted upon her, except death, with legal impunity. (*Against Neaera*, 87)[70]

Juxtaposing this reconstruction of the missing first part of the law with the provisions concerning the adulteress preserved in *Against Neaera*, one can see that they can plausibly represent parts of one statute. Indeed, they fit together as a coherent whole, which covers all aspects of the offense. First the statute deals with the fate of the

---

[68] This is, as discussed above, on the analogy of the treatment of the adulterer before the court. See *Against Neaera* 66.

[69] Following Aristotle's summary of the statute in *Ath. Pol.* 52.1.

[70] Ἐάν τις μοιχὸν λάβῃ [ἄνευ ἐγχειριδίου] χρῆσθαι ὅ τι ἂν βούληται ἢ ἀπαγαγεῖν τοῖς ἕνδεκα· ἐὰν μὲν ὁμολογῇ θάνατον εἶναι τὴν ζημίαν, ἂν δ' ἀμφισβητῇ εἰς τὸ δικαστήριον...
Ἐάν τις μοιχὸν λάβῃ, χρῆσθαι ὁμολογοῦντι αὐτῷ ὅ τι ἂν βούληται, ἂν δ' ἀμφισβητοῦντι, ἀπαγαγεῖν τοῖς ἕνδεκα...

[Dem. 59.87]...Ἐπειδὰν δὲ ἕλῃ τὸν μοιχόν, μὴ ἐξέστω τῷ ἑλόντι συνοικεῖν τῇ γυναικί· ἐὰν δὲ συνοικῇ, ἄτιμος ἔστω· μηδὲ τῇ γυναικὶ ἐξέστω εἰσιέναι εἰς τὰ ἱερὰ τὰ δημοτελῆ, ἐφ' ᾗ ἂν μοιχὸς ἁλῷ· ἐὰν δ' εἰσίῃ, νηποινεὶ πασχέτω ὅ τι ἂν πάσχῃ, πλὴν θανάτου.

adulterer, next it turns to the question of the husband and his relation to his wife (he must divorce her so as to prevent fraudulent or frivolous action),[71] and finally it turns to the penalties, in the form of civic disabilities, which the wife is made to suffer. Finally, the statute provides severe penalties for both the adulteress and her husband if they disregard its provisions. Again, I aim not at reconstructing the precise wording of the actual statute (an impossible task), but rather at fitting together what seem to be close paraphrases of pieces of it, in order to show that the general contours of the proposed solution represent a complete and plausible legislative scheme. On this view, Athenian law classified adultery under the provisions for summary arrest (*apagoge*), which treat the adulterer taken in the act as a *kakourgos*.

III

Thus far the argument has clarified two major issues: the scope of the conception of adultery itself, and the nature of the provisions which regulated such conduct. Yet three large issues concerning the law of adultery remain unaddressed. These concern the legal treatment of the adulterer *not* taken in the act, the mental element (if any) required for conviction, and the extent to which these legal provisions found application in daily life. Unfortunately, the extant evidence does not permit elaborate treatment of any of these questions. This section suggests tentative interpretations of those fragmentary indicia which do exist.

(*i*)

Athenian criminal law empowered any citizen to bring a prosecution for certain specified offenses. This class of offenses (*graphai*) included theft of public funds, bribery, sycophancy, and hubris. Aristotle also includes adultery in his partial list of *graphai* (*Ath. Pol.* 59.2–4), and scholars have generally interpreted this to mean that the law provided a public action (*graphe moicheias*) against the adulterer. This interpretation is certainly possible, but previous accounts have

---

[71] Roman law required that the husband divorce his wife, and that, if he killed either the adulteress or adulterer, he must also kill the other. See D.48.5.30, 33, and see the similar provisions in the Middle Assyrian Laws and the Code of Hammurabi (Driver and Miles 1975: 36ff. and Tablet A sec. 15, and see the fundamental contribution of Roth, 1988). The Athenian legislation must be understood in this light.

overlooked that it is not the only possible (or plausible) interpretation. Indeed, numerous grounds suggest the preferability of
an alternative account, maintaining that there was no public action
for the prosecution of adultery.[72]

To begin with, apart from Aristotle, no classical source either
refers to an actual prosecution, or even mentions the provision. This
would not matter so much if Aristotle's testimony was unambiguous,
but it is not. Above, I discussed a public action (*graphe*) which could
be brought against someone holding the adulterer for ransom. We
possess both the text of this law, as well as evidence about its use.
Aristotle only mentions *one graphe* concerning adultery, and there is
no reason to suppose that this was not the one he had in mind.
Otherwise one must argue that he refers to an action for which we
have *no* other evidence, and fails to list the one which we know
existed.

Substantive grounds support the plausibility of this reading of the
evidence. Athenian law, I would suggest, did not punish adultery
because of the inherent moral wrongness of the act of the adulterer.
There are no "sexual offenses," in the modern sense, in Athenian
law. Thus the legislation discussed above does not aim at the legal
enforcement of moral or religious notions of right sexual conduct.
Rather, it regulates the violence perceived as implicit in the ideology
and practice of adultery in Athenian society: the penetration of the
house, at night,[73] by a stranger, with consequences ranging from
dishonor to blood feud.[74] For this reason, extant Athenian discussions
of the punishment of adultery focus upon the law providing for the
summary arrest of the adulterer/*kakourgos*, and the law of justifiable
homicide. Both of these represent legislative responses to the
problems arising out of the kind of self-help that involves the
apprehension of the offender in the very act.[75]

A final obstacle to the idea that adultery was conceptualized as a
public offense, prosecutable by any citizen, arises out of the

[72] In Roman law the movement was from familial jurisdiction before the *lex Julia* to the
public action it instituted. In the fourth century, the *Codex Theodosianus* restricted the right
of accusation to close kin (9.7.2).

[73] On the association of night with adultery (as with theft), see Euripides, *Hippolytus* 418,
where Phaedra calls night the accomplice of adultery. This passage (408ff.) makes the
connection with shame and dishonor manifest.

[74] Athenian law, in short, focused on the public consequences of illicit sexuality, not on the
private, moral transgression. See Evans-Pritchard (1951: 120) on the Nuer.

[75] As noted above, the law of justifiable homicide probably simply represents an older
legislative scheme which did not distinguish between different sexual offenses.

treatment of the adulteress. It is particularly striking that Athenian law inflicted no physical punishment on the adulteress taken in the act. Her husband had to divorce her, and she was debarred from religious life. These are serious penalties, but they stop far short of the death and disfigurement meted out by other ancient legal systems. In Roman, Biblical, Assyrian, and Babylonian law (as in Albanian and Bedouin customary law), when a man killed an adulterer the woman also had to be put to death.[76] In abstaining from extending the death penalty to the adulteress it did not rely on private vengeance against her. Indeed, the law explicitly assumes that this will not be the case, for it commands the husband to divorce her upon pain of disenfranchisement (*atimia*).[77] The law does punish the adulteress taken in the act by barring her from public religious life, but such women could, and did, remarry.[78]

In short, the Athenian law of adultery did not aim at regulating adultery as a form of sexual misconduct, but rather as a source of public violence and disorder.[79] The summary arrest procedure sharply limited the exercise of self-help, and the public action that could be brought *on behalf* of the adulterer prevented its abuse. This limitation of self-help, and the fact that the husband could not, with impunity, kill his wife must have operated to diminish the outbreak of the blood-feuds to which such self-help, in such situations, too

---

[76] See Digest 48.5.33; Chelhod (1971: 121); Hasluck (1954: 213).

[77] As one character remarks in Euripides' *Melanippe*, "Punish this woman. The reason why women are troublesome is, that when a man finds he has a bad wife he doesn't kill her" (Fr. 499).

[78] As Demosthenes' *Against Neaera* and Euripides' *Electra* show: "When an adulterer corrupts his neighbor's wife and is forced to marry her ... " (*Electra* 920ff.). This passage from drama must be taken with considerable caution. However, it is interesting in at least two respects. First, it fits in with the Athenian legal context in which the husband was required to divorce his wife, and with the other evidence suggesting that remarriage was possible (on remarriage, see Thompson [1972]). Second, the remark about the adulteress and adulterer being forced to marry, though very tentative in the Athenian evidence, resonates with the comparative material; see Hasluck (1954: 213) and Chelhod (1971: 121ff.).

[79] Ruggiero reaches similar conclusions in his pioneering study of adultery in Renaissance Venice (discussed further in Chapter 6): "Once again the Forty seemed to be concerned not with eradicating a moral vice but with reconstituting the family unit and protecting property... Adultery was an aspect of sexual life that perhaps more than any other functioned as a safety-valve for a society in which marriage and marital values melded only imperfectly with social realities" (1985: 69).

often gives rise.[80] As in Republican Rome, there was, I suggest, no public action for adultery alleged to have taken place in the past.[81]

(ii)

A puzzling aspect of the procedure of summary arrest for adulterers remains unexplicated. This concerns the requirement that the responsible magistrates (the Eleven) ask the accused adulterer if he acknowledges his guilt.[82] A modern reader might well wonder about the purpose of such a requirement, for it seems strange to imagine that anyone would not deny the charges so as to postpone immediate execution. This was not as simple as it sounds, however. The circumstances of summary arrest created an overwhelming appearance of guilt: the husband, together with a group of witnesses, brought the accused, probably bound and still naked, to the magistrates.[83] In the face of such testimony, the accused could probably not hope to succeed without invoking a recognized or plausible defense whose verification would require a trial.[84] Euphiletus' speech provides an example of one type of allegation that, in all likelihood, fell into this category: collusive and fraudulent accusation. Thus Euphiletus assures the court that there was no other source of enmity (4, 43–5) between him and Eratosthenes, that he did not himself lure Eratosthenes into a trap (37–42), and that he did not drag him in from the street and then murder him (27). While the necessity of defending oneself against such charges demonstrates the risks that self-help might entail, another such category of defense sheds light on more significant issues of substantive law and legal theory. Here, the central issue involves not the motivation of the accuser, but rather the intent of the accused.

[80] In the classical tradition, the most famous literary example is the aftermath of Paris' adultery with Helen. For modern examples, see Campbell (1979: 185–203), Chelhod (1971: 244), and the synthetic treatment of Black-Michaud (1975).

[81] It has been suggested that adultery was also subject to a private lawsuit, but there is no concrete evidence in any classical source for this.

[82] As pointed out above, it is possible that the law also required the aggrieved husband to pose this question.

[83] In customary Albanian law, as among the Bedouin, the naked bodies of the adulterer and adulteress provided the irrefutable proof which, displayed to the community, served to avoid blood-feud. Hasluck reports that in the twentieth century, after the customary law period, the Albanian government still accepted the evidence of the bodies lying together (1954: 212).

[84] Mistakes could occur whereby someone entering the wrong house might be mistaken for a thief or adulterer. Theophrastus gives a (comic) example, describing the man who goes outside to defecate during the night, and, half-asleep, stumbles into the wrong house; *Characters* 14.5.

Modern systems of criminal law incorporate a mental element into the definition of most serious offenses.[85] Theft, for example, can only occur when there is an *intent* to steal. Other offenses require different mental states, like recklessness, or negligence. If adultery, in Athenian law, required the adulterer to intend to have intercourse with another man's wife, an allegation of the lack of such intent would have constituted another category of question requiring a trial to settle. Lest one object that such considerations presuppose a degree of sophistication unknown to ancient legal systems, the Middle Assyrian Laws regulating adultery (fourteenth century BC) contain such provisions: "If a married woman has come out of her house and gone to a man, where he is dwelling, (if) he has lain with her (and) *knew that she was a married woman*, the man and also the woman shall be put to death."[86] Interestingly enough, a later section that seems to regulate cases where the husband takes the adulterer in the act in his house omits this requirement, perhaps on the grounds that the nature of the circumstances precluded confusion as to the status of the woman.[87] The question arises, then, whether a comparable mental element was required for a conviction for adultery in Athenian law.

In all likelihood, the Athenian adultery statute did not contain an explicit reference to a mental element. A passage from Aristotle, to be discussed shortly, makes this sufficiently clear. This is not particularly significant, however, for Athenian statutes normally contain no definition of the offenses they specify. This is generally true in most pre-modern legal systems, and the Assyrian statutes discussed above represent exceptions to the general rule.[88] For example, an Athenian theft statute provided that if someone stole they would receive a certain punishment, but it fails to define what

[85] For present purposes the question of whether the mental element is an issue of definition (a *Tatbestandsmerkmal* in German criminal law), or a matter to be raised as an excuse (a *Schuldfrage*), is irrelevant. Given the nature of the Athenian legal system such fine theoretical distinctions were not likely to play a significant role, even if they had been recognized by someone like Aristotle. On this distinction in modern American and German law, see Fletcher (1978: 552–669) and Jescheck (1978: 339ff.). The only systematic treatment of problems concerning the mental element in Athenian law is Maschke's *Die Willenslehre im Griechischen Recht*.

[86] Tablet A, section 13: Driver and Miles (1975: 387), and cf. sections 14–16.

[87] Section 15, *ibid* 389. Section 14 also deals with adultery consummated outside the marital dwelling, and it specifically requires that the man know the woman to be married.

[88] In general, before the modern period only homicide statutes specify mental states. Even in modern American law, criminal statutes sometimes fail to state what mental state is required. See Fletcher (1978: 341ff.) on the uniqueness of homicide legislation.

constitutes stealing. Since Athenian law operated without jurists, professional judges, or a system of precedent, any of which might have provided authoritative definitions, there were no technical definitions as in modern, or even Roman, law. The conception of adultery possessed by the jurors or lay magistrates involved in a particular case decided the issue.[89] Of the extant authors who deal with legal issues, Aristotle and Plato (and particularly the former) seem to have been most aware of the problems this situation might cause. Indeed, Aristotle addresses this point directly, and some of his texts furnish the only evidence for assessing its relevance for the law of adultery.

A passage in the *Rhetoric* (1374a) provides a convenient starting-point. Aristotle argues here for the necessity of precise definitions of offenses in criminal prosecutions. If there are no such definitions, he reasons, men accused of adultery may admit to having had intercourse, but deny that the intercourse constituted adultery. He does not indicate what sorts of cases he has in mind here, but a passage from the *Eudemian Ethics* provides the necessary explanation (1221b). After having characterized adultery as intercourse with married women, Aristotle goes on to say that some men admit to intercourse, but deny committing adultery since they acted in ignorance or under compulsion. The context of the passage suggests that Aristotle means ignorance of the fact that the woman was married, and this supposition is confirmed in another passage from the *Nicomachean Ethics*. Aristotle, in discussing the question of attribution of wrongdoing to a man's character, says that a man may have intercourse with a woman "knowing who she is," yet not out of deliberate choice (1134a). The phrase "knowing who she is" appears as the counterpart of the ignorance mentioned in the *Eudemian Ethics*, and probably means "knowing that she is married."

Aristotle's point is that the lack of knowledge of the woman's status negates the intention which the law requires.[90] Since some sources indicate that some Athenian men may have prostituted their

---

[89] Athenian juries (which might number 500, 1000, or even more) were not only untrained in law, but also could not discuss the case amongst themselves before taking their decision.

[90] His example from the law of theft, arguing that an intent to deprive the owner of the property is required, makes clear that Aristotle understood the problem as one of intent. A second passage (1138a) confirms the centrality of the woman's marital status as a constitutive element of the offense. Arguing that no one is guilty of injustice without committing an unjust act, he says that "No one can have adultery with his own wife, nor burgle his own house, nor steal his own property" (and cf. *Magna Moralia* 1196a).

wives, one can imagine circumstances under which a man might not know that he was technically committing adultery.[91] The oration *Against Neaera* also reveals that some men used such ambiguity to extort payment through "discovering" such adultery. Indeed, in *Against Eratosthenes*, Euphiletus explicitly says that he did not arrange the apprehension of Eratosthenes as a way of making money "to raise (himself) from poverty to wealth" (4). The further fact that the Athenian law of justifiable homicide (and perhaps the adultery statute as well) extended its coverage to intercourse with concubines kept for the purpose of having free children, would have made such a condition even more necessary. Such circumstances, where knowledge of the woman's exact status might appear tenuous, created even greater opportunities for confusion. If Aristotle's characterization of the law represented the general societal conception that judges and magistrates applied, then an adulterer taken in the very act of intercourse and brought to the Eleven, as in *Against Eratosthenes*, could admit having intercourse (he could hardly deny it), but could deny having committed the offense because of his ignorance of the marital status of the adulteress. Further, he could also allege that the husband had fraudulently lured him into the house on other pretexts. In a society whose legal procedures, and non-existent investigative magistracy and forensic technology, made questions of proof based upon circumstantial evidence extraordinarily problematic, such allegations would have been extremely difficult to disprove except in cases where the adulterer was taken in the very act.

The possibility of such factual complications helps reveal the reasons for the procedural preference of Athenian criminal law for this form of summary arrest procedure which greatly simplified the process of prosecuting many serious crimes. Such reasons no doubt play a significant part in explaining why Athenian law did not recognize a public action for theft, adultery, robbery, or burglary based upon accusation by means of a written indictment (*graphe*).[92] Some scholars tend to think that "normal" public prosecutions (by *graphe*) must have existed for crimes like theft and adultery, but such interpretations may rest on modern presuppositions about the prosecution of crime. Whereas modern society views the "norm" as

---

[91] See Paoli (1976: 313).

[92] This preference for summary prosecution through self-help also helps to explain why we do not possess a single forensic oration (or reference to one) arising out of a prosecution of any of these offenses.

identification of an offender, based upon an "after the fact" investigation, in many pre-modern legal systems apprehension at the time of the commission of the offense constituted the dominant means of prosecution (very often the only practicable one). This is particularly the case for offenses like adultery, theft, and burglary where, once the offender had escaped from the premises, proof might be rendered almost impossible.

(iii)

For reasons like those just mentioned, we know almost nothing about the actual patterns of apprehension, punishment, or vengeance in regard to adultery at Athens. Scholars often suggest that some relaxation in the treatment of adulterers forms the background to the prosecution of Euphiletus for homicide, but the oration itself offers no evidence on this point. The fact that someone prosecuted Euphiletus for homicide may have to do with technical aspects of the law of adultery that remain obscure (see above, Section II), or to other unknown factors peculiar to this case. In our ignorance of any other prosecutions for adultery, or for the murder of adulterers, comments on the typicality of this case remain pure speculation. There exists, however, evidence which indicates that Athenians recognized that not all husbands acted as Euphiletus did. Existing sources, impoverished as they are, indicate at least two other patterns of responses.

Some husbands, it appears, chose to do nothing – whether out of shame, fear, indifference, or some other motivation. Aristotle, in his treatise on rhetoric, claims that some men are ashamed to disclose the sexual transgressions of their wives (*Rhetoric* 1373a). Likewise, Aeschines, in the oration *Against Timarchus*, refers to men who choose to cover the seduction of their wives in silence, and a character in Euripides' *Hippolytus* makes the same general observation (470f.). Comparative evidence from modern Mediterranean communities indicates that such a strategy is not uncommon in these societies that so highly prize male honor and female chastity. Indeed, as Chapter 3 showed, on some accounts, the worst sort of *cabron* (cuckold) is the man who knows of his wife's infidelity and does nothing, not the man who lives in ignorance of such deceit.

Though fear of the various possible consequences of apprehension and its concomitant scandal may have kept many men from exacting legal or extra-legal vengeance, other motives could also play a role.

Some men, it appears, sought to derive financial benefit from their wives' illicit sexual activity. Thus Euphiletus feels compelled to argue that he did not seek to derive a monetary profit from his wife's infidelity (Lysias 1.4). He clearly refers here to ransom, a practice which the oration *Against Neaera* (Demosthenes 59.41–2) refers to at some length. These two accounts represent a range of possibilities, from men who prostituted their wives and perhaps occasionally extorted ransoms from men they thought easy targets, to others who genuinely discovered the adultery, but considered a profitable ransom the most convenient form of revenge. Adultery, it appears, often had a monetary dimension.[93] This was also the case at Rome, and the Augustan legislation dealt with this issue at some length. As Ulpian commented, "Anyone who makes a profit from his wife's adultery is punished, for it is no small crime to have pimped for one's wife."[94] Athenian law, in contrast apparently did not punish the taking of ransom, only, like Roman law, the failure to divorce the adulteress. Thus Aristotle describes two adulterers, one who must pay for his satisfaction, the other who pursues the activity for profit (*N.E.* 1130a25).

Comparative evidence indicates that in some Spanish communities, for example, men of higher social station often pursue long-term adulterous relationships with lower class women. Some husbands acknowledge the relationship and the monetary advantage it brings, others pretend not to notice and accept the profit indirectly. As mentioned in Chapter 3, some communities regard such situations as one of the "burdens of poverty." There is, however, little Athenian evidence that permits generalizations about such practices. Two passages in Aristotle's *Rhetoric* refer to adultery as an activity appropriate to the rich, or nouveaux riches,[95] and the (pseudo-) Platonic dialogue *Eryxias* describes adulterers who pay their neighbors' wives (396e). Aristophanes' *Plutus* and *Thesmophoriazusae*, on the other hand, comically portray young men who receive money from older women[96] – perhaps the situation to which Aristotle refers when he says that some adulterers aim at profit. Herodes' *Mimes* provides many similar examples, but again, the anecdotal nature of the evidence inhibits social historical analysis.

Such testimony, however, does reveal the complexity of the social

---

[93] In Aristophanes' *Plutus* an adulterer is caught in the act and gets off by paying (168).
[94] D.48.5.30.3. Roman law also punished the wife who accepted recompense for her husband's adultery, but Daube has argued that this is a later development (1972: 374–5).
[95] 1372a, 1391a, and cf. 1401b and 1416a.
[96] 980ff., and 344, and cf. *Clouds* 1070.

context of adultery. In this light, the content of the relevant legal norms begins to appear as a deceptively simple answer to the question of how Athenian society regulated the social practice of adultery. For this reason, one should exercise great caution before proposing historical explanations based upon a presumed decrease in the severity with which adultery was punished. Yet such is the explanation often given for why Euphiletus found himself pleading for his life before a homicide court. It is true that an oration of Isaeus refers to an adulterer "suffering that which is appropriate" (8.44), where the context makes clear that he lived to cavort again. But despite various accounts of the moral decline of Athens (Isocrates, Aristotle, etc.), this does not imply that earlier periods had punished adultery with a greater and more regularly imposed severity. Since there exist no contemporary sources describing the treatment of adultery in earlier periods, such generalizations remain futile. Further, comparative evidence shows that one should regard informants' accounts of a decline in standards with great caution.

In many societies where anthropologists have studied the actual treatment of adultery, it appears that strict norms commanding revenge are seldom followed. As in Aristophanes' *Clouds*, descriptions of higher standards in the past often represent nothing more than prescriptions about the present.[97] In modern Mediterranean societies, for example, informants often maintain that in earlier times blood always flowed to avenge adultery. Some anthropologists have accepted such statements at face value, even where, as is very often the case, informants also make greatly exaggerated claims about the frequency of such revenge or punishment in their own day.[98] In Greek, Spanish, North African, Near Eastern, and southern Italian communities where informants uniformly affirm the continuing validity of such norms, one regularly finds many actual cases that reach quite different conclusions.

Mohsen, for example, in her treatment of the Egyptian semi-nomadic Awlad ꝺAli, describes the way in which "The responsibility for retaliation in the case of adultery... is divided between the

[97] See for example Sanders' (1962: 133, 156–7) description of a Greek village, where people say that in earlier times things were much stricter, children were more respectful, girls didn't dare set foot out of the house, etc. Aristophanes satirizes this proclivity in *Clouds*, in the famous passage where the "Just Argument" characterizes the good old days when boys were masculine and modest in contrast to contemporary degeneracy.

[98] See for example Hasluck (1954: 264–5) who recounts at length legendary tales of bloody revenge for marital infidelity in eighteenth- and nineteenth-century Albania. Since firsthand accounts of behavior in more recent times reveal more varied responses, one infers a lessening of standards.

woman's nearest kinsman and her husband."[99] She affirms that honor requires the death of both the adulteress and the adulterer. She then notes, however, that in fourteen cases of adultery she examined during her fieldwork, none resulted in the killing of the adulteress, and only three in the killing of the adulterer. She explains this discrepancy between norms and practice by claiming that the "division of the right of revenge explains the infrequency of drastic actions taken in cases of adultery."

Comparative evidence, however, shows that this is a typical pattern: often the adulterer is not killed, even more often the wife is spared.[100] This is not due to the division of responsibility, which is not present in other societies that have the same pattern, but rather to the way in which individuals manipulate ideal and practical norms and expectations to suit their particular purposes. Mohsen further notes that in all three cases where the husband killed the adulterer, he had to pay blood-money to the deceased's family. This, of course, contradicts the "right" of the husband to kill, in a manner not totally unlike the situation in Lysias' *Against Eratosthenes*. One recalls here Bourdieu's comments on the danger of taking "rules" to represent an "objective" reality.[101]

One must, of course, give jural norms, the "imperatives" of honor, and other ideal and ideological formulations their due. But they do not make the whole story. This chapter has described the little we know about the *legal* regulation of adultery at Athens, but this concluding section demonstrates the limits of such a positivistic account. Those abstract norms of law and morality, those "codes" and "rules" do not determine behavior. They are one aspect of the normative resources in relation to which individuals manage appearances and orient their conduct. To understand the social meaning of adultery, and the law of adultery, one must locate them in the patterns of social practices informing male–female relations in general; that is, in the politics of sex and gender. This constitutes the task of the next chapter.

---

[99] Mohsen (1970: 226).

[100] See e.g. Fernea (1969: 148, 261) for examples of this discrepancy. She notes the universally affirmed customary law that requires the death of a dishonored woman, but in all the cases she observed it was not carried out. She notes that only one of the older women she knew claimed that during her lifetime such a killing actually took place.

[101] Bourdieu (1977: 1–71). I do not mean to imply that such murders "of honor" never take place. Italian homicide statistics reveal that, particularly in the South, they remain one of the primary causes of violent death. There is doubtless wide regional variation in the actual incidence of such homicides in Mediterranean societies.

CHAPTER 6

Adultery, women, and social control

The previous chapter described the legal norms and procedures which regulated adultery at Athens. The final section of that discussion, however, suggested that the social practices involving adultery were rather more complex than the prohibitions of the criminal law might imply. Although the law provided that the husband, or the appropriate magistrates, could put to death the adulterer taken in the act, some aggrieved spouses were perceived as responding with silence, extortion, or complicity. Although social norms of honor and shame linked the woman's sexual modesty to the honor of her husband and other male relatives, some women were thought to buy the favors of young men, and some men to acquiesce in the financial advantage they might gain from their wives' infidelity. Rather than inquiring what such practices tell us about the normative evaluation of sexual relations, a positivistic, instrumental approach to social control would dismiss all such conduct as "violations" of social and legal rules, as deviations from the norm. As Chapters 2–4 suggested, however, such rules represent but one facet of social control in "face-to-face" societies: they influence, but do not determine, the social practices through which they, and the social order, are reproduced. Further, though they may reflect the norms of ethical and legal ideals, they may vary widely from other normative expectations which play a central role in patterns of social conduct. In the case of adultery, then, one must investigate the dynamic interrelation of these normative structures and social practices within the larger social context constituted by what Chapter 3 described as the politics of gender, reputation, and spatial differentiation.

In sketching this social context, the seemingly banal questions of "how and why" furnish a convenient starting-point. If, as much contemporary scholarship holds, women were strictly confined to

133

their houses, watched by their husbands, and accompanied in their every movement by relatives or slaves, how did they form adulterous relationships and then consummate them? Further, why did men and women run the considerable risks that adultery entailed? After all, as Lysias' *On the Murder of Eratosthenes* makes clear, some husbands, at least, were not loath to exercise the summary procedures provided by the law, and other passages attest to the ill-treatment which adulterers were likely to suffer if apprehended. Indeed, the question of motivation arises with particular force for men, since, according to many scholars, the only significant romantic attachments for men were homosexual, and sexual gratification, in this slave society, was ubiquitous and cheap. After all, if Andromache's description of her life in Euripides' *Trojan Women* is taken as typical, one wonders why and how adultery happened at all, let alone achieved its pre-eminence in the pantheon of sexual misconduct:[1]

I made good reputation my aim...As Hector's wife I studied and practiced the perfection of womanly modesty. First, if a woman does not stay in her own house, this very fact brings ill-fame upon her, whether she is at fault or not; I therefore gave up my longing to go out, and stayed at home; and I refused to admit into my house the amusing gossip of other women...Before my husband I kept a quiet tongue and modest eye; I knew in what matters I should rule, and where I should yield to his authority.

This statement is all too often regarded by scholars as representative, yet it contrasts markedly with the many assertions of the sexual intemperance of women and the frequency of adultery one finds in the sources. It also stands in stark opposition to the evidence discussed above concerning the financial aspects of adultery: husbands who accept payment, women who pay men, etc. As a character in Euripides' *Stheneboea*, mouthing a commonplace, puts it, "Many a man, proud of his wealth and birth, has been disgraced by his wanton wife." What accounts for these antithetical descriptions of the married woman and her role? An examination of this and

---

[1] Although in modern Western society it is rape which has become the pre-eminent or paradigmatic sexual crime, in Athens this was not the case. The Athenian orators, for example, frequently refer to adultery, but do not mention a single case of rape involving an Athenian woman of citizen-standing. Indeed, Mediterranean societies typically evidence an almost obsessive concern with adultery. In New Comedy rape does often figure in the plot, usually involving maidens at festivals where it is often not clear to what extent the intercourse may have involved seduction. Such festivals were one of the few occasions where normal patterns of social control for unmarried women might be relaxed.

other related contradictions concerning the characterization of women may serve as a first step towards understanding adultery and the context in which it occurred.

Conflicting characterizations of women in the ancient sources have caused considerable confusion, which scholars have dealt with in two ways. The more primitive method denies the force of the antinomy, explaining it away in some fashion. Thus Flacelière accepts the Andromachean typology at face value:

Whereas married women seldom crossed the thresholds of their own front door, adolescent girls were lucky if they were allowed as far as the inner courtyard since they had to stay where they could not ʰe seen – well away even from the male members of the family.[2]

He admits, though, that Aristophanes presents a very different picture of Athenian women, but concludes that this must represent a change towards greater freedom in the late fifth century – a rather desperate expedient since we have almost no evidence *before* the last quarter of the century.[3] More recently, Gould and Humphreys acknowledge the contradiction, but Humphreys rather unsatisfactorily explains that "This contradictoriness must be to some extent a product of the nature of our sources, which are heavily dominated by cultural themes in which women are seen through a grid designed to fit men."[4] Gould, on the other hand, relates the contradiction to profound cultural conflicts concerning women and their sexuality, conflicts expressed with particular force in myth. These conflicts arise out of a central cultural ambiguity about women and sexuality, based upon a dynamic of dependence and hatred, desire and fear, which, it will be argued below, is typical of Mediterranean societies. A satisfactory explanation, however, must go beyond the realm of myth, important as that may be, and attempt to explain these contradictions in terms of what Giddens calls the "structural properties" of social systems.[5] Looking at similar difficulties that have arisen in describing the social role of women in the contemporary Mediterranean world may prove helpful in addressing this task.

Anthropologists, predominantly male, had long formulated a view of Mediterranean women as secluded, powerless, and isolated from

---

[2] 1965: 55.   [3] 1965: 69.
[4] Humphreys (1983: 49). For a contrary view, see Henderson (1975: 206).
[5] 1986: Chapter 1.

the life of their society. A later generation of researchers, however, challenged this widely accepted thesis. Clark, for example, in her social anthropological study of a modern Greek village, acutely formulates the contrast between these different interpretations of the role of women in traditional Mediterranean societies:

When we began our field study at Methane it was soon evident that characterizations of Greek women in some of the ethnographic accounts did not fit the women we were encountering. While we had read about powerless, submissive females who considered themselves morally inferior to men, we found physically and socially strong women who had a great deal to say about what took place in the village. The social and economic affairs of several households were actually dominated by older women, including the house of village officials.[6]

Clark's explanation of this contradiction focuses on the way in which the gender and marital status of the researcher largely determine the information to which he or she has access.[7] A significant body of recent research has confirmed these findings, revealing how conceptualizations of the role of women vary according to the perspective of the informant and the rhetorical nature of the context in which the view is expressed. Both perspectives exist within this social context, and both reflect the values and norms of the society. What is misguided is to try to identify one as "correct," on the assumption that such norms and values must form a coherent "system," free of ambiguity, ambivalence, or conflict. A further source of difficulty in anthropological assessments of women in Mediterranean societies arises from the related problem of failing to differentiate firsthand observation from informants' accounts, based as they often are upon the conscious and unconscious manipulation of norms and cultural ideals so as to convey a particular point of view. In assessing the status of women, as well as related questions like seclusion, classical scholars have perhaps often fallen prey to the same trap, failing to distinguish between ideology and (sometimes conflicting) normative ideals on the one hand, and social practices on the other.[8] Too often normative ideals are taken as objective structures which determine

[6] Clark (1983: 122). See also the pioneering article by E. Friedl (1967).
[7] See Whitehead and Conaway (1986) for the most recent studies on this question.
[8] Two of the most penetrating analyses of the manipulation of such categories are P. Bourdieu's classic study, *Outline of a Theory of Practice* (1977: 36–43, 58–71), and Comaroff and Roberts, *Rules and Processes* (1981).

behavior rather than as what Bourdieu calls "official representations of practices," which are manipulated according to the strategic exigencies of particular practical contexts.[9] Seeing the way such norms operate as an element of social practices illuminates the otherwise perplexing contradictions.

The two Athenian authors who were most acutely aware of the problems of women in their society, Aristophanes and Euripides, were also fully cognizant of such contradictions: that is, the contradiction between conflicting normative idealizations of woman: desire and fear, dependence and hatred, Medea and Andromache, and the further conflict between these positive and negative ideals on the one hand, and the life of the society on the other. Euripides, in *Medea, Trojan Women, Bacchae, Hippolytus*, and other plays, deliberately embodies in drama these conflicting positions. In *Melanippe*, a play noted in antiquity for its collection of antithetical characterizations of women, one character thus exclaims "The worst plague is the hated race of women." "Except for my mother I hate the whole female sex."[10] On the other hand, in the same play a woman asserts that

Women manage homes and preserve the goods which are brought from abroad. Houses where there is no wife are neither orderly nor prosperous. And in religion – I take this to be important – we women play a large part... How then can it be just that the female sex should be abused? Shall not men cease their foolish reproaches, cease to blame all women alike if they meet one who is bad?[11]

The way in which Euripides repeatedly plays upon the conflicts inherent in these views, stereotypes, and ideals should have indicated to classical scholars that great caution is required in evaluating the portrayal of women in Athenian sources. He depicts a society whose values reflect profound ambivalence about women and their sexuality, and his conscious dramatic manipulation of ideologically determined stances shows the way in which neither Andromache's speech, nor nominally non-fictional accounts like that in Xenophon's *Oeconomicus*, can be taken at face value as reflecting "how it really

[9] See Bourdieu (1977: Chapter 1), and Comaroff and Roberts (1981).
[10] Frgs. 496, 500, translated by Vellacott (1975: 97).
[11] Translation by Vellacott (1975: 97). These views are expressed in fragments, but they can nonetheless serve as examples of the way in which Euripides employed antithetical views of women in his plays. Thus they are not employed here in an attempt to reconstruct the plot or authorial intention of the play. Familiar examples of such antithetical portrayals of women abound in *Medea, Hippolytus, Hecuba*, etc.

was."[12] If Euripides used this conflict as the fuel of tragedy, Aristophanes no less brilliantly placed the same antitheses and ambiguities at the center of some of his most serious comic creations. In *Lysistrata*, *Ecclesiazusae*, and *Thesmophoriazusae* much of the sexual humor derives from the way in which he exploits the contradictions between the cultural ideal and real life, between woman as men think she should be, woman as men fear she is, and the mothers, maidens, wives, and widows of everyday existence.

Scholars like Zeitlin, King, Segal, and Loraux have explored such contradictions by looking to myth and literature as symbolic expressions of the cultural organization of gender.[13] Charles Segal for example emphasizes the ambivalent image of women in Greek myth and literature in terms very similar to those employed by modern Mediterranean anthropologists:

As the one who bears and cares for children and tends house and hearth, she is at the center of what is secure, nurturing, life-giving; but in her passionate and emotional nature and the violence of her sexual instincts which she is felt as little able to control, she is regarded as irrational, unstable, dangerous. Hence she is seen as an integral part of the civic structure on the one hand, but also regarded as a threat to that structure on the other... She has her place within the sheltered inner domain of the house, but also has affinities with the wild, savage world of beasts outside the limits of the city walls.[14]

Such analyses, based upon tragedies like *Medea*, *Bacchae*, and *Agamemnon*, have greatly contributed to our understanding of those plays, and of the ideological conceptualization of women's sexuality. Such an approach, however, possesses only a limited capacity for relating the conflicts and ambiguities it uncovers to concrete questions concerning the social practices which instantiate the regulation of sexuality, the social and legal position of women, etc. As recent anthropological work has emphasized, in analysing the

---

[12] To translate loosely Ranke's "Wie es eigentlich gewesen ist," on which, see Finley's critique of such approaches (1985a: 47–66).

[13] King (1983: 124), for example, claims that "The Greeks saw 'woman' as a contrast between the undisciplined threat to social order and the controlled, reproductive *gyne* [woman/wife]. The presentation of female maturation as a movement from the first to the second expresses the hope that women can safely be incorporated into society in order to reproduce it." See also Just (1975: passim), Detienne (1981: 106) and Zeitlin (1982: 135).

[14] 1978: 185. This ambivalence is widespread: it is not uniquely Greek, nor uniquely Mediterranean, though prevalent in the Mediterranean world. See Poole (Ortner and Whitehead 1981: 116–65) and Godelier (1987: Part 1) for the Baruya of New Guinea, and Gregor (1985: Chapters 2, 3, 7, 8, 10) for the Mehinaku of the Amazon Basin.

cultural articulation of gender one must look beyond literature to the realm of practices and the normative structures[15] implicit within them. A multi-dimensional approach requires the exploration of the relationship between the realm of symbolism and ideology, as expressed in literature, and myth, and the politics of gender and reputation constituted by the individual and collective conduct which makes up the life of the society. As Whitehead puts it in her seminal discussion,

> Sexual behaviors that occur within the context of normative expectations tell us something about normative expectations, but very little about human desire; and, conversely, spontaneous (non-instituted) sexual expressions indicate the presence of characteristic desires without giving us any clear message about the operations of the formal cultural system.[16]

Yet, if the conflicting portrayals of women in the sources all reflect something about the norms and values of classical Athens, how is one to relate these products of ideology to the social practices which they inform? It was suggested above that in order to understand adultery one would have to broaden the inquiry to include the sexual role of women. Now the scope of the discussion must be further expanded to cover the broader normative context encompassing female sexuality, a context defined by the politics of space, reputation, and gender, and the related antinomies of public and private, and honor and shame. Using comparative evidence one may sketch a series of social practices, norms, and beliefs which illuminate the Athenian evidence and the contradictions which classical scholars like Gomme and Gould found within it. The ensuing discussion will thus focus on three themes in order of decreasing generality: the normative application of honor and shame and the public/private dichotomy to sexuality, the sexual and social roles which such an application implies, and the dynamic relationship between ideals and practices in the description and embodiment of these roles. Finally, the argument will return to the topic of adultery, placing it within this larger context.

Chapter 3 sketched the patterns of values, norms, and social practices which define prestige and reputation in many modern Mediterranean communities. Within that context the values and beliefs associated with honor and shame occupy a prominent place,

---

[15] It is worth repeating that I use the word "structure" here, following Bourdieu and Giddens, in the sense elaborated in Chapter 2.   [16] Whitehead (1981: 81).

and one may begin investigating the politics of gender by recalling those central features of honor and shame that connect to sexuality. The crucial point here is that the honor of men is, in large part, defined through the chastity of the women to whom they are related.[17] Female honor largely involves sexual purity and the behavior which social norms deem necessary to maintain it in the eyes of the watchful community. Male honor receives the active role of defending that purity. A man's honor is therefore involved with the sexual purity of his mother, sisters, wife and daughters – of him chastity is not required. The vigilance of men is necessitated therefore by the free play which social norms give to the expression of masculinity through the seduction of the women of others, and also by the view of female sexuality which posits that women need to be protected from themselves as well. As Pitt-Rivers puts it:

The frailty of women is the inevitable correlate of this conceptualization, and the notion is not, perhaps, displeasing to the male who may see in it an encouragement of sexual conquest. Thus an honorable woman, born with the proper sentiment of shame, strives to avoid the human contacts which might expose her to dishonor; she cannot expect to succeed in this ambition unsupported by male authority. This fact gives justification to the usage which makes the deceived husband, not the adulterer, the object of ridicule and opprobrium ...[18]

Closely associated with these beliefs is the fear of unbridled female sexuality, which only the force of social convention and male vigilance can restrain. Because the "bride's virginity and the wife's fidelity are the basic moral assumptions on which the family is built,"[19] the expression of this sexuality in illicit ways may bring humiliation and dishonor to a family and lineage.[20] Viewed from this

---

[17] Ortner and Whitehead (1981: 16, 21) argue for the essential linkage of gender systems and prestige: "A gender system is first and foremost a prestige structure itself." More specifically, "most societies have some sources of male prestige that ... are relatively disconnected from relations with women. But in perhaps the majority of cases, male prestige is deeply involved in cross-sex relations. Women may be cast as the prize for male prowess or success; having a wife may be the prerequisite to full adult male status; good or bad liaisons with women may raise or lower one's status; the status of one's mother may systematically affect one's status at birth; the sexual comportment of one's sisters and daughters may polish or dull one's honor; and so on." See also Abu-Lughod (1986: 85ff.).

[18] Pitt-Rivers (1977: 23).   [19] See Chapter 3, n. 132.

[20] See e.g. Campbell (1979: 271), Jamous (1981: 66), and Brandes (1975: 234–6): "In San Blas, a family's honor is probably more dependent on the sexual conduct of its women than on any other single factor ... The fact that personality attributes are considered to run in the blood ... means that virtually all of a woman's consanguines are affected by her behavior as well." In Euripides' *Hecuba* (1186), one finds the same genetic attribution of wrongdoing in women to inheritance – it is their nature.

perspective, women are perceived as powerful and dangerous. Indeed, many Mediterranean societies conceptualize them as the sexual embodiment of the demonic. Thus Bourdieu notes the proverbial saying in Kabylia, where women are associated with the left, men with the right hand, that "Shame is the maiden," and women are often called the "cows of Satan" or "the devil's snares."[21] Similarly, du Boulay notes that in Ambeli women are "of the left," "from the devil,"[22] and thus represent the weak link that endangers the family. As the Greek saying has it, "Houses, mansions, and cottages with tiny windows are lost by means of women."[23]

Such beliefs serve to connect an ideology of gender to a politics of reputation by means of a dark conceptualization of women's sexuality that serves as the connecting link. Women are thought to embody a seething sexuality that can ignite an uncontrollable response in men.[24] To preserve the social order, this potentially destructive force must be controlled and mediated through the institution of the family, which, when properly contained and channeled, it serves to reproduce.[25] The male role, then, is to ensure the chastity on which men's reputation, in large part, depends:[26]

A wife's infidelity threatens the moral reputation of her entire family. But it affects no one so profoundly as her cuckolded husband, who is charged with the responsibility of harnessing her rampant sexuality and confining it within the secret walls of their bedroom.[27]

The burden of this social responsibility weighs heavily upon men, who, because of the very separation of male and female spheres of activity, feel that their wives and daughters could always be deceiving them, as the Sarakatsani say, "forty times each day."[28]

---

[21] Bourdieu (1977: 44–52).
[22] Du Boulay (1974: 139); Brandes (1975: 219) reports that in Andalusia "Women are of the Devil," and cf. Campbell (1979: 277).
[23] Du Boulay (1974: 139), and cf. Maher (1974: 91ff.) and Abu-Lughod (1986: 114). As these sources reveal, the association of women with the demonic is not a product of Christianization. The theme is just as prevalent in the Muslim Mediterranean.
[24] Mernissi (1975:4,10,16) describes Moroccan men's traditional fear that women's sexuality makes men lose their self-control, giving in to the forces that represent chaos. Women are perceived as almost impossible to satisfy (10, 16). See also Berger (1962: 120–2) and Lloyd and Fallers (1976: 258–9).
[25] Fuller (1961: 52), and see Abu-Lughod (1986: 145ff.). King emphasizes this point for Athens (1983: 111); see her references to the collections of passages maintaining that the unmarried girl must be tamed, broken, domesticated. [26] Brandes (1975: 236).
[27] Brandes (1975: 227); cf. Campbell (1979: 277–8). [28] Campbell (1964: 278).

Fear, anxiety, and hostility result from this social and ideological dynamic. Anxiety, for example, is manifested in extreme concern about paternity. In San Blas, for example, one never says that a baby looks like its mother, for this calls the paternity of the father into question.[29]

Apart from obsessive fear of adultery, of entering that most humiliating of all social states, cuckoldry,[30] men also feel threatened by their direct contact with the powerful sexual potential that their honor requires them to superintend.[31] Brandes relates how in San Blas men believe that women trap men through seductive wiles and a modest exterior into marriage. Then they try to kill them with their voracious sexual appetites so that they may live off their pension and insurance premiums and indulge their sexual appetites unencumbered by the restrictions of marriage.[32] The seductive power and sexual voraciousness of women is deadly for men because it depletes the substance of their life force. Thus in Greece, Italy, and Spain, one finds the widespread belief that the genitals are the source of a man's strength and will, semen its substance. The depletion of this vital fluid leads to one's demise. Brandes emphasizes that this is not a Christian moralization of sexuality:

In San Blas, I have observed no concern among men that coitus or sexual contact of any kind with women is immoral or contrary to religious standards ... in other words, men are totally unconcerned that women will lead them into sin. What does worry them, however, is that their wives will, through sexual activity, deprive them of their strength and youth, and drive them to an early grave.[33]

This sentiment finds expression in many proverbs and sayings, such as "Si quieres llegar a viejo, Guarda la leche en el pellejo." (If you want to reach old age, Keep your milk within your skin.)[34] Pitt-Rivers reports the same beliefs in the areas of Andalusia he

[29] Brandes (1975: 228).

[30] See also Maher (1974: 101). To become a cuckold is to become feminized; the goat is the female animal, and female goats, unlike female sheep, have horns (Brandes, 1975: 229–30).

[31] This applies, of course, not only to wives, but daughters as well. Women are weak and cannot control their potent sexuality, so men must guard them closely (Williams 1968: 83; Berger 1962: 119–21). This is the reason informants typically give for child betrothal and early marriage (Berger 1962: 122; Prothro and Diab 1974: 29ff.; Maher 1974: 150; Friedl 1958: 133; Sanders 1962: 158; Granquist 1931: 45). See Menander, *Epitrepontes* 1114–16, for the same sentiment.   [32] Brandes (1975: 224–5).

[33] 225–6. On semen and the dangers of frequent sexual activity in Greek thought, see Rousselle (1988: 39). This view of semen can lead to other patterns; see for example Godelier (1987: 52–3) on the Baruya.   [34] Brandes (1975: 226).

studied, where men fear the insatiable appetites of widows, even septuagenarians.[35] This ideology of gender, based upon fear and hostility, does not represent an exclusively male preoccupation, but operates in a dynamic between the sexes. Campbell relates that unmarried kinswomen console the bride, just before the wedding, about the horrors that are to come. They say that they will never marry and submit, and the bride responds that she will hide a knife on her person and castrate her husband on their wedding night.[36] Furthermore, as Brandes rightly claims (1975: 235), because of the power of women to "ruin" a lineage,[37] this ideology of gender should not "be dismissed as a mere rationalization for the political and economic exploitation of women. Rather it must be understood on its own terms as a strong motivating force in determining relationships between the sexes."[38]

Similar patterns of norms, values, and practices associated with the politics of reputation and gender characterize ancient Athenian society as well. The nexus of honor, shame, and sexuality informs, for example, the passages from Euripides quoted above, such as "Many a man, proud of his wealth and birth, has been disgraced by his wanton wife."[39] This is not simply a literary formula, for in the Attic orators it is not uncommon to attack an opponent by referring to the unchastity of his women.[40] Further, numerous orations reveal the way men feel dishonored when their women are compromised.[41] For example, the cuckolded husband in Lysias' *On the Murder of Eratosthenes* claims that the adulterer he killed disgraced his children

[35] 1977: 82; see also du Boulay (1974: 123).

[36] Campbell (1979: 276). As will appear below, the myths and literature of classical Greece are also replete with such dark fantasies.

[37] As Pitt-Rivers (1977: 80) argues, "It is only too easy to understand then that men, conscious and resentful of their vulnerability through the actions of their womenfolk, should be eager to credit them with the faults of character that are, however ill-founded, commonplace in the literature of the Mediterranean, faults which justify their exclusion from the political sphere and the authority of their menfolk over them."

[38] See also Prothro and Diab (1974: 117ff.).

[39] On the dishonor and shame of adultery for the woman and the *oikos*, see Euripides, *Hippolytus* 408ff. The infidelity of the adulteress dishonors her husband and their children: *Hippolytus* 420-1, 715-20. Thus Phaedra feels shame (*aischune*) at her desire for infidelity (*Hippolytus* 246, and cf. 317 *miasma*); death shall bring her honor, *time*, 329, and cf. 385, 405-6, 411.

[40] See e.g. Demosthenes 18.129, Demosthenes 22.61, Aeschines 2.149, and cf. Theophrastus, *Characters*.

[41] Men are dishonored by *hubris* when they cannot protect the sexual integrity of their wives and children: [Dem.] 17.3-4, and cf. Euripides, *Hippolytus* 411ff. Cf. Lysias 3.6, 23, 29, 46, where breaking into a man's home at night violates his honor.

and humiliated him by entering his house and seducing his wife.[42]
Indeed, the code of honor and shame is enshrined in the law of
homicide, which allows a man to kill anyone found having intercourse with his wife, mother, sister, daughter, or legal concubine.[43]

As in modern Mediterranean societies, in Athens men's perception
of female sexuality complicated the task of guarding the honor of a
family. Greek literature abounds with references to men's view of the
dangers of women's sexuality. To begin with, women are associated
with the left, darkness, cold, and evil; men with the right, good, hot,
and light.[44] According to Aristotle, *malakia* (softness, weakness, lack
of self-control) afflicts women's nature (*N.E.* 1150b12–16, *H.A.*
608a35ff.). Thus the good wife has been taught by her family to be
self-controlled, restrained (*sophron*; Xenophon, *Oec.* 7.14).[45] When
Aristotle (*H.A.* 608a22–b18) analyzes the differences between men
and women, he concludes that women are more passionate,
shameless, deceitful, and false of speech, etc.[46] In *Lysistrata* (11–12)
women are described as *panourgoi* (ready to do anything, deceitful,
wicked), and the play is replete with references to men's view of the
animality and debauched sexuality of women's nature (387–9, 405,
476, 1014–15, and cf. *Clouds* 49ff.).[47] Indeed, male perceptions of
women's unchastity appear as a commonplace in drama,[48] and,
linked with the values of honor and shame, make clear how women

---

[42] Dishonor, revenge, and social disorder are seen as typical results of sexual wrongdoing
against the wives of other men; Aristotle, *Politics* 1311b7–20; Isocrates, *Nicocles* 36–7, and
cf. *Panegyricus*.

[43] See Chapter 5 above. The husband's revenge for dishonor requires that the adulterer suffer
humiliation (Xenophon, *Mem.* 2.1.5). An oration of Hyperides claims that it is unbelievable
that someone would not be killed on the spot for making compromising remarks to a free
woman: "What brother would not have killed him?" (*Lycophron* 6); and cf. Demosthenes
23.79; 59.12; and Menander, *Dyskolos* 22.

[44] See Lloyd (1983: 82), Kember (1973: 90). Aristotle associates the male with greater heat,
and the lack of heat explains why females have no semen. See e.g. *G.A.* 729aff. and
Horowitz (1976: 192). Women in tragedy are often portrayed as linked to chthonic powers
and associated with death and darkness: Euripides, *Bacchae*, *Medea* 395–409; see also King
(1983: 113ff.).

[45] If women start having intercourse too early their sexual appetite will be too great; see
Detienne (1981: 105) and Just (1975: 165) for further references.

[46] Women are more afflicted by the "disease of desire" than men (Euripides, *Andromache*
220–1). Hecuba, in Euripides' play of that name, says that women, through treachery, use
violence to prevail over men (882–4).

[47] Medea is referred to as a tigress and bull, and cf. Euripides, *Andromache* 269ff. Animal
metaphors are frequently applied to Clytaemnestra in the *Oresteia*, and cf. *Hippolytus* 645–8
and *Hecuba* 1180–2. See also Zeitlin (1982: 145).

[48] For the conventional view of women's unchastity see Euripides, *Ion* 1090ff.; *Hippolytus*
406ff., 616–68; and *Medea* 420ff.

must be guarded so as to protect the family and, ultimately, the social order.[49] As Electra accuses her mother, "Any woman who works on her beauty when her man is gone from home indicts herself as being a whore. She has no decent cause to show her painted face outside the door unless she wants to look for trouble."[50]

Further, as in contemporary Mediterranean communities, this "empowerment" of women to ruin a family generates considerable sexual hostility.[51] Woman is a hated thing (*misema*), says Hippolytus, voicing a traditional sentiment.[52] Euripides also repeatedly portrays women who resent male hostility and the social and political subordination connected to it. Medea speaks at length on this theme, and the same sentiment appears in a number of his plays: "Life is harder for women than for men; they judge us, good and bad together, and hate us" (*Ion* 398–400, and cf. *Hecuba* 1180–6). Like the men of San Blas, described by Brandes, who fear that this resentment will lead women to seek the freedom of widowhood, Athenian drama depicts male fantasies of murderous brides and wives, like Clytaemnestra, Medea, the 50 Danaids who, save one, kill their husbands on their wedding night, or the Lemnian women who massacre all the men on their island. As a character in Euripides' *Ion* claims, "Many a woman, when driven to it, has used the knife or poison against her husband."[53] The debates about the viciousness or virtue of women in Euripides indicate the probable depth of this ideological conflict in Athenian society,[54] and this evident ambivalence of attitudes has fueled controversy in the contemporary study of Athenian sexuality. Most feminist scholarship has portrayed Athenian society as misogynistic in its very essence, and has

---

[49] Euripides, *Hippolytus* 408ff., *Hecuba* 879–87, 1180ff. Recent scholarship has argued that this sentiment informs the discussion of virginity and the diseases of virgins in the Hippocratic Corpus; see King (1983: 113ff.), Lloyd (1983: 69), and Rousselle (1988: 37ff.). Zeitlin (1982: 135), for example, claims that the Hippocratic text which describes how "the female can only be controlled through irrigation of the womb by male semen... and by pregnancy which keeps it in place..." should be read socially as saying that stability comes through control exercised by men and through the production of legitimate children through marriage.   [50] Euripides, *Electra* 1072–5.   [51] Cf. Parker (1983: 101).

[52] As Hesiod put it, woman is a *kalon kakon*, "good evil" (*Theogony* 585; see Loraux 1978: 53ff.). For the traditional view, see also Hesiod, *Works and Days* 586–7; and Vernant (1981: 51).

[53] See Euripides, *Hecuba* 876–88, *Hippolytus* 478; Aeschylus, *Agamemnon* 1231: "the female that kills the male," *Choephoroi* 599–601, 621ff.; Aristophanes, *Thesmophoriazusae* 559ff.; and cf. Antiphon 1, 9–10, 26–7. See Burkert on the association of blood, violence, and castration with the Thesmophoria (1985: 244).

[54] E.g. *Andromache* 270ff., 945ff.; *Hecuba* 1180; *Ion* 396ff. 1090ff.; *Bacchae* 215–25, 260ff.

emphasized the central role of men's fear of women.[55] On the other hand, Mary Lefkowitz, one of the most important figures in this area, has rightly pointed up the inevitable exaggeration of many one-sided feminist accounts. Though she may go somewhat too far in discounting male fear of female sexuality (1986:112), her fundamental point is well taken.

The underlying problem with such debates is that the conflicts which delimit the politics of gender at Athens can only be understood as part of a larger whole. Debates about Athenian misogyny ring hollow so long as they confine themselves to the world of literature and myth. Athenian sexual ideology *was* shot through with contradiction and ambiguity. Indeed, such is the nature of ideology in all cultures, for it reflects the chaos hidden beneath the surface of social action.[56] Accordingly, the discussion must now move to locate the politics of gender in that broader context of social practices.

To this point, the discussion has sketched some of the ideological parameters of the politics of gender in both classical Athens and the modern Mediterranean, and indicated the way in which values and beliefs associated with honor and shame constitute, to use the theoretical vocabulary of Chapter 2, central structural principles of this social system. Further, it has identified certain paradoxical aspects of the conceptualization of gender relations, and suggested that they may be connected to issues of social control and the sexual division of labor and space. Now, to illuminate further these connections, the argument will focus in some detail on these important facets of the social roles connected with honor and shame, namely the sexual aspect of the antinomy of public and private spheres. It may be helpful to begin by contrasting ancient and modern views, and then move to consider some confusions in classical scholarship which comparative evidence can help to dispel.

Chapters 3 and 4 elaborated the general identification of the public sphere with men and the private sphere with women as characteristic of both traditional Mediterranean societies and classical Athens. Xenophon and pseudo-Aristotle, for example, expound at length on how, by their very natures, men are suited for

---

[55] See e.g. Keuls (1986) and Padel (1983: 3ff.).

[56] As Brandes (1975: 218–19) argues, "The curious paradox is that, even though women in San Blas are restrained and restricted by society, men nonetheless feel severely threatened by them, or at least they are encouraged by the ideology to feel so...It is an ideology that reverses the state of affairs that exists in the realm of actual behavior."

the outside, women for the inside.[57] Men are associated with commerce and politics, the marketplace, café, fields, and so on, the women with the home. The man's role requires him to be outside; as Xenophon puts it, men who stay at home during the day are considered womanish (*Oec.* 7.30).[58] The woman's role, on the other hand, requires her to stay indoors. In Bourdieu's formulation,

The opposition between the inside and the outside ... is concretely expressed in the clear-cut distinction between the feminine area, the house and its garden, and the masculine area, the place of assembly, the mosque, the café, etc. In the Kabyle village the two areas are distinctly separate ...[59]

The sexual differentiation of space operates within a framework of norms and values constructed around the poles of honor and shame. The house is the domain of secrecy, of intimate life. As indicated above, whether in classical Athens or in traditional Spanish, Greek, Italian, or Moroccan communities, honor requires that its sanctity be protected, and the mere fact that strangers gain entrance to it, avoiding the vigilance of male members of the family, itself calls the chastity of the women into question. Any violation of the house is an attack on the honor of its men and the chastity of its women, even if the intruder is only a thief.[60] The separation of women from men and the man's public sphere within this protected domain is the chief means by which sexual purity is both guarded and demonstrated to the community.[61] Thus, apart from Andromache's eloquent testimony to the connection of honor and seclusion, husbands in Aristophanes typically grow angry on discovering that their wives have been out, and their immediate suspicion is of sexual transgression (e.g. *Thesm.* 397ff., 410ff., 519, 785–91). Dubisch relates that in modern Greek communities a common euphemism for adultery is to say that a woman deceives her husband in the street.[62] In *Ecclesiazusae* a wife, regaled by her husband when she

---

[57] Xenophon, *Oeconomicus* 7.17–40; [Aristotle], *Oeconomica* 1343b25ff.

[58] On men who are ridiculed for staying around the house, see Maher (1974: 112), Gilmore (1987b: 14), and Loizos (1975: 92). For a comparative perspective, see Gregor (1985: 23).

[59] Bourdieu, in Peristiany (1966: 221). In *Outline of a Theory of Practice* Bourdieu examines the way in which such categories operate in a fluid manner in the complex pattern of social and political strategies, rhetoric, and action (41–71, 159–197). See also Herzfeld, in Dubisch (1986: 215–33) and Gilmore (1987b: Chapters 1–3).

[60] See e.g. Demosthenes 23, Lysias 1 and 7, and the discussion in Chapter 5.

[61] See Campbell (1979: 185, 203, 268–74, 301–20); du Boulay (1974: 121–200); Handman (1983: 171–5).

[62] (1986: 200). Maher (1974: 84–5, 91) reports similar values and beliefs in Morocco. See also Menander, Fr. 546: "Respectable women should stay at home, the street is for whores."

returns from assisting a friend in childbirth, asks him "Do you think
I've been to see my lover (*moichos*)?" (520, and cf. 1008).[63] Similarly,
a woman informant in modern Greece rhetorically asks, "Do you
know...how a man rejoices and how he loves his wife when he finds
her always in the house?"[64]

Not only ought women to remain within, but they must also guard
themselves from contact with any men who pass by or call for their
husbands. Thus, in Theophrastus (*Char.* 28.3), insulting a woman by
saying she addresses those who pass by on the street, or that she
answers the door herself, or that she talks with men, are all roughly
equivalent to saying "This house is simply a brothel," or "They
couple like dogs in the street."[65] Lycurgus also comments on the
unworthy behavior of women showing themselves at the door of
their house (*Against Leocrates* 40), using the same category as the
Babylonian Talmud (*Sota* 1.7) employs to describe paradigmatically
the adulteress: "She stood at the door of her house to show
herself."[66] Lysias, in a rhetorical variation on the familiar topos,
emphasizes the honor of women who had led such orderly lives that
"they are ashamed to be seen even by their kinsmen" (3.6–7).
Again, such normative judgments of women's conduct seem typical
of many Mediterranean communities. Davis, for example, in his
study of the modern Italian village of Pisticci, reports that "Several
men told me that I was the first man not their kinsman to cross their
thresholds."[67] This statement is, of course, no more literally true
than Lysias' rhetorical exaggeration of "proper" feminine modesty,
but rather an expression of a cultural ideal.[68]

Some scholars, however, have taken statements like those of Lysias
as veracious descriptions of actual conduct, using them to support
their portrayal of the isolated and secluded Athenian woman. How,
then, can one distinguish ideology and social practice in such

---

[63] Cf. Handman (1983: 164–6).

[64] Du Boulay (1974: 131). Similarly, Godelier (1987: 44) reports that Baruya girls are told
during initiation "Get home before your husband, that way he won't suspect you of
screwing around outside."

[65] Cf. a female informant's account in Williams (1968: 76–7): "A good girl walks in the street
and doesn't speak to anyone...The bad one, she tries to talk to everybody even if a man
doesn't greet her."

[66] But in Menander's *Dyskolos*, women, probably of poorer families, answer the door
themselves. See also Demosthenes 47.37–8, 53 and Euripides, *Electra* 340ff. for the propriety
of women inviting men into the house.   [67] Davis (1973: 48–9).

[68] See e.g. Dubisch (1986: 200): "Ideally, a woman should be confined to the house, leaving
its boundaries only as necessity demands and never for idle or frivolous reasons."

passages? The problem with the ancient evidence, as I noted above, is that it is like a jigsaw puzzle where most of the pieces are missing. In recovering the missing "picture" to aid in reconstructing the "puzzle" of male–female relations in classical Athens, evidence from social anthropology can be of invaluable assistance in providing models of social systems. The model which can provide the most plausible explanation of the evidence we do have can therefore help to reconstruct the social practices which produce it. I have sketched such a model above, and, with further elaboration, I believe it can provide the basis for a critique of certain important misconceptions concerning the public/private dichotomy and the role and status of women in Athenian society.

To begin with, there is a marked tendency to take the public/private dichotomy as an absolute ontological category and hence to confuse separation and seclusion.[69] That is, it does not follow that because, generally speaking, the man's sphere is public/outside, and the woman's is private/inside, women live their lives in total isolation from all but their slaves and their family. Separation of spheres of activity does not imply physical sequestration, and consequently utter subjection, as does seclusion.[70] While it is undeniable that women did not operate in the public and political spheres in the way that men did, it does not necessarily follow that they did not have public, social, and economic spheres of their own, nor that these categories were not fluid and manipulable as opposed to rigid and eternally fixed. Scholars too often assume this to be the case, however, misled by the well-known, ideologically determined texts like Andromache's speech or Xenophon's picture of the ideal wife, and do not attempt to test critically the validity of these models. Thus Flacelière (1965: 55) assumed that women never left the house and adolescent girls never even reached the courtyard. Much recent scholarship follows a similar interpretation. Thus Tyrrell, in a formulation that is not at all untypical, uncritically accepts Xenophon's idealized description arguing that "'The outer door of the house is the boundary for the free woman.' Segregated from women of other households, with only female relatives by marriage and slaves for company [one wonders how the relatives got there!], women tended to the domestic chores of running the house

[69] For a review of the literature see Foley (1981b: 148ff.).
[70] Maher (1974) shows the psychological strain which true seclusion produces, but also indicates how most women's lives are led according to very different social patterns.

for their husbands.''[71] Walcot also speaks of the seclusion of women, but he sensibly notes that "we have no way of being certain how far social reality corresponded to the social ideal of female seclusion.''[72]

I, however, would argue that we do have a way of making such distinctions, for social anthropological studies of modern Mediterranean societies show that the patterns of male–female role divisions in classical Athens are typical products of forms of social organization prevalent in traditional Mediterranean communities. Because of the tendency to view Greek society as somehow isolated from the rest of Western civilization, scholars like Eva Keuls[73] tend to view such patterns as unique, bizarre, or even pathological, when in fact they are quite normal aspects of certain kinds of social systems. It is within such an intellectual framework that the significance of adultery in Athenian society becomes clear, for it is the larger structure which makes the sexual purity of the wife of paramount importance for the reputation and standing of a family.

In taking separation to imply seclusion, the prevailing view tends to ignore a considerable body of evidence which indicates that Athenian women participated in a wide range of activities which regularly took them out of their houses. These included working in the fields (Aristophanes, *Peace* 535, Demosthenes 57.45), or as vendors, midwives, innkeepers, or bakers (Demosthenes, 57.30–1, 34; Aristophanes, *Acharnians* 478, *Wasps* 497, 1380–92, *Frogs* 1346, *Lysistrata* 445, 456ff., *Thesmophoriazusae* 346ff., 447ff.).[74] In an oration of Demosthenes a man testifies that his mother worked as a nurse, and he goes on to say that many Athenian women do the same, or work in the vineyards or at the loom (57.35, 45; see also Plato,

[71] W. Tyrrell (1984: 45); likewise Padel, in Cameron and Kuhrt (1983: 8); Cantarella (1986: 46), and Zeitlin (1982: 129). Keuls (1985: 87–8, 110) argues that not only did respectable women almost never leave the house, but also that for a man, the women's quarters of his own house were "largely unknown territory." Such views of Athenian culture necessarily tend to exaggerate the actual physical isolation of women, often while acknowledging in some way that this is only an ideal. Foley (1981b: 130), for example, concedes that "Poorer women may have participated in agriculture, and certainly sold goods at markets," but hastens to add "Respectable women left the house *only* [my emphasis] to visit neighbors, aid in childbirth, or to attend religious rituals – marriages, funerals, and festivals." The word "only" hedges a rather major qualification here. Further, the equation of respectable with wealthy, poor with unrespected is typical of much contemporary scholarship, and reflects scholarly preoccupation with the lives of the upper strata as "Athenian society," despite the fact that they were almost certainly a relatively small minority. See also Just (1975: 165).

[72] P. Walcot (1984: 37–47). Cf. Humphreys (1983: 16), and Gould (1980: 38–59).

[73] E.g. *The Reign of the Phallus* (1985).

[74] On women called in to assist in childbirth or tend the sick, see G. Lloyd (1983: 79).

Theaetetus 149). Finally, a widow in Aristophanes' *Thesmophoriazusae* (445) works to support her five children. How many other Athenian women found themselves in similar positions during the many periods of protracted warfare?

In fact, there is no need to list all the passages on the various economic activities of women for they were collected as long ago as 1922 (Herfst: 1922). Such a pattern, of course, is just what one would expect in a poor region like the Mediterranean, where most families could not dispense with the labor of women and children. Bourdieu (1966: 222) comments on the widespread mistaken belief that North African women are secluded in the house, when economic necessity requires that they work outside.[75] One particularly associates such expectations of seclusion with countries like Saudi Arabia or Iraq, but Altorki's recent study (1986: 23) advances the general thesis that women's freedom of movement varies directly with their contribution to the subsistence economy: "The demand for female labor outside the house lessens the restrictions on women's mobility."[76] Aristotle makes the same point with considerable force in the *Politics*, when he says that in a democracy it is impossible to prevent the women of the poor from going out to work (1300a4–9). Athenian law, moreover, made it a delict to rebuke any citizen, male *or female*, with selling in the marketplace (Demosthenes 57.30–1).

In Athens, married and unmarried women often worked outside their homes because economic survival required it. Contemporary evidence from communities where the men engage in migrant work for part of the year shows that this situation generally increases the economic role of women.[77] This is likely to have been true in Athens during those many years when a significant part of the male population, including those men from poorer families who served in the navy, were away on campaign for many months.[78] As will appear, however, whether in classical Athens or the modern

[75] For Morocco, see Maher (1974: 113, 150–1) and S. Davis (1980: 92–4). Gilmore (1987b: 1–3) comments upon the widespread, but mistaken belief that Andalusian women, in conformity with the cultural ideal, remain at home. See also Friedl (1962: 22–3), Sanders (1962: 77, 87, 94), Cutileiro (1971: 107), and Williams (1968: 79).

[76] Altorki (1986: Chapter 4) also shows that even the women of wealthy Saudi families participate in a wide range of social networks that take them out of the house. Indeed, the social function of the anonymity the veil provides is to make such movement possible.

[77] See e.g. Sweet's study of Lebanon (1967: 175).

[78] If the Aristophanic plays about women provide even a dim reflection of cultural conflicts, the war years seem to have produced a greater concern about women's political, economic, and social role.

Mediterranean, there may be a wide discrepancy between economic realities and ideological statements about what sorts of things women *ought* to do. As social anthropologists from Malinowski on have recognised, however, informants often offer such normative ideals as matter-of-fact descriptions of how things actually are. In Malinowski's case, his investigation of incest among the Trobrianders taught him that failure to appreciate this rhetorical fact could result in a massive misconstrual of the patterns of social behavior.[79]

In Athens, women's activities which took them out of the house were not exclusively economic. They might include going to their favorite soothsayer (Theophrastus, *Char.* 11.9–10, 16.12), participating in a sacrifice (Aristophanes, *Acharnians* 253), or in religious festivals. Women traveled to Eleusis to be initiated, and women alone arranged for major festivals like the Thesmophoria (Isaeus 8, 19–20; 3, 80; 6, 49), which required them to spend three days and nights outside of their house without any male intervention. Indeed, historians have failed to explore the social implications of the fact that Athenian women's networks were organized enough to carry out the full range of activities associated with such an undertaking, including election of officials and a governing council, rehearsals, supplies, finances, etc.[80] In fact, Athenian priestesses were public officials, and were subject to the same public audits as male officials (Aeschines 3, 18). This degree of organization and subjection to public scrutiny and accountability suggests that women were well able to cope with the demands of their sphere of public life. Indeed, it is scarcely imaginable that any of this could take place if they were confined to the home and embarrassed to be seen by any men other than close relatives. In Athenian society religion occupied an important place in civic life, and within it women played a central role.

Further, as is the rule in many Mediterranean communities, apart from the wealthy, women also performed the daily task of bringing water from the well and washing clothes in the fountain, a task organized to bring women together for conversation (Aristophanes,

---

[79] Malinowski (1929: 503–72).
[80] Zeitlin emphasizes the important role of women in Athenian religious life (1982: 130). They served as priestesses of Athena, and the wife of the *archon basileus*, the *basilinna*, along with fourteen other priestesses, had a central role in the Anthesteria (Parke 1977: 110ff.) and filled important public functions. On women's festival celebrations see Menander, *Epitrepontes* 451ff, 474ff. For an investigation of the special role of women in religious life in modern Greek communities, see Dubisch (1983).

Lysistrata 327–31; Euripides, *Electra* 75, 109–11, *Hippolytus* 124–30; Herodotus 5.12).[81] They participated in funeral processions (Demosthenes 43.63, Lysias 1.8),[82] went to the public baths, attended the public funeral orations (Thucydides 2.45.2) and were brought by their fathers, husbands, or sons into court to arouse the sympathy of the judges (Aeschines 2.148, 152; Plato, *Apology* 34c–35b; Demosthenes 19.310; 21.99, 186; 25.84; Aristophanes, *Wasps* 568–9, *Plutus* 382). When relatives were convicted, women relatives, including those of "respectable" families, were not ashamed to gather outside, and women visited their imprisoned relations (Andocides 1.48; Lysias 13.39–41; Plato, *Phaedo* 60a). Some women themselves appeared before the archon or arbitrators to testify (Isaeus 3.78; Demosthenes 40.11). They participated with friends and relatives in wedding processions and feasts where the bridesmaids danced and male guests might talk with the bride (Hyperides, *Lycophron* 3–6; Isaeus 3.76, 79; 8.18, 20; Aristophanes, *Acharnians* 1056, 1067–8, *Peace* 1195, 1316; Euripides, *Alcestis* 935–61, *I.T.* 1140; Menander, *Dyskolos* 855, 950).[83] Husbands expected their wives to go out, and those wealthy enough gave them slaves to accompany them, as Theophrastus' satire of the parsimonious husband reveals (*Char.* 22.10, 13).[84]

The passages just enumerated indicate that, although women did not participate in exclusively male activities like war and politics, they were not confined in their houses in "oriental seclusion," never seeing anyone outside their immediate family (as some scholars

[81] Carrying water and washing clothes in communal streams and fountains are activities that fall exclusively to women in most pre-industrial societies. In the late sixth century public fountain houses were constructed in Athens, and scores of vase paintings depict women fetching water, as described in *Lysistrata* 327ff. (See Keuls, 1985: 235ff.) The vases show the social interaction of the women as they work, younger girls playing, and men approaching the women there: the same combination of activity as anthropologists have found across the modern Mediterranean. See e.g. Fuller (1961: 51), S. Davis (1980: 94), and Riegelhaupt (1967: 117). Freeman (1970: 54ff.) emphasizes that such activities (going to fountains, washing, etc.) are used "specifically for associational purposes." Unexamined assumptions about the literal seclusion of women have led to derivative mistakes in interpreting such vase paintings – for example, by assuming that any woman represented at the fountain must be a slave or prostitute because "respectable" women never left the house.

[82] Lefkowitz (1982: 155) points out the way in which funeral rites brought women into contact with men and women outside their own families.

[83] See Sutton (1981: 177ff., 190ff.), and Keuls (1985: 107) on the vase paintings depicting such festivities with family friends and phraters.

[84] It is commonly taken to be an absolute rule that men did the shopping, but in Aristophanes Fr. 318, a husband is angry with his wife when she comes home tired from a festival and has not gone shopping for food.

rather romantically think of it, having little idea that, in fact, "oriental seclusion" also includes activities like carrying water, visiting friends and neighbors, participating in festivals, and so on). Indeed, one of the most important activities of women included visiting or helping friends and relatives. As men had their circle of friends, a substantial body of evidence indicates that, as in modern Mediterranean societies which also separate the male and female spheres, Athenian women formed intimate friendships, particularly with neighbors. The largely anecdotal evidence, viewed in the light of the model outlined above, indicates that women of the neighborhood visited one another constantly (Demosthenes 55.23-4, 53.4, 58.40). The descriptions of the varied purposes of such visits – to borrow food, utensils, jewelry, clothes or money, or to assist in childbirth or some other moment of need (Theophrastus 10.13; Aristophanes, *Ecclesiazusae* 446-8, 460, 528; Lysias 32.10; Euripides, *Electra* 1130; Plato, *Theaetetus* 149) – assume that this represents a common pattern. The theme of neighbors' participation in one another's affairs runs all through Menander's *Dyskolos*, including the kind of mutual borrowing suggested above (see particularly 475-508). The exchange of information is typically an important aspect of such contacts, and the commonplace condemnations in Athenian drama of women's excessive gossiping and visiting imply that such activities were taken for granted (see e.g. Euripides, *Hippolytus* 384, 395ff., 646ff., *Andromache* 944ff.; Menander, *Dyskolos* 481ff.; Theophrastus, quoted in Stobaeus 16.30; and cf. Aeschines, 1.127-8).[85] Indeed, Aristotle criticizes Athenian radical democracy because, he claims, women dominate the home and carry abroad gossip about their men (*Politics* 1313b). Women in *Lysistrata* (300ff.) talk about the difficulty in getting out to visit friends, not because of any prohibition, but rather the press of domestic responsibilities. Indeed, the underlying assumption of the passage is that they can and do visit in this way. This sort of evidence suggests that Athenian women, like their modern Mediterranean counterparts, participated in a variety of overlapping networks encompassing religious, economic, and social activities.[86]

---

[85] For modern comparisons see du Boulay's (1976) and Handman's (1983) classic treatments of lying, slander, and gossip. See also S. Davis (1980: 94).

[86] See e.g. J. Davis (1973: 69) on co-operation in the neighborhood: "the women lend utensils, food, even cash to each other without reserve. They make bread together, hire a seamstress together, fetch water together, or, if one has got a cistern and the other not, give water freely...When the husband comes home the women do not go away."

Chapters 3 and 4 showed how this intimacy of friends, centered around the neighborhood, formed one of the major mechanisms of social control, operating through the politics of reputation. These patterns of neighborly relations also constituted one of the contexts in which adulterous relationships typically arose. Athenian women were able to form such relationships because they were not physically isolated from their community, and their daily activities took them out of their houses and brought them into contact with men, whether in the agora, at a festival or wedding, or in the house of a friend or neighbor. Of course, the barriers imposed by the politics of reputation and the values of honor and shame shaped the limits of such encounters. Indeed, they existed to do so. The discussion of the sexual dimension of the intrusion of friends and neighbors into the private sphere of the family set out in Chapter 4 explores the context in which some Athenians, at least, perceived such encounters typically to take place. Recall, for example, Aristotle's statement, that it is particularly easy to have an adulterous relation with the wife of a friend or neighbor (*N.E.* 1137a5; *M.M.* 1188b17),[87] or Demosthenes' assertion that Athenian law allows a man to kill even his friends if they commit *hubris* against or seduce the women of his family (23.53–6).[88] The association of adultery with neighbors is common enough in the ancient world, as the Commandment not to covet thy neighbor's wife makes clear.

Adultery served as a focus of obsessive sexual fears in the ancient and modern Mediterranean precisely because women regularly engaged in activities which brought them into some sort of contact with other men. In "face-to-face" societies, those "moral communities where public opinion arbitrates reputation,"[89] this contact is most intimate, and most unavoidable, in the neighborhood.[90] It must have been even greater for those many Athenians who lived in small houses crowded close together or in tenement-like dwellings (see *Thesmophoriazusae* 273, *Knights* 1001; [Xen.] *Ath. Pol.* 1.17; Thucydides 3.74). Ehrenberg (1962: 214–15) aptly summarizes the intimacy of the neighborhood and deme: "Everybody knew everybody else, and the circumstances of all the families were known

---

[87] For the connection of sexual access enhanced by proximity, see also Menander's *Georgos*, where a young man has illicit intercourse with the girl next door. In *Samia*, a young man rapes and later marries a girl neighbor.

[88] *Hubris* has a strong sexual connotation here, on which, see Chapter 7.

[89] Gilmore (1987b: 3).

[90] See Freeman (1970), Handman (1983: 105–25), and du Boulay (1974: 169–229).

to everybody."[91] Anecdotally, Hyperides (*Lycophron*) describes how a friend could come and go in his friend's home, and talked to the wife. An oration of Antiphon (1.14) describes how a friend has a room in the family's house, where he regularly stays when visiting Athens and, finally, in Menander's *Epitrepontes*, when a husband moves out because of his wife's unchastity he moves into his neighbor/friend's house next door.[92]

Ruggiero's major study of sexual crimes in Renaissance Venice is instructive in its description of similar patterns of conduct: "Neighborhood, occupation, and friendship provided the context for adultery especially at the lower social levels, demonstrating that the noble ideal of isolating married women was unattainable for the more humble" (1985: 60). Ruggiero cites numerous cases where friendship and the intimacy of neighbors provided the means by which the adulterer initiated the relationship. For example, when a man was prosecuted in 1441 for a long adulterous liaison, "he was reported to have been a close friend of Bembo's [the husband], coming and going 'like a brother' in his house."[93]

One possible objection to this interpretation is that certainly some Athenian families could afford enough slaves so that the women *could* stay at home. Athenian and comparative evidence, however, suggests that they may well have nonetheless pursued relationships with other women in social and public religious networks extending beyond their families. Whether in ancient Rome, or in the Thesmophoria or the cult of Athena at Athens, or in the Church organizations of the Andalusian communities studied by Pitt-Rivers, it is women of the upper strata who figure most prominently in women's roles in religious life.[94] Indeed, the assertion of their high status, while requiring that they refrain from all economic activity, at the same time demands that they participate in the public and social activities appropriate to their station.[95] Moreover, what Maher, in her interesting study *Woman and Property in Morocco*, terms

[91] Members of the phratria regularly knew the women of a family: Isaeus 3.76, 79; 6.10.; 8.18, 20.

[92] And see Demosthenes 43.63; 53.4; 58.40; Isaeus 8.18; 2.3; 3.13; Aristotle, *M.M.* 1188b17, *N.E.* 1137a5, 1166a30, 1171ab, 1172a; Aeschines 3.174; Lysias 7.15ff.; Aristophanes, *Plutus* (250, 613ff.).

[93] 1985: 63, and, in general, 59–68. Recall the Demosthenic oration (discussed in Chapter 4) which describes the intimate friend (πάνυ οἰκεῖος) to whom a man entrusted his house and family when going away on business, and Aristotle's statement about the ease of having an adulterous relationship with the wife of a friend (*N.E.* 1137a5; *M.M.* 1188b17).

[94] Parke (1977: 110ff.).   [95] See e.g. Aswad (1967: 149).

"ostentatious seclusion," primarily occurs among a few nouveaux riches families where the husband is anxious to demonstrate that he has enough money literally to isolate his wife. Even there, however, this normally only occurs in large cities when a woman has married a man who lives far from the village where she grew up, and hence finds herself isolated from the supportive network which sustains most women.[96] Fernea vividly describes how even upper-class women, "secluded" in the harem of the sheik in an Iraqi village, participate in such networks: receiving female visitors, visiting in turn, participating in festivals, or going on religious pilgrimages (as at Athens, religious festivals are the great social events for women).[97] Of course, as Fernea reports, the principle is that women remain at home, but the practice is quite different. However, the practice upholds the rule by being carried out with extreme discretion while recognizing, in principle, the validity of the norm.[98] Fernea's narrative provides a wonderful example of Bourdieu's point about the strategic manipulation and interpretation of norms, in portraying how these women manage to lead rich lives within this normative framework that their behavior at once avoids, re-interprets, manages, and reproduces.[99]

In his classic study of Portuguese rural society, Cutileiro discusses similar patterns of conduct, and makes explicit their connection to social prestige: "The wife should remain secluded at home. This is only possible among the wealthy, however. Wealthy wives are much more restricted to their houses, and the layout of these houses makes their seclusion even greater." Though Cutileiro does not seem particularly aware that he is citing normative precepts rather than social descriptions, his further comments reveal that these arrangements do not imply real seclusion, for he adds that such women devote their time to "needlework, churchgoing, charity work, visiting, and last, but not least, sheer idleness."[100] Not having to

---

[96] Maher (1974: 2–3, 61, 117, 150–1), and cf. Williams (1968: 67–83). Maher's treatment also reveals the importance of distinguishing seclusion and separation. Seclusion, in those few cases where it does literally occur, tends to reduce the woman to a state of utter subjection. Separation, on the other hand, even in societies like that of rural Iraq or Saudi Arabia where it is very strictly enforced, allows women to sustain themselves in extensive supportive social networks. On Iraq, see Fernea (1969), and on Saudi Arabia, Altorki (1986: Chapter 3).

[97] Fernea (1969: 107, 130, and, generally, 24–172), and see Friedl (1967: 100–1). For Athens, see Zeitlin (1982: 130).   [98] See Fernea (1969: 130, 143).

[99] Fernea (1969: 50), and see also Altorki (1986: 51–122) on Saudi women.

[100] Cutileiro (1971: 107).

work outside the home, or, better yet, work at all, is a great mark of economic status.[101]

As classical scholars have typically assumed that separation necessarily implies seclusion, so earlier ethnographic accounts often built upon similar premises.[102] Recent studies of Spanish, Portuguese, Italian, Greek, Turkish, Iraqi, Lebanese, and Moroccan societies have shown, however, that such assumptions may be wildly inaccurate.[103] The paper by Clark on gender bias quoted above represents an attempt to show some of the reasons for such confusion. To take but one further example, one might refer to the article by Lloyd and Fallers on sex roles and the public/private dichotomy in Edremit, Turkey. In this paper, while confirming that the "world of women...in Edremit is the private world of the house and the courtyard," they document the wide range of women's activities and relationships and the autonomy of the women's sphere. They employ these observations as the basis for a re-evaluation of the thesis for isolation advanced by Forster in his study of Italian towns:

What he [Forster] meant to suggest was that men's monopoly of the town's public space made it possible for them to interact...unencumbered by the contingencies of their individual ties with women. It must follow from this, he apparently reasoned, that the women were pining away, each in her own home, awaiting the return of their lord and master...Now this, as we have shown, is not the case in Edremit. If relations among males are relatively unencumbered by their relations with females, it is also the case that females' relations with each other are similarly, if in lesser degree (since male authority and possession of public space do inhibit women's movements), free of male interference. Our point is not the familiar one

[101] Aswad's (1967) study of aristocratic women in the Middle East makes this point with great clarity, and demonstrates the need to differentiate between urban and rural elites. Whether in urban or rural settings, however, all women are part of informal communications/gossip networks and it is largely through them that information spreads through the village.

[102] Many such ethnographic accounts are based exclusively upon what male informants told the male anthropologist about women whom he had no opportunity to observe or talk with. See e.g. Berger (1962: 119–21) and Marx (1967: 103–7). Because the complicated networks of women's relations were not accessible to them (because of the very fact of separation), earlier anthropologists often assumed that such networks did not exist and that separation meant virtual isolation.

[103] E.g. Portugal: Cutileiro (1971); Spain: Pitt-Rivers (1971), Gilmore (1987), Freeman (1970); Italy: Maraspini (1968), J. Davis (1973); Greece: Campbell (1979), du Boulay (1974), Friedl (1962, 1967), Handman (1983), Kennedy (1986); Turkey: Lloyd and Fallers (1976), Stirling (1966); Lebanon: Williams (1968); Fuller (1961); Iraq: Fernea (1969); Morocco: Maher (1974), Mernissi (1975), S. Davis (1980); see also Bourdieu (1977), Pehrson (1967), and Abu-Lughod (1986).

that women, submissive in public, manage to influence their fate by domestic scheming, manipulation and henpecking. Our point is rather that women in Edremit have an institutional structure and sense of solidarity of their own, parallel to those of men which give them a substantial field for self-assertion and a psychological independence of men...[104]

These conclusions represent a widespread pattern found in most traditional Mediterranean societies. In such communities the sexual politics of space and labor are far more complex than the thesis of seclusion and isolation would allow. The assumption that close association with the house means that women are confined within its physical boundaries cannot account for actual social patterns. For example, though, "It is commonly assumed that in North African society the woman is shut up in the house. In fact this is completely untrue because the peasant woman always works out of doors."[105] Further, the operation of these principles of sexual politics limits the opportunities for men to control closely the activities of their women. Men tend to keep away from the house, because association with it makes them objects of suspicion to their neighbors.

This latter point is no less true in classical Athens (see e.g. Xenophon, *Oec.* 7.2.30), where, as Chapter 4 showed, men's role requires them to spend their time outside of the domestic sphere. As a woman of the Marri Belouch says, "What do the men know about the household affairs? They are away from home a lot... What do they know about what their women do?"[106] The Athenian sources which discuss the management of the house explicitly affirm this autonomy of sexual/spatial spheres by relegating such responsibility exclusively to the wife.[107] Kennedy (1986: 123) makes this point succinctly in her discussion of the sexual division of space in modern Greece:

Men and women spend relatively little time with each other, know little about each other's domains, and have a great deal of animosity towards each other in general... Men see women as mysteriously able to exploit

---

[104] Lloyd and Fallers (1976: 260).   [105] Bourdieu (1966: 222).

[106] Pehrson (1967: 60). See also du Boulay (1974: 129) and Fernea (1969: 255). For just this reason, in Athens men are often portrayed as obsessed with the trustworthiness of their wives (see e.g. Aristophanes, *Thesmophoriazusae* 414ff., 789ff.), the "guardians of the house," whose duties Xenophon lovingly enumerates (*Oec.* 7.17).

[107] In addition to the passages from Xenophon's and pseudo-Aristotle's treatises on household management cited above, see Aristotle, *N.E.*1161a–1162a. In *Politics* 1313b32–5 he complains that in the Athenian radical democracy women rule the home.

potentially unlimited sexual power to build up or destroy men's honor...Although men are allowed greater individual freedom in all activities than women are, men are in many ways outcasts from their homes and lead relatively solitary – although public – lives.

Indeed, part of men's fear of adultery arises from their ignorance about what their wives do. The cuckolded husband in Lysias' *Against Eratosthenes* remained ignorant of his wife's infidelity until enlightened by a malicious informant. The suspicious husbands caricatured by Aristophanes, who look under the bed for *moichoi* and want to know where their wives have been (e.g. in *Thesmophoriazusae* 397, 410–14, 519), do not seem to act on the basis of a conviction that their wives spend all of their waking moments locked up in the women's quarters, "ashamed to be seen even by their kinsmen," to quote Lysias again (3.6).[108] Furthermore, the perception that Athenian husbands, like their modern Mediterranean counterparts, typically relaxed their concern after the birth of the first child also testifies to the relative independence of women within the realm of their domestic, economic, religious, and social activities.[109] It was precisely the autonomy of the women's sphere, and women's relative freedom within its boundaries, which, together with the power of women to destroy the reputation of a lineage, fueled male anxieties. Moreover, this autonomy also meant that women were the primary agents of social control in regard to their sex. First, women were responsible for the discipline and socialization of female children, and it was this process which prepared girls to accept their subordinate social and political role.[110] Secondly, although scholars often speak of women being "confined," "supervised," "guarded,"

---

[108] Indeed, the plausibility (as opposed to the veracity) of stories of the sexual misconduct of women presupposes considerable freedom. The concern about adultery, and the belief that it frequently occurs, both imply that women have enough independence to carry off such affairs without being found out. In addition to the caricatures of Aristophanes, see the accusation that Alcibiades regularly brought free women into his house (pseudo-Andocides 4.14, and cf. Andocides 1.124–6).

[109] As exemplified in Xenophon, *Oeconomicus*, Lysias 1, and Aristotle, *N.E.* 1161a–1162a. Typically, marriage and bearing a first child bring a woman to full sexual and social status; see Fuller (1961: 55), Pehrson (1967: 59), and Maher (1974: 117, 156). Euphiletus recounts that he fully accepted his wife only after she had given birth to their first child, and he had seen that she didn't spend her days chatting at the doorstep (Lysias 1.6).

[110] Godelier (1987: 50–1, 160–1) emphasizes the way in which the ideology of sex and gender, as promulgated by women in their initiation, operates to reproduce the system in which they are subordinated to men. "In fact, the female initiation emerges as the complement or projection of the men's initiation into the world of men; it is the women's share in the task of promoting a single order and law, that of male domination."

"controlled" and so on, the discussion of such actions usually assumes, or implies, that the agents of control are men. But how can husbands guard or confine their wives or daughters if the man's role demands that he stay away from the house? In fact, women's information networks play a central role in the politics of reputation that, as was seen in Chapters 3 and 4, form the primary means of implementing community vigilance in the form of social control.[111] As Cutileiro (1971: 137) says of the Portuguese village he studied,

Since women remain in the villages most of the time, whereas men go to work outside, neighborly relations are basically feminine relations... Supervising children's play, borrowing cooking utensils or provisions... are some of the favors exchanged among poor neighbors, but the exchange of favors does not exhaust the features of the neighborhood relationship. Neighbors are basically watchers of their neighbors' behavior.

In Athens, where women participated in the same kind of neighborhood networks, Medea appears to express the same sentiment when, referring to "the world's censorious eyes," she comes out of the house to address the rumors about her situation: "Women of Corinth, I would not have you censure me, So I have come..." (214-18).[112] It was, no doubt, this fact that led Aristotle to criticize Athenian society because men's reputations depended upon the gossip of women. Women, he claims, rule the home and carry abroad reports about the men (*Politics* 1313b). Further, Aeschines (1.127-8) argues that gossip makes the private deed become public knowledge. Hence some men hide the adultery of their wives (1.107).[113] Literary sources also portray women's gossip as a medium for fostering or destroying other women's reputations.[114] Thus Athenian women were not, as they have too often been portrayed, mere passive objects of monolithic masculine domination, but were themselves agents in processes of social control that governed both their lives and the lives of men as well (Chapter 7 will address more specifically how such patterns operated in regard to male sexuality). Through such practices, to apply Godelier's (1986: 50) discussion of

---

[111] J. Davis (1973: 22).

[112] As one of Gilmore's (1987b: 7) informants puts it in her description of malicious gossip, "The worst of all are your neighbors." Chapter 4 collects the Athenian evidence.

[113] See also Aristophanes, *Frogs* 1052.

[114] In Euripides' *Alcestis* (300) a stepmother's slander against her stepdaughter could ruin her chances for marriage. Such themes run all through plays like *Hippolytus*. For contemporary Morocco, see S. Davis (1980: 93).

the Baruya to Athens, "women produce their own consent to the order by which they are dominated."[115]

Combining this clarification of the meaning of separation of roles and spheres with the point made above about the distinction between cultural ideals and social practices can do a great deal to illuminate the situation of women at Athens – these women who never cross the threshold yet somehow appear to participate in a wide range of activities and relationships. Women *should* not leave the house but participation in their independent sphere of social, religious and economic activities requires that they do so. How is the conflict resolved? In fact, it is not resolved, but rather consciously manipulated in a serious game that is played according to a complex set of rules and prohibitions.[116] Some examples may help to clarify the point. Mothers in the Lebanese village of Harouch say of their daughters that they never leave the house. This is the cultural ideal dictated by the code of honor and shame, according to which the honor of a woman is measured by "the closeness she keeps to her house and the distance she maintains towards strangers."[117] Thus one mother says "We are here in the house and we have nothing to do with anyone; we just stay in the house and see our neighbors."[118] One wonders, of course, how the neighbors got there.

It bears repeating that such practices ought not to be conceptualized as determined by a clear set of rules, rigidly applied. As Bourdieu, in a passage discussed in Chapter 3, argues in his critique of such an "objectivist" conception of social rules, not only are rules flexible and manipulable, but there are also points of incoherence or opacity. In Kabylia, the hour of *azal*, during the heat of the day, is a sort of "dead" time. The streets are deserted, the men are resting where they work, and

...no one can say whether the public space of the village belongs to man or

---

[115] Fernea (1969: 128–9) emphasizes the way women are acutely aware of the power of malicious gossip. Solidarity presses them to resist, but the temptation is great; cf. Kennedy (1986: 123–35). See Euripides, *Hippolytus* 384, on gossip as a pleasure of life, but a pleasant evil, and cf. 395ff. See also *Andromache* 944ff. on the destructive effects of women visiting and gossiping, and Menander, *Dyskolos* 384ff. on the corrupting effects of women's company.

[116] The strategic manipulation of such categories is one of the major themes of Bourdieu's (1977) and Goffman's (1963a, 1971) studies of social interaction. For examples, see Fernea (1965: 256–66), and Fuller (1961: 58).

[117] Williams (1968: 76–7). And see also du Boulay (1974: 159, 191), and S. Davis (1980: 92–3): "The ideal, although not always practicable, pattern remains for the girl to stay in the house."   [118] Williams (1968: 76–7).

to woman. So each of them takes care not to occupy it: there is something suspicious about anyone who ventures into the streets at that hour... Furtive shadows slip across the street from one house to another: the women, equally unoccupied, take advantage of the limited presence of the men to meet together or visit one another.[119]

Thus, in practice, what statements to the effect that the women never leave the house in fact mean is that they never leave the house without a purpose, a purpose that will be regarded as legitimate in the eyes of the watchful community, for example, going to the fountain, going to work in the fields, visiting a neighbor, etc.[120] But, as Williams (1968: 77) notes of the girls of Harouch, "I have watched our neighbor's daughter dump a full water jar behind the stables so that she can briskly set out for the tower while the boy she likes is on the road." As another scholar puts it,

The very fact that there is a well-recognized dividing line between the two sexes engenders an atmosphere of artful intrigue or flirtation in disguise, which in itself provides its own form of village recreation. Young men stand silently on the verandah and look down on the fountain where the girls lean to fill their pitchers. The young girls, in their turn, make more trips to the fountain than necessary.[121]

The ruse and the lie serve to legitimate activities which, though violating the norms of ideal conduct, are nonetheless accepted as long as deviance follows legitimating strategies rather than taking the form of defiance and challenge. Du Boulay and Handman have explored such patterns of behavior most astutely in their well-known studies of modern Greek villages.[122] Handman (1983:164–5) recounts how men always suspect their women of lying, but how else should a woman go to visit a neighbor for a chat other than saying that she has to borrow something, whether true or false? Most pleasurable activities for women are legitimated by lies, a necessity which, according to Handman, becomes a sort of reflex. The result is a complicated game of sexual politics whereby women preserve a sphere for themselves through the ruse and the lie, which the men know and accept, but attempt to limit and control through their

---

[119] Bourdieu (1977: 161). See also du Boulay (1974: 190–200), and Dubisch (1986: 129).
[120] See Brandes' (1975: 145–54) description of the relationship between women's friendships, the neighborhood, and social control. Women who do not spend sufficient time participating in neighborhood networks become objects of suspicion.
[121] Fuller (1961: 47).
[122] Du Boulay (1974: Chapters 8 and 9), Handman (1983: 147–198). See also Herzfeld (1983: 171).

suspicion and questioning. Herzfeld (1983: 171) concludes his study of the strict code concerning virginity in Greek rural communities with a similar interpretation: "Pre-marital sex may break the *rules* but...as long as it remains secret it does not challenge the code. Indeed, violators have a vested interest in denying the vulnerability of the code, since this allows them to pour scorn on any suspicion that may be directed against them...The eternal verities are thus maintained by those whose individual actions would seem...to flout them most outrageously."

These practices recall the women of Athens described by Aristophanes: the wives in the *Ecclesiazusae* (520, 1008) and *Thesmophoriazusae* (414, 519, 785–800) whose husbands find them out of the house and want to know what they have been doing. The husbands know that they go out, but they should not *be found* to have been out, particularly not at an inappropriate time or without an appropriate purpose;[123] or the woman in *Peace*, peeking out of the door to see the man she admires walking down the street (978–85, and cf. *Thesmophoriazusae* 797–9, and Theocritus 3.7); the young girl waiting at home for her lover while her mother is out (*Ecclesiazusae* 920, and cf. Euripides, *Ion* 1520); the man hanging around outside the house of a married woman waiting to catch another glimpse of her at the window (*Thesmophoriazusae*).

These scenes represent patterns of adulterous or pre-marital courtship where gifts, messages, and entreatments are conveyed through slave intermediaries (Lysias 1; Aristophanes, *Thesmophoriazusae* 339ff., *Ecclesiazusae* 610; Hyperides, *Lycophron* 2; Euripides, *Hippolytus* 645ff.). Isaeus (3.14) says that no man would dare to serenade a married woman, implying that this form of courtship is too overt. Theophrastus, on the other hand (*Characters* 12.4), gives as an example of the tactless man one who serenades his lover at the wrong time. Such courtship could lead to a wide variety of relationships: the young adulteress of Lysias' *On the Murder of Eratosthenes* who consummates her relationship in the same way as

---

[123] See Fernea (1969: 77), who reports that women go visiting together, but prefer that their husbands don't find them not at home. They take pains to be there when the husband returns. Cf. Bourdieu (1977: 160) and Dubisch (1986: 200). Maher (1974: 91) describes how frequently Moroccan couples quarrel over the woman "going out"; for men, women wanting to go out is "tantamount to infidelity." A fragment of Hyperides (207) makes a similar point by saying that it is all right for a woman to adorn herself for her husband, but a cause for alarm when she does so before going out. Again, the passage assumes that women do go out.

the couple caricatured by Aristophanes (*Thesmophoriazusae* 478ff., 790ff.); young Alcibiades who was pursued by upper-class women and engaged in a variety of other affairs (Xenophon, *Mem.* 1.2.24; Lysias 14.26, 29, 41; Andocides, *Against Alcibiades* 10); the widow seduced in Demosthenes' oration *Against Stephanus I* (27, 39, 71, 84); the adulterer who deceives a woman with promises he doesn't fulfill, the rich old woman who takes young lovers, and the young woman who accepts gifts and then betrays her lover (Aristophanes, *Thesmophoriazusae* 340–5, and cf. Herodes, *Mime* 5). Whether these particular affairs occurred or not is unimportant, for credibility required that they not violate audience expectations of possible behavior. Like the examples of "deviant" reactions to adultery enumerated at the end of the last chapter, they are utterly inconsistent with idealized views of Athenian women, but none-theless reflect the rich texture of social practice. Athenian maidens never saw males who were not close relatives, in the same way that the girls of Harouch never left the house. Yet Aristophanes is surely closer to the truth when he describes the daughter in *Acharnians* (253) on the way to a sacrifice with her mother and father, fully conscious that she is on display to prospective suitors.[124]

Such examples are from literature, of course, but as Dover briefly notes, such women "may be much nearer the norm of Athenian life than those cloistered ladies who were 'embarrassed by the presence even of a male relative.'"[125] Because of their preoccupation with the lives of the wealthy, however, many scholars have not thought through the implications of such evidence for their general position on "Athenian Women." In fact, such bits and pieces of evidence from Aristophanes offer better evidence of the daily life of ordinary women than do the set-piece speeches of a Medea or Andromache, or Xenophon's idealized vision of gentry life. Of course such passages are part of a comedy, and of course they were written by a man. But

---

[124] Antoun (1968: 682–3), in his treatment of female modesty in the eastern Mediterranean, illuminates the dynamics of such behavior: "The abandonment of [a norm in] particular actions may be justified explicitly or implicitly by the realization of the same norm in a wider context. Thus, although girls are not allowed to look attractive for fear of tempting males, they are dressed up at an early age by their mothers until puberty 'in order to attract attention to themselves and secure a husband'...Here violation of the norm prohibiting adornment is in order to bring early marriage and in so doing avoid a much more serious breach of modesty..." Antoun's example helps to explain the contradiction between the norm requiring the most extreme modesty for girls and the kind of behavior Aristophanes describes. Indeed, here again, Aristophanes derives his humor from just the exploitation of this conflict.   [125] Dover (1973: 69).

a portrayal of women talking at the fountain in the morning is not
a product of comic distortion, though some of their conversation,
with its often grotesquely exaggerated sexual humor, may be.
Moreover, vase paintings, passages from the orators and Aristotle,
and comparative evidence support the accuracy of the description,
which, though the product of a male imagination, derives much of
its force from the plausibility and verisimilitude of its social setting.
It bears repeating that Aristophanes' dramas are not an unthinking
product of male ideologies, but rather a conscious manipulation and
satire of them. The catalogue of women's treacherous ploys in
Thesmophoriazusae (335–51, 383–432), for example, transparently
functions this way. In short, I would argue that Aristophanes offers
considerable insight not only into Athenian sexual politics, but also
into the perceived social practices that form the practical basis of
such politics. Further, as this discussion shows, comparative evidence
from modern Mediterranean communities can play a crucial role in
distinguishing these types of social action.

The same duality, the same manipulation of categories and
behavior as described above for the social sphere also applies to
economic and political activities. Bourdieu (1977: 39–51), for
example, shows the way that among the Kabyle norms and
definitions in the contexts of kinship, marriage alliances, legal
disputes, and feuds are articulated in a rhetorical manner so as to
meet the strategic exigencies of the occasion; or, for example, in
Lebanon, the women of Harouch claim that they only work in the
house – a rare occurrence that is a great sign of status. But once
Williams met one of the girls, who had previously told her that she
only worked in the house, coming back from a day of labor in the
fields: "Before I even had a chance to speak, she hastened to explain
that she had gone out to supervise the hired hands for an hour... She
told me then as she had done many times before, that her work is
'only in the house'" (1967: 67; cf. 79). Statements by authors like
Xenophon about women's work being confined to the house should
be taken in the same light. Indeed, Xenophon's description clearly
applies to the wealthy family with a host of servants. Aristotle's
statement that the wives of the poor *must* go out to work reveals the
underlying economic necessity that touched the bulk of the
population. That in Athens, too, status concerns were connected to
such economic distinctions appears clearly enough from the law,
alluded to above, that prohibited anyone from denigrating an

Athenian man or woman for working in the marketplace. The social reality behind such legislation appears from Aristophanes' use of comic license to deride Euripides because his mother sold produce in the agora (*Thesmophoriazusae* 387–8, 455–6).

A further way in which confusion as to the nature and meaning of separation has created problems in the understanding of Greek sexual roles brings the discussion back to the "hows and whys" of adultery. Many classical scholars have assumed that, in this society where men and women led separate lives, the marital relation was viewed instrumentally as simply a means for producing legitimate children, involving little affection, let alone love or deep emotional attachment.[126] Humphreys (1983: 17), for example, asserts that in Athens friendship and romantic love are only found in male–male relationships, and Keuls (1985: 99) argues that Athenian men "virtually disregarded the category of sexual pleasure in marriage"; or, as Flacelière says, "It seems fairly clear that there was little intimacy, intellectual contact, or ever real love between husband and wife in classical Athens."[127]

Such conclusions are not to be taken too seriously, for there is abundant evidence from Aristotle, Xenophon, Isocrates, Euripides, Aristophanes, Lysias, and vase paintings[128] which makes clear that some men, at least, were perceived as both passionately enamored of women and deeply emotionally and sexually attached to their wives.[129] Moreover, it is the reciprocity of marital sexual love[130] which accounts for the sexual jealousy men and women were

[126] E.g. Cantarella (1986: 39–51).

[127] Flacelière (1965: 55). Gould also adopts this view (1980: 56ff.). Lefkowitz (1986: 67) is one of the few scholars who has made the case for a contrary interpretation.

[128] Sutton (1981: iv, 170ff., 224ff.) argues that wedding scenes on classical Athenian vases emphasize "the emotional and physical union of the bride and groom as the basis of the household." They do this by emphasizing the union and romantic attachment between the married couple (232ff.). Attic funerary inscriptions testify at the least to the conventionality of portraying the closeness of the marital relationship (Lefkowitz 1986: 28, 67).

[129] Parke's (1977: 160) discussion of how garlic was used by Athenian women to keep their husbands away during festivals attests to marital sexuality. On this use of garlic see Aristophanes, *Thesmophoriazusae* (494–6), and Detienne (1978: 102). Aristotle (*Politics* 1335a) assumes the importance of marital sexuality, and see Xenophon, *Oec.* 10.4, 10.12. Strepsiades' account (*Clouds* 41ff.) of his sexual relationship with his wife is a comic tribute to the intensity of marital sexual relations. It assumes such a sexual relationship to derive its humor. See also Menander, *Dyskolos* (788–90); Xenophon, *Symposium* 9.7. Marital sexuality is also vital to the plot of *Lysistrata* (45–50, 155, 167, 210, 706ff., and cf. *Ecclesiazusae* 600ff.), on which see Henderson (1975: 94), Dover (1973: 71) and Ehrenberg (1962: 194).

[130] Xenophon, *Symposium* 8.3, *Oeconomicus* 10.12–13; Euripides, *Medea* 570ff., 1377–9, *Suppliants* 1024ff.; *Thesmophoriazusae* 1021, 1205f., and see Lefkowitz (1986: 68).

perceived as feeling towards unfaithful spouses.[131] This explains why adultery is described in the sources as an offense which undermines the *philia* (love, friendship, attachment) between husband and wife (Xenophon, *Hiero* 3.4). Aristotle, for example, describes marriage as a partnership based upon the natural *philia* between husband and wife. Whereas other animals mate for reproduction, more varied and deeper ties bind human pairs together (*N.E.* 1161a, 1162a15).[132] Thus it is not only the external explanation provided by the code of honor and shame that accounts for the hatred directed to adulterers, but also the internal explanation that focuses upon the violation of the relationship of trust and affection between husband and wife.

This dual level of explanation may also be appropriate in understanding the motivation of the men who ran the risks which adultery entailed. The adulterer is a man of honor in the sense that he increases his own status, accentuates his masculinity, by dishonoring other men by seducing their women. Aristotle thus characterizes adultery as typical of the hubristic nouveaux riches (*Rhet.* 1391a). This, as Pitt-Rivers has shown, is the Spanish understanding of Don Juan, as a punctilious man of honor, interested only in the conquests which magnify his own stature and reputation.[133] The very seclusion of women that is designed to protect them is a sexual challenge to other men, who, in Athens as in other Mediterranean societies, were willing to run considerable risks to achieve their ends. On the other hand, this explanation is not the whole picture. Men did not become adulterers simply for sexual gratification; in Athens there was little need of this. But, on the other hand, because of the early age of marriage for girls, married women or widows were the only free women who were likely to be available for a relationship which did not have to be bought. This is still the case in many

[131] In Xenophon, *Symp.* 4.8, a man is afraid that his wife will think that he has been with another woman. For women's resentment at men's infidelity see Euripides, *Medea* 556, 569ff., *Andromache* 179–82, 464ff., *Hippolytus* 150f., *Electra* 1025–37; Isocrates 3.40; Isaeus 6.19–21; Aristophanes, *Peace* 1130f. See also the debate about marital fidelity in *Andromache* 220ff. (and cf. 465, 905, 945) and the discussions of sexual monogamy in Aristotle, *Politics* 1335b38ff.; *Oeconomica* 1344a; Isocrates 3.36–42. Jealousy outside of marriage is explored by Fantham (1986).

[132] Aristotle views marriage as a partnership, and says that something like social justice prevails in it, since the married couple are nearly equals. This, he argues, distinguishes this relation from that of master–slave and father–son, where relations of justice do not obtain. Hence, he concludes, the woman is not like a slave or child in the marital relation (*Magna Moralia* 1194b25, and cf. *Politics* 1259b). He elaborates on this view in the *Nicomachean Ethics* where he argues that men and women have separate spheres, and the woman rules in hers. [133] See e.g. Pitt-Rivers (1977: 23).

modern Mediterranean societies, where unmarried men often prefer to pursue relationships with young married women, for a variety of reasons.[134] Likewise, for the many young women who were unfortunate enough to find themselves in marriages in which, because of differences in age and other problems associated with arranged marriages, *philia* was not a possibility, adultery might be the only opportunity they would ever have for a romantic–erotic attachment.

Ruggiero's (1985) analysis of the motivations for adultery in Renaissance Venice reflects similar patterns. As in Athens, in Venice girls of 13 or 14 were married off by their families to men of about 30. The women were supposed to be modest and stay at home, while their husbands enjoyed the benefits of the double standard. In inquiring why men and women ran the risks that adultery entailed, Ruggiero concludes that "Women as well as men went outside their marriages to find sexual satisfaction often at considerable economic and social risk." But more was involved than sex, he argues, for "The adultery records demonstrate repeatedly that at least some people expected a certain level of affection in marriage or were prepared to change their marriage situation to secure such a relationship" (64). Indeed, "More typically... adultery cases reveal couples seeking affection outside of marriage, presumably, in part, because they had not found it there" (65).

Another related factor appears from the many references to the jealousy (and envy?) which women felt towards the sexual freedom of their husbands (evidence which has too often been ignored).[135] As Clytaemnestra says in Euripides' *Electra*, when "a husband looks elsewhere and slights his lawful wife, she will copy him, and find herself another friend. And then the glance of public censure lights on us; the husbands are to blame but they are not concerned" (1036–40).[136] In any society with arranged marriages, restricted courtship, and a double standard, adultery is a likely outlet for the emotional and sexual frustrations which such arrangements often produce. In Athens these various motivations were obviously strong

---

[134] Berger (1962: 123) claims that young men are more likely to look for married women than unmarried girls because of easier access, and no problems of pressure to marry and "fatherless" pregnancy. This was also Pepys' preference in seventeenth-century England.

[135] See e.g. Keuls (1985: Chapter 4).

[136] The other passages are set out in n. 126 above. For a similar explanation of modern Greek women's motivation in extra-marital affairs, and the way in which such affairs contribute to the male attitudes that provoke women's resentment, see Kennedy (1986: 123ff.).

enough to induce men to face torture or death (Xenophon, *Mem.*
2.1.5; Aristotle, *N.E.* 1117a; Isaeus 8.44; Demosthenes 21.78–9;
37.45–7; 47.38, 53, 60), and women to risk major civic disabilities
and social disgrace. The accepted notion of Athenian men as only
interested in courtesans, prostitutes, and boys, and Athenian women
as isolated, passive, and disinterested in sexual attachments, requires
serious rethinking.[137]

This examination of the social context of adultery has led, I hope,
not only to a fuller understanding of adultery itself, but also of the
complexity of male–female sexual relations at Athens. Attempts to
account for such sexual relations in terms of social and legal rules,
which determine conduct and classify according to binary categories
of obedience and violation, cannot do justice to the ambivalence and
conflict that characterize normative expectations about sexual
conduct. Further, such an account remains insensitive to the
strategic dimension of social action, the way in which individuals
exploit and manipulate the incoherence of the normative categories
their culture offers them so as to achieve their private ends. Moving
to the realm of male sexuality, the next chapter will pursue this
analysis of the strategies, conflicts, and contradictions that lie at the
heart of Athenian sexual politics, or, for that matter, of any complex
social practice.

---

[137] See Lefkowitz's (1986: 39) revisionist account of Athenian sexual politics.

CHAPTER 7

Law, social control, and homosexuality in classical Athens

The preceding two chapters have investigated the processes of social control associated with male–female sexual relations, particularly adultery. This chapter turns to the area of sexual relations between men, and attempts to show how the politics of reputation and gender also govern this complex field of social practices. Further, the discussion of homoeroticism pursues the theme of the ambiguity, ambivalence, and manipulability of norms, values, expectations, and practices introduced above. Here, Giddens' comment about the centrality of contradiction as a characteristic of social systems can usefully serve as a guiding light for the investigation.

Recent scholarship has succeeded in greatly advancing our understanding of "Greek Homosexuality." Kenneth Dover and Michel Foucault have argued that the modern dichotomization of sexuality as heterosexuality/homosexuality does not apply to the ancient world, and they have shown how distinctions between active and passive roles in male sexuality defined the contours of the permissible and impermissible in paederastic courtship and other forms of homoerotic behavior. Among the Greeks, we are told, active homosexuality was regarded as perfectly natural: sexual desire was not distinguished according to its object. There was, however, a prohibition against males of any age adopting a submissive role that was unworthy of a free citizen.[1]

Some Athenians in the classical period may have unjudgmentally thought that some men by nature liked boys, others women, still others both, but it does not follow that the normative categories of sexual roles associated with the dichotomy of homosexual/heterosexual were entirely absent. Further, though the delineation of active and passive roles was certainly important it was by no means

[1] Dover (1980: 60–8, 81–109), Foucault (1984: 47–62), Cantarella (1988: 35–78), and Halperin (1990).

the only determinant of social norms related to sexual roles and homoerotic behavior. What other normative expectations influenced homoerotic behavior, how such expectations influenced processes of social control, and how these processes, together with patterns of compliance, avoidance, manipulation, and interpretation, operated to reproduce the social system of homoerotic relations also remains largely unexplored.[2] Thus, despite the fundamental contributions of Dover, Foucault, Halperin, Cantarella, and others, major issues remain that the new orthodoxy that has followed in the wake of Dover's work does not resolve.

Foucault, for example, whose interpretation relies heavily upon Dover, has addressed some of these problems, but his interpretation manifests a desire to deny the force of any norms or values other than those associated with the dichotomies of active/passive and excess/moderation. This desire, in my opinion, arises largely from his programmatic need to locate a period largely free of the evils out of which the modern Christian problematization and "auto-regulation" of sexuality can develop. While Dover's account follows the traditional strategy of attributing differing attitudes towards paederasty to class distinctions, as manifested in the audiences and milieus associated with Platonic and Socratic circles, as opposed to the comic poets, Foucault recognizes that such an explanation does not go deep enough.[3] Although he closely follows Dover's account of the social institutions and attitudes associated with paederasty, he emphasizes the extent to which sexuality was already a source of unease in that the naturalness of undifferentiated sexual desire was, for men, bounded by the dual limits of excess and passivity.[4]

Foucault's explanation of this conflict is, however, ultimately unsatisfying in that in the end it rests upon his account of philosophical speculation about pleasure, moderation and self-mastery in Plato, Xenophon, and Aristotle. The development of what he calls the principle of "auto-regulation," as embedded in the cultural ideal of the self-controlled man, operates to restrain that universal sexual drive which, Foucault argues, is seen as naturally tending towards excess. This tendency, he goes on, if realized, would place the sexual subject in a role of submission to pleasure, of slavery to passion in Plato's phrase, that is unworthy of a free man. Thus, by

---

[2] The most recent work of Winkler (1990) and Halperin (1990) considers some of these questions, though from a perspective rather different from the present study.

[3] Dover (1980: 148–51).   [4] Foucault (1984: 56–7).

"not yielding, not submitting, remaining very strong and prevailing over pursuers and lovers through firmness, temperance and resistance," the young man affirms his masculine worth. However, both Foucault and Dover seem to think that after sufficient struggle the boy may, under certain circumstances, give in.[5] Thus, although Foucault raises the issue of ambivalence, he does not pursue it because his intellectual pre-inclinations lead him to underestimate the extent of the unease which he has correctly identified. Foucault, like many other scholars, is committed to finding that in Greek culture homoeroticism is regarded as natural, that a heterosexual/ homosexual bivalence and accompanying modes of normalization do not exist, and that an ideal of asceticism and self-mastery over the body arises in philosophical speculation. Accordingly, he does find just these things which he needs for the larger story which makes up the enterprise of his history of sexuality, but in the process his account becomes a bit too univocal and homogenized.

In my opinion, an exploration of Greek homosexuality ought to begin by insisting very strongly on the profundity of the conflicts which permeated Athenian values and practices in this area. The argument which follows will show that current interpretations do not do justice to the complexity of these social patterns and will argue that Athenian homoeroticism must be understood in the context of a theory of social practice which emphasizes the centrality of cultural contradiction and ambivalence.

Beginning with the classical studies of Malinowski among the Trobrianders, an increasing number of anthropological theorists have focused on conflict and contradiction as central features of cultural systems.[6] Malinowski first recognized the importance of identifying the conflict between cultural ideals and social practices implicit in the accounts which informants give of their culture. Later anthropologists like Bourdieu, Barrett, Turner, and Godelier have moved to a more sophisticated understanding of conflict and ambiguity as structural principles of culture. Chapter 9 will address the general theoretical question of cultural conflict and contradiction more fully, but the point here is that the historian should not always attempt to explain away every contradiction or ambiguity as if socio-

---

[5] The precise position is not always clear; see e.g. Dover (1980: 81–109).

[6] Malinowski (1929: 565–72), Bailey (1969: 125ff.), Turner (1967: 5–44), Handman (1983: 191), Gellner (1981: 114–16), Bourdieu (1977: 1–142), Godelier (1986: Chapters 2, 3, 6, 7).

historical explanation were a riddle which admits of a univocal solution.

As Malinowski discovered in his work on the incest taboo, and as later scholars have shown, such normative ambiguity is perhaps nowhere so pervasive as in the realm of sexuality.[7] For Malinowski the moment of illumination came when he was forced to confront such a contradiction on the occasion of a public incest scandal involving a brother–sister relationship (the worst imaginable case by Trobriand standards). His informants had repeatedly assured him that such behavior was regarded as the supreme abomination and thus never had occurred. Having taken this testimony at face value, Malinowski was forced by these events to reconsider his premises. He realized that his informants had not been lying, but had sincerely described their society as they wanted it to appear to be, rather than acknowledging the multivalent force of brother–sister incest in family life, ideology, and myth. Indeed, his study of the Trobriand creation myth, where society comes into being through brother–sister incest, revealed fundamental tensions in normative ideals, tensions which also manifested themselves in Trobriand sexual practices. Affirming that such tensions and contradictions should not be dismissed or explained away, Malinowski's account reveals their centrality for an understanding of cultural complexity.[8] The same principle holds good for the historian. Conflict and contradiction must likewise be the starting-point for Athenian homoeroticism.

The Athenians themselves were not unaware of such ambiguities and conflicts. To begin with, according to Xenophon Greeks acknowledged that laws and customs regarding paederasty varied widely between different states. Some prohibited it outright, others explicitly permitted it.[9] Further, in his *Symposium* (182aff.), Plato put into the mouth of Pausanias an encomium of love which explicitly addresses the conflicts within Athenian norms and customs regulating paederasty. Whereas for the rest of Greece the laws and customs pertaining to paederasty are clear and well-defined, explains Pausanias, those of Athens and Sparta are "poikilos" – intricate, complicated, many-hued. He goes on to say that Athenian legislation in this area is admirable, but difficult to understand; the difficulty consists in the simultaneous approbation and censure which social

[7] E.g. Handman (1983: 191), Gregor (1985: Chapters 2, 3, 4, 5, 10).
[8] Malinowski (1929: 494–572).   [9] *Lakonian Constitution* 2.12–14, *Symposium* 8.34–5.

norms and legal rules attach to the pursuit of a paederastic courtship.

Whatever its philosophical or other merits, Pausanias' famous explanation that society only condemns the unchaste love of Aphrodite Pandemus while justly praising the noble (i.e. unconsummated) love of Uranian Aphrodite, does not dispel the contradiction which it has correctly identified. Part of the difficulty is that Pausanias' speech conflates at least two distinct categories of norms and institutions. For although he repeatedly uses words like *nomos* (law, custom), it is often not clear whether he is referring to law, or to custom in the sense of traditional social practice. It may be appropriate, then, to start by examining Athenian legislation on this subject and then move to a comparison of the legal norms with social codes and practices.

Preliminarily (though in discussing Athenian attitudes towards homoeroticism, scholars often note that at Athens there was no law forbidding unremunerated homosexual intercourse between consenting males) this statement requires some qualification. As Chapter 9 will show, the fact that the law does not prohibit a particular sexual act does not imply that it is favored, but may arise out of the delimitation of a sphere of private activity which is thought to be beyond the legitimate scope of legislative activity. Thus, although most Athenians seem to have regarded incest as an abomination, there is no law which prohibits or punishes it. Likewise, most scholars would agree that, in general, Athenians would have regarded the idea of sexual intercourse between two middle-aged male citizens as disgusting. Such conduct, however, was not felt to transgress the public sphere which the law protects.[10] This point will become clearer after the description of the Athenian statutes, but what deserves emphasis here is that the lack of statutory prohibition does not in itself imply permissive or positive attitudes.

The legal provisions regulating various forms of homoerotic behavior may be grouped in three categories: laws relating to prostitution, laws relating to education and courtship, and, finally, general provisions concerning sexual assault. These are only categories of convenience, however, and there can be considerable overlap between them.

The laws concerning male prostitution may be considered first.

---

[10] See e.g. Halperin (1990).

One statute partially disenfranchised any Athenian citizen who engaged in homosexual intercourse for gain, whether as a boy or an adult; he lost his right to address the Assembly and to participate in other important areas of civic life.[11] Secondly, if a boy was hired out for sexual services by his father, brother, uncle or guardian, they were subject to a public action, as was the man who hired him (Aeschines 1.13–14). Thirdly, a general statute prohibited procuring and applied to any freeborn child or woman.[12] Finally, Aeschines several times suggests that the man who hired an Athenian male for sexual services was likewise liable to severe penalties, but it is not clear whether he is referring to the second statute described above which pertains to boys, or to a separate one. Moreover, many of the passages suggest that he may be extending his description of the law for particular rhetorical purposes (e.g. Aeschines 1.11, 45, 72, 90, 163).

The second category of laws pertained to education and set out a series of detailed prohibitions designed, among other things, to protect schoolboys from the erotic attentions of older males. These laws regulated all the contacts which boys had with adult males during the period at school, and provided for the appointment of public officials to ensure that proper order was maintained. According to Aeschines, the law forbade the schools to open before sunrise or stay open after dark, and strictly regulated who might enter and under what circumstances (Aeschines 1.9–14). Finally, another law prohibited slaves from courting free boys.[13]

The third kind of statutory prohibition is rather more problematical than the first two and has received scant attention in regard to the regulation of homoerotic conduct. Here I refer to the law of *hubris* (insult, outrage, or abuse). Current scholarship on paederasty commonly asserts that there was no law prohibiting an Athenian male from consummating a sexual relationship with a free boy without using force or payment. This point is usually adduced as the cornerstone of the standard interpretation.[14] This interpretation, however, implicitly rests upon the assumption that such a

---

[11] Aristotle, *Ath. Pol.* 18.2; Demosthenes 19.200, 257; 22.21, 31–3; Aeschines 1.3, 13–14, 18–19, 29; Aristophanes, *Knights* 88off; Isocrates, *Panathenaicus* 140–1; Andocides 1.100–1.

[12] Aeschines 1.14; cf. Aristotle, *N.E.* 1131a7.

[13] Perhaps the *nomoi* (laws) referred to by Pausanias also regulated courtship. There is, however, a great deal of ambiguity in the text. Plato repeatedly uses the vocabulary of statutes and legislation, but at many points he clearly refers to societal attitudes and customs.   [14] E.g. Dover (1980: 64ff., 88ff.) and Foucault (1984: 238).

prohibition would have been embodied in a statute specifically prohibiting intercourse between boys and men. Since we know of no such statute, it follows that this class of homoerotic conduct remained unregulated. Yet such an assumption ignores another possibility, which is that homosexual intercourse between a man and a boy was prosecutable by the boy's family under the law of *hubris*. That is, the fact that a boy consented to a sexual transaction with a man may not have prevented the family from prosecuting such an act as an injury to its, and the boy's, honor, in the way that Roman law permitted prosecutions for sexual insults to family members. More specifically, the traditional view leaves unanswered a series of questions concerning the way in which Athenian law viewed sexual relations between minors and adults. Did Athenian law acknowledge an age of consent in its conceptualization of sexual assault and seduction? If the consent of the boy was not a bar to prosecution did *any* consummated sexual relationship with a boy constitute *hubris*? Did Athenian law have some notion equivalent to statutory rape in modern legal systems, whereby intercourse with a child under a certain age constitutes rape regardless of whether or not the child consented?[15]

An affirmative answer to any of these questions would require one to reassess the standard view that the active role in paederastic relations was absolutely free from any taint of disapprobation. If the consent of the boy was not an issue, then the use of force or monetary inducements would be irrelevant, for intercourse with a boy of a certain age would constitute *hubris per se*. Thus any intercourse with a free boy younger than a certain age would give his father an action against the man. When an adult male consented to such an act, it would not be appropriate for his family to bring such an action.

Evidence from philosophical and legal contexts presents a view of *hubris* consistent with such an interpretation.[16] First of all, it must be emphasized that the noun *hubris* and the verb *hubrizein* have a strong sexual connotation. This is only natural in a society which, as was seen above, closely linked honor to sexuality in such a way that

---

[15] See e.g. *People v. Hernandez* (1964) 61 C. 2d 529, 339 P. 2d 673. In the traditional statutory formulations, consent negates a required element of the offense (see *Regina v. Morgan*, House of Lords (1976), A. C. 182) or operates as an affirmative defense. An allegation that the victim consented to intercourse is, however, irrelevant in a prosecution for statutory rape where the age of the victim obviates any enquiry into his/her state of mind. For hints of Athenian attitudes, see Aeschines 1.139–40.

[16] I rely here on the more thorough treatment of the law of hubris in Cohen (1991a).

sexually compromising a woman or child damaged the reputation of the family as a whole, and particularly its men. Many authors, for example, refer to captive women and children being taken off to suffer *hubris*, and here, as in numerous other references, this clearly implies being subjugated to the sexual will of others.[17] Such passages reveal the way in which the inability to protect the sexual integrity of the family dishonors the men who bear this responsibility. Scholars usually do not refer to *hubris* in connection with paederasty because they believe *hubris* to require violent insult or outrage.[18] They have not paid sufficient attention, however, to the way in which the law of *hubris* may have provided the principal criminal penalties for rape. But although rape is often characterized as *hubris*,[19] so is seduction. Euphiletus, for example, refers to the *hubris* which the lover of his wife has committed against him (Lysias 1.4, 17, 25), and an oration of Demosthenes involves a prosecution for *hubris* (*hubreos graphe*) brought by a son on account of the seduction of his mother.[20]

Such contexts perfectly match Aristotle's definition of *hubris* as any behavior which dishonors and shames the victim for the pleasure or gratification of the offender (*Rhetoric* 1378b). Indeed, it is in this connection that Aeschines introduced the law of *hubris* into the catalogue of statutes which he enumerated as regulating paederasty in Athens in the fourth century B.C. In fact, when he first refers to the law of *hubris* he characterizes it as the statute which includes *all* such conduct in one summary prohibition: "If anyone commits *hubris* against a child or man or woman or anyone free or slave..." (Aeschines 1, 15). Accordingly, Athenian sources qualify both rape

---

[17] Thucydides 8.74; Plato, *Laws* 874c; Herodotus 3.80, 4.114; Aristotle, *N.E.* 1115a23, *Rhetoric* 1314b, 1315a15–20, 1373a35; Demosthenes 17.3–4, 19.309, *Letter* 4.10–11; Dinarchus 1.23; Isocrates 3.36, 4.114, *Letter to Archidamus* 10.

[18] See e.g. Dover (1980: 34–9). Fisher (1976, 1979) rightly recognizes that it can cover both rape and seduction, but he does not pursue the point.

[19] See e.g. Dinarchus, 1.23; Andocides 4.15; Demosthenes 10.27; 18.130; 23.56, 141.

[20] Demosthenes 45.4; 27.39; and cf. 23.53–6. Scholars commonly accept at face value Lysias' comparison of rape and seduction, where he argues that the law treats the latter far more seriously (Lysias 1.32–6). The problem here is that Lysias is using a common rhetorical technique of comparing laws from two different categories. He says that the law concerning *bia* (force) only awards double damages, while the law of adultery involves a capital offense. But the law he quotes about *bia* is a private suit for damages, while the action for adultery he refers to belongs to the most serious category of public offenses. The proper comparison would be with the public action for *hubris*, which did permit the death penalty. Lysias distorts the legal situation so as to emphasize the horror of adultery by showing that it is even worse than rape.

and seduction of women and children as acts of *hubris*, for both violate the sexual integrity and honor of the family.

Sexual relations with children, particularly for pay, dishonor them, and under this statute such shame and dishonor for the gratification of the offender constitutes *hubris*. Given the strong sexual connotations of the words *hubris* and *hubrizein* in ordinary language, Aeschines' argument seems perfectly reasonable, particularly in the case of minors, whose consent may be felt to be irrelevant.[21] In fact, apart from the particular case of children, numerous passages from Greek orators indicate that using a male in a passive sexual role dishonors him and thus qualifies as *hubris*. Of course, in the case of adults, voluntary consent may undercut the attribution of blame to the offender, and indeed, such men who consent are often described as committing *hubris* against themselves by their submission, hardly grounds for prosecution.[22] But in the case of a boy, such consent would have been regarded as irrelevant, and thus the attribution of wrongdoing adheres to the man who dishonors the boy, whether through rape or seduction. As in the modern law of statutory rape, the consent of a boy younger than a certain age would not negate the charge of *hubris*.

This picture of the sexual aspects of *hubris* finds additional support in Aristotle's description of shameful actions which cause dishonor to those who suffer them. He gives, as his example of such conduct, providing sexual services with one's body, and explicitly states that such shameful actions involve submitting to *hubris* (*N.E.* 1148b29). As was seen, Demosthenes and Lysias characterize both seduction

---

[21] This may have provided one incentive for *erastai* (lovers taking the active role) to limit their demands to intercrural intercourse, as Dover suggests they did. This would have been less likely to be regarded as *hubris* because it involved no penetration. Vase paintings portray boys and men having intercrural intercourse facing one another. Thus the boy does not adopt the submissive "female" position which also connotes *hubris*. However, as will appear below, there are strong reasons for skepticism about the practical force of such limitations.

[22] Aeschines 1.29, 40, 116, and the portrayal of the Persian defeat at Eurymedon discussed below, pp. 184–5... On the humiliation of submission to intercourse see F. Bailey (1969: 123) who relies on studies of primate behavior: "The males of one troop sort themselves out into patterns of dominance and subordination. If annoyed by a challenge – perhaps inadvertent – from an inferior, the dominant male will stare fixedly at him; the inferior should then look away. If he does not, the dominant male will move as if to charge; the weaker baboon should then cringe down to the ground... failing that there will be a charge and a chase... The weaker baboon may still avoid being bitten by turning its back, presenting its hindquarters and allowing itself to be mounted, just as a female is mounted in copulation." See Dundes and Falassi (1975: 188–9) on the role of mock homosexual rape in the rivalry of gangs of young men during the Palio in Siena. For similar associations in the Biblical context, see G. Bailey (1975: 32–4).

and adultery involving free women as *hubris*, and Aristotle unequivocally applies the same standard to boys when he says that some males enjoy homosexual intercourse because they were subjected to *hubris* as boys.[23] Clearly he does not mean that they acquired the habit of passivity because they were forcibly raped. Rather, they were subjected to *hubris* whether they consented for monetary gain or any other motivation. Thus, although they may have consented to such intercourse, their consent did not disqualify the act as *hubris*. Likewise, Demosthenes, in the oration *Against Androtion* (58), applies to adult males precisely the same judgment as Aeschines, arguing that the man who prostitutes himself must submit to *hubris*. Finally, Xenophon says that using men as women constitutes *hubris* (*Mem.* 2.1.30).

In short, Aeschines' characterization of the law of *hubris* as potentially providing penalties for certain homoerotic relations is not inconsistent with a good deal of other evidence. Since the law of *hubris*, like most other Athenian criminal statutes, provided no definition of the offense, *hubris* was whatever the mass bank of lay judges was prepared, without benefit of discussion or juristic advice, to regard as such. Given the wide variety of authors who denote subjecting a boy to the passive role in intercourse as *hubris*, such judgments may well represent the community consciousness which formed the only basis for determining in a particular prosecution whether or not a given act constituted *hubris*. Given the paucity of our sources, there is no way of knowing, however, if, or how often, the law was actually applied in this way. It would not be surprising if few prosecutions were brought for non-coercive *hubris* involving boys, for the very fact of prosecution would have provided the basis for future disenfranchisement.

Having briefly surveyed this wide range of legislation pertaining to homoerotic behavior it is easy to understand why Plato made Pausanias characterize Athenian law as many-hued, intricate, and difficult to understand in contrast with other Greek cities which either prohibited or permitted paederasty in a straightforward way. Now, if legal norms are one reflection or embodiment of the values, attitudes and ideology of a society (or parts of a society), what do these Athenian laws reveal about the values and beliefs of the social order which they defined and regulated? Scholars have not

[23] Aristotle, *N.E.* 1148b29; Demosthenes 23.56; Lysias 1.4, 16, 25.

addressed this question despite its crucial importance in unraveling the way in which homoeroticism was regarded at Athens.

The set of legal norms embodied in these statutes reflects a social order which encompassed a profound ambivalence and anxiety in regard to male–male sexuality; a social order which recognized the existence and persistence of such behavior but was deeply concerned about the dangers which it represented. The chief of these dangers was the corruption of the future of the polis, represented by the male children of citizen families. Boys who, under certain circumstances, participated in sexual intercourse with men were believed to have acted for gain and to have adopted a submissive role which disqualified them as potential citizens.[24] Likewise, adult citizens who prostituted themselves were subject to the same civic disabilities and opprobrium. These laws represented one of the severest sanctions which such a society could impose, and reflect the high level of concern for the preservation of the citizen body.

Further, several passages in Aristophanes refer to the possibilities for extortion and political advantage which such laws created, and of which Aeschines' prosecution of Timarchus was an actual example. In order to ensure that those who, in the words of Aeschines, are "hunters of young men," do not deplete the supply of new citizens, a group of laws aimed at deterring others from leading boys and young men into disenfranchisement: hence the various statutes, most of them capital offenses, regarding procuring, prostitution, regulation of schools, etc. Clearly, such laws imply severe censure both of the boy or young man who allowed himself to be led astray, as well as of those who were doing the leading, whether by means of financial incentives or other means.[25] At school, boys did not enjoy the supervision of their families, and the law protected them in this setting by providing the death penalty for those who sought to take advantage of this opportunity. Surely such a law does

---

[24] See for example Xenophon, *Symposium* 8.34ff. This point marks the great difference which separates Athens from cultures where homosexual intercourse plays a mandatory role in the initiation of young males. Although some scholars (for example, Bremmer [1980], and Sergent [1984]) wish to trace Athenian paederasty back to such a process of initiation, such public submission to intercourse, as required of Melanesian initiates, could have resulted in the disenfranchisement of young Athenians. On the variety of Melanesian rituals and attitudes, see Herdt (1984).

[25] Koch-Harnack's (1983: 77–9, 93–4) discussion of courtship reveals the way in which the giving of animals and money seems to be portrayed as interchangeable in Attic vase painting. She emphasizes the reciprocal nature of the transaction which the exchange of such "gifts" implies. See also Aristophanes, *Birds*.

not arise in a society which regards paederastic courtship and seduction as unproblematic? A man might do whatever he wished with a slave boy or foreigner; this was not the law's concern. Sons of citizen families, however, were felt to require the law's protection to help ensure their sexual integrity.

In many societies, such as those described by anthropologists like Herdt and Godelier, where homoerotic relations play a central role in the "making" of men out of boys, law and custom strictly delimit the boundaries of the licit. Thus among the Baruya men may use boys of a certain age only for oral intercourse (anal intercourse is strictly prohibited), and such relations must cease after initiation is complete and the boy has become a man and marries.[26] In Athens, however, law and custom did not assign a legitimate initiatory role to sexual intercourse with boys even under narrowly defined circumstances. Instead the law forbade a whole range of activities which could lead to the corruption of boys, and the law of *hubris* may have made prosecution at least a theoretical possibility for any consummated act of intercourse with minors.

In short, the range, variety, and overlapping of the Athenian statutes seem to reflect a society which was attempting over a period of time to cope with persistent patterns of behavior which were felt to jeopardize the well-being of the city. The mechanisms of the public law were deployed to deter and punish such conduct and to protect free boys.

Protection from their fathers or relatives who might hire them out, protection from their schoolmasters and chorus leaders, protection from seducers, protection from themselves: such legislation reflects strong underlying tensions about homoerotic behavior, tensions which manifest a community in conflict about its values and practices. The law may reflect such underlying conflicts but (and this is particularly the case in the sexual sphere) it is always an inadequate mechanism by which to resolve them. Hence it is not surprising that one knows of so few cases in which this impressive panoply of statutes was actually applied. Some of the reasons for this seeming disjunction between the normative potential which the law represented and the actual will to apply it may emerge from an examination of the cultural ideal, norms, and practices which, together with the law, reproduce the social fabric.

---

[26] Godelier (1987: 51–63).

In light of the discussion of *hubris* above, it is not surprising that these norms, practices, and beliefs operate within the politics of reputation, whose normative poles are honor and shame. Indeed, the fundamental antinomy that underlies all of the most important accounts of homoerotic courtship is that of honorable vs. shameful eros.[27] As Pausanias puts it in Plato's *Symposium* (182e), the *erastes* (the wooing, pursuing lover) gains honor by his success and is humiliated by defeat in his pursuit.[28] Likewise, the victory of the *erastes* means the defeat of the *eromenos* (the pursued beloved), for "it is shameful to gratify an *erastes*."[29] As Gouldner puts it, honor is a "zero-sum" game; the increase of one man's honor is at the expense of another's.[30] Unscrupulous *erastai* enhance their reputation by publicizing their victory: "...it may be expected that a lover, conceiving that everyone will admire him as he admires himself, will be proud to talk about it and flattering his vanity by declaring to all and sundry that his enterprise has been successful" (Plato, *Symposium* 232a, and 234a).

Indeed, that honor and shame define the normative boundaries of homoeroticism (and sexuality in general) is implicit, and often explicit, in all our sources from Plato, Aristotle, and Xenophon to the orators and drama.[31] Sexual submission is shameful and slavish; it dishonors and humiliates a free male.[32] Thus, as it constitutes public slander to say that a man's mother was a whore, the same is true of saying that his father or his son prostituted himself (Demosthenes 22.61). Similarly, Aristotle (*Ath. Pol.* 18.2) depicts the plot of Aristogeiton and Harmodius against the Athenian tyrant, Hippias, as arising out of an insult about the effeminacy of

---

[27] Plato, *Symposium* 181a–5b; Xenophon, *Symposium* 8.8–13; Aeschines 1.155–160; Demosthenes, 61.1–6, 18–22.

[28] Courtship could also involve fierce competition among admirers for the "favors" of the *eromenos*: Plato, *Phaedrus* 232b–d. Orations by Lysias (3.5–30, 4.5–11) and Demosthenes (54.14) elaborate the connections of erotic rivalry, *hubris*, and reputation.

[29] Plato, *Symposium* 182a, 183c–d.

[30] Gouldner (1965: 49). Winkler (1990) comments on the centrality of "zero-sum" competition in Athenian culture. Dover (1964: 31) emphasizes competitive features of courtship. As Professor Dieter Nörr correctly pointed out to me, however, this is not always a "zero-sum game" in the strict sense. That is, one party's honor may be enhanced at the expense of the other, but this does not imply that the diminishment is always total.

[31] Aristotle, *Rhetoric* 1370b, 1378b, 1383b–4b, *Politics* 1311b; Plato, *Symposium* 182, 217, *Phaedrus* 251; Xenophon, *Agesilaus* 5.7, *Symposium* 4.52ff., 7.9ff., 8.23–35, *Memorabilia* 1.2.29, 1.3.11; Lysias 3, *passim*; Demosthenes, 61.1, 3, 5–6, 17–20; Aristophanes, *Clouds* 1085.

[32] Aristotle, *Rhetoric* 1315a15–20, 1378b, 1384a; [Demosthenes] 10.27; *Letter* 4.10–12; 22.58.

Harmodius; or, as Isocrates comments, those boys who preserve their youth untrodden (*abaton*) by the base are honored greatly.[33]

Though scholars have recognized the importance of honor and shame as dominant values in Greek society, some of the consequences which arise through their operation according to a "zero-sum" rule in the area of homoeroticism deserve elaboration. Indeed, such an elaboration permits a clearer understanding of the divergent attitudes and practices in Athenian homosexuality. As was shown above, honor is largely defined by reference to sexuality, both for men and for women. The honor of a man is measured through the sexual purity of his wife, mother, sisters, and daughters, and likewise through the virility to which his public behavior gives testimony. Thus, in the Andalusian communities studied by Pitt-Rivers and Brandes, a man of honor is a man who has *cojones* (testicles); a man without honor is *manso* – tame, castrated, woman-like.[34] For men and women, "The natural qualities of sexual potency or purity and the moral qualities associated with them provide the conceptual framework on which the system [of honor and shame] is constructed."[35] Thus the politics of reputation overlap with the politics of gender, for a male can become, morally speaking, a female (according to Aristotle, in the case of a eunuch also physiologically). This is most readily accomplished by acquiring the reputation of adopting the submissive, passive role that, ideologically speaking, characterizes women. The man who submits is a victim of *hubris*; he becomes woman-like, and hence dishonored, or even disenfranchised.[36] An Athenian vase painting makes this point rather graphically when it symbolically depicts the Persian defeat at Eurymedon by showing a Persian soldier bent over while an Athenian warrior approaches him from behind, erect phallus in hand.[37] As Dundes, Brandes, and other anthropologists have shown, the same attitudes still pervade many Mediterranean cultures today, where phrases like *tomarlo por culo* ("to take it by the ass") and *bajar*

---

[33] *Helen* 58. For the same sentiments in a Roman setting, see Cicero, *Pro Milone* 9, *Pro Caelio* 3.6–8, *Pro Sestio* 8.18, 17.39, 54.16.   [34] Pitt-Rivers (1977: 22).

[35] Pitt-Rivers (1977: 23). Campbell (1979: 269–70), for example, reports that a man who possesses *andrismos* (virility) must be *barbatos* (well-endowed with testicles).

[36] This, essentially, is Aeschines' argument against Timarchus.

[37] Schauenburg (1975).

los pantalones ("to lower the trousers") refer to the defeat and subordination which symbolically transforms a man into a woman.[38]

Now, apart from defeating other men in battle or athletic competition, an obvious way in which a man may demonstrate his virility in an agonistic society like this is in competition for the favors of women.[39] There is one hitch here, however: success in this competition is purchased at the price of dishonor for the man who has failed to protect the woman whose favors have been received. Honor is a "zero-sum" game. Thus, since sexual conquest serves as a demonstration of masculinity, the adulterer or seducer gains in stature, but at the expense of others; the husband becomes the *cabron*, the cuckold. Thus Aristotle says that *hubris* against the women or sons of a family are wrongs that a man would be ashamed to disclose.[40] Isocrates even claims that desire for revenge for such wrongs is a major cause of civil strife, for only through revenge can sullied honor be redeemed (*Cyprians* 36).[41] Xenophon's account of the treatment of adulterers is also informed by this "zero-sum" model, for he says that the adulterer suffers *hubris* and humiliation at the hands of the husband, because the husband must dishonor the man who has dishonored him. In comedy, at least, this might be accomplished by a painful mock homosexual rape.[42] Whether or not such practices were comic inventions, the implicit cultural valuations are clear enough.

The greater the value attached to female purity, the keener the competition for the precious commodity, the greater the honor which is gained by conquest.[43] This is why, as Pitt-Rivers (1977: 92) points out, in this culture Don Juan is the punctilious man of honor, a judgment which has far-reaching implications for the whole range of sexual relationships:

Don Juan, the destroyer of reputations – this is the basic sense of his title *burlador* – whose aspirations to self-aggrandizement were founded upon the notion that the honor you strip from others becomes yours. In an agonistic society such as this, not only marriage but all romantic relations between the sexes have implications in the political realm even though they are

---

[38] Brandes (1981: 232–3) offers the most succinct analysis of this, and cf. Dundes (1975: 188–9).   [39] See the rivalry described in Lysias 4.

[40] *N.E.* 1173a, and cf. *Politics* 1311a–b.   [41] And cf. *Lochites* 6–9.

[42] Aristophanes, *Clouds* 1083.

[43] Seneca notes the way in which some men are attracted to adultery by the difficulty and danger: "Laetatur ille adulterio, in quod invitatus est ipsa difficultate."

seldom recognized. Thus the tenderest sentiments come together in the complex of honor with considerations of ethics, religion, prestige, economics and social pre-eminence to form a system of behavior that determines the distribution and redistribution of respect among the families of which the community is composed.

Now, as the foregoing analysis of Athenian legislation should have made clear, the Athenians were well aware of the "implications in the political realm" which sexual relations could have. Just as in Andalusia a man working in the employ of a widow (widows are regarded as sexually voracious) suffers in regard to his honor because he is seen to be subject sexually – "the one who is mounted" rather than "the one who mounts"[44] – so the Athenian male who adopts the passive, submissive role, the role of the woman, is likewise dishonored.[45] In Athens, agonistic sexuality could scarcely manifest itself in the competition for women for a variety of reasons. First, institutionalized courtship of unmarried women was non-existent, and clandestine courtship was difficult and somewhat impractical, since girls were married very young to prevent just such "accidents" and were zealously guarded during the brief period between pubescence and marriage.[46] As appeared above, adulterous unions were an attractive option to some men, but fraught with danger.[47] On the other hand, rivalry for prostitutes and slaves[48] was hardly a path to honor for an Athenian "gentleman" (*kalos kai agathos*), especially because they were automatically in a submissive and inferior position anyway and at the economic disposal of all who could pay.[49]

Public sexual competition for honor, then, had largely to be directed towards boys (particularly since chasing after prostitutes was in itself judged as shameful according to conventional norms). This fact established the basic dynamic of paederastic courtship, a dynamic which necessarily threatened to put the boy *eromenos* in the role of a woman; pursued rather than pursuing, defensive rather than aggressive, submissive rather than dominant, mounted rather

---

[44] Pitt-Rivers (1977: 82).
[45] Plato, *Gorgias* 494e; Demosthenes 22.58; Aristotle, *N.E.* 1148b–9b.
[46] See Maher (1974: 150), and the discussion in Chapter 6 above.
[47] See Xenarchus Fr. 4 (Edmonds 1961: vol. II, 594–7) and Philemon Fr. 4 (Edmonds 1961: vol. IIIa, 6–9) on the sexual options available to men with heterosexual inclinations. Note the way that, as in the *Lysistrata*, homoerotic relations are not viewed as a satisfactory alternative outlet for the sexual drives in question.
[48] Demosthenes 54.14; Lysias 3 and 4.   [49] See also Xenophon, *Hiero* 1.27ff.

than mounting. The dangers of submission increased the scarcity value of victory, which in turn fueled the keenness of the competition and heightened its emotional overtones.[50] The way in which this dynamic turned paederastic courtship into an *agon* for honor in which the *erastes* sought to gain honor by making the boy a woman, and the *eromenos* to do the same by showing himself to be a man, must now be addressed. First, however, some preliminary remarks on gender and sexual roles may be appropriate.

What does it mean, "to make a boy a woman"? It is necessary to distinguish two related aspects of this claim. The first concerns the sexual act itself and the way in which the roles of the two participants are seen, while the second involves the larger social context of courtship and the role patterns associated with it. Although it has become quite fashionable to deny that any Greeks thought homoeroticism to be unnatural and that modern categories of homosexuality/heterosexuality can be applied to classical Greece, one should not make such universal assertions too facilely. Sexual roles in both of the senses distinguished above were defined in terms of a male/female dichotomy and judged by norms that were felt by some to be at once social and natural. Some scholars concede that Plato may have felt this way, but endeavor to portray his perspective as entirely idiosyncratic, standing in opposition to the entirety of Athenian society.[51] This vision of a monolithic sexual normativity is, however, reductionist and incomplete.

To begin with the first sense of "making a boy a woman," there is ample evidence to show that the Levitical formulation "to lie with mankind as with womankind" (*Lev.* 20:13) represents a way of categorizing homosexual intercourse that was not unknown in Athens.[52] Indeed, Xenophon refers to the hubristic practice of "using men as women," and Plato argues that the man who adopts the passive role in homosexual intercourse can be rebuked as the impersonator of the female, a situation which is "against nature"

---

[50] Barrington Moore's (1984: 66) discussion of Malinowski's treatment of sexuality is illuminating here: "Romantic intensification of erotic attraction...can occur only where there are strong obstacles to erotic satisfaction. Where several partners are available and the failure to obtain the joys and services of one partner may be no more than a prelude to success with another, the form of intense passion will not occur." This, it seems to me, helps to account for the excesses of paederastic courtship attested by the sources: sleeping on the boy's doorstep, going without food, etc.   [51] See e.g. Winkler (1990).

[52] See Daube (1986: 447–8) on the meaning of this phrase. See Herdt (1984: 118, 220) for descriptions of the way in which the younger partner is seen as taking the woman's role.

(*para phusin*).[53] Aristotle also characterizes such submission as dishonorable, shameful, and unmanly (*Rhetoric* 1384a). Such usage was not confined to philosophical circles, for Aeschines accuses Timarchus of making himself a woman by adopting a passive sexual role (1.111), a state which he also says is against nature (1.185, *para phusin*). Demosthenes likewise accuses the sexually submissive of effeminacy, a frequent subject for Aristophanic satire. A fragment of Hyperides (Fr. 215) is even more explicit, arguing that nature would be surprised at a man misusing his body by acting like a woman. Such a man, he continues, abuses nature's kindness by, having been born a man, changing himself into a woman.

In a lengthy passage in the *Laws* (836–41) Plato does, indeed, go further than this, in making an analogy to nature and the mating patterns of animals. He argues that, as it is natural for a male and female to mate, and natural that male animals do not seek other males, so it is unnatural when men do not follow their example (836c). It should be emphasized that Plato does not merely characterize *passive* behavior as unnatural for men, but rather sexual relations between men *per se*, although the passive role is seen as more shameful.[54] Such judgments are clearly based upon an implicit sexual norm of male–female intercourse, and they put the passive man or boy into the submissive role which is, according to nature, that of the female.

This characterization also represents the view of Aristotle, a view which is the basis for the analysis of procreation in his treatise on the *Generation of Animals*. What underlies that entire work is the same analogy that Plato uses in the *Laws*: in their procreative capacities human beings are like animals and it is natural for male to mate with female – natural in the sense of instinctual. In the *Nicomachean Ethics* (1162a20) he carries the analysis even further, arguing that the *philia* between man and wife is according to nature (*kata phusin*) because man is by nature even more of a pairing creature than a political one. They pair not only as animals, for begetting offspring, but also to order their lives around this mating. Thus, concludes the *Politics* (1252a26–31), it is a natural necessity for male and female to join together.

---

53 Xenophon, *Memorabilia* 2.1.31; Plato, *Laws* 836e, 841d.
54 The evidence for this point appears in the concluding part of this chapter.

To return to the *Generation of Animals*, that text defines these gender categories not only in terms of physiological differentiation, but also with reference to the principle which underlies them. Thus Aristotle says that after castration a male organism changes to become very much like the female; a judgment not far removed from Pitt-Rivers' statement that in the Mediterranean to have *cojones* is the essence of masculinity and the presupposition of honor. In the Greek context eunuchs were commonly judged in this light, and boys, who were regarded as being incapable of emitting semen or performing intercourse, were not truly male (*G.A.* 728a; *Problems* 879a).[55] At the more general level, Aristotle goes on to characterize the underlying principles of masculinity and femininity as based upon the dichotomy of active and passive sexual roles, and this characterization enables one to distinguish two levels of his analysis of what is natural in sexual relations.

In the first instance, it is natural that the physiological male mate with the physiological female. This is natural both in the sense that it represents the basic reproductive pattern of living organisms and also because nature has developed our sexual organs towards the fulfillment of this procreative purpose. The second level concerns the roles which are adopted within the procreative act based upon the principles of activity and passivity. At the level of physiology the infertile male is likened to a woman because he lacks the capacity to produce semen, the active ingredient required for procreation (*G.A.* 728–9). At the level of sexual role behavior, the man who adopts a submissive, passive role is unmanly, woman-like, and he therefore dishonors and shames himself. Since a boy also cannot produce semen, physiologically speaking he is not yet a man (*G.A.* 728a). Indeed, a passage in the *Metaphysics* (1019b) argues that boys and eunuchs are both like impotent men, though impotent in different senses, and the *Politics* concludes that a boy is an undeveloped citizen, possessing male virtues only in unfinished form (1260a11–33; 1260b20). Further, when he lends himself to sexual intercourse with a man it *necessarily* places him in the role of the female, the object to

---

[55] This view of the boy is widespread. See Herdt (1984: passim), and particularly the passage at 220: "Male cults have been known in Melanesia for a long time, and I think they share a common, basic, and underlying theme. To put it as simply and colloquially as possible, it is this: 'Girls will be women' but 'boys *will not* necessarily be men.' One may indeed say that male and female are opposed to each other as nurture to nature and thus the cultural necessity for promoting masculinity, of finishing through ritual an "unfinished, possibly ambiguous biological entity'."

which desire is directed. Yet, because he is not female, in the normal case he will experience no pleasure in the act,[56] and hence must be providing services with his body for gain, an act which dishonors and shames him, placing him in a submissive role which is against nature.[57] On the other hand, if he does experience pleasure this is characterized in one Aristotelian text as due to a physiological disorder, and hence unnatural in another sense.[58] The *Nicomachean Ethics*, however, emphasizes the relation of nature to habit. Here Aristotle claims that the disposition towards submitting to physical union with men is one of the bestial dispositions, a categorization arising from the contrast between natural pleasure and natural depravities. Such persons suffer from a diseased state brought about by habitual indulgence. Thus, he continues, women adopt the passive role from nature, but for men it is unnatural and morbid.[59]

What this brief survey of views reveals is that despite the variations as to details, for those who took procreation as their starting point the "natural" pattern which provided the norm for sexual activity was the mating of male with female. Males who pursued other males were a category (or, as Xenophon puts it, a *tropos*, or disposition, way of life) defined in relation to a heterosexual norm.[60] Whereas males who submitted to other males were regarded as disgraced, the way in which the former category was judged was more controversial. But the force which the procreative heterosexual norm had for them too is perhaps most vividly seen in a text which seeks to honor such behavior: Aristophanes' famous encomium of love in Plato's *Symposium*.

Aristophanes presents heterosexuality and homosexuality as categories which are indeed both defined by nature: some individuals are naturally drawn to members of the opposite sex, others are attracted by their own sex. Further, he claims that males of the latter category are more virile, and superior to other men. But in order to justify this positive evaluation, he must create a fantastic new natural order which ignores the traditional one with its implicit valuation of heterosexuality. Hence he conjures up his famous

---

[56] Xenophon, *Symposium* 8.22.   [57] Aristotle, *Rhetoric* 1384a; Aeschines 1.185.

[58] *Problems* 879bff.

[59] See *N.E.* 1149a15 and b25 for further examples of the distinction between natural and diseased bodily pleasures. Another passage (1150b10) holds that, although most men can resist effeminate pleasures, the unrestrained man pursues "bodily pleasures contrary to the proper norm" (*para ton orthon logon somatikas hedonas*).

[60] Xenophon, *Anabasis* 4.7.

creation myth, which is elaborated so as to reach the conclusion that the youths who seek pleasure with men are not shameless, *as opinion holds*, but rather the more virile (191d–2a). The need to present a new creation myth, an entirely new model of nature, so as to justify this positive valuation, testifies eloquently to the power of the norm felt to be implicit within the traditional view.

Aristophanes' speech is interesting in yet a further respect. When he descends from the level of myth he comments that the homoerotic man is by nature (*phusis*) not inclined to marry and beget children, but is compelled to do so by law and custom (*nomos*, 192b). In the first instance, this formulation reveals that Athenians were prepared to categorize human beings according to the dichotomy homo-sexuality/heterosexuality, both in the biological *and* social–sexual spheres. Thus Aristophanes' speech explicitly distinguishes between those who *by nature* want to have intercourse only with women, marry, and beget children, and those who desire to have sexual relations and spend their lives only with other men. The former presumably include those who classify homoerotically inclined youths as "shameless"[61] and would pass similar judgments on permanently unmarried adult males who openly consorted only with boys.[62] In showing how such men felt compelled by social pressure to act against their natural inclinations and marry, the passage unequivocally demonstrates the social force that such normative judgments could have and bears further witness to the ambivalence in Athens concerning the kinds of sexual behavior considered natural, shameful, or honorable.

Aristophanes' speech also raises the question of the second of the two senses in which a boy can be made into a woman, the social–sexual sense as opposed to the physiological. For Aristophanes reveals that, for this society, law, custom, and opinion dictated that

---

[61] 192b, and see e.g. Plato, *Phaedrus* 255a4–6. *Symposium* 192a–b reads, in a way, like a plea for greater understanding by those whom social pressure constrains to conform to sexual norms; not Plato's own plea, but his representation of one contemporary position on homoeroticism.

[62] Note that the passage also implicitly accepts the normative classification that men be attracted only to boys and not other adult males. Aristophanes' speech explicitly says that, when these homoerotically oriented boys grow up, they in turn take boys as their lovers. Such norms do distinguish between legitimate and illegitimate objects of desire, for a male past the age of physical maturation (first beard growth) is generally regarded as "out of bounds." On the age of beard growth and its relation to sexual roles, see Moller (1987: 751). As discussed in Chapter 3, modern Mediterranean societies frequently express similar disapproval and suspicion of men who do not marry.

the natural role of every man was to be a husband and father. Heterosexuality is institutionalized as the foundation of the most basic social unit, the family.[63] This fact is perhaps most forcefully expressed in the Aristotelian *Oeconomica* and the *Nicomachean Ethics*. The *Ethics*, as noted above, holds that the *philia* between man and wife is a natural instinct. This instinct is the basis of the family and the division of labor; men and women cohabit both to reproduce the race and to provide the basic necessities of life (1162a15–30). In the *Oeconomica* (1343a–44a), the opening passages repeatedly emphasize that it is according to nature that a man and a woman join together to form a family. From the differentiated economic tasks and spheres which are sexually appropriate to husband and wife devolve the social roles which make up the patterns of community and family life.[64] It is in this broader context that the homoerotic valuation of boys became problematic, for while they were in the process of being educated to be citizens and warriors they were also subjected to patterns of courtship and norms of behavior which assimilated them to women.

In his discussion of the Athenian festival of the Oschophoria, Vidal-Naquet has commented upon the role of the two ephebes who dress as women.[65] He explains that the young man before his initiation as a warrior is not yet virile, not yet truly male:

It is a well known fact that the transvestism, of which we find an example in the Oschophoria, was, for archaic Greek societies... a means to dramatize the coming of the young man to the age of virility and marriage. The classic example... is that of Achilles at Skyros, disguised as a girl but unable to resist the sight of arms.

What is implicit in this passage is the equation, at least on the symbolic level, of the uninitiated male with the female. Similarly, Godelier (1987: 33) reports that in the first stage of Baruya initiation each boy is dressed half as a man, half as a woman. Symbolically, this costuming emphasizes the fact that an uninitiated male is essentially

---

[63] When sexuality is viewed from the starting point of the ideology of the family, the perspective, though not monogamous, seems inevitably heterosexual. Hence the famous tripartite division of the Demosthenic oration, *Against Neaera*, 122: "Mistresses we keep for pleasure, concubines for the daily care of our persons, but wives to bear us legitimate children and guard our households." One might object that the speaker does not mention boys only out of a sense of shame, but doesn't that just reinforce the point?

[64] A similar view of the foundation of the family is, of course, expressed by Xenophon in his *Oeconomicus*.   [65] Vidal-Naquet (1981: 167–8); and see Delcourt (1958: 1–27).

female: he must be made into a man, a complex social and biological process which takes many years.[66] The equating of the boy with the female went beyond the symbolic level, however, as Aristotle indicates when he says that in regard to form a boy is like a woman.[67]

Given this ambivalent view of the sexual identity of boys, it is not surprising that in Attic vase painting courtship of boys and courtship of women were depicted in an almost identical manner.[68] Apart from one major difference (the depiction of the sexual consummation of courtship), the stages, gestures, rituals, and gifts of courtship were much the same whether the object was a boy or a woman.[69] Indeed, it seems that a sort of displaced courtship, leading to a sort of displaced marriage, is the appropriate context in which to understand the assimilation of the boy to a woman both in terms of his sexual identity, his role in courtship, and, in a mixed way, his social role in general. An example may help to clarify this notion of displaced courtship and marriage.

In an unjustly neglected article entitled "Sexual Inversion among the Azande," Evans-Pritchard describes the case of a warrior society in which the age of marriage for men is quite late, as at Athens, from the late twenties to the thirties.[70] Since girls were betrothed very young, the only way in which young men could obtain heterosexual satisfaction was through adultery. But that was what Evans-Pritchard terms "a very dangerous solution to a young man's problem," since husbands often tortured and mutilated adulterers taken in the act.[71] The solution to this dilemma was, according to

[66] See also Herdt (1984: 220), and Poole (in Herdt, 1982: 107–9). It bears repeating that there appears to be no evidence at Athens for the ritualized homosexuality that Herdt, Godelier, Poole, Read, and others have found to be at the core of male initiation in some Melanesian societies. In those communities a complex socio-biological ideology requires that boys be grown into men through the regular ingestion of the semen of their elders. A boy not so nourished would remain, socially speaking, a female because he would not have gone through initiation, but biologically, it is felt, he could also not grow into a man.

[67] *G.A.* 728a. In addition, boys are also linked to that other category of submissive beings, slaves, by the linguistic usage which refers to both with the same word, *pais*, which can also refer to a female child. For a discussion of slavery and paederasty, see Golden (1984).

[68] I have refrained from relying heavily on vase paintings of homoerotic conduct because of the problems of interpretation posed by such an undertaking. Apart from matters of stylization and artistic convention, the principal of these is that the vase paintings all date from at least one hundred years before the literary evidence on which accounts of Athenian homoeroticism must rely.

[69] Dover (1980: 81ff.), Koch-Harnack (1983: 59–82), Foucault (1984: 244–7).

[70] See also Godelier's (1987: 52–4) description of similar relations between Baruya initiates and their older partners.

[71] Evans-Pritchard (1970: 1429). For the parallels at Athens, see the discussion in Chapter 5 of the dangers of adultery.

Azande informants, for young men to marry boys when they went into the king's service as warriors: not marry in the legal sense, but rather to court a boy who would then move into the warrior's house as his lover. The pair often referred to each other as "husband" and "wife," with the man helping to educate the boy and the boy providing sexual and other services. When the period of military duty was over the warrior would end the relationship, return to his village, and marry. The boy would, in his turn, become a warrior and repeat the process in the "male role." After the termination of this relationship and marriage sexual activity was purely het-erosexual. Significantly, all the Azande informants insisted that intercourse with the boys was only intercrural; they all expressed disgust at the suggestion of anal penetration.[72] Similar patterns in Melanesia suggest that institutionalized patterns of homoerotic relations involve sharp distinctions between licit and illicit activities, usually including anal intercourse among the latter.[73]

Evans-Pritchard's account suggests a number of interesting parallels with the situation at Athens. There too, late marriage of men, early marriage of the closely guarded adolescent girls, and the dangers of adultery combined to make boys an attractive alternative – but with a difference. Those Athenian men who pursued boys were not merely seeking immediate sexual gratification (nor, of course, were their Azande counterparts) since, as Xenophon put it, in this slave society cheap sexual fulfillment was available at every corner.[74] Devereux has remarked that courtship behavior is almost universal because it seems to fulfill a deep human need,[75] and in Athens courtship and the erotic relationship which it aims at was only possible with boys. This courtship, as Plato, Aeschines, Xenophon, and Demosthenes reveal, was institutionalized in the sense that it was governed by *nomoi* (customs/laws/prescriptions) which many Athenians viewed as distinguishing honorable and shameful con-duct.[76] When the boy was seen as having become a man physiologically – after the growth of his first beard – he was no

---

[72] Evans-Pritchard (1970: 1430).   [73] Godelier (1987), Herdt (1984).
[74] *Memorabilia* 2.2.4. For one obol according to Philemon Fr. 4.
[75] Devereux (1968: 82).
[76] I don't mean governed in the sense of "determined." These *nomoi* helped to define the parameters of normative expectations within which individuals pursue their own ends. Texts like Demosthenes' *Erotic Essay*, Aeschines' prosecution of Timarchus, or the speeches in Plato's *Phaedrus* reveal the way conventional standards were interpreted and manipulated according to the purposes and strategies of particular individuals.

longer an appropriate object for pursuit (Plato, *Protagoras* 309); his ambiguously defined androgynous sexuality had become definitively male.[77] Once again the heterosexual norm was the standard by which roles and behavior were judged. Even Aristophanes' speech in the *Symposium* implicitly accepts this dichotomization of sexual roles by concluding that when boys came of age they would then become pursuers of youths themselves. Similarly, Aeschines (1.41) claims that a man named Misgolas is generally regarded as having an upright character, but shameful and peculiar sexual tastes because he desires young men (not boys). Men, *pace* Foucault, were not appropriate objects of desire, nor should they submit to being objects of desire. Hence permanent male–male sexual partnerships were not a socially legitimate substitute for marriage.

Thus the Athenian boy seems to have found himself in a situation which, like the Athenian code of conduct itself, is aptly described by Pausanias' term *poikilos* – intricate, many-hued, ambiguous. While he was being educated to be a warrior and a citizen the Athenian boy was also, in many ways, cast into a feminine social role, as the vase paintings depicting courtship imply. Thus the ideal boy was supposed to be modest and chaste, avoid contact with adult males who were not relatives or close friends of the family, keep his eyes lowered and blush when made the object of attention, etc.[78] Their families protected them from male attention as if they were daughters, but since, if they were to become men, they could not be confined to the house like a daughter, a *paedagogus* watched over them:

Yet we find in practice that if a father discovers that someone has fallen in love with his son, he puts the boy in the charge of a tutor and won't let him talk with lovers; the tutors receive strict injunctions to forbid it. And friends of his own age reproach him if they see anything of that kind going on, and their elders will neither stop their being rude nor tell them the reproach is undeserved.[79]

---

[77] Some sources also indicate that it was considered shameful for men past a certain age to be interested in boys: Lysias 3.1, Aeschines 1.11. Halperin (1990: 2–3) explains that when a boy comes of age he is no longer desirable. This occurs when the hair of the thighs and beard becomes fully developed, i.e. when they become manly and unwomanlike. See Moller (1987) for a comparative study of age and beard growth.

[78] Plato's *Lysis* and *Charmides*, and Xenophon's *Symposium* describe this ideal.

[79] Plato, *Symposium* 183c–d, and cf. *Phaedrus* 231e, 240, 255a. In Xenophon's *Symposium* 4.24–6 the father appoints a tutor for the boy who has a crush on a schoolmate, and cf. 4.52ff., and 8.19ff. Aeschines says that parents appoint a *paedagogus* to protect their sons (1.187), and

Thus the sexual purity of the boy was protected by the family under the same code of honor and shame as that which applied to women, but for Athenian boys, unlike their Azande and Baruya counterparts, sexual purity was defined as not assuming the woman's role in sexual intercourse. The attention paid to a beautiful boy might enhance his reputation, but suspicion of submitting to *erastai* could destroy it.[80] Moreover, the politics of sexual reputation applied to boys just as to women. As Aristotle puts it, some men prefer to shroud in silence their dishonor from the *hubris* done to their wives or daughters *or sons* rather than accept the publicity and humiliation of a lawsuit. The reputation of a boy was determined by the inferences drawn from his public behavior with men.[81] Just as in a modern Mediterranean village (or in classical Athens) a girl who lingers at the fountain or takes longer than necessary to return from the fields compromises her honor and becomes the object of gossip and slander,[82] so a boy who was seen spending much time alone with a man, particularly at his house, or drinking with him, or alone with him in a deserted place (particularly after dark) was compromised, and might even become the object of blackmail.[83] Propriety (or rather, a strategy for maintaining one's reputation by avoiding damaging gossip), as Xenophon informs us, ideally required that the lover inform the boy's father of his inclination and see the boy in public, in the presence of the father or other relatives.[84] Indeed, the first two speeches about homoerotic courtship in Plato's *Phaedrus* provide a perfect example of the strategic manipulability of these norms, expectations, and appearances: arguing opposite sides of the same question, both speakers utilize the same normative repertoire in support of their position.

Hence courtship was an elaborate and public game of honor, a "zero-sum" game in which the *erastes* won honor by conquering, the

---

cf. Aristophanes, *Birds* 137–42, Xenophon, *Memorabilia* 1.5.2, Aristotle, *N.E.* 1119b14. See also Vlastos (1987: 95–6).

[80] See Vlastos (1987: 95–6) on *eros kalos* and its hazards for the boy.

[81] See Demosthenes 61.17–21 on the boy's conduct and reputation.

[82] See Fuller (1961: 47) and Campbell (1979: 86, 190–201).

[83] Lysias 14.25; Aeschines 1, 42, 51, 60, 75–6, 82, 90; 3.162; Plato, *Theaetetus* 144e, *Symposium* 217c, *Phaedrus* 232a–b, 234a–b, *Charmides* 155a, *Euthydemus* 275b; Aristotle, *Rhetoric* 1348b; Aristophanes, *Clouds* 995ff., *Knights* 880. Also, Aeschines (1.75–6) claims that a boy having money for gambling, flute-girls, and the like would give rise to inferences that he must be receiving money in return for his "favors." [84] Xenophon, *Symposium* 8.11–20.

boy by attracting much attention but not submitting.[85] As Isocrates comments (*Helen* 58), those boys who preserve their youth untrodden (*abaton*) by the base are honored greatly.[86] Similarly, Aristotle characterizes paederastic relationships as a kind of non-reciprocal friendship: one pursues for pleasure, the other allows the pursuit because his lover may prove useful.[87] The common result is that the *erastes* complains that his affection is not returned (because he is not being sexually gratified), while the *eromenos* complains that the *erastes* promised everything and doesn't deliver (*N.E.* 1164a). In this dynamic, the *erastes* is shamed by his failure to conquer, the boy by his submission, all of this behavior being judged by the community through its manifestations in the public arena of reputation, honor, and shame.[88] For, as Aeschines argues in his prosecution of Timarchus, no one can "prove" what took place between two individuals in private, so the judges must base their decision on their own general knowledge of the accused's reputation, a reputation based upon inferences from the behavior the community does see.[89] Aeschines, of course, manipulates the "facts" and normative expectations to blacken Timarchus' reputation, just as his opponent would to exonerate himself. Thus paederastic courtship at Athens was not unlike, in some ways, the gallant courtship of married women in other times and places in Europe. There too, honor was the stake of the game, and the public aspect of the politics of reputation was likewise present: society tolerated deviance from the ideal norms so long as the forbidden acts remained secret and the rules were obeyed. Madame X might have been "known" to be the mistress of Chevalier Y with no unpleasant consequences until she was publicly compromised by an accident, indiscretion, or her lover's gossip; thereupon her reputation was destroyed and she was cast out from society irremediably.[90]

In Athens an ideal solution was offered to the dilemma of the "zero-sum" game of honor, an ideal indicated by the descriptions of chaste courtship in Plato, Xenophon, and Demosthenes.[91] According

---

[85] For the honor which a boy receives by being admired and sought after for his beauty, see e.g. Plato, *Charmides* 154c; Aeschines 1.134; Demosthenes 61.10–14; and Vlastos (1987: 95–6).   [86] See also Aeschines 1.136–9, 155–60; Demosthenes 61.5–6, 16–20.

[87] *E.E.* 1245a25; cf. 1238b and 1243b15.

[88] Demosthenes 61.15–21; Aeschines 1.74–93.   [89] Aeschines 1.74–93.

[90] This is the hypocrisy which Tolstoy inveighs against in *Anna Karenina*. Laclos' *Les Liaisons Dangereuses* provides the most penetrating portrayal of this pattern.

[91] Plato, *Symposium, Phaedrus*; Xenophon, *Symposium*; Demosthenes 61.

to this ideal an equilibrium was reached whereby the *erastes* and *eromenos* could both maintain their honor. The *erastes* was granted "favors" by his *eromenos*, but the *eromenos*, striving "to allow others no grounds for suspicion of wrongful conduct,"[92] stopped short of granting (or appearing to grant) favors which would dishonor him.[93]

Dover and Foucault argue that the *eromenos* only allowed intercrural intercourse and never anal penetration, but, as Vlastos (1987: 96) points out, "If submitting to anal copulation carries a stigma, the boy would always be under suspicion of it. Who is to know what goes on between him and his lover in the privacy of their *amours*?" Indeed, as pointed out above, the community can only rely upon gossip and the observation of *public* behavior to form judgments about what point a particular relationship has reached on the axis of honorable/shameful eros:[94]

A lover is bound to be heard about and seen by many people talking with his beloved..., so that when they are observed talking to one another, the meeting is taken to imply the satisfaction, actual or prospective, of their desires. (Plato, *Phaedrus* 232a–b)

This presents serious risks for the boy, for his reputation (and even civic rights) may be compromised by incorrect inferences and irresponsible gossip. Hence the evident concern in our sources about *erastai* who "kiss and tell."[95] Further, the maddening ambiguity of our sources about the precise boundaries of licit and illicit "favors" which *eromenoi* grant, mirrors the conflict and ambiguity on which the politics of reputation thrive. It is precisely the contradictory and ambiguous nature of normative expectations which, as Bourdieu has shown, permits individuals to manipulate standards and circum-

---

[92] Demosthenes 61.19.
[93] Aristotle's discussion of the problematics of gratification in the *Prior Analytics* (68a40–69) reveals the complexity of the competing motivations and sentiments in which man and boy might be enmeshed: every lover, says Aristotle, prefers his lover to be disposed to gratify him without doing so rather than to gratify him against inclination. Since the boy feels no pleasure and no natural inclination to intercourse, it follows that the boy is not inclined and the lover should not want him to submit. This example, of course, proceeds from an implicit standard case: the lover wants to, the boy is not inclined. What the lover really aims at, according to Aristotle, is that the boy be willing to engage in intercourse, because this reveals that his *philia* is being returned. This willingness manifests reciprocity of sentiment, because the readiness cannot be due to desire. Cf. *N.E.* 1157a and 1171b30 for Aristotle's representation of the essentially chaste pleasures (ideally) of the *eromenos–erastes* relation: the *erastes* derives pleasure from looking at the *eromenos*, the *eromenos* from receiving the affection of the *erastes*.
[94] See du Boulay (1976: 389–406), and the discussion of gossip and reputation in Chapters 3 and 4.   [95] Plato, *Phaedrus* 232a, 234a.

stances for their own purposes, whether following strategies of justification or criticism. Aeschines' long disquisition on the role of gossip, inference, and public "knowledge" in establishing Timarchus' reputation for sexual depravity provides a powerful illustration of this potential.[96]

While texts like Plato's *Symposium* and *Phaedrus* reveal that some Athenians, at least, felt able to resolve to their own satisfaction the contradictions implicit in their sexual code by means of this sort of ideal equilibrium, other sources offer a different picture. Indeed, it appears that some Athenians viewed this solution as hollow, raising again Malinowski's problem of distinguishing competing cultural ideals and practices. For there may be disagreement within a culture as to what is practice, what is ideal, and how each is to be valued. Thus at Athens some boys rejected paederastic relations altogether, some attempted to uphold the distinction between honorable and shameful relations, and others gave themselves openly.[97] Wilamowitz-Möllendorf referred to Pausanias' speech as the "Ehrenkodex der athenischen Knabenliebe," but Victor Ehrenberg has aptly commented that "There is little in common between the blushing boys of Plato's dialogues, and the world of unnatural lust which the comedians depict."[98]

Thus Aristophanes in *Clouds* (961ff.) depicts the way in which such cultural ideals of chaste and virile youth are projected into the past to create a false history which is nothing more than ideology. Indeed, he appears to have been acutely aware of the problem of the contrast between ideal and practice, for in a number of passages he attempts to expose the hypocrisy of the paederastic ideal by contrasting it with stark reality (a view of reality strongly supported by Attic vase painting). In *Birds* and *Wealth* he refers to the general courtship practice of giving gifts of animals to the *eromenos*, and he seems to suggest that it is pure hypocrisy to regard it as distinguishable from the prostitution which the law forbids:

And they say that boys do the same, not for their lovers but for gold. Not those of good family, but the prostitutes. The well-bred ones don't ask for money. What then? A good horse or hunting dogs. Being ashamed to ask for money they disguise their vice with a name.[99]

---

[96] As, in their own way, do the first two speeches in Plato's *Phaedrus*.
[97] Demosthenes 61.1, 5–19. This is also implicit throughout Plato's *Phaedrus* and *Symposium*, and Xenophon's *Symposium*.
[98] Wilamowitz-Möllendorf (1920: Vol. 1, 365); Ehrenberg (1962: 100).
[99] *Plutus* 153–9, and cf. *Birds* 704f.

Criticisms of the paederastic ideal are not limited to comedy, and, contrary to contemporary orthodoxy, are also not confined to passivity. Xenophon (*Memorabilia* 1.2.9, and 1.3.11), for example, relates how Critias loved the boy Euthydemus and tried to use him like those who enjoy the erotic pleasures of the body. Socrates turned him away saying this to be slavish and not fit for a respectable man because he was asking to be given that which is wrong. One can, of course, attempt to dismiss this as peculiar to Socrates, but these two passages are part of Xenophon's defense of Socrates' character, and here he seeks to show his moral uprightness by demonstrating that he was sexually self-restrained and considered the seduction of boys harmful and dangerous. If this view were entirely without resonance in the conventional morality of most Athenians, Xenophon could hardly use it as part cf his defense of Socrates. Moreover, Xenophon expresses the same view (*Memorabilia* 2.1.24) when he has Vice personified counsel intercourse with boys and Virtue responds by saying that using a man as a woman is wrong, for such people are committing *hubris* all night (cf. *Rhetoric* 1384b and *Mem.* 2.6.21, 33). In these passages not only is it wrong to submit, but it is also wrong to demand submission.[100] As Xenophon's *Symposium* says, *erastai* feel ashamed of what they want the most.[101] Thus the good *erastes* makes his affection public and tells the boy's father, and this is how it ought to be (*hoionper chre einai*), the normative ideal. Only shameful, unchaste love demands to be kept secret (8.8). Since the lover who demands submission wants what will cause the greatest disgrace for the boy, he hides the matter from the boy's family and may even resort to force. Many bad results have arisen from such shameful relations, and thus Athenian conventions (*nomima*) make unchaste paederasty disgraceful (8.19–34).

Similarly, Demosthenes (61.1) maintains that the good (*dikaios*) *erastes* would neither do something shameful nor request it; many boys, however, refuse to associate with their admirers because of the men who defile (*lumainein*) such relationships. Likewise, Aeschines (2.166) says that a man should be ashamed of the reputation of being a pursuer of young men, and the speaker in an oration of Lysias (3.4) asks the judges not to think ill of him for chasing a boy at his age (and cf. Aeschines 3.162). Finally, Isocrates (*Helen* 58) argues that those

---

[100] In the *Symposium* Xenophon also claims that the open homoerotic relations of Theban and Elean warriors are condemned by Athenian custom (*nomima*) with the severest reprobation.

[101] 4.15–16; and see Aristotle, *Metaphysics* 1019b20.

who hire themselves out are held in greater dishonor than those who do wrong against the bodies of others, a sentiment echoed by Plato in the *Phaedrus* (234b). Clearly, on this view the passive partner is worse, but both are dishonorable.

A final passage from Xenophon brings together these themes of honor and shame, public and private, as they inform the politics of reputation. Whether the story is historically accurate or not in no way influences its capacity to reflect Xenophon's perception of Greek values. In his life of the Spartan king Agesilaus, Xenophon relates how Agesilaus avoided being slandered about having homosexual relations by always lodging in public places where everyone would think such doings would be impossible. Agesilaus, cognizant of the politics of reputation and the power of gossip, thus took care to justify his behavior in advance by arranging the circumstances so as to prefer a particular set of inferences. Secrecy and privacy are associated with sexual transgression, so he confined his activities to public places where he could claim, like many speakers in Athenian orations, that his behavior was open for all to see. What his actual sexual preferences were matters little. What is significant is the way that he attempted to manipulate judgments about those preferences by playing upon the normative expectations that determine reputation. Further, it is likewise clear that Agesilaus felt that being regarded as a paederast would be a subject for slander that could damage his reputation.

What then is one to conclude about a culture whose laws expressed a deep rooted anxiety about paederasty while not altogether forbidding it?[102] A culture in which attitudes and values ranged from the differing modes of approbation represented in Plato's *Symposium* to the stark realism of Aristophanes and the judgment of Aristotle that, in a man, the capacity to feel pleasure in a passive sexual role is a diseased or morbid state, acquired by habit, and comparable to biting fingernails or habitually eating earth or ashes.[103] A culture is not a homogeneous unity; there was no one "Athenian attitude" towards homoeroticism. The widely differing attitudes and conflicting norms and practices which have been discussed above represent the disagreements, contradictions, and

---

[102] Plato, *Symposium* 182ff.; Xenophon, *Symposium* 8.35.

[103] *N.E.* 1148b. One could argue that the passage applies to all pleasure from homoerotic sexual intercourse, but I here limit the claim to its unequivocal application to the passive role.

anxieties which make up the patterned chaos of a complex culture. They should not be rationalized away. To make them over into a neatly coherent and internally consistent system would only serve to diminish our understanding of the "many-hued" nature of Athenian homosexuality.

CHAPTER 8

The prosecution of impiety in Athenian law

The three preceding chapters have discussed the manner in which Athenian society encompassed two areas of problematic sexual practices: adultery and homosexuality. Building upon these investigations, the next chapter will attempt to analyze the way in which the regulation of such sexual behavior relates to more general questions of political ideology, particularly to democratic theory. So as not to leave this general discussion of the enforcement of morals vulnerable to the criticism that it relies exclusively upon material concerning sex and gender, the present chapter takes up aspects of the legal regulation of religious behavior.[1] Although modern discussions of the enforcement of morals often confine themselves to the realm of sexual morality, the nature and scope of the statutory provisions for the enforcement of socio-religious norms is, in most legal systems, one of the most significant criteria by which to evaluate various aspects of the relationship of the individual and the family to the state and to the society as a whole.[2] This is no less the case in classical Athens where the processes which regulate religious practices and beliefs are of central importance for an understanding of issues like the relation between law and morals, the place of individual liberty and freedom of conscience, and the link between democracy and toleration. Indeed, Plato's *Republic* and *Laws* bear witness to the recognition of the importance of religious conformity, as, in its own way, does the trial of Socrates. Discussion of these broader questions will occupy much of Chapter 9. This chapter addresses a number of preliminary, more concrete problems which

---

[1] A full treatment of impiety in Athenian society remains outside the scope of this study. This chapter thus aims at addressing those aspects immediately relevant for issues concerning the regulation of the public and private spheres.

[2] See e.g. Rawls' (1974: 205–21) treatment of the problem of intolerance and of the permissible coercion of the individual (or groups) in religious matters.

determine the course of any further theoretical speculation. These problems concern the meaning and normative application of the word *asebeia* (impiety) in legal and other contexts, and may be formulated as four related questions:

1 How does the ordinary language usage of the word *asebeia* relate to its legal definition? Does *asebeia* in the legal sense encompass conduct like failing to honor one's parents, failing to prosecute certain crimes, failing to fulfill an oath, perjury, etc.?

2 Was there a clear legal definition of *asebeia*? If not, why is such the case? Is it simply because the concept of *asebeia* is so vague and undefinable, as some scholars have suggested?[3]

3 What is the range and application of actions for *asebeia* which served as a means to enforce religious and social norms? In other words, what kind of conduct was, and properly could be, prosecuted as *asebeia*? Did *asebeia* only apply to actions and ritual violations, and is the prosecution of Socrates for his beliefs thus to be seen as a deviation from the norm, or did the action for *asebeia* represent a mechanism for ensuring social and religious conformity in all its aspects?

4 Finally, how does Athenian practice in regard to impiety relate to Plato's legislation in the *Laws*? Is Plato's legislation on religious conformity idiosyncratic and to be seen as "totalitarian" when measured against the "tolerance" of democratic Athens?

It is appropriate to begin with the first question posed above, concerning the relation of the ordinary language/cultural conception of *asebeia* to its legal usages. Plato's dialogue *Euthyphro* offers what is perhaps the best available evidence on this issue. Set just before Socrates' trial for impiety, it depicts Socrates' attempt to lead Euthyphro, who is bringing an action for murder against his own father, to a definition of just what impiety is. Euthyphro's relatives accuse him of committing impiety by bringing such a prosecution, and he, like Socrates, claims that he is innocent of such an accusation. Socrates asks him to justify this claim, and the first general definition of *asebeia* which he prods Euthyphro to produce probably represents the unreflective ordinary language conception of the Athenian citizen who is sure that he knows what such concepts mean.

---

[3] See Thalheim, *RE*: 1530–1; Lipsius (1905: 359–60); Finley (1969: 162ff.).

On Euthyphro's formulation, piety is that which is pleasing to the gods, impiety (*asebeia*) is that which is not pleasing to them (7a). Such a definition, as Socrates points out, is not particularly helpful at the conceptual level, and, more importantly, it indicates the extent to which the range of actions connoted by *asebeia* is simply the product of unarticulated cultural conceptions. As a Justice of the United States Supreme Court intimated about pornography, one may not be able to define it, but one knows it when one sees it. Most Athenians, Plato points out, think they know what such words mean, but even though this "knowledge" will decide the fate of those accused of impiety (like Socrates), it rests, in Plato's view, upon the shakiest of foundations.

One can, of course, turn to more sophisticated treatments, but the philosophical definition of *asebeia* found in the Aristotelian *Virtues and Vices* (1251a30) is scarcely more illuminating: *asebeia* consists in wrongdoing against gods and demons, parents, the dead, and the fatherland. In fact, an examination of all occurrences of the word *asebeia* in classical Athenian sources reveals a range of usage as broad as that suggested by the foregoing definitions, but, as will be seen, it is reasonable to suppose that the legal scope of the term is narrower. Indeed, the central cases are, as usual, fairly clear; the question is how to delineate the borderlines.

To begin with, among these apparent extended usages a number of passages in the Athenian orators use *asebeia* or its cognates as strong synonyms for "wrongdoing" or "wrongdoer." The contexts of these remarks reveal no reference to actual religious transgressions, so these usages appear to follow a common rhetorical technique whereby orators seek to label their opponents as impious, violent, dissolute, or larcenous as a general tactic of reprobation.[4] Likewise, one can also dismiss another group of exaggerated usages, as when Isocrates (*Panath.* 203) refers to one of his students as impious because he praised the Spartans. This surely stretches even the broad definition of the *Virtues and Vices*, and hardly seems likely to form the basis of an actual legal prosecution. Leaving such cases aside, then, one can identify a number of categories where ordinary language and standard legal usages almost certainly overlap. Such categories include profaning the mysteries;[5] offenses against cults or temples such as improper sacrifices, or violation of ritual prohibitions;

[4] See e.g. the rhetorical exaggeration in Lysias 12.24, or Antiphon, *Tetralogy* 2a.3, 9, 11.
[5] See e.g. Andocides, 1, passim; Xenophon, *Hell.* 1.4.4.

entering a temple or participating in a festival or ritual or holding a sacred office from which one is debarred;[6] violating a temple by sacking it, murdering someone within its boundaries, or dragging a suppliant from its altar;[7] and violating or destroying sacred objects like the Herms.[8] Likewise clearly within the central conception[9] of *asebeia* fall the more intangible offenses of not honoring or believing in the gods of the polis, or introducing new gods, but the scope of these categories of impiety deserves detailed attention and the evidence for them will be examined below.

Apart from these central cases where one can feel quite confident of a congruence between ordinary language and legal usage, there are a number of categories which are more problematic. Numerous passages from a wide variety of authors attest, for example, that the violation of oaths constitutes *asebeia*. This includes various kinds of violations, such as perjury, or judges violating their oath of office by convicting a man innocent of homicide, or acquitting one guilty of homicide, or deliberately forswearing oneself.[10] Other passages suggest that some Athenians, at least, regarded associating with a parricide, not prosecuting a homicide, or certain offenses against parents as impious.[11] Euthyphro's kin, it will be remembered, accused him of impiety for daring to prosecute his father for homicide.

A final problem concerns the relation between impiety and theft of sacred property. Athenian law distinguished theft of sacred property (*hierosulia*) from other sorts of theft.[12] Of course, precisely that violation of the religious sphere which makes *hierosulia* a separate category of theft also links it with the general concept of offenses against religion connoted by *asebeia*. Indeed, broadly conceived offenses like *hubris* and *asebeia* readily lend themselves to such conceptual ambiguity, and the evidence suggests that *asebeia*

---

[6] Demosthenes 22.72, 78; 23.51, 55, 147, 197, 227; 59.77, 116–17; Andocides 1.71, 132; Lycurgus, *Against Leocrates* 129; Thucydides 6.27, 53; Herodotus 6.81.

[7] Aristotle, *N.E.* 1126a; Isocrates, *Paneg.* 156; Xenophon, *Hell.* 4.4.3; Herodotus 1.159, 2.139, 8.129; Thucydides 4.97–8; Lysias 2.7, 10; Lycurgus, *Against Leocrates* 81, 147; and cf. *IG* 2418.   [8] Thucydides 6.27, 53.

[9] Throughout, I am using the contrast between "central" or "standard" cases and "borderline" cases in the sense elaborated by H. L. A. Hart (1961: 16–17).

[10] Aristotle, *Rhetoric* 1377a20–4, 1416a30; Lycurgus, *Against Leocrates* 76; Demosthenes 21.104–5, 120; 23.79; 59.82; Xenophon, *Cyr.* 8.8.3; Andocides 1.30–33; Antiphon 5.88.

[11] Demosthenes 22.2–3 (and cf. 24.7); Plato, *Republic* 615c, *Symposium* 188c, *Euthyphro* 1–7; Lycurgus, *Against Leocrates* 94; [Aristotle], *Virtues and Vices* 1251a30.

[12] See generally Cohen (1983: Chapter 3), and Demosthenes 24.177; 22.69.

and *hierosulia* did indeed overlap. It is far from clear, however, whether every case of *hierosulia* would also constitute *asebeia*, and, if not, where the distinction lay. It is surprising that the scholarly literature largely ignores such issues, but the question remains: how ought one to go about resolving such difficulties?

In the only classical Greek text to address this problem specifically, Aristotle, in his *Rhetoric* (1374a), argues that borderline cases cannot be decided without a definition of the offense. Further, the context of his discussion makes clear that this proviso applies to most of the cases which I have just enumerated. This passage in the *Rhetoric*, moreover, clearly assumes that, in terms of actual practice, deploying such a definition was problematic. Where, then, could Athenians find a legal definition of offenses like *asebeia*? And if they were not interested in such questions of definition (as a perusal of the orators would lead one to believe), why is that the case? These questions introduce the second of the four issues enumerated above: the meaning of *asebeia* in legal contexts.

Scholars have advanced two theories about the legal definition of *asebeia*. Since Lipsius' classic account in the nineteenth century most classicists and legal historians have accepted that the variety of cases included within the scope of *asebeia* arises from the vague and undefinable quality of the concept itself.[13] As one German scholar formulates the standard interpretation, "The great multiplicity of cases in which this form of prosecution was applied is attributable to the indefiniteness and elasticity of the concept of *asebeia* itself."[14] On the other hand, at least one scholar has expressed the view that there was actually a clearly defined notion of *asebeia* in Athenian law and that prosecution was only allowed in precisely defined cases.[15] This suggestion, however, has had little influence on prevailing opinion and rests on rather tenuous interpretations of the evidence. If it is correct, then, that a fundamental ambiguity seems to inhere in the Athenian conceptualization of impiety, what I would like to suggest is that this apparent plasticity has as much to do with certain general characteristics of the Athenian legal system as it does with the broadness of the term itself. Indeed, I would argue that the principal difficulties which arise in defining *asebeia* are inherent in the manner

---

[13] Lipsius (1984: 359–60), Derenne (1930).
[14] Thalheim (*RE*: 1530–1): "Die grosse Mannigfaltigkeit der Fälle, in denen diese Klage zur Anwendung kam, erklärt sich aus der Unbestimmtheit und Dehnbarkeit des Begriffes der *Asebie* selbst." [15] Rudhardt (1960).

in which Athenian legal norms were formulated, interpreted, and enforced, and thus apply, to a lesser or greater extent, to all offenses. Clarification of this point requires returning to the passage from Aristotle's *Rhetoric* discussed above.

In this important, yet neglected, text, Aristotle argues for the necessity for precise definitions of offenses (1374a). He asks how, without a definition of the offense, can one decide if a particular case of illicit intercourse falls under the law of adultery (*moicheia*), or theft of sacred property under the law of *hierosulia*? Such problems of statutory interpretation arise, he says, for example when a defendant admits that he had intercourse with a woman, but denies that it was adultery because he did not know the woman was married; or he admits that he stole certain property but denies that this constitutes *hierosulia* because the property was not consecrated. Only an authoritative and clear definition of *moicheia*, which explicitly states whether knowledge of the woman's marital state is a requirement for conviction, or one of *hierosulia* which indicates that the stolen property must be consecrated, concludes Aristotle, can resolve such questions. If one recalls the difficulties experienced in *Euthyphro* in arriving at anything like a definition of *asebeia*, and transposes such confusion into a judicial context, one can readily appreciate the force of Aristotle's observations.

Now the reason why Aristotle must argue for the need for defining offenses arises on the one hand from a characteristic which Athenian law shares with most pre-modern legal systems, and, on the other hand, from peculiarities all its own. It is common to almost all pre-modern statutory schemes that, with the frequent exception of homicide, criminal statutes do not define the offenses for which they provide procedures and penalties. Thus the typical formulation is: "If a man steals...," "If a man commits adultery...," "If some one commits hubris..."[16] As was seen above in Chapters 5–7, such formulations leave considerable room for speculation about whether or not a particular act in fact constitutes adultery or hubris. The underlying problem is that such statutes do not *define* the conduct which constitutes theft, or rape, or insult, but rather *assume* a definition which such words imply. Of course, many legal systems provided institutional mechanisms by which borderline or difficult cases could be discussed or judged, and definitions arrived at so that

---

[16] Homicide statutes sometimes do define the elements of the offense, on which see Fletcher (1978: Chapter 5).

they might be applied in particular cases. The Roman jurists, with their legal training and specialist literature, and the highly articulated Talmudic tradition of legal exegesis, represent perhaps the two most prominent instances of such institutions in the Western legal tradition.

In Athens, however, institutional arrangements hindered such developments. First, there is the absence of professional judges, jurists, or learned scribes. Public and private cases in Athens were judged by ordinary citizens who constituted both judge and jury. Thus these lay judges, sitting in mass courts of 500 or more, did not enjoy the benefits of authoritative interpretations of statutory provisions in particular cases. Further, they could neither debate the legal points of a case among themselves, nor institutionalize their decision through a written decision or learned commentary. They simply heard the arguments for both sides and then cast their votes. In short, the only applicable definitions of offenses were those residing in the collective consciousness of the community, as manifested through the 500 or more citizens who happened to be sitting on a particular day to hear a particular case. Once again, Plato's *Euthyphro* perhaps offers the best testimony for the kind of statutory definitions implied by such an arrangement. In short, the Athenian legal system remained institutionally incapable of providing an exact definition by which difficult cases could be decided; for example, whether a thief who had touched but not yet walked off with the property had committed theft, or whether prosecuting one's father for homicide constituted *asebeia*.

Another passage, despite its rhetorical overtones, adds an important dimension to the problem under consideration. In Lysias' oration *Against Alcibiades* the speaker reminds the judges that since this is the first such case to be decided they are acting not only as judges but also as lawmakers, for their decision will determine the attitude of the city for all time. This argument clearly implies a recognition that the decisions of the court in individual cases play a role in shaping the definition of offenses, albeit necessarily in a very imperfect way. The Athenians thus acknowledged the lawmaking aspect of judicial decisions, and when in a novel case a particular kind of conduct was found to constitute *asebeia*, such a finding may well have influenced or expanded the culturally implicit definition of the offense. On the other hand, in a case where the judgment was widely felt to be unjust, the decision may have operated to clarify the implicit cultural definition by restriction. In fact, in a "face-to-face" community where a significant proportion of the citizens served on the annual jury panel of 6000, the results of novel or striking cases would be common knowledge, and could encourage or discourage others who contemplated similar prosecutions. What all this implies for those uncertain categories of *asebeia* enumerated above is that the number of such passages which link such conduct to *asebeia* is testimony, although sometimes rhetorically distorted, to the un-articulated social norm which would determine the contours of the legal definition. Adequate evidence exists for actual cases of *asebeia* arising out of violations of festivals, temples, or cults, or, in the case of Socrates, out of the expression of impious beliefs. As to the other categories like perjury, or offenses against parents, in the absence of evidence for actual prosecutions one can only speculate as to the extent to which a particular statement accurately reflects the contemporary norms and values which gave the hollow statutes their content.

Against this background, we may now turn to the third question raised above, concerning the range of the application of the law of *asebeia* in the process of the enforcement of religious and social norms. That actions for impiety were brought for various kinds of conduct is clear from the historical record of actual prosecutions. That such prosecutions could have significant political overtones is likewise evident from the scandals of 415, involving the mutilation of the Herms and profanation of the Mysteries. Indeed, these events have received sufficient scholarly attention in accounts of the Pelopon-nesian War, Athenian religion, and the law of impiety. At issue here, however, is whether the law of impiety extended beyond such conduct, and included the realm of belief and opinion. Although in the nineteenth century Fustel de Coulanges (1980: 219–23) had already argued that the ideas of religious freedom and toleration were completely alien to the ancient city, modern scholarship has largely chosen a different standpoint from which to evaluate the social and political aspects of this offense.[17] On the whole, the general view seems to be that *asebeia* was properly concerned with ritual conduct and actions and not with beliefs. Seen from this perspective the trial of Socrates, the most famous stumbling block for

[17] In *Economy and Society*, Weber(1968: vol. I, 209) similarly argues that the modern notion of freedom of conscience was unknown in antiquity.

such an interpretation, is dismissed as an aberration, a "political case," arising out of a concatenation of unusual circumstances.[18]

Similarly, some scholars, relying on late sources, have portrayed a series of such "heresy trials"[19] in the second half of the fifth century, but they usually explain these events as products of the peculiar intellectual and political climate of that period.[20] I would argue, however, that such interpretations perhaps reflect more about the ideology which determines what modern scholars have wanted to find in democratic Athens than it does about the legal and social realities of which *asebeia* is a part. The fundamental question, in my view, is what sort of coercive political and social matrices underlay religious life in Athens, and I think it is far from clear that "Impiety did not normally lie for unorthodoxy of belief; Athens was singularly free of the unlovely habit of persecuting men for their opinions, and, indeed, it would be difficult to say what religious unorthodoxy at Athens consisted in."[21]

In fact, a variety of evidence suggests that belief was a central component of the Athenian notion of piety, and that the expression of contrary, unorthodox opinions about religious matters could fall well within the scope of *asebeia*. Thus Isocrates claims that in regard to the lies of the poets about the gods, both those who say such things and those who believe them commit *asebeia* (*Busiris* 40). He does not go on to recommend that they be prosecuted, but his characterization of their conduct reflects the way in which expression of belief alone could fall into the category of impious behavior. As appeared above, and as the trial of Socrates makes all too plain, there was no *legal* barrier to initiating such a prosecution. In the same vein, Lysias, in one of his orations (6.17), argues that "Diagoras committed impiety *in word* against sacred things and festivals which were alien to him, whereas Andocides committed impiety *in deed* towards those in his own city." Similarly, a passage in Aristotle's *Rhetoric* (1399b7) quotes Xenophanes as saying that "those claiming that the gods are born, commit impiety just as much

---

[18] See e.g. Allen (1980: 17–18): "Athenian religion was not a matter of creed and dogma, but of ritual observance, of *dromena*, things done, rather than *legomena*, things said ... Impiety, in short, normally lay for definite kinds of acts."   [19] Dodds (1971: 189).

[20] See e.g. Nilsson (1961: 791).

[21] Allen (1980: 17–18). For the position that democratic Athens was fundamentally tolerant and open in regard to expression of unorthodox opinion, see Dover (1976: 41), Lloyd (1979: 256–7) and Finley (1985b: 122). Ostwald (1986: Chapter 3) advances a different view of secularism and popular sovereignty in the Athenian state.

as those who claim that the gods die." The cultural definition of impiety at Athens clearly did not confine itself to the realm of ritual conduct and the like.[22]

As noted above, some scholars have sought to identify a sort of "witch-hunt" in the late fifth century. They have commonly sought evidence about the role of prosecutions for impiety in the suppression of unorthodox religious and intellectual thought in the supposed trials of Protagoras and Anaxagoras. These trials, and a decree about impiety supposedly brought forward by a man named Diopeithes, form the backbone of such interpretations. For example, these events play a central role in Dodds' portrayal of Athenian political intolerance, as well as in Finley's defense of Athenian institutions.[23] In the literature on Greek law, MacDowell's handbook on Athenian law bases its account of *asebeia* largely on these trials. However, the evidence for the trials and the decree comes exclusively from late sources, based solely upon evidence from Plutarch and Diogenes Laertius and *not* upon any contemporary Athenian evidence.[24] The decree of Diopeithes, for example, is attested only in Plutarch's life of Pericles, written many centuries after these events. And as to the trial of Anaxagoras, reading the historian Diogenes' puzzled description of all the various contradictory accounts of the trial should give one pause before accepting any of this tradition as true.

In my opinion, in the study of Athenian law, evidence from late authors like Plutarch should be ignored unless it is possible to examine critically their sources and unless we have corroborative evidence also from contemporary Athenian sources.[25] Apart from this radical methodological principle, this entire tradition of impiety trials rests upon an extremely fragile and dubious evidentiary foundation. Since Kenneth Dover has demonstrated this at length in his definitive treatment of the subject, there seems little point in rehearsing these issues yet again.[26] In short, it seems to me that in

---

[22] See also Xenophon, *Mem.* 1.1–1.2, *Apology* 24; Hyperides Fr. 14; Plato, *Euthyphro* 2b–c, 5a, 16a.   [23] Finley (1985b: 122), Dodds (1971: 189).

[24] MacDowell (1978: 200–1) bases his account solely upon evidence from Plutarch and Diogenes Laertius. He makes no argument for the reliability of these sources, nor does he account for the great variety of conflicting accounts about these trials. Dover's (1976: 29ff.) exhaustive treatment of the sources for these trials, and his conclusion that the whole tradition is without demonstrable foundation, are treated below in n. 26.

[25] I argue for this position at some length in Cohen (1989).

[26] The first account of the prosecution of Anaxagoras is found in Diodorus Siculus (12.39.2). Dover (1976: 29ff.) shows the unreliability of Ephorus' account, on which Diodorus

regard to legal matters one cannot rely upon these trials or upon the decree under which they supposedly occurred. This leaves us, apart from the passages mentioned above, with the Socratic tradition, which does offer sufficient relevant material.

There is no cause here to offer a comprehensive account of the trial of Socrates. The fundamental points to be made are that the definition of *asebeia* as unorthodox belief forms the basis of the trial in the accounts of Xenophon and Plato, and that this fact has been obscured somewhat by the desire of modern scholars to demonstrate the innocence of Socrates. Indeed, in doing so they have often confused two questions which must be clearly distinguished. The first is whether the accusations against Socrates accurately reflect his beliefs; this is a biographical question which is irrelevant for present purposes. The second question, which has all too often been obscured by the first, is whether such accusations, *if true*, could properly form the basis for a conviction for *asebeia* in Athenian law. A brief examination of the *Euthyphro* and the accounts of the trial in Xenophon and Plato will reveal that this latter question must be answered affirmatively.

Socrates, at the beginning of *Euthyphro*, characterizes the charges against him as based upon an accusation of innovating or inventing in regard to the gods and not recognizing/accepting the gods of the city (3b–c). The word used here for "recognize" or "accept" or "believe in" is *nomizein*, and some scholars have tried to show that here it means "honor" and refers to conduct and not to belief or opinion. *Nomizein* can have both meanings, but the context makes it clear that belief is what is at issue here.[27] Thus Euthyphro answers Socrates by saying that it is his *daemon*, the divine voice which speaks to him, which forms the basis of the accusation of innovating in

apparently based his narrative. Diogenes Laertius gives several versions, and, as Dover points out, neither Ephorus, Diogenes Laertius, nor Plutarch knew exactly what happened to Anaxagoras (1976: 31) – the accounts are varied and contradictory. Of course, one can speculate about the sources upon which such later authors based their accounts. This, however, would in no way mitigate the fundamental problem that there is hopeless disagreement among the late sources. Indeed, Diogenes Laertius explicitly acknowledges this. In such a situation, particularly where there is not a shred of Athenian evidence, arguments about what sources Plutarch had at his disposal, or how reliable, in general, this or that author is, seem unable to make up for our fundamental inability to provide concrete, specific criteria and evidence to evaluate which elements, if any, of this tradition are true. In such a situation, constructing interpretations of Athenian law upon such flimsy foundations seems unwise.

[27] Fahr (1969) exhaustively treats the range and meaning of *nomizein*. Cf. Ostwald (1986: 137), whose interpretation focuses on ritual acts.

regard to religious matters (3b–c). In the whole of the dialogue, this idea of innovative, non-traditional beliefs repeatedly characterizes the accusation against Socrates. Indeed, Socrates' own admission supports this characterization, when he says that he cannot accept the traditional stories about the gods, such as Zeus' wrongdoing against his father (5e–6d). Surely this statement refers to the charge that he does not accept/believe in the traditional gods. Socrates then, like Plato, departs from accepted beliefs in rejecting the tradition of the Olympian deities as a kind of quarrelsome *oikos*, and this rejection forms the basis for the charge of not accepting (*nomizein*) the gods of the city.

Euthyphro's discussion of *asebeia* is, of course, framed against the backdrop of Socrates' trial. Though the dramatic date of the dialogue places it just before the trial, Plato clearly intends the discussion of impiety to be read against the conviction of Socrates. Like his other dialogues devoted to this subject (*Apology* and *Phaedo*), *Euthyphro*, in part, serves as a defense of Socrates, part of Plato's martyrology.[28] It is striking, then, that in this long discussion of piety and impiety the one argument which is *never* made is that the accusation against Socrates is inappropriate. The whole argument here, and in Plato's and Xenophon's other works defending Socrates,[29] implicitly rests upon the supposition that the *legal* basis of the prosecution is legitimate; that if the facts were as alleged they would indeed constitute *asebeia*. The argument against the charges aims solely at showing that they misrepresent the beliefs and character of Socrates, who was actually extremely pious, virtuous, temperate, just, etc. This is especially significant in *Euthyphro*, where the dialogue focuses on the meaning of piety and impiety. Neither Socrates nor Euthyphro ever hint that innovating in regard to the gods, or rejecting traditional beliefs and myths, are not constitutive of *asebeia*; indeed, the whole argument assumes that they are.

The same point arises from the first part of Plato's *Apology* (23) where Socrates discusses his attitude towards speculation about the universe and the causes of natural phenomena.[30] Such scientific

---

[28] Xenophon's and Plato's accounts of Socrates' death closely fit the pattern of other martyrologies. Compare for example Zagorin's (1982: 149) account of Crespin's martyrology of the victims of Catholic persecution in France: "Reporting the ghastly scenes of executions along with touching human details, extracts of letters and conversations, and professions of belief, these narratives communicate the dedicated spirit of the men and women who accepted death for faith."

[29] See e.g. Xenophon, *Mem.* 1.1.5–6.   [30] Likewise in Xenophon's *Apology*.

inquiry seems to have generated considerable hostility in certain periods of the fifth century because of the challenge it represented to traditional religious beliefs. Thus Xenophon is insistent in pointing out that Socrates had no interest in such matters, and that when he did take an interest it was only to criticize them (*Mem.* 1.1.9–16). This defensive and contradictory formulation testifies to Xenophon's anticipation that ordinary Athenians were likely to associate such speculation with *asebeia*. It was, moreover, such ordinary citizens who served as judges in the courts and decided, without legal instruction, what was impious and what was not. Likewise, Plato's version of Socrates' defense reveals that such scientific skepticism could be regarded as impious. Thus Plato has Socrates ask one of his accusers "Do you suggest that I do not believe that the sun and moon are gods, as is the general belief of all mankind?" Meletus replies that Socrates, in fact, believes that the sun and moon are made of stone. Meletus thus implies that such beliefs support the accusation of impiety, and all Socrates can do is deny that he had such beliefs. Such passages employ the verb *nomizein* (e.g. 26d), demonstrating unequivocally that what is at stake is belief in the gods, not rituals, not actions, but conviction, opinion, and expression.

Thus, I would suggest, to dismiss Socrates' prosecution as a deviation, as a political case, and an exception or distortion of the law, is misguided. Personal and political motivations may have played an important role in the decision to prosecute. But this was likely the case with most prosecutions in the Athenian legal system. Such motivations in no way suggest the illegitimacy or inappropriateness of the legal basis of the prosecution. The impulse to discount the conviction of Socrates as an exception, a "political case," perhaps arises from a desire to buttress the case for his innocence, and to preserve some idyllic notions about Athenian democracy. The fact is, as Peter Garnsey has persuasively argued, that ancient societies were, on the whole, intolerant in religious matters.[31] Athens represents no exception to this generalization. Plato's *Euthyphro* makes clear that such charges of unorthodox belief were appropriate enough under the heading of *asebeia*. Plato, in his defense of Socrates through many dialogues, never argues otherwise, never suggests that this is an unjustifiable extension of the law. The same is true of Xenophon. For the Athenian courts that decided whether particular

[31] Garnsey (1983).

conduct fell within the purview of a statutory offense, not accepting the traditional beliefs about the gods could count as *asebeia* and could properly be punished as such.

The foregoing, if correct, casts new light on the provisions concerning religious conformity in Plato's *Laws* (907–9). This text sets out a comprehensive legislative scheme for the governance of an ideally constituted Greek polis. Its criminal statutes include a law of impiety which differs from that of Athens in distinguishing offenders of good character who act out of inner conviction, from those of depraved character who practice fraudulent arts of sorcery, prophecy, and the like. As at Athens, Plato's statute offers no definition of *asebeia*. The penalty for the second kind of impiety is life imprisonment in a severe penal institution (909b). The atheist of good character, however, must spend up to five years in a house of correction where he receives instruction and admonition. If, upon release, he again commits the same offense, he is punished with death (909a).

The standard interpretation of Plato's treatment of impiety in this dialogue is that it is a reactionary and totalitarian deviation from the way things were in tolerant democratic Athens. The main evidence for this is that, in the *Laws*, even the man who in good conscience refuses to accept the communal religious beliefs is put to death if he cannot be re-educated. Socrates, it is often pointed out, fell into precisely this category, so scholars conclude that late in life Plato's reactionary views even led him to betray his revered teacher. But in terms of the emphasis upon belief, and the underlying theory of the rights of the individual in religious matters, how different is Plato's legislation from Athenian law? Hasn't Plato just systematized the traditional notion of *asebeia* and fitted it into his larger political theoretical framework? As at Athens, in Plato's society the law of *asebeia* forbids the expression of impious beliefs. Indeed, both societies regard certain kinds of unorthodoxy in religious matters as a public offense which threatens the community as a whole, not as a matter of private conviction. In fact, Socrates himself did not challenge the rightness of the Athenian law of impiety under which he was indicted. In the *Crito* he explicitly states that the laws are just, and that he has been wronged not by them, but by the men who have prosecuted and convicted an innocent man (50a–2a, 54c). It misrepresents his views, in my opinion, to regard him as rejecting the principle that the polis has the right to govern the religious affairs of its citizenry. Plato's provisions on impiety, then, represent no fundamental departure from the principles and assumptions which inform the classical Athenian law of *asebeia*.

The foregoing discussion of Plato has only suggested a possible line of inquiry. To provide a definitive interpretation would require a full discussion of social and religious regulation in the *Laws* and the *Republic*. It seems, however, that one should pause before contrasting Plato's "totalitarian" conception of impiety with an "enlightened" Athenian one which may never have existed. The means of social control in Athens may have been quite different from the institutionalized form Plato envisioned. Nonetheless, as the trial of Socrates shows, Athenian legal institutions, by deriving the normative content of the statutes they enforced from community conceptions of proper and deviant conduct, provided an apt means for the regulation of religious unorthodoxy.

CHAPTER 9

The enforcement of morals

Chapters 4–8 have set out an interpretation of the means of social control by which Athenians regulated certain aspects of their sexual and religious activities. Building upon the preceding discussion of particular anthropological and social theoretical approaches to social action, this interpretation emphasized the complexity of the dynamic relation linking law, norms, practices, and ideology in a "face-to-face" society. Reversing this movement from a general discussion of social action to very specific inquiries into homo-eroticism, adultery, impiety, and the like, this concluding chapter shifts back to a more abstract level and attempts to draw together some of the strands of argument developed earlier. Specifically, it suggests a fundamental connection between the ideology of Athenian democracy and the patterns of social control elucidated above. Further, it addresses the theoretical question of the role of ambiguity, conflict, and contradiction in social ideologies and practices, and argues that such contradiction is not to be understood as an "aberration," but rather as a central characteristic of social systems and the practices which reproduce them.

I

Privacy, democracy, and the enforcement of morals

Modern Western political thought, conditioned by the liberal tradition, perceives an intimate connection between privacy and the enforcement of morals. Indeed, in contemporary American constitutional law, the development of a fundamental right to privacy has served as one of the principal means used to defeat legislation on moral matters. More broadly, Anglo-American jurisprudence has framed the debate over the enforcement of morals through the question of whether, to use the famous phrase of the British government's Wolfenden Report on homosexuality and prostitution, "There must remain a realm of private morality and immorality which is, in brief and crude terms, not the law's business." The publication of the Wolfenden Report in 1956, with its call for the decriminalization of homosexuality and prostitution, gave rise to a storm of controversy and debate. That debate underscored the centrality of the concept of privacy in determining whether or not there are realms of social life which must remain beyond the regulative reach of the criminal law. The Wolfenden Report's best known critic, Lord Devlin, maintains that there are *no* such limits:

Society is entitled by means of its laws to protect itself from dangers, whether from within or without... Societies disintegrate from within more frequently than they are broken up by external pressures. There is disintegration when no common morality is observed and history shows that the loosening of moral bonds is often the first stage of disintegration, so that society is justified in taking the same steps to preserve its moral code as it does to preserve its government and other essential institutions. The suppression of vice is as much the law's business as the suppression of subversive activities... There are no theoretical limits to the power of the State to legislate against treason and sedition, and likewise I think there can be no theoretical limits to legislation against immorality.[1]

The analogy of treason and immorality implies that *any* form of immorality can be punished, because immorality as such tends to undermine the "moral consensus" on which the health of the state depends. Clearly, this view tends to dissolve completely the distinction between public and private spheres of conduct, removing any limit that considerations of privacy might impose upon the state. Although Chapter 4 indicated the importance of this distinction in Athenians' conceptualization of their society, the attempt to obliterate that distinction in the name of preserving the social and political order is also not foreign to Athens. Indeed, I will argue that a major thrust of the arguments advanced against Athenian radical democracy focused upon precisely this issue. Concomitantly, proponents of radical democratic thought advanced the relative sanctity of the private sphere as one of the central tenets of their theory of government.

[1] Devlin (1965: 13-14).

Apart from the fact that recognizing this ideological conflict can broaden our understanding of Athenian politics and political philosophy, it is also of considerable theoretical interest. Athenians who concerned themselves with such matters appear to have conceived of the notion of a protected private sphere as one of the constitutive characteristics of a democratic society. For radical democrats, arguing for the right of the state to interfere in this area involved attacking the notion of democracy itself.[2] In classical Athens the valuation of democracy was a debatable issue. In contemporary political culture it is not, and those, like Devlin, who argue for the unlimited power of the state to regulate morals maintain that such regulation is compatible with democratic principles. The ideology of Athenian radical democracy, however, points up the essentially anti-democratic nature of any legislative ideal which undermines the barriers between legitimate public interest and purely private concerns.[3] Of course, Athenian democrats also held that conduct by public citizens which endangered the state should be prohibited.[4] They conceived, however, of the nature of such conduct in a way fundamentally different from their critics, taking great care to preserve the private sphere, while protecting the public interest.[5] The following analysis will draw upon the preceding discussions of the regulation of immorality at Athens, showing how Athenian law articulates this democratic view of public and private. Having established this legislative pattern, the focus will then shift to the ideology of Athenian democracy and its critics.[6]

---

[2] There were, of course, competing theories of democracy. Some theorists considered themselves critics of radical democracy, but proponents of a better form of democratic constitution. When I characterize Isocrates, for example, as a critic of Athenian democratic theory, I am referring specifically to his opposition to radical democratic theory, and, more particularly, to its position regarding state controls of morals, education, and private life. I do not mean to imply that the concept of democracy in Athenian society and thought is reducible to the conflict this chapter examines. Rather, it attempts to analyze a specific set of issues concerning the way in which radical democrats and their opponents (of various persuasions) conceptualized the general problem of state regulation of certain aspects of the lives of citizens.

[3] That is, such legislative ideals are characterized as anti-democratic, though their proponents might not consider them to be so.

[4] The trial of Socrates furnishes the most controversial example of this.

[5] Naturally, in practice Athenian democracy sometimes fell far short of this ideal. I am speaking here of ideology, of Athenians' self-conception.

[6] Caution is always required in starting with a modern problem and trying to see how it was dealt with in another historical or cultural setting. In regard to the relation of law, morality, and privacy at Athens, however, several reasons indicate that such concerns are not decisive. First, Chapter 4 has shown that a highly articulated sense of public and private

Public order and private vices

Viewing Athenian criminal legislation on sexual matters as a whole, the extant evidence strikingly testifies to its relative paucity. In comparison with the impressive lists of sexual offenses found, for example, in the Near Eastern codes, Athenian laws on such matters are relatively few, and, apart from adultery, primarily concern sexual transactions involving force, and the abuse of children. Noticeably absent from the Athenian codes[7] were the kind of statutes familiar to the Near Eastern and the late Roman and Canon Law traditions which straightforwardly provided that if a man had intercourse with an unmarried woman, another man, a beast, a close female relative, or a married woman, he was to be put to death. The Jewish and late Roman/Canon Law traditions criminalized such conduct because of religious and theological presuppositions which identified certain kinds of immoral conduct as a sin against God. In my opinion, Athenian law, on the other hand, in principle did not punish immoral behavior *as such*, rather only immoral behavior which either harmed those unable to protect themselves or directly transgressed against the clearly demarcated public sphere.

Recall, for example, the earlier discussion of Athenian legislation pertaining to homoerotic behavior. Among a plethora of provisions, no statute prohibited sexual intercourse between two male adults. Yet Chapter 7 clearly showed that accepting a passive homoerotic role could entail dishonor and social and legal censure for an adult Athenian male. As Aristotle comments, "Men are ashamed of suffering... those things which bring dishonor and disgrace. These are such things as providing a service with one's body or for shameful deeds, which includes submitting to an act of *hubris*; and also those things tending to licentiousness, whether voluntary or involuntary..." (*Rhetoric* 1384a13ff.). Further, it was shown that at least some Athenians considered that the Athenian man who uses another Athenian male "as a woman" (Xenophon, *Mem.* 2.1.30) also

---

as social and political categories existed at Athens. Next, this dichotomy of public and private was seen to be related to the realm of morality in a number of important ways (sexuality, friendship, Aristotle's independent spheres of justice, etc.). Finally, adultery law was conceived of as protecting the private sphere, and it is inconceivable that such a society, with a legal system seen as being organized around public wrongs and private wrongs, would not confront the problem of the relation of law and morals, no matter in what way it might have tried to resolve it.

[7] To the limited extent of our knowledge of Athenian legislation.

engaged in shameful behavior, despite his active role. This is also surely the case where the passive partner has reached a mature age: two middle-aged Athenian citizens found in sexual congress would both have been the object of censure and dishonor. The point here is that although such behavior could arouse the strongest terms of moral reprobation and censure, Athenian legislation does not penalize such moral "transgressions." Legal consequences do attach to conduct like prostituting a young boy, or prostituting oneself, but the nature of the consequences reveals the force of the public/private dichotomy in Athenian political and legal thought.

Aeschines' oration, *Against Timarchus*, catalogues all the Athenian statutes which define such behavior.[8] These provisions protect young boys from molestation at school and at the gymnasium, and provide that if any boy is hired out for homosexual activities by his father or guardian, both the father and the client are liable to the statutory penalties. Acting as a procurer for a free boy also seems punishable by death, and Aeschines also discusses the law of *hubris*, which prohibits the rape or violent sexual misuse of both children and adults (as well as, perhaps, seduction in the case of children). Finally, the laws provide that any Athenian citizen who prostitutes himself or allows himself to be kept by another man with whom he has a sexual relationship, cannot hold a wide range of religious, public, and administrative offices, or address the Assembly. If someone violates this prohibition, the penalty is death or disenfranchisement.

This is an imposing array of offenses, but it appears exclusively concerned to protect minors and to exclude from political life those who had accepted a sexual role unworthy of an Athenian citizen. Athenian law left males of all ages free to dispose of their bodies as they saw fit, despite the moral censure and disgrace which attached to sexual passivity and prostitution. Specifically, the law only punished those who contributed to the sexual activities which served to remove a man from the ranks of full citizens. Similarly, the Athenian men who had prostituted themselves as youths (or adults) were not tried and punished *unless* they engaged in political and religious activities from which the law debarred them. Only if they entered the prohibited spheres of public life did they become indictable under the law.[9] Thus Athenian legislation left a private

---

[8] Aeschines 1.7–8.
[9] Thus the man who prostitutes himself does not suffer the legal *penalty* of *atimia*. Prosecution can *only* ensue *after* he enters the prohibited public sphere. He does not *legally* lose vital civic

sphere of homoerotic activity unregulated, except where it infringed directly upon the public life of the city: when a boy lost his future rights of citizenship, or when a man who had shown himself to be unfit to participate in the management of the state's affairs nonetheless did so. The extent of the concern is demonstrated by the severity of the penalty.[10] The legal disabilities attaching to such behavior, if enforced, could have serious consequences for a political community like that of classical Athens, and these laws seem to have attempted to protect young boys and men, as far as was possible, from falling victim to them. It is frequently pointed out that the apparent uniqueness of the prosecution of Timarchus indicates that they were not regularly enforced, but we have no way of knowing how many men *refrained* from participating in political life because they had such a past.[11] In any event, the discussion in Chapter 7 of the complexity of the social norms and practices associated with homoeroticism reveals why such enforcement may have been either rare or unnecessary. More importantly, it underscores that in regard to the enforcement of morals, an examination of the relevant statutes only illuminates one dimension of the problem.

One response to the preceding argument might be to point immediately to adultery as a counter-example, for, after all, isn't adultery viewed today as a private matter which most modern states have declared to be beyond the scope of criminal law? While this objection might hold true for the way in which modern Western societies view adultery, it does not do justice to the way in which adultery was regarded in classical Athens (or in the Roman and Canon legal traditions).

Athenian criminal law, as Chapter 5 demonstrated, punished adultery under the law of *kakourgoi*, which provided that certain offenders could, *if taken in the act*, either be killed with impunity or

rights until convicted by a court of exercising them impermissibly. Until prosecution and conviction he merely exercises them at his risk. Thus impermissible homosexual conduct was not *punishable* by *atimia*, rather legal penalties only attach to the assumption of prohibited civic roles.

[10] As Dover (1978: 6) rightly suggests, a man who transgressed the rules of "legitimate eros detaches himself from the ranks of male citizenry and classifies himself with women and foreigners; the prostitute is assumed to have broken the rules simply because his economic dependence on clients forces him to do what they want him to do; and conversely, any male believed to have done whatever his senior homosexual partner(s) wanted him to do is assumed to have prostituted himself."

[11] We also have no way of knowing how many other prosecutions were brought under the statute.

summarily taken off to the Eleven for execution, unless they could successfully assert their innocence. Chapters 5 and 6 suggested further that adultery fell under this category of most serious offenses not because of its inherent heinousness, but because of the danger which the confrontation of the husband and the adulterer apprehended in the act represented for public order. Thus the wife taken in adultery suffers no criminal penalties, although the law commands her husband to divorce her. Whereas it is a feature of Roman, Byzantine, Biblical, and Assyrian law that the adulterer can only be killed if the adulteress is also put to death, in Athens the law provided only for the punishment of the man.[12] The point here is that adultery was seen, in its essence, as a violation of the house and its honor, an assault upon a protected sphere.[13] By Athenian standards this is a dangerous transgression against the social order, and one which could lead to feud and civic violence if not regulated by the law. Thus the law permits the males of a family to apprehend and execute (or take to the Eleven for summary execution) *only* those adulterers taken in the very act of intercourse. This exercise of *Hausgewalt* was limited to adulterers (or thieves so apprehended). After the fact, an adulterer against whom the most unequivocal evidence could be brought remained immune from this procedure.[14] The adulterer's offense, when he is taken in the act, is not conceptualized as a private dispute or a transgression against sexual norms, but rather as a dangerous violation of public order. The adulteress, on the other hand, who is not guilty of such a violation, remains beyond the boundaries of criminal prosecution, except in certain special circumstances which must now be examined.

It is striking that the woman, though certainly regarded as, morally speaking, more reprehensible than the adulterer (having betrayed her family and irremediably stained its honor), did not suffer similar legal penalties. She was barred from participating in public religious life, and the law also required that her husband divorce her, in part, no doubt, to prevent collusive allegations of

[12] This applied in Roman law to the lawful exercise of self-help by the father. The husband, on the other hand, could kill neither of the adulterous pair, except that he could kill the adulterer if he was of sufficiently low status. See D.48.5.24–5.

[13] See Lysias 1.36.

[14] This explains, in the case of theft, for example, the often remarked discrepancy between the summary execution of the thief, as opposed to the relatively trivial double fine in the case of a normal prosecution when the thief was not taken in the act. See Cohen (1983: Chapter 3).

adultery.[15] Unlike in Roman law, however, no legal provision prevented her from remarrying.[16] The most significant feature of this law for present purposes is, of course, that aspect which it shares with the law regarding homosexuality described above. Like the man who has prostituted his body, the adulteress is not punished directly by the law, as is the adulterer, but is rather excluded from that sphere of civic life which is the equivalent of politics for men. Again, like the male prostitute (or other homosexuals falling under its provisions), the law only punishes her directly when she defies this ban and intrudes upon the prohibited public sphere. Our sources leave us in no doubt that such a woman is viewed as defiled and utterly morally reprehensible (at least according to "official" morality), but the law confines itself to ensuring that, as the speaker in *Against Neaera* (86) puts it, "Our sanctuaries be kept free from pollution and profanation." In sum, while the adulterous act of the male intruder is seen as more than a private sexual transgression, but rather a flagrant and dangerous violation of house, family, and honor, the adulterous conduct of the wife, on the other hand, merely disqualifies her from that sphere of public life appropriate to women. Like the male citizen prostitute, she has rendered herself unfit for participation in civic life, but only suffers physical punishment if she ignores the prohibition against such participation.

The argument advanced here concerning immorality, privacy and the criminal law at Athens finds further support in the area of incest. In Greece, the Oedipus tale, and its dramatic representations, make clear enough that intercourse between mother and son was regarded as a religious abomination and morally reprehensible in the highest degree. Other Athenian sources indicate that the incest taboo, as one would expect, extended to fathers and daughters, brothers and sisters, and mothers-in-law as well.[17] Further relationships may or may not have been included within the social incest taboo, but that sexual relations or marriage between persons within these degrees of relationship were regarded as serious moral transgressions seems quite certain. Among the categories of voluntary sexual behavior, incest is perhaps the offense most universally

---

[15] I do not mean to imply that these are insignificant penalties. Chapter 6 demonstrates the significance of public religious life for Athenian women.

[16] Chapters 5 and 6 present the evidence which shows that such remarriages seem to have occurred. On Athenian remarriage, see Thompson (1972).

[17] See e.g. Aristotle, *Politics* 1262a25ff.

prohibited in ancient, primitive, and modern legal systems. What is extraordinary about Athenian law, is that this does not seem to be the case, at least in the classical period.

Plato's *Laws* and Xenophon's *Memorabilia* provide the most unequivocal evidence on this point. Although I am well aware of the dangers of inferring from Plato's legislation to Athenian law, in this case there seems to be no real problem, for the discussion in *The Laws* focuses first upon how people in actual society, as opposed to Plato's imaginary state, are disposed towards this matter. As the Athenian interlocutor says (838),

We are aware, of course, that even nowadays most men, in spite of their general disregard for the law, are very effectively prevented from having relations with people they find attractive. And they don't refrain reluctantly either, they're more than happy to... when it's one's brother or sister whom one finds attractive. And the same law, *unwritten though it is*, is extremely effective in stopping a man sleeping – secretly or otherwise – with his son or daughter.

He goes on to say that obedience to these unwritten laws is maintained without sanction, by means of socialization. People grow up hearing

the doctrine that these acts are absolutely unholy, an abomination in the sight of the gods, and that nothing is more revolting. We refrain from them because we never hear them spoken of in any other way... when we see a Thyestes on the stage, or an Oedipus... we watch these characters dying promptly by their own hand as a penalty for their crimes.

A passage in Xenophon's *Memorabilia* (4.4.19–22) explicitly supports this interpretation, for the rule that "Parents never have sexual intercourse with their children" is used as an example of unwritten law. Further, the passage explicitly contrasts the punishments imposed by the gods for violations of unwritten law with the penalties for other offenses ordained by man. In addition, there are two further passages in the orators which offer indirect confirmation, although I would not want to press them very hard. The accusation against Callias in Andocides' *On the Mysteries* (124–6) shows that in Athens it was thought an abomination to have sexual relations with one's mother-in-law, and, given the detailed description of Callias' act and its consequences, one could expect here the traditional reference to the penalties with which such behavior is punished, if there were any. As one might have expected on the basis of the passages from Plato and Xenophon, however, the only source of potential fear for Callias seems to be religious, namely from the Two Goddesses. The other passage, from Lysias (14.29), provides similar, albeit weak, evidence for the brother–sister relation.

One might, of course, object that although no legal statute prohibited incest, the unwritten laws were enforced by other means. In the first place, whether or not this might have been the case for the fifth century is an open question, for, to my knowledge, no concrete evidence exists for that period. In any event, a reform of the Athenian law codes in 403/2 specifically prohibited the enforcement of any unwritten law. The only other possible mode of prosecution would have been an action for impiety, but this might as well have run up against the prohibition against unwritten laws. In light of the evidence cited above and the absence of *any* known prosecutions for incest, this possibility appears rather remote. What seems more likely is that, as Plato suggests, the weight of socialization and the force of social disapproval fulfilled their task, at least in most cases. For the rest, it seems that such consensual unions would have remained beyond the scope of the criminal law (except, perhaps, in certain cases involving minors).

In regard to sexual transgressions, then, Athenian law seems to limit itself to two kinds of regulation. Sexual transactions accomplished by force, or against minors, were punished outright. Here, the laws against *hubris*, the prostitution of minors, and so on, define public offenses thought to deserve the severest penalties. On the other hand, consensual sexual conduct between adults remained unregulated except where it transgressed public order. Thus behavior regarded as purely private immorality, such as homoerotic acts between adult male citizens, incest, or the adultery of women, may have aroused social censure, but did not give rise to public prosecutions. On the other hand, adulterers taken in the act were liable to summary punishment, and men or women barred from certain public spheres might suffer if they ignored the ban.

This interpretation comports well with the general distinction Demosthenes makes between private lawsuits and public prosecutions. Why, he asks, if someone defrauds another on a contract for a deposit, does the law allow only double compensation to the injured party, whereas in the case of theft there is an additional fine to the public treasury? His answer is "that the legislator regarded every deed of violence as a public offense also committed against

those who are not directly concerned" (*Against Meidias* 44–5).
According to Demosthenes' analysis, serious transgressions in the
private sphere do not fall within the scope of the criminal law
because, there being no element of force, violence, or coercion,[18] they
do not involve harm to the community as a whole. In another
passage he refers again to the contrast between laws regarding
private as opposed to public life, and asserts that, whereas the laws
regarding private relations are characterized by being benevolent,
gentle and tolerant, those regarding relations with the state are, and
ought to be, harsh and pre-emptive (*Against Timocrates* 192–3).

The case of impiety, however, serves as a reminder that this
delineation of public and private realms followed different contours
from those indicated by the modern liberal tradition. Since Kant,
the principle that moral and religious matters are regulated *in foro
interno* has enjoyed increasing ascendancy in Western societies. In
classical Athens, while belief alone may not have presented an object
of legislative or judicial concern, the expression of unorthodox
religious belief could well do so. The action for impiety reminds us
that Athenians, particularly in times of social crisis, might consider
many aspects of religious practice and belief as intimately connected
to the public order. Socrates' conviction under this statute testifies
that although the dichotomy of public and private informed
Athenian political ideology and practice, the conceptualization of
what activities pertained to each sphere might differ considerably
from modern convictions. The following section will pursue this
question of political ideology in greater detail.

Privacy and the rule of law

In the Athenian view democracy is made possible by the rule of law.
That the democratic state will perish if the law is undermined is a
commonplace in the Athenian orators.[19] Indeed, the laws are seen as
guaranteeing that liberty which is thought to be the essential
characteristic of life in a democratic state, a characteristic which
many Athenians thought of as a civic virtue peculiar to their polis.
Of particular significance for present purposes, this liberty closely
connects to the conceptualization of a protected private sphere. The

---

[18] Cf. Aristotle's classification of voluntary and involuntary transactions in *N.E.* 1131a–2a.
[19] E.g. Demosthenes 21; 25.26ff.

laws, then, define and limit the right of the law to interfere in the lives of citizens by delineating areas of public interest and private concern (of course, the Athenian orators show how these categories were fluid enough to be manipulated for rhetorical and political purposes). In the extant fourth-century political and legal orations, perhaps our best evidence for political ideology, this liberty (*eleutheria*) has two aspects. The first is free speech (*parresia*), and what is meant here is the right of all citizens to participate in the affairs of the state, to address the Assembly, etc. Some passages also characterize this freedom of speech as an attribute of Athenian private life as well.[20]

The second aspect of liberty finds expression in the sentiment that under the radical democracy each man lives as he chooses, subject only to the pressures of social, as opposed to legal, norms. This involves the right of each citizen to conduct his private life as he sees fit, provided he obeys the laws of the city which protect public order and regulate various aspects of men's relations with one another. Thus Demosthenes (25.25) reports that Aristogeiton argued that "in a democracy a man has a right to do and say whatever he likes as long as he does not care what reputation such conduct will bring him, and that no one will kill him at once for his wrongdoing." This characterization is so widespread in our sources that there is little doubt that the phrase about doing what one pleases was a political slogan used by proponents and critics alike.[21] At the level of ideology, Thucydides' version of Pericles' Funeral Oration (2.37) furnishes the classical statement of the relationship of Athenian democratic politics to tolerance in private life:

Our constitution is called a democracy because power is in the hands not of a minority but of the whole people. When it is a question of settling private disputes, everyone is equal before the law ... And just as our political life is free and open, so is our day-to-day life in our relations with each other. We do not get in a state with our neighbor if he enjoys himself in his own way, nor do we give him black looks which, though they do no real harm, still do hurt people's feelings. We are free and tolerant in our private lives; but in public affairs we keep to the law.

[20] Demosthenes 9.3; Plato, *Republic* 344a; [Xenophon], *Ath. Pol.* 1.2.
[21] Demosthenes 22.51; Lysias 25.33; Isocrates, *Panath.* 131, *Areop.* 20; Aristotle repeatedly uses this phrase as a way of characterizing democratic societies, e.g., in *Politics* 1310a30, quoting Euripides' expression of the same sentiment, and 1319a; 1316b25; 1317b10; Plato, *Republic* 557b, 560–1, 563b, *Laws* 700a; also, democracy was considered *praoteros*, which, in this context, it would be not unreasonable to translate as "more tolerant."

The crucial role of the rule of law as the foundation of democracy often provides the focus of comparison with other forms of constitution, and particularly with those two which Athenians often characterized as lawless: tyranny and oligarchy.[22] Isocrates (*Paneg.* 113), for example, comments that under the tyrannical reign of the Thirty at the end of the Peloponnesian War, no Athenians were far enough from public life to be safe. Aristotle (*Politics* 1313bff.) also describes tyranny as preserving itself by preventing private associations and spying upon men's private lives in a variety of ways. Thus descriptions of tyranny and oligarchy typically characterize them as states in which law does not restrain those who hold power from using naked force to satisfy their personal desires for women, boys, money, or land. Such rulers enter men's houses at will, robbing, kidnapping, or killing to get what they want.[23] Indeed, in Plato's *Gorgias*, Polus' and Callicles' characterizations of the enviable life of the tyrant emphasize precisely this total lack of restraint in fulfilling one's desires.[24] The tyrant, in their view, must be the happiest of men because he can rape, rob, murder, and banish at will.

This autocratic terror describes the state of affairs which obtains when the law does not provide a sphere of security where the state may not intrude. In the Athenian democratic view, tyranny and oligarchy are antithetical to the rule of law. Thus Athenians' descriptions of their immediate experience of such political lawlessness under the terror of the Thirty Tyrants employ just such terms: the Thirty forcibly entered men's homes, stole their wealth, dragged them off for execution without trial, etc.[25] This point must be stressed, for whereas under oligarchy or tyranny law does not restrain the violation of the private sphere and the sanctity of the house, democracy, its proponents claim, places these realms beyond the reach of public officials.[26]

Thus the role of law, according to the Athenian conception of radical democracy, is not to enforce an *intrusive* order regulating all aspects of life, but rather to provide a *delimiting* order which defines the boundaries beyond which the state or private individuals (hubris, calumny, assault, theft) may not enter one's private domain (house, sexuality, family, friendships, property, livelihood, etc.). The demo-

---

[22] See e.g. *Politicus* 291dff.   [23] Plato, *Republic* 343ff., *Gorgias* 471–3; Lysias 12.
[24] *Gorgias* 471ff., 490ff.   [25] Isocrates, *Pan.* 113; Lysias 12, 8–17, 29–33.
[26] Demosthenes, 18.132, 20.15, 22.52, 24.197; and cf. 18.111–12, 123, 19.255ff, 22.62–3; Aristotle *N.E.* 1180a, *Politics* 1317b, 1319b23ff.

cratic polis, then, does not attempt to root out immorality, but rather to keep its harmful effects out of the public sphere. This interpretation finds striking confirmation in Demosthenes' explanation of the law permitting the prosecution of those citizens who have prostituted themselves, but nonetheless enter political life. Demosthenes argues that this law is characteristic of democratic, as opposed to oligarchic, legislation, for it does not seek to *punish* the behavior of such men, but instead aims at preventing corrupt citizens from influencing political life. As he specifically says, such a prohibition is not onerous, "and he [the lawgiver] could have established many harsher penalties *if his purpose had been to punish such men*" (*Against Androtion*, 30–1, my emphasis).

The critique of radical democracy and the enforcement of morals

From our perspective, the Athenian laws which regulated many aspects of social and religious life may appear as extensively interfering in the private lives of citizens. What matters, however, is that Athenian radical democrats apparently felt that the legal order nonetheless preserved a sacrosanct private sphere and that critics of radical democracy clearly felt that private life remained too free. In particular, their concern centered on sexuality, the family, and education as related areas which the state should subject to more stringent discipline. In examining the discourse of democracy's critics, the discussion will focus upon three representative thinkers and texts: Isocrates' *Areopagiticus*, Aristotle's *Politics*, and Plato's *Laws*. It is convenient to begin with Isocrates, if only because his argument presents the fewest complexities.[27]

To begin with, Isocrates characterizes Athenian radical democracy as a state where freedom means lawlessness, freedom of speech is mistaken for equality, and license "to do what one pleases" is taken for happiness.[28] From this critique he then moves to a discussion of the well-governed state, validating his views by projecting them backwards onto the glorious Athenian past. He begins by suggesting that in the past the state was wisely governed because there was a harmony between good government and good

---

[27] I do not mean to imply here that Isocrates, Aristotle, and Plato all shared the same opinions about democracy in general. Rather, the argument focuses upon their response to particular propositions which critics and proponents alike associated with Athenian radical democracy in this period. [28] *Areopag.* 20, and cf. *Panath.* 131.

conduct in private life (*Areopag.* 28). He goes on to suggest four reasons for this:

(1) supervision of males not only during boyhood, but also manhood. In earlier times, he claims, the institution of the Areopagus supervised morals and behavior, unlike in contemporary Athens (*Areopag.* 37).

(2) These Athenians recognized, he continues, that virtue does not come from a multitude of detailed laws, but from the habits of everyday life. Too many laws signify moral degeneracy, for it is by good morals, not by many laws, that a state is well governed. Therefore, the task facing Athens is to produce moral rather than lawless citizens (*Areopag.* 40).

(3) The state should exercise care over all citizens, but particularly the young. Vocations should be assigned, not left to individual choice.

(4) The former political institutions supervised the lives of all citizens. They brought the disorderly before the Council, which punished them *as they saw fit, not always waiting until they broke the law to punish them* (*Areopag.* 47).

This earlier, "stricter constitution" (*akribestera politeia*, 57, as Isocrates calls it) clearly reveals the way in which the autonomy of the private sphere (expressed in the phrase "live as you like") represents one of the fundamental defects of Athenian democracy. The only remedy requires placing the private sphere fully within the supervision of the state. Privacy is thus seen as a barrier which must be removed. It is of particular significance that the rule of law, which democratic apologists saw as the foundation of democracy, is dispensed with. Wrongdoers are punished as those in power see fit, sometimes even when they have not committed an offense but are thought likely to do so.[29] In short, in his *Areopagiticus*, Isocrates argues for a close supervision of morals and private behavior by an aristocratic council. He extols the day when the Council of the Areopagus had acted as an all-powerful moral censor, in contrast with the contemporary degeneracy and corruption brought about by the radical democracy: "The Athenians of that day were not watched over by many preceptors during their boyhood only to be

---

[29] Isocrates' proposal seems to emulate the perceived powers of the Spartans' ephors to punish any citizens they considered to be guilty of wrongdoing.

allowed to do what they liked when they attained their manhood; on the contrary, they were subjected to greater supervision in the prime of their vigour than when they were boys" (37).

In his *Politics*, Aristotle follows a similar strategy. Democracy, he says, has a false conception of liberty. Democrats, he claims, imagine that liberty consists in doing whatever one pleases, so that in a democratic state everyone lives as he likes (1310a30). A democratic constitution, he continues, accordingly attracts many supporters because it leaves private life unregulated, allowing lawlessness (*anarchia*) among slaves, women, and children, and letting all live as they like (1319b30ff., and cf. 1319a). This state of affairs, he argues, endangers the state, for through their private lives (*dia tous idious bious*) men cause revolutions. A well-governed state, then, must appoint magistrates to inspect whether the citizens' way of life is unsuited to the respective form of constitution (1308b20). A poorly governed state, on the other hand, shows no concern for the moral character of individuals, letting them live as they please. Thus the well-governed state considers civic virtue and vice. This follows from the principle that what characterizes human, as opposed to animal, associations is that man alone perceives good and bad, just and unjust. Moreover, it is unanimity in regard to these things which makes a household or a city (*he de touton koinonia poiei oikian kai polin*, 1253a16).

For Aristotle, what follows from all this is that the well-governed state regulates private life through the law. In the *Nicomachean Ethics* he asks how, given that the many act rightly only out of fear of penalties, the state is to become virtuous. Like Plato, he believes that education furnishes the only means for achieving such virtue, and so he argues that education must be regulated by law. This is the same position he takes in the *Politics* (1337ff.), where he argues that education should be public and not private (*koinen kai me kat' idian*).[30] Further, in the *Nicomachean Ethics*, he continues that education in virtue must not stop with youth, and the practices of adults must therefore also be regulated by law. Indeed, such regulation must concern citizens' entire lives, for the many are more amenable to

---

[30] Recall the debates in the nineteenth century in which liberals like Mill argued that liberty required that education be private; see also Donzelot (1979) on this issue of state interference with the family in the nineteenth century. It is not insignificant that the reason that Aristotle advances to support this educational policy is the claim that citizens belong to the polis and not to themselves.

punishment than to moral ideals. Sparta, this discussion in the *Ethics* concludes, is the only state whose laws properly regulate upbringing and practices, whereas in other states each lives as he likes, like the Cyclops of Homer's Odyssey, each laying down the law for his children and spouse.

Having set out this striking critique of the lawlessness and anarchy of democratic cities, where citizens can "live as they like," the *Politics* describes the pattern of regulation which should be employed in the ideal state. Fundamentally, this involves the elimination of the private sphere through scrupulous legal regulation of every major aspect of sexuality, education, and the family. The contrast with the patterns of Athenian legislation sketched above should be readily apparent. First of all, Aristotle argues, there must be magistrates to supervise those whose lives center on the private sphere: women, children, and slaves:[31]

A Controller of children, a Controller of women, and officers with sovereign powers to discharge responsibilities similar to these, are an aristocratic feature (of constitutions), not a democratic one, for in a democracy who could prevent the wives of the poor from going out?[32]

Next, all aspects of marriage must be regulated: age, choice of partners, manner and time of intercourse, age of children, etc. The law must also provide that deformed children be exposed. The number of children is to be limited, and if custom prohibits exposure, then abortion is required by law. During the age of procreation marital fidelity is to be required, and a married man who has intercourse with another woman or man during this period is to be punished. Education is to be taken over by the state, and even indecent talk and pictures are to be prohibited lest they harm children. Once again, Aristotle presents the antithesis of democratic tolerance ("live as you like") through the comprehensive regulation of the private sphere by means of the legal enforcement of morals so as to achieve that unanimity in regard to good and bad, just and unjust, which is indispensable for the well-governed city. Thus the relative autonomy of the private sphere represented, for proponents and critics alike, one of the fundamental features of Athenian democracy. For those, like Plato and Aristotle, who thought this form of government disastrous, this autonomy of the private was an obstacle that had to be removed. Indeed, in his last dialogue, *Laws*,

[31] *Politics* 1269b–70a, 1299b19, 1300a5–10, 1323a.   [32] *Politics* 1300a4f.

Plato explicitly addresses the need to overcome privacy in all its aspects if the good society is to flourish.

Plato's last dialogue, *Laws*, is a massive treatise on political theory, which sets out and defends a detailed constitution for a model state. In many significant respects it represents a major rethinking of many of the principles advanced in his *Republic*. One strand of thought which the two dialogues share, however, involves the thoroughgoing regulation of the private sphere of the family, marriage, education, and sexuality. In this, as in many other areas, *Laws* provides a far more detailed plan for such regulation than did the *Republic*. Indeed, in *Laws* control of religion and morals forms part of the detailed legislative program designed to ensure order and stability in the state.

The Cretan city Plato imagines in *Laws* regulates the economic, social, political, religious, and familial lives of its citizens from birth to death. Like the *Republic*, it places tremendous emphasis upon education and socialization. This emphasis distinguishes Plato's approach to social control and the enforcement of morals from Aristotle's. Indeed, perhaps no other political theorist has so fully understood the implications of a multi-dimensional conceptualization of order as Plato. In particular, this is a key to an understanding of *Laws*, and a factor which elevates that work far beyond Aristotle's *Politics* as a work of constructive political theory. More specifically, Plato and Aristotle implicitly rely upon different theories of the way in which a state can maintain and enforce normative orders. Aristotle's perspective largely centers on the effect of external coercion operating through law and other enforcement institutions. He recognizes the internal perspective on order, but thinks it likely to be ineffective in maintaining the state against the disorderly many. Therefore, he concludes in *Politics*, the state must regulate all aspects of life through law and magistrates since unregulated socialization is unlikely to produce virtue (i.e. obedience).

Plato, on the other hand, adopts a multi-dimensional perspective in which the internal aspect of normative order is dominant. Committed to moral voluntarism as he is, he believes that the law fails when it must resort to pure coercion. Hence, in *Laws*, only as a last resort is the ineducable offender simply eliminated from the community: he cannot function as part of a moral society. As the discussion on impiety in Chapter 8 revealed, Plato places great weight upon the education of the impious man of good character. Such a person possesses the moral potential for citizenship, and only if he commits the same offense again after his period of re-education is he to be executed. The offender of degenerate character, however, receives, on his first offense, a sentence of life imprisonment in complete isolation from the rest of the community (*Laws* 908–9). The creation of the internal order which makes, for Plato, this moral society possible is the task of education, understood in the broadest sense. The law itself reflects this perspective, for in *Laws*, each statute begins with a preamble designed to persuade the citizens of the importance of the provision. Plato assigns great importance to such institutions as the preambles, for they separate true law and good government from mere coercion and despotism. For Plato, in the good state law should need to serve only an educational function. Punishment, the secondary, coercive aspect of law, prunes the community of those diseased members whom education cannot reach. Above all, however, education and law must inform every aspect of social life. No private sphere can remain unregulated, for, on Plato's view, it is here that the state stands or falls.

II

Norms, contradiction, and social control

The foregoing sections have explored the legal regulation of the private sphere at Athens, as well as democratic and anti-democratic ideological perspectives on such regulation. As Chapters 2–8 made clear, however, this "legal" perspective on the regulation of social life addresses only one dimension of social control. These earlier chapters emphasized the complex interaction of normative structures and social practices in "face-to-face" societies. The law, it was seen, represents only one pole of social normativity, and indeed, a pole which often has little to do with actual social norms and patterns of social control. It was further argued that any view of social control which accounts for such processes primarily in terms of coercive force imposed from above through legal institutions, cannot do justice either to the role of agency in reproducing the social system of which legal institutions are but a part, or to the strategic, manipulative nature of the social action which is the medium of social reproduction. Finally, through examining the legal and extra-legal parameters of social control as they inform social practices related to various forms of illicit sexuality, it appeared that the normative systems which define such parameters are shot through with ambiguity, conflicts, and contradictions. Indeed, it is precisely these qualities which furnish individuals with the opportunity to manipulate the standards of their culture in pursuit of their own ends. The result cannot be described in terms of a neat set of "rules" which somehow "govern" (i.e. determine) social life. The remaining part of this section will briefly attempt to draw together some of these strands of argument by relating them to the attempts of anthropologists and sociologists to understand the role of contradiction and ambiguity in social life.

Anthropological theory provides a number of different models for understanding the nature of contradiction. The earlier discussion of Malinowski's work among the Trobrianders provides perhaps the most simplistic formulation of the problem. To Malinowski, the "values" of the culture represented a coherent set of norms, but individuals often chose to ignore or violate these norms in actual life. This way of understanding the discrepancy between what individuals say their culture requires of them and how they in fact behave continues to influence anthropological thought.[33] Bourdieu has perhaps developed this line of interpretation in the most sophisticated way. He also emphasizes the difference between official and unofficial, practical versions of events (e.g. marriages, insults, etc.). On his account, however, "official" or "ideal" norms do not enjoy the preferred ontological status seemingly assigned them by Malinowski and others. For Bourdieu they do not constitute a logically coherent system of rules, and they have no objective existence outside of their instantiation in the interpretative and manipulative practices which reproduce them. Understanding this dynamic explains the apparent conflict between the objective rules adduced by anthropologists ("cross-cousins must marry") and the frequency with which they are "violated."[34]

[33] Cf. Bailey (1971), and Blok (1969: 7). Tentori (1976: 284) describes the contrast in the southern Italian town of Matera between what he calls the formal standard, which a show is made of respecting, and the "real standard" which is reflected in practice, though it often contradicts the formal one. See also Brandes (1981) and Comaroff and Roberts (1981).

[34] Bourdieu (1977: 37): "The ethnologist is in a particularly bad position to detect the distinction between official and practical kinship: as his dealings with kinship...are restricted to cognitive uses, he is disposed to take for gospel truth the official discourse which informants are inclined to present to him as long as they see themselves as spokesmen mandated to present the group's official account of itself. He had no reason to perceive that

Viewed in this way, behavior appears as more than rule-determined adherences and violations. As Goffman argues, "In general then, we can say that a rule tends to make possible a meaningful set of non-adherences, only one of which is an infraction, the others being functions made possible by our ability to discriminate (and to trust others to discriminate) among types of non-adherences."[35] Bourdieu, following a similar interpretation, offers an example that well illustrates the point.

The completion of the construction of a house in Kabylia is always concluded by a meal in honor of the mason. The meal, according to Bourdieu, symbolizes the (in the ideal) non-economic relation of the parties whereby the labor is seen as an unsolicited gift. One mason, however, refused the meal and demanded payment in lieu of it:

Whereas the greatest indulgence was accorded to the subterfuges used by some to minimize the cost of the meals... – a departure from principles which at least paid lip-service to their legitimacy – the reaction could only be scandal and shock when a man took it upon himself to declare that the meal had a cash equivalent, thus betraying the best-kept and worst-kept secret (one that everyone must keep), and breaking the law of silence which guarantees the complicity of collective bad faith in the good faith economy.[36]

Particularly interesting here is the notion of "collective bad faith" which enables the complex of behaviors associated with simultaneous norm-validation and norm-non-adherence to exist. As seen above, such a pattern seems to inform illicit homoerotic and adulterous conduct in classical Athens. The greatest anger is reserved for those who betray, i.e. expose the truth of, the system which keeps the veil of propriety (e.g. chaste love, unconsummated wooing, intercrural intercourse, etc.) in place: hence the particular importance that one's public behavior only admit of inferences indicating that the norms are being adhered to, even (or especially) in cases where everyone knows they are not. This "management of appearances" becomes particularly difficult in societies like classical Athens, or the rural Greek villages studied by Handman and du Boulay, where the lie, slander, and secrecy are the rule, and the community is often anxious to place the worst possible interpretation upon behavior. Bourdieu's analysis aptly describes the way in which such a system,

he is allowing the *official definition* of social reality to be imposed on him – a version which dominates or represses other definitions." See also his discussion of the Kabyle calendar (1977: 106).   [35] Goffman (1971: 61, n. 54).   [36] Bourdieu (1977: 173).

built upon contradiction, collective lies, euphemism, and the repression of the conflicts generated by these, can maintain itself.

Useful though such an analysis may prove in underscoring the importance of a voluntaristic view of agency in any account of social action, other interpretations can also help illuminate the dynamics of social control. Gellner's account of North African societies, for example, argues for just the kind of normative multi-valence which, I argued above, informs Athenian practices relating to sexuality: "Accounts of societies in terms of the beliefs and values of their members often assume that each member has *one* set of beliefs about the world, and *one* set of values. This seems to be a major mistake."[37] Gellner's discussion emphasizes the way that tribesmen, for example, can acknowledge the validity of competing sets of tribal and non-tribal values: "They recognize the standards of purity in terms of which their own tribal society fails, yet at the same time they wish to remain as they are, indefinitely. They are quite aware of the conflict and contradiction, yet at the same time the contradiction is not articulated clearly or stressed. It is there, yet is clouded in decent obscurity."[38] Athenian attitudes towards homoeroticism and women encompass similar contradictory sets of beliefs and values. While such implicit conflicts and ambiguities may have remained in "decent obscurity" in ordinary life, they were systematically brought to light by figures like Plato, Euripides, and Aristophanes. Clearly, many plays of these two dramatists would have failed their impact if the cultural contradictions and conflicts about women and homoerotic love which they exploited were not already widely recognized. Also, recall again Pausanias' tortured account of the "many-hued" nature of Athenian attitudes towards legitimate and illegitimate eros.

In her fine account of secrecy, sexuality, and social control in rural Greece, Handman argues for a differentiated account of the status of the sexes, "under the rubric of a morality, or rather of several moralities which are often contradictory and which one can manipulate."[39] In the end, she concludes that her village is a "paragon of ambiguity," though her explanation of the ambiguity is particularistic rather than general. The failure to recognize the

---

[37] Gellner (1981: 114). [38] Gellner (1981: 116).

[39] Handman (1983: 191). On the manipulability of the normative repertoire, and the relation between rules and individuals' interpretation and manipulation of them, see also Comaroff and Roberts (1981).

general significance of such ambiguity and conflict accounts for the difficulty which historians often experience in explaining the contradictions which they find everywhere in their sources. Such conflicts too often have to be explained away with one source being "correct" and the other being "inaccurate," or "unrepresentative," on the assumption that there was really only one Athenian view of women or homoeroticism, or that the "status" of women is a singular objective reality, a "right" answer or "historical truth" waiting to be discovered. As Euripides, Aristophanes, and Plato make clear, however, Athenians themselves had a far more differentiated view of their culture and the conflicts, ambiguities, and contradiction inherent within it. The point is that they, like other Athenians, as individual bearers of that cultural repertoire, manipulated the categories which it provided them for their artistic, philosophical, and political purposes, just as the Kabyle manipulated "public" and "private," according to Bourdieu's description.

Therein, I would argue, lies the cultural meaning of many of the exaggerations, lies, distortions, and fabrications with which the orators are replete. For the historian, the question is not that of determining the social reality "behind" the lies: it is forever lost to us whether or not a particular marriage, or adoption, or making of a will in Isaeus actually took place. Similarly unachievable is a definitive statement of the status of women at Athens: even without knowing what many different opinions Athenian women may have had of the matter, Euripides and Aristophanes surely make plain enough how many competing and contradictory beliefs and values informed this question. A more important task facing the historian who addresses such issues consists in understanding the way in which legal, social, and moral categories were manipulated so as to influence the normative judgments of the community according to the standards of the politics of reputation.[40] It is such inquiries, I believe, which can help us recover the normative order of Athenian life at the level of social practice, differentiating between competing views of ideology, values, and practices, as they were understood by those whose lives were given shape by these structures, and who in turn reproduced and reshaped them through their actions.

[40] See Altorki's (1986: 149–50) final chapter, "Ideology and Strategy": "The individual, therefore, has a great deal of strategic scope to pursue interests; but although his or her strategy may be idiosyncratic, for it to be truly social...it can never be inconstruable – others must be able to understand it as a variation on cultural themes."

Bibliography

Abrams, P. (1982) *Historical Sociology* (London)
Abu-Lughod, L. (1986) *Veiled Sentiments* (Berkeley)
Adkins, A. (1960) *Merit and Responsibility* (Oxford)
  (1972) *Moral Values and Political Behaviour in Ancient Greece* (London)
Alexander, J. (1983) *Theoretical Logic in Sociology*, 4 vols. (Berkeley)
Allen, R. (1980) *Socrates and Political Obligation* (Minneapolis)
Altman, I. (1977) "Privacy Regulation", *Journal of Social Issues* 33, 66–84
Altorki, S. (1986) *Women in Saudi Arabia* (New York)
Annas, J. (1980) "Aristotle on Pleasure and Goodness", in Rorty
Anthropological Quarterly, Special Issue, (1967) *Appearance and Reality: Status and Role of Women in Mediterranean Societies*
Antoun, R., and Haruk, I., eds. (1972) *Rural Politics and Social Change in the Middle East* (Bloomington)
Antoun, R. (1968) "On the Modesty of Women in Arab Villages", *American Anthropologist*, 70, 671–97
Arendt, H. (1958) *The Human Condition* (Chicago)
Ariès, P. and Béjin, A., eds. (1985) *Western Sexuality* (Oxford)
Aswad, B. (1967) "Key and Peripheral Roles of Noble Women in a Middle Eastern Plains Village", *Anthropological Quarterly* 40, 139–51
Baal, J. van (1975) *Reciprocity and the Position of Women* (Amsterdam)
Baer, G. (1964) *Population and Society in the Arab East* (London)
Bailey, F. G. (1969) *Stratagems and Spoils* (New York)
  (1971) ed., *Gifts and Poison* (New York)
  (1973) *Debate and Compromise* (Oxford)
  (1977) *Morality and Expediency* (Oxford)
Bailey, G. (1975) *Homosexuality and the Western Christian Tradition* (London)
Balikci, A. (1965) "Quarrels in a Balkan Village", *American Anthropologist* 67, 1456–69
Banfield, E. (1958) *The Moral Basis of a Backward Society* (New York)
Baroja, J. (1958) "The City and the Country: Reflections on Ancient Commonplaces", in Pitt-Rivers
Barrett, R. (1974) *Benabarre, The Modernization of a Spanish Village* (Prospect Heights, Illinois)
Barrett, S. (1984) *The Rebirth of Anthropological Theory* (Toronto)
Beauchet, L. (1897) *Histoire du Droit Privé de la République Athénienne* (Paris)

Behar, R. (1986) *Santa Maria del Monte* (Princeton)

Bell, R. (1979) *Fate and Honor, Family and Village* (Chicago)

Belmonte, T. (1979) *The Broken Fountain* (New York)

Benn, S. (1971) "Privacy, Freedom, and Respect for Persons", in Pennock and Chapman, 1–26

Ben-Yehuda, N. (1982) *Deviance and Moral Boundaries* (New York)

Berger, M. (1962) *The Arab World Today* (New York)

Berneker, E. (1968) (ed.) *Zur Griechischen Rechtsgeschichte* (Darmstadt)

Berque, J. (1955) *Structures Sociales du Haut-Atlas* (Paris)

(1957) *Histoire Sociale d'un Village Égyptien* (Paris)

Black-Michaud, J. (1975) *Cohesive Force* (Oxford)

Blok, A. (1969) "Peasants, Patrons, and Brokers in Western Sicily", *Anthropological Quarterly* 42, 155–70

(1974) *The Mafia of a Sicilian Village* (New York)

(1981) "Rams and Billy-Goats: A Key to the Mediterranean Code of Honour", *Man* 16: 427–40

Boehm, C. (1984) *Blood Revenge* (Philadelphia)

Bohannan, P. and Middleton, J., eds. (1968) *Marriage, Family and Residence* (New York)

Boissevain, J. (1969) *Hal Farrug, A Village in Malta* (New York)

(1974) *Friends of Friends* (New York)

Bonner, R., and Smith, G. (1970) *The Administration of Justice from Homer to Aristotle* (New York)

Bosquet, G. (1966) *L'éthique sexuelle de l'Islam* (Paris)

Boswell, John (1980) *Christianity, Social Tolerance and Homosexuality* (Chicago)

Boswell, J. (1906) *Life of Samuel Johnson* (London)

Bouce, P., ed. (1982) *Sexuality in Eighteenth Century Britain* (Manchester)

Bourdieu, P. (1962) "Célibat et condition paysanne", *Etudes Rurales* 5–6, 32–135

(1966) "The Sentiment of Honour in Kabyle Society", in Peristiany

(1977) *Outline of a Theory of Practice* (Cambridge)

(1979) *Algérie 1960* (Cambridge)

(1980) *Le Sens Pratique* (Paris)

(1990) *In Other Words* (Stanford)

Brandes, S. (1975) *Migration, Kinship, and Community* (New York)

(1980) *Metaphors of Masculinity: Sex and Status in Andalusian Folklore* (Philadelphia)

(1981) "Like Wounded Stags: Male Sexual Ideology in an Andalusian Town", in Ortner and Whitehead

(1987) "Reflections of Honor and Shame in the Mediterranean", in Gilmore, 121–34.

Braudel, F. (1972) *The Mediterranean and the Mediterranean World in the Age of Philip II* (New York)

Bray, A. (1982) *Homosexuality in Renaissance Britain* (London)

Brelich, A. (1969) *Paides e Parthenoi* (Rome)

Bremmer, J. (1980) "An Enigmatic Indo-European Rite: Paederasty", *Arethusa* 279–98

Brewer, R. and Styles, J., eds. (1980) *An Ungovernable People* (London)

Brundage, J. (1987) *Law, Sex, and Christian Society in Early Modern Europe* (Chicago)

Buffière, F. (1982) *Eros adolescent* (Paris)

Burgmann, L. (1983) *Ecloga* (Frankfurt)

Burkert, W. (1985) *Greek Religion* (Oxford)

Calame, C. (1977) *Les choeurs de jeunes filles en Grèce archaïque* (Rome)

Callier, C. (1966) "Soajo, Une Communauté Féminine Rurale de l'Alto-Minho", *Bulletin des Etudes Portuguaises* 27, 237–78

Cameron, A., and Kuhrt, A., eds. (1983) *Images of Women in Antiquity* (Detroit)

Campbell, J. (1979) *Honour, Family, and Patronage* (Oxford)

Canguilhem, G. (1978) *On the Normal and the Pathological* (Dordrecht)

Cantarella, E. (1972) "Adulterio", in *Studi G. Scherillo* (Milan)
  (1976) *Studi Sull'Omicidio* (Milan)
  (1979) *Norma e Sanzione in Omero* (Milan)
  (1986) *Pandora's Daughters* (Baltimore)
  (1988) *Secondo Natura* (Rome)
  (1991) "Moicheia", in *Symposion 1990* (Graz)

Carmichael, C. (1974) *The Laws of Deuteronomy* (Ithaca)

Cartledge, P. (1981a) "Spartan Wives: Liberation or License?", *Classical Quarterly* 31, 84–105
  (1981b) "The Politics of Spartan Pederasty", *Proceedings of The Cambridge Philological Society* 17–36
  (1986) Review of MacDowell (1986), *LCM* 11, 142–4

Caspi, M. (1985) *The Daughters of Yemen* (Berkeley)

Chelhod, J. (1971) *Le Droit dans la Société Bedouine* (Paris)

Clark, M. (1983) "Variations on Themes of Male and Female: Reflections on gender bias in fieldwork in rural Greece", *Women's Studies* 102, 117–33

Cockburn, J., ed. (1977) *Crime in England* (London)

Cohen, D. (1983) *Theft in Athenian Law* (Munich)
  (1985) "A Note on Aristophanes and the Punishment of Adultery in Athenian Law", *ZSS* 385–7
  (1989) "Models and Methods in the Study of Greek Law", *ZSS* 106, 81–105
  (1991a) "Sexuality, Violence, and the Athenian Law of Hubris", *Greece and Rome*
  (1991b) "Athenian Attitudes Towards Homosexuality", *Past and Present*

Cole, S. (1981) "Could Greek Women Read and Write?", in Foley
  (1984) "Greek Sanctions Against Sexual Assault", *Classical Philology* 79, 97–113

Comaroff, J. and Roberts, S. (1981) *Rules and Processes* (Chicago)

Coon, C. (1931) *Tribes of the Rif* (Cambridge, Mass.)

Cooper, J. (1980) "Aristotle on Friendship", in Rorty

Coward, D. (1980) "Attitudes to Homosexuality in Eighteenth Century France", *Journal of European Studies* 231–55

Crook, J. (1984) *Law and Life of Rome* (Ithaca)

Cutileiro, J. (1971) *A Portuguese Rural Society* (Oxford)

Darnton, R. (1984) *The Great Cat Massacre* (New York)

Daube, D. (1947) *Studies in Biblical Law* (Oxford)

  (1969) *Roman Law* (Edinburgh)

  (1972) "The Lex Julia Concerning Adultery", *The Irish Jurist* 7, 373–80

  (1978) "Biblical Landmarks in the Struggle for Women's Rights", *The Juridical Review* 90, 177–97

  (1986) "The Old Testament Prohibitions of Homosexuality" *ZSS* 103, 447–8

Davis, J. (1973) *Land and Family in Pisticci* (New York)

  (1977) *People of the Mediterranean* (London)

Davis, N. (1975) *Society and Culture in Early Modern France* (Stanford)

Davis, S. (1980) "The Determinants of Social Position among Rural Moroccan Women", in Smith

Deacon, A. (1934) *Malekula* (London)

DeDieu, J. (1987) "The Inquisition and Popular Culture in New Castile", in Haliczer

Delaney, C. (1987) "Seeds of Honor, Fields of Shame", in Gilmore

Delcourt, M. (1958) *Hermaphrodite* (Paris)

Derenne, E. (1930) *Les Procès d'Impiété* (Paris)

des Villettes, J. (1964) *La Vie des Femmes dans un Village Maronite* (Tunis)

Detienne, M. (1978) *The Gardens of Adonis* (New Jersey)

Devereux, G. (1968) "Greek Pseudo-Homosexuality and the 'Greek Miracle'", *Symbolae Osloenses* 42

Devlin, P. (1965) *The Enforcement of Morals* (London)

Dimen, M. (1986) "Servants and Sentries: Women, Power, and Social Reproduction in Kriovrisi", in Dubisch

Dodds, E. (1973) *The Ancient Concept of Progress* (Oxford)

  (1971) *The Greeks and the Irrational* (Berkeley)

Donzelot, J. (1979) *The Policing of Families* (New York)

Dover, K. (1964) "Eros and Nomos", *Bulletin of the Institute of Classical Studies* 9, 31–42

  (1968) *Aristophanes: Clouds* (Oxford)

  (1973) "Classical Greek Attitudes to Sexual Behavior", *Arethusa*, 59–73

  (1974) *Greek Popular Morality* (Oxford)

  (1976) "The Freedom of the Intellectual in Greek Society", *Talanta* 7, 25–54

  (1978) *Greek Homosexuality* (New York)

Drier, E., ed. (1983) *Recht, Moral, Ideologie* (Frankfurt)

Driver, G., and Miles, J. (1952) *The Babylonian Laws* (Oxford)

  (1975) *The Assyrian Laws* (Aalen)

du Bois, P. (1982) *Centaurs and Amazons* (Ann Arbor)

du Boulay, J. (1974) *Portrait of a Greek Mountain Village* (Oxford)

  (1976) "Lies, Mockery, and Family Integrity", in Peristiany

  (1986) "Women: Images of their Nature and Destiny in Rural Greece", in Dubisch

Dubisch, J. (1983) "Greek Women: Sacred or Profane", *Journal of Modern Greek Studies* 1, 185–202
   ed. (1986) *Gender and Power in Rural Greece* (Princeton)
Dundes, A., and Falassi, A. (1975) *La Terra in Piazza* (Berkeley)
Durkheim, E. (1964) *The Division of Labor in Society* (New York)
Dworkin, R. (1966) "Lord Devlin and the Enforcement of Morals", 75 *Yale Law J.*, 986
Dwyer, D. (1978) *Images and Self-Images: Male and Female in Morocco* (New York)
Edgerton, R. (1988) *Rules, Exceptions, and Social Order* (Berkeley)
Edmonds, J., ed. (1961) *The Fragments of Attic Comedy*, 3 vols. (Leiden)
Ehrenberg, V. (1962) *The People of Aristophanes* (New York)
Elias, N. (1989) *Über den Prozess der Zivilisation*, 2 vols. (Frankfurt)
Emmison, F. (1970) *Elizabethan Life: Disorder* (Essex)
   (1973) *Elizabethan Life: Morals and the Church Courts* (Essex)
Epstein, L. (1967) *Sex Laws and Customs in Judaism* (New York)
Erdmann, W. (1979) *Die Ehe im Alten Griechenland* (New York)
Eser, A. and Fletcher, G., eds. (1987–8) *Rechtfertigung und Entschuldigung*, 2 vols. (Freiburg)
Esposito, J. (1982) *Women in Muslim Family Law* (New York)
Evans-Pritchard, E. (1951) *Kinship and Marriage among the Nuer* (Oxford)
   (1970) "Sexual Inversion among the Azande", *Am. Anth.*, 1428–35
Fahr, W. (1969) *Theous Nomizein* (Hildesheim)
Fantham, E. (1975) "Sex, Status, and Survival in Hellenistic Athens: A Study of Women in New Comedy", *Phoenix* 29, 44–74
   (1986) "*Zylotupia*: A Brief Excursion into Sex, Violence, and Literary History", *Phoenix* 40, 45–57
Febvre, L. (1982) *The Problem of Unbelief in the Sixteenth Century* (Harvard)
Ferguson, J. (1958) *Moral Values in the Ancient World* (London)
Fernea, E. (1969) *Guests of the Sheik* (New York)
   (1980) *A Street in Marrakech* (New York)
Finley, M. (1952) *Land and Credit in Athens* (New York)
   (1969) *Aspects of Antiquity* (New York)
   (1975a) *The Ancient Economy* (Berkeley)
   (1975b) *The Use and Abuse of History* (London)
   (1977) *The World of Odysseus*, 2nd ed. (London)
   (1980) *Ancient Slavery and Modern Ideology* (London)
   (1985a) *Ancient History: Evidence and Models* (New York)
   (1985b) *Democracy, Ancient and Modern* (New Brunswick)
Firth, R. (1973) *Symbols: Public and Private* (Ithaca)
Fisher, N. (1976) "Hybris and Dishonour I", *Greece and Rome* 23, 177–93
   (1979) "Hybris and Dishonour II", *Greece and Rome* 26, 32–47
Flacelière, R. (1965) *Daily Life in Greece* (London)
Flandrin, J.-L. (1979) *Families in Former Times* (Cambridge)
Fletcher, G. (1978) *Rethinking Criminal Law* (Boston)
Foley, H. (1981a) (ed.) *Reflections of Women in Antiquity* (New York)
   (1981b) "The Conception of Women in Athenian Drama", in Foley

Forster, R. and Ranum, O., eds. (1978) *Deviants and the Abandoned in French Society* (Baltimore)

Fortes, M., ed. (1972) *Marriage in Tribal Society* (Cambridge)

Foucault, M. (1979) *Discipline and Punish* (New York)
   (1980) *The History of Sexuality*, vol. 1 (New York)
   (1984) *L'Usage des Plaisirs* (Paris)

Foucault, M. and Farge, A. (1982) *Le Désordre des Familles* (Paris)

Freeman, S. (1970) *Neighbors* (Chicago)

Fried, C. (1968) "Privacy", *Yale Law J.* 77, 475–93

Friedl, E. (1958) "Some Aspects of Dowry in Boeotia", in Pitt-Rivers
   (1962) *Vasilika* (New York)
   (1967) "The Position of Women: Appearance and Reality", *Anthropological Quarterly* 40, 97–108

Fuller, A. (1961) *Buarij* (Cambridge, Mass.)

Fuller, E. (1986) "Hardwick v. Bowers: An Attempt to Pull the Meaning of Doe v. Commonwealth's Attorney Out of the Closet", *Miami L. Rev.*

Fustel de Coulanges, N.D. (1980) *The Ancient City* (Gloucester, Mass.) (Original French publication 1864)

Gade, K. (1986) "Homosexuality and the Rape of Males in Old Norse Law and Literature", *Scandinavian Studies* 58, 124–41

Gagarin, M. (1979) "The Athenian Law against Hybris", *Arktouros* (Berlin)

Gardner, J. (1986) *Women in Roman Law and Society* (Bloomington)

Garfinkel, H. (1984) *Studies in Ethnomethodology* (Cambridge)

Garnsey, P. (1983) "Religious Toleration in Classical Antiquity", *Proceedings of the Cambridge Philological Society*

Geddert, H. (1984) *Recht und Moral* (Berlin)

Geertz, C., Geertz, H., and Rosen, L. (1979) *Meaning and Order in Moroccan Society* (Cambridge)

Gellner, E. (1963) "Sanctity, Puritanism, Secularity, and Nationalism in North Africa", in Peristiany
   (1969) *Saints of the Atlas* (Chicago)
   (1981) *Muslim Society* (Cambridge)

Gennep, A. van. (1960) *The Rites of Passage* (Chicago)

Gernet, L. (1976) *Anthropologie de la Grèce antique* (Paris)
   (1976) Introduction to Budé edition of Plato's *Laws* (Paris)

Ghiselin, M. (1974) *The Economy of Nature and the Evolution of Sex* (Berkeley)

Giddens, A. (1979) *Central Problems in Social Theory* (Berkeley)
   (1986) *The Constitution of Society* (Berkeley)
   (1987) *Social Theory and Modern Sociology* (Cambridge)

Gilmore, D., ed. (1987a) *Honor and Shame: The Unity of the Mediterranean* (Washington D.C.)
   (1987b) *Aggression and Community* (New Haven)

Ginzburg, C. (1982) *The Cheese and the Worms* (Harmondsworth, Middlesex)

Giovannini, M. (1986) "Female Anthropologist and Male Informant: Gender Conflict in a Sicilian Town", in Whitehead and Conaway, 103–16
   (1987) "Female Chastity Codes in the Circum-Mediterranean: Comparative Perspectives", in Gilmore

Glotz, G. (1973) *La Solidarité de la Famille* (New York)

Godelier, M. (1987) *The Making of Great Men* (Cambridge)

Goffman, E. (1961) *Asylums* (New York)

  (1963a) *Behaviour in Public Places* (Glencoe)

  (1963b) *Stigma* (Englewood Cliffs)

  (1967) *Interaction Ritual* (New York)

  (1971) *Relations in Public* (New York)

  (1973) *The Presentation of Self in Everyday Life* (New York)

Golden, M. (1984) "Slavery and Homosexuality at Athens", *Phoenix* 38, 308–24

Gomme, A. (1967) *Essays on Greek History* (New York)

Goody, J. (1968) "A Comparative Approach to Incest and Adultery", in Bohannan and Middleton

  (1977) *Production and Reproduction* (Cambridge)

  (1983) *The Development of the Family and Marriage in Europe* (Cambridge)

Goria, F. (1975) *Studi sul Matrimonio dell' Adultera nel Diritto Giustiniano e Bizantino* (Turin)

Gould, J. (1980) "Law, Custom, and Myth", *JHS* 38–59

Gould, T. (1963) *Platonic Love* (London)

Gouldner, A. (1965) *Enter Plato* (New York)

Granquist, H. (1931, 1934) *Marriage Conditions in a Palestinian Village*, 2 vols. (Helsingfors)

Gray, T. (1983) *The Legal Enforcement of Morality* (New York)

  (1980) "Eros, Civilization, and the Burger Court", *Law and Contemporary Problems* 43, 87

Greenawalt, K. (1974) "Privacy and its Legal Protection", *Hastings Center Studies* 2, 45–68

Gregor, T. (1974) "Publicity, Privacy, and Mehinaku Marriage", *Ethnology* 13, 333–49

  (1977) *Mehinaku* (Chicago)

  (1985) *Anxious Pleasures* (Chicago)

Hafen, R. (1983) "The Constitutional Status of Marriage, Kinship and Sexual Privacy", *U. of Michigan Law Review* 81, 463

Haliczer, S., ed. (1987) *Inquisition and Society in Early Modern Europe* (Ottawa)

Halperin, D. (1989) *One Hundred Years of Homosexuality* (New York)

Halperin, D., Winkler, J., and Zeitlin, F., eds. (1990) *Before Sexuality* (Princeton)

Halperin, J. (1958) *A Serbian Village* (New York)

Hamburger, M. (1971) *Morals and Law, The Growth of Aristotle's Legal Theory* (New York)

Hampshire, S., ed. (1978) *Public and Private Morality* (Cambridge)

Handman, M.-E. (1983) *La Violence et la Ruse* (Aix-en-Provence)

Hansen, M. (1976) *Apagoge, Endeixis, and Ephegesis Against Kakourgoi, Atimoi, and Pheugontes* (Odense)

  (1981) "The Prosecution of Homicide in Athens: A Reply", *GRBS* 22, 11–30

Harrison, A.R.W. (1968) *The Law of Athens*, vol. 1 (Oxford)

Hart, H. (1961) *The Concept of Law* (Oxford)
  (1963) *Law, Liberty, and Morality* (Stanford)

Hasluck, M. (1954) *The Unwritten Law of Albania* (Cambridge)

Hastrup, K. (1975) "The Sexual Boundary-Danger: Transvestism and Homosexuality", *Journal of the Anthropological Society of Oxford* 42–55

Hay, D., et al. eds. (1975) *Albion's Fatal Tree* (New York)

Hayek, F. (1977) *Law, Legislation and Liberty* 3 vols. (London)
  (1978) *New Studies* (London)

Hegel, G. (1981) *Philosophy of Right* (Oxford)

Henderson, J. (1975) *The Maculate Muse* (New Haven)

Herdt, G. (1981) *Guardians of the Flutes: Idioms of Masculinity* (New York)
  ed. (1982) *Rituals of Manhood* (Berkeley)
  (1984) *Ritualized Homosexuality in Melanesia* (Berkeley)

Herfst, P. (1922) *Le Travail de la Femme* (Paris)

Herman, G. (1987) *Ritualized Friendship and the Greek City* (Cambridge)

Herzfeld, M. (1980) "Honor and Shame: Problems in the Comparative Analysis of Moral Systems", *Man*, 339–51
  (1983) "Semantic Slippage and Moral Fall: The Rhetoric of Chastity in Rural Greek Society", *Journal of Modern Greek Studies* 1, 161–72
  (1984) "The Horns of the Mediterraneanist Dilemma", *American Ethnologist*
  (1985) *The Poetics of Manhood* (Princeton)
  (1986) "Within and Without: The Category of the Female in the Ethnography of Modern Greece", in Dubisch
  (1987) "As in Your Own House: Hospitality, Ethnography, and the Stereotype of Mediterranean Society", in Gilmore

Hill, C. (1975) *The World Turned Upside Down* (Harmondsworth, Middlesex)
  (1985) *The Experience of Defeat* (New York)

Hoffman, B. (1967) *The Structure of Traditional Moroccan Society* (The Hague)

Hopkins, K. (1978) *Conquerors and Slaves* (Cambridge)
  (1983) *Death and Renewal* (Cambridge)

Horowitz, M. (1976) "Aristotle and Woman", *Journal of the History of Biology* 9, 184–213

Houlbrooke, R. (1979) *Church Courts and the People* (Oxford)

Hruza, E. (1979) *Die Ehebegründung nach Attischem Recht* (New York)

Humphreys, S. (1983) *The Family, Women, and Death* (London)

Ithurriague, J. (1931) *Les Idées de Platon sur la condition de la femme* (Paris)

Jackson, B. (1972) *Theft in Early Jewish Law* (Oxford)

Jamous, R. (1981) *Honneur et baraka, Les Structures sociales traditionnelles dans le Rif* (Cambridge)

Jescheck, H. (1978) *Lehrbuch des Strafrechts, Allgemeiner Teil* (Berlin)

Just, R. (1975) "Conception of Women in Classical Athens", *Anthropological Society of Oxford Journal*, 6, 153–70

Kamen, H. (1985) *Inquisition and Society in Spain* (Bloomington)

Kember, O. (1973) "Anaxagoras' Theory of Sex Differentiation and Heredity", *Phronesis* 18, 1–14

Kennedy, R. (1986) "Women's Friendships on Crete", in Dubisch

Kenny, M. (1962) *A Spanish Tapestry: Town and Country in Castile* (Bloomington)

Keuls, E. (1985) *The Reign of the Phallus* (New York)

King, H. (1983) "Bound to Bleed: Artemis and Greek Women", in Cameron and Kuhrt

Koch-Harnack, G. (1983) *Knabenliebe und Tiergeschenke* (Berlin)

König, R. (1982) "Das Recht in Zusammenhang der sozialen Normensysteme", in Lüderssen and Sack

Lacey, W. (1968) *The Family in Classical Greece* (London)

Lagerborg, R. (1926) *Die Platonische Liebe* (Leipzig)

Latte, K. (1920–1) "Schuld und Sühne in der griechischen Religion", *Archiv für Religionswissenschaft* 20, 254
  (1968a) "Beiträge zum griechischen Strafrecht", in Berneker
  (1968b) *Kleine Schriften* (Munich)
  (1932) "Moicheia", *RE* 2446–9

Lawson, J. (1964) *Modern Greek Folklore* (New York)

Le Roy Ladurie, E. (1982) *Montaillou* (Middlesex)

Leach, E. (1954) *Political Systems of Highland Burma* (London)
  (1961) *Pul Eliya: A Village in Ceylon* (Cambridge)

Lefkowitz, M. (1986) *Women in Greek Myth* (Baltimore)

Lefkowitz, M., and Fant, M., eds. (1982) *Women's Life in Greece and Rome* (London)

Legendre, P. (1974) *L'Amour du Censeur* (Paris)

Levy, H. (1958) "Inheritance and Dowry in Classical Athens", in Pitt-Rivers

Lipsius, J. (1984) *Das Attische Recht und Rechtsverfahren* (Hildesheim)

Lison-Tolosana, C. (1966) *Belmonte de los Caballeros* (Oxford)

Lloyd, A., and Fallers, M. (1976) "Sex Roles in Edremit", in Peristiany

Lloyd, G. (1979) *Magic, Reason, and Experience* (Cambridge)
  (1983) *Science, Folklore, and Ideology* (Cambridge)

Loizos, P. (1975) *The Greek Gift: Politics in a Cypriot Village* (New York)

Loraux, N. (1978) "Sur la Race des Femmes et Quelques-unes de ses Tribus", *Arethusa*, 11, 43–87
  (1981) *Les Enfants d'Athéna* (Paris)

Lüderssen, K. and Sack, F., eds. (1982) *Abweichendes Verhalten*, vol. 1 (Frankfurt)

Luhmann, N. (1972) *Rechtssoziologie*, 2 vols. (Hamburg)
  (1984) *Soziale Systeme* (Frankfurt)

McClees, H. (1920) *A Study of Women in Attic Inscriptions* (New York)

MacCormack, C., and Strathern, M., eds. (1980) *Nature, Culture, and Gender* (Cambridge)

MacDowell, D. (1963) *Athenian Homicide Law* (Manchester)
  (1976) "Hybris in Athens", *Greece and Rome*
  (1978) *The Law in Classical Athens* (London)

(1986) *Spartan Law* (Edinburgh)

Macfarlane, A. (1981) *The Justice and the Mare's Ale* (London)

Maher, V. (1974) *Women and Property in Morocco* (Cambridge)

Malinowski, B. (1929) *The Sexual Life of Savages* (New York)

Maraspini, A. (1968) *The Study of an Italian Village* (Paris)

Marchant, R. (1969) *The Church Under the Law* (Cambridge)

Marcus, G., and Fisher, M. (1986) *Anthropology as Cultural Critique* (Chicago)

Marrou, H. (1956) *History of Education in Antiquity* (New York)

Martin, J. (1987) "Popular Culture and the Shaping of Popular Heresy in Renaissance Venice", in Haliczer

Marx, E. (1967) *Bedouin of the Negev* (New York)

Maschke, R. (1979) *Die Willenslehre in Griechischem Recht* (New York)

Mauss, M. (1967) *The Gift* (New York)

Melikian, L., and Prothro, E. (1954) "Sexual Behaviour of University Students in the Arab Near East", *Journal of Abnormal and Social Psychology*, 59–64

Menefee, S. (1981) *Wives for Sale* (Oxford)

Mernissi, F. (1975) *Beyond the Veil: Male-Female Dynamics in a Muslim Society* (Cambridge, Mass.)

Merton, R. (1964) *Social Theory and Social Structure* (New York)

Mohsen, S. (1970) "Aspects of the Legal Status of Women Among the Awlas 'Ali", in Sweet

Moller, H. (1987) "The Accelerated Development of Youth: Beard Growth as a Biological Marker", *CSSH* 29, 748–62

Mommsen, T. (1965) *Römisches Strafrecht* (Graz)

Monter, E. (1981) "Sodomy and Heresy in Early Modern Switzerland", *Journal of Homosexuality*, 41–53

(1987) *Enforcing Morality in Early Modern Europe* (London)

Moore, B. (1984) *Privacy* (London)

Morris, H. (1976) *On Guilt and Innocence* (Berkeley)

(1985) "A Paternalistic Theory of Punishment", in J. Murphy, ed., *Punishment and Rehabilitation* (Belmont, California)

Morton, A. (1979) *The World of the Ranters* (London)

Mosse, G. (1982) "Nationalism and Respectability: Normal and Abnormal Sexuality in the Nineteenth Century", *Journal of Contemporary History*, 221–46

Murphy, R. (1970) "Social Distance and the Veil", in Sweet

Nagel, T. (1969) "Sexual Perversion", *Journal of Philosophy* 61, 5–17

Nalle, S. (1987) "Popular Religion in Cuenca on the Eve of the Catholic Reformation", in Haliczer

Neufeld, E. (1951) *The Hittite Laws* (London)

Nilsson, M. (1961) *Geschichte der griechischen Religion*, vol. 2 (Munich)

Nörr, D. (1977) "Planung in der Antike", in *Freiheit und Sachzwang, Beiträge zu Ehren Helmut Schelskys* (Opladen) 309–334

(1986) *Causa Mortis* (Munich)

Note (1985) "Survey of the Constitutional Right to Privacy in the Context of Homosexuality" *U. of Miami Law Review* 40, 521

Note (1985) "The Constitutional Status of Sexual Orientation", *Harvard Law Review* 98, 1285

O'Neil, M. (1987) "Magical Healing, Love Magic and the Inquisition in Late Sixteenth Century Modena", in Haliczer

O'Neill, B. (1987) *Social Inequality in a Portuguese Hamlet* (Cambridge)

Opp, K. (1983) *Die Entstehung Sozialer Normen* (Tübingen)

Ortner, S., and Whitehead, H., eds. (1981) *Sexual Meanings: The Cultural Construction of Gender and Sexuality* (Cambridge)

Ostwald, M. (1986) *From Popular Sovereignty to the Sovereignty of Law* (Berkeley)

Otis, L. (1981) *Prostitution in Medieval Society* (Chicago)

Ozment, S. (1983) *When Fathers Ruled: Family Life in Reformation Europe* (Cambridge, Mass.)

Padel, R. (1983) "Women: Model for Possession by Greek Daemons", in Cameron and Kuhrt

Paoli, U. (1959) "Zum attischen Strafrecht und Strafprozessrecht", *ZSS* 76, 97–112

(1976) *Altri Studi di Diritto Greco e Romano* (Milan)

Parent, W. (1983a) "Recent Work on the Concept of Privacy", *American Philosophical Quarterly* 20, 341

(1983b) "Privacy, Morality, and the Law", *Philosophy and Public Affairs* 12, 269–88

Parke, H. (1977) *Festivals of the Athenians* (London)

Parker, R. (1983) *Miasma* (Oxford)

Parsons, T. (1964) *Social Structure and Personality* (Glencoe)

(1968) *The Structure of Social Action* (New York)

Patai, R. (1959) *Sex and the Family in the Bible and Middle East* (New York)

Patterson, O. (1982) *Slavery and Social Death* (Cambridge, Mass.)

Patzer, H. (1982) *Die Griechische Knabenliebe* (Wiesbaden)

Pavlides, E. and Hesser, J. (1986) "Women's Roles and House Form and Decoration in Erossos, Greece", in Dubisch, 68–96

Pehrson, R. (1967) *The Social Organization of the Marri Beluch* (Chicago)

Pennock, J. and Chapman, J., eds. (1971) *Privacy* (New York)

Peristiany, J., ed. (1963) *Contributions to Mediterranean Sociology* (Paris)

ed. (1966a) *Honour and Shame* (Chicago)

(1966b) "Honour and Shame in a Cypriot Highland Village", in Peristiany.

ed. (1976) *Mediterranean Family Structures* (Cambridge)

Photiadis, J. (1965) "The Position of the Coffee House in the Social Structure of the Greek Village", *Sociologia Ruralis* 45–56

Piers, G., and Singer, M. (1963) *Shame and Guilt* (Springfield)

Pitt-Rivers, J. (1958) (ed.) *Mediterranean Countrymen* (Paris)

(1966) "Honour and Social Status", in Peristiany

(1971) *People of the Sierra* (Chicago)

(1977) *The Fate of Shechem or the Politics of Sex* (Cambridge)

Poole, F. (1981) "Transforming 'Natural' Woman: Female Ritual Leaders and Gender Ideology among Bimin-Kuskusmin", in Ortner and Whitehead

(1982) "The Ritual Forging of Identity", in Herdt

Prothro, E., and Diab, L. (1974) *Changing Family Patterns in the Arab Near East* (Beirut)

Quaife, G. (1979) *Wanton Wenches and Wayward Wives* (London)

Radcliffe-Brown, A. (1965) *Structure and Function in Primitive Society* (New York)

Raheja, G. (1988) *The Poison in the Gift* (Chicago)

Rawls, J. (1974) *A Theory of Justice* (Boston)

Rawson, B. (1986) (ed.) *The Family in Ancient Rome* (Ithaca)

Read, K. (1965) *The High Valley* (New York)

Reay, B., ed. (1985) *Popular Culture in Seventeenth Century England* (London)

Richards, D. (1977) "Unnatural Acts and the Constitutional Right to Privacy", *Ford Law Review* 45, 1281

(1979) "Sexual Autonomy and the Constitutional Right to Privacy", *Hastings Law Journal* 30, 957

Riegelhaupt, J. (1967) "Saloio Women: An Analysis of Informal and Formal Political and Economic Roles of Portuguese Peasant Women", *Anthropological Quarterly* 40, 109–26

Romanucci-Ross, L. (1986) *Conflict, Violence, and Morality in a Mexican Village* (Chicago)

Rorty, A., ed. (1980a) *Essays on Aristotle's Ethics* (Berkeley)

(1980b) "Akrasia and Pleasure", in Rorty

Rosenfeld, H. (1960) "On Determinants of the Status of Arab Village Women", *Man*, 66–70

Ross, E., and Rapp, R. (1981) "Sex and Society: A Research Note from Social History and Anthropology", *Comparative Studies in Society and History* 23, 51–72

Rossiaud, J. (1978) "Prostitution, Youth, and Society in the Towns of Southeastern France in the Fifteenth Century", in Forster and Ranum

Roth, M. (1988) "She Will Die by the Iron Dagger: Adultery and Neo-Babylonian Marriage", *Journal of the Economic and Social History of the Orient*

Rousselle, A. (1980) "Observation féminine et idéologie masculine", *Annales, ESC* 5, 1089–1115

(1988) *Porneia* (Oxford)

Rudhardt, J. (1960) "La définition du délit d'impiété", *Museum Helveticum*, 87–105

Ruggiero, G. (1985) *The Boundaries of Eros: Sex Crime and Sexuality in Renaissance Venice* (Oxford)

Runciman, W. (1983) *A Treatise on Social Theory* 1 (Cambridge)

Sanders, I. (1962) *The Rainbow in the Rock* (Cambridge, Mass.)

Savalli, I. (1983) *La Donna nella Società della Grecia Antica* (Bologna)

Schaps, D. (1979) *Economic Rights of Women in Ancient Greece* (Edinburgh)

Schauenburg, K. (1975) "Eurymedon Eimi", *MDAI* 90, 97–121

Schluchter, W. (1985) *The Rise of Western Capitalism* (Berkeley)

Schneider, C. (1977) *Shame, Exposure, and Privacy* (Boston)

Schneider, J. (1971) "Of Vigilance and Virgins: Honor, Shame, and Access to Resources in Mediterranean Societies", *Ethnology*, 1–24

Schneider, P. (1969) "Honor and Conflict in a Sicilian Town", *Anthropological Quarterly* 42, 130–54

Schoemann, F., ed. (1984) *Philosophical Perspectives on Privacy* (Cambridge)

Schuller, W. (1985) *Frauen in der Griechischen Geschichte* (Konstanz)

Schwartz, B. (1968) "The Social Psychology of Privacy", *American Journal of Sociology* 73, 741–52

Segal, C. (1978) "The Menace of Dionysus: Sex Roles and Reversals in Euripides' Bacchae", *Arethusa* 11, 185–202

Sergent, B. (1984) *L'homosexualité dans la mythologie grecque* (Paris)

Shapiro, H. (1981) "Courtship Scenes in Attic Vase Painting", *AJA*, 133–43

Sharpe, J. (1983) *Crime in Seventeenth Century England* (Cambridge)

 (1986) *Crime in Early Modern England 1550–1750* (London)

Shostak, M. (1983) *Nisa* (New York)

Silverman, S. (1968) "Agricultural Organization, Social Structure and Values in Italy: Amoral Familism Reconsidered", *American Anthropologist* 70, 1–20

 "Stratification in Italian Communities", in L. Plotnicov, ed. (1979) *Essays in Comparative Social Stratification* (Pittsburgh)

 (1974) "Bailey's Politics", *Journal of Peasant Studies* 2, 111–21

Simmel, G. (1950) *The Sociology of Georg Simmel* (K. Wolff, ed.) (Glencoe)

 (1971) *On Individuality and Social Forms* (Chicago)

Simon, B. (1978) *Mind and Madness in Ancient Greece* (Ithaca)

Skocpol, T., ed. (1984) *Vision and Method in Historical Sociology* (Cambridge)

Smith, J., ed. (1980) *Women in Contemporary Muslim Societies* (Lewisburg)

Spina, L. (1986) *Il Cittadino alla tribuna* (Naples)

Stirling, P. (1966) *Turkish Village* (New York)

 (1969) "Honor, Culture, Theory, and Some Doubt", *Tot de Taal-, Land-En Volkenkunde* 118–33

Stone, L. (1977) *The Family, Sex, and Marriage in England 1500–1800* (New York)

Strathern, M., ed. (1987) *Dealing with Inequality* (Cambridge)

 (1988) *The Gender of the Gift: Problems with Women and Problems with Society in Melanesia* (Berkeley)

Sutton, R. (1981) *The Interaction between Men and Women Portrayed on Attic Red-Figure Pottery*, diss.

Sweet, L. (1967) "The Women of 'Ain Ad Day", *Anthropological Quarterly* 40, 167–83

 ed. (1970) *Peoples and Cultures of the Middle East* (New York)

Tentori, T. (1976) "Social Class and Family in a Southern Italian Town", in Peristiany

Thomas, K. (1963) "History and Anthropology", *Past and Present* 24, 3–24
  (1973) *Religion and the Decline of Magic* (Harmondsworth, Middlesex)

Thompson, E. (1966) *The Making of the English Working Class* (New York)
  (1971) "The Moral Economy of the English Crowd", *Past and Present* 50, 76–136
  (1974) "Patrician Society, Plebeian Culture", *Journal of Social History* 7, 382–405
  (1975) *Whigs and Hunters* (New York)

Thompson, W. (1972) "Athenian Marriage Patterns: Remarriage", *Cal. Studies in Classical Antiquity*, 211–24

Thonissen, J. (1875) *Le Droit Pénal Athénien* (Brussels)

Tönnies, F. (1909) *Die Sitte* (Frankfurt)

Turner, V. (1957) *Schism and Continuity in an African Society* (Manchester)
  (1967) *The Forest of Symbols* (Ithaca)

Tyrell, W.B. (1984) *Amazons* (Baltimore)

Unger, R. (1975) *Knowledge and Politics* (New York)
  (1976) *Law in Modern Society* (New York)
  (1987) *Politics, A Work in Constructive Social Theory*, 3 vols. (Cambridge)

Vellacott, P. (1975) *Ironic Drama* (Cambridge)

Vernant, J.-P. (1981) *Mythe et Société* (Paris)

Vidal-Naquet, P. (1981) *Le chasseur noir* (Paris)

Vlastos, G. (1987) "Socratic Irony", *CQ* 79–96

Walcot, P. (1973) *Greek Peasants, Ancient and Modern* (Manchester)
  (1984) "Greek Attitudes Towards Women: The Mythological Evidence", *Greece and Rome*, 33–47

Watson, A. (1981) *The Making of the Civil Law* (Cambridge, Mass.)
  (1984) *Sources of Law, Legal Change and Ambiguity* (Philadelphia)
  (1985) *The Evolution of Law* (Baltimore)

Weber, M. (1958) *The Protestant Ethic and the Spirit of Capitalism* (New York)
  (1968) *Economy and Society*, 2 vols. (Berkeley)
  (1977) *Critique of Stammler* (New York)

Weinstein, W. (1971) "The Private and the Free", in Pennock and Chapman, 27–55

Weisser, M. (1976) *The Peasants of the Montes* (Chicago)

White, H. (1973) *Metahistory* (Baltimore)

Whitehead, H. (1981) "The Bow and the Burden Strap: A New Look at Institutionalized Homosexuality in Native North America", in Ortner and Whitehead

Whitehead, T. and Conaway, M., eds. (1986) *Self, Sex, and Gender in Cross-Cultural Fieldwork* (Urbana)

Wilamowitz-Möllendorff, U. von (1920) *Platon*, 2 vols. (Berlin)

Williams, J. (1968) *A Lebanese Village* (Cambridge, Mass.)

Winkler, J. (1990) *The Constraints of Desire* (London)

Wolff, H. (1944) "Marriage Law and Family Organization in Ancient Athens", *Traditio* 2, 43–95

(1946) "The Origin of Judicial Litigation among the Greeks", *Traditio* 4, 31–87

(1968) "Die Grundlagen des griechischen Eherechts", in Berneker

(1974) *Opuscula Dispersa* (Amsterdam)

Wylie, K. (1973) "The Uses and Misuses of Ethnohistory", *Journal of Interdisciplinary Studies* 3, 707–20

Yalman (1966) Review of *Turkish Village*, *Journal of Balkan Studies*

Zagorin, P. (1982) *Rebels and Rulers*, Volume I: *Society, States, and Early Modern Revolution* (Cambridge)

Zeid, A. (1966) "Honour and Shame among the Bedouins of Egypt", in Peristiany

Zeitlin, F. (1978) "The Dynamics of Misogyny in the *Oresteia*", *Arethusa* 11, 149–81

(1981) "Travesties of Gender and Genre in Aristophanes' Thesmophoriazusae", in Foley

(1982) "Cultic Models of the Female: Rites of Dionysus and Demeter", *Arethusa* 15, 129–57

Index

adultery, 53, 63, 67, 68, 73, 85, 89, 98–132, 134, 142, 147, 150, 155–6, 160–1, 165, 167–9, 170, 180, 193–4, 221, 223–5, 227

Aeschines, 81, 90, 94, 96, 111, 129, 161, 176, 178, 179, 180, 181, 188, 194, 195, 197, 199, 200, 222

Agesilaus, 81, 82, 201

agora, 72, 73, 80, 167

Alcibiades, 77, 165

ambiguity of social norms, 12, 20, 21, 31, 33, 55, 67, 117, 128, 135–7, 145–6, 171, 173, 174, 181, 191, 198, 206, 207, 218, 237, 239

Andalusia, 60, 61, 142, 186

Andocides, 73, 211, 226

animals, relation to human reproduction, 188, 199

Aristophanes, 108, 120, 130, 131, 135, 137, 138, 147, 151, 160, 164, 165, 166, 167, 181, 190, 191, 195, 199, 201, 239, 240

Aristotle, 71, 75, 76, 77, 79, 80, 83, 86, 88, 101, 107, 112, 118, 122, 123, 127, 129, 130, 144, 151, 154, 155, 161, 166, 168, 172, 178, 179, 183, 184, 185, 188, 189, 190, 193, 196, 197, 201, 207, 208, 211, 221, 230, 233, 234, 235

Athenian Assembly, 72, 73, 77, 80, 176

belief, religious, 210, 211, 213, 215, 216, 228

Bourdieu, 23, 30, 31, 32, 33, 43, 44, 59, 68, 69, 74, 78, 80, 137, 141, 147, 151, 157, 162, 166, 173, 198, 237, 238, 240

boys, 170–1, 176–7, 180–2, 184, 186, 189, 191–200

Brandes, S., 88, 142, 143, 145, 184

brothers, 53, 64

Campbell, J., 96, 143

Cantarella, E., 100, 172

castration, 189

chastity, 41, 47, 63, 129, 140, 141, 147

children, 100, 103, 107, 128, 160, 167

citizens, 2, 71, 72, 73, 181, 192, 209, 215, 220, 222, 229, 231, 232, 233, 234, 235

community, 3, 5, 7, 12, 15, 41–2, 46–57, 60, 62–5, 68–9, 73, 79, 80–3, 87, 91–3, 95–6, 140, 147, 161, 163, 180, 182, 192, 197, 198, 209, 210, 216–17, 223, 228, 235, 236, 238, 240

community standards, 3, 19

competition, 54, 56, 58, 85, 185–7

concubines, 101, 106, 128

contradiction, role of in norms and practices, 12, 31, 33, 135–7, 146, 171, 173–5, 218, 237–40

conventions, 65, 94, 200

courtship, 16, 30, 40, 41, 164, 169, 171, 175, 182, 183, 186, 187, 192, 193, 194, 195, 196, 197, 199

criminal law, 18, 21, 72, 126, 128, 219, 223, 225, 227, 228

cuckolds, 62–3, 67, 129, 141–3, 160, 185

daughters, 50, 52, 87, 97, 106, 140, 141, 161, 162

Davis, J., 57, 148

democracy, 9, 97, 151, 154, 203, 215, 218–34

Demosthenes, 5, 71, 72, 75, 80, 82, 88, 93, 97, 100, 103, 105, 107, 118, 155, 165, 178, 179, 180, 188, 194, 200, 227, 229, 231

desire, sexual, 135, 137, 139, 171, 172, 188, 189, 191, 195

deviance, 5, 7, 23, 28, 30, 163, 197

discretion, role in social life, 85, 92, 93, 95, 157

divorce, 107, 110, 124, 130

Dover, K., 100, 165, 171, 172, 173, 198, 212

du Boulay, J., 81, 82, 88, 93, 95, 96, 141, 163, 238

enforcement of morals, 1–8, 18, 20, 22, 25, 203, 218–40
Euripides, 88, 129, 134, 137, 138, 143, 145, 167, 169, 239, 240
Evans-Pritchard, 193

family, 14, 39–42, 45, 52, 55–7, 61, 67, 75–8, 83–7, 93–4, 98, 113, 132, 140–1, 145, 150, 155, 174, 177, 178–9, 185, 192, 196, 203, 224–5, 231, 234–5
festivals, 73, 86, 152, 154, 157, 210, 211
Foucault, M., 171–3, 195, 198
friendship, 78–9, 84, 86–9, 90, 93, 96, 156, 167, 197
funerals, 86

gender, social construction of 36, 51, 57, 60, 71, 133, 138–41, 143, 146, 158, 184, 187, 189
Giddens, A., 26, 28, 29, 68, 135, 171
girls, 81, 103, 108, 135, 149, 160, 163, 165–6, 168, 186, 193–4
Godelier, M., 161, 173, 182, 192
Goffman, E., 28, 29, 30, 34, 238
gossip, 49–51, 55, 64–9, 83, 86, 90–1, 93–5, 134, 154, 161, 196–8, 201
Gregor, T., 91, 92, 93, 95

Halperin, D., 172
Handman, E., 93, 163, 238, 239
Herdt, G., 182
homicide, 14, 15, 73, 86, 100–10, 113–14, 117–19, 123, 128, 144
homoeroticism, 81–2, 171, 173–5, 181–7, 190–1, 194–201, 223, 225, 239, 240
honor, 36–7, 39–40, 54–7, 59, 60, 62–4, 66–8, 72–3, 79–83, 85, 92, 95–7, 113, 116, 129, 131–3, 139–44, 146–8, 155, 162, 168, 177, 179, 183–9, 196–7, 201, 224–5, *see also* shame, reputation
house, 42–7, 58, 62, 65–6, 74–6, 79–80, 82–4, 87–9, 94, 112–13, 116, 123, 126, 144, 147–52, 158–9, 161–6, 195, 224–5, 230, 238
hubris, 82, 83, 89, 116, 122, 155, 176–80, 183–5, 208, 221–2, 227
Hyperides, 80, 156, 188

ideology, 4–6, 25, 35, 83–4, 90, 97, 123, 136, 139, 141, 143, 146, 148, 174, 180, 218–20, 228–30, 240
immorality, 219, 220, 225, 227, 230
impiety, 73, 84, 204–17, 227–8, 235
incest, 152, 174, 175, 225–7

inference, in evaluations of conduct, 64–6, 81–2, 92, 94–7, 196–8, 201, 238
initiation, 182, 192
insult, 61, 68, 69, 178, 183
intercourse, sexual, 63, 99–108, 112, 116, 126–8, 175–7, 180–2, 187–9, 191, 194, 196, 198, 200, 221, 224–6, 234, 238
Isaeus, 77, 84, 85, 86, 90, 97, 131, 164, 240
Isocrates, 75, 76, 77, 81, 82, 96, 184, 185, 197, 200, 205, 211, 230, 231, 232

kinship, 87, 106, 166

law, 2–7, 15–25, 54, 79–80, 83–4, 151, 155, 175, 178, 180–2, 191, 208, 219, 224–40
Lefkowitz, M., 146
legitimacy, 19, 100, 102, 103, 107
lies, 34, 64, 95–6, 163, 238, *see also* secrecy, gossip
love, marital, 107, 167–70
Lysias, 78, 85, 86, 87, 89, 93, 101, 105, 106, 107, 108, 110, 114, 115, 118, 119, 120, 132, 134, 143, 148, 160, 164, 179, 200, 209, 211, 227

MacDowell, D., 101, 212
Malinowski, B., 152, 173, 174, 199, 237
marriage, 75, 85, 102, 103, 106–7, 142, 166–9, 185–6, 193–5, 225, 234, 235
masculinity, 140, 168, 185, 189
Mediterranean, anthropology of, 36–69, 135–6, 138–41, 144, 146, 148, 150–2, 154, 159, 166, 169, 184, 189, 196
Mehinaku, 91, 92, 94, 95
men, 43–7, 51, 60–3, 66, 68, 72–4, 79, 80, 97, 113, 127, 129, 130, 134, 140–7, 159–61, 167–72, 177–82, 184–5, 187–96, 200
misogyny, 137–8, 140–6
modesty, 43, 60, 61, 87, 133, 134, 148
mothers, 50, 52, 96
myth, 135, 138–9, 146, 174, 190–1

nature, 144, 171, 187–9, 190–2
Neaera, 107–10
neighborhood, 44, 47–52, 57, 89–90, 154, 156, 161
neighbors, 48–50, 52, 65, 67, 85–90, 93–4, 156, 161
norms, 16–9, 21–3, 27, 29–31, 33, 41, 53, 56–8, 60, 65–6, 68, 91, 94, 103–4, 109, 131–3, 136–7, 139–40, 143, 147, 157, 163, 171–2, 174–5, 180–2, 187, 192, 196–7, 203, 207, 210, 224, 229, 236–40

passive, sexual role, 171–2, 179–80, 184, 186–90, 194, 198, 200–1

Pitt-Rivers, J., 39, 40, 53, 56, 61, 140, 142, 168, 184, 185, 189

Plato, 35, 73, 75, 76, 77, 80, 86, 87, 96, 97, 127, 172, 174, 180, 183, 187, 188, 190, 194, 196, 199, 200, 201, 203, 204, 205, 209, 213, 214, 215, 216, 217, 226, 227, 230, 231, 233, 234, 235, 236, 239, 240

pleasure, 77, 167, 172, 178, 190–1, 197, 201

potency, 61–3, 184

practices, social, 16, 20–32, 41–69, 79–97, 133, 136–9, 146, 149, 161–2, 164, 166, 218, 223, 233–40

prestige, 51, 54, 55, 57, 73, 139, 157

privacy, 35–7, 66, 70, 74, 79, 83–97, 201, 218–19, 225, 232, 235

private, 37–44, 66, 69, 70–86, 90–1, 95, 97, 139, 146, 149, 155, 158, 175, 197, 201, 219–22, 227–40, *see also* public

prostitution, 170, 175, 180–1, 199, 219, 222, 225, 227

public, 15, 29, 37–47, 54, 57–8, 70–83, 91–2, 95, 110, 122–4, 147, 149, 156, 159–60, 163, 175, 184, 186, 196–8, 201, 219–40, *see also* private

public opinion, 46, 53, 55, 58, 59, 60, 69, 73, 97, 155, *see also* reputation, gossip

purity, sexual, 53, 60, 82–3, 140, 147, 150, 184–5, 196

rape, 52, 100, 104–5, 177–9, 185, 222, 230

religion, 21, 98, 103, 110, 124, 137, 152, 154, 156, 203, 205–6, 211–25, 231, 235, *see also* belief

remarriage, 124

reputation, 36, 41–6, 49–57, 59–69, 72–4, 78–81, 83, 86, 90–1, 93–7, 133–4, 139, 141, 143, 150, 155, 160–1, 168, 178, 183–4, 196–8, 200–1, 229, 240, *see also* gossip, honor, lies, secrecy, shame

revenge, 111, 113, 116–17, 124, 129–32, 185

Ruggiero, G., 89, 156, 169

Sarakatsani, 51, 57, 60, 61, 62, 102, 103, 141

seclusion, of women, 136, 147, 149–51, 153–4, 157–9, 168

secrecy, 43, 48, 55, 64, 66, 69, 81, 90, 92–6, 147, 161–4, 201, 238–9, *see also* gossip, lies

seduction, 67, 100, 102, 105, 109, 129, 140, 177–9, 182, 200, 222

semen, 142, 189

separation, of male and female spheres, 141, 147, 149–51, 158, 162, 167

sexuality, 38, 82–3, 89, 135, 137–46, 161, 188–95, 231, 234–5, 237, 239

shame, 36, 54–5, 58, 60–4, 73, 79–85, 90, 97, 133, 140–1, 144, 179, 183–4, 196–7, 201, *see also* honor, reputation

slaves, 73, 153, 156, 176, 186, 233, 234

social control, 17, 34, 36, 42, 49–52, 54–69, 70, 80–2, 86–7, 90–7, 133, 140–6, 155, 160–3, 172, 195–8, 217, 218, 235, 236, 239

social order, 16–18, 23–6, 52, 69, 133, 141, 145, 224

socialization, 25, 32, 160, 226–7, 235

Socrates, 80, 200, 203, 204, 205, 210, 211, 213, 214, 215, 216, 228

solidarity, familial, 56, 61, 76, 86

structure, 22–8

theft, 53, 72, 84, 104, 112, 114, 118–20, 122, 125–6, 128

Thompson, E., 21, 24–5

Thucydides, 64, 79–80, 229

Timarchus, 181, 188, 197, 223

values, 16–17, 28, 79–81, 92, 97, 136–9, 143–4, 146–7, 155, 173, 180, 182, 184, 201, 210, 237, 239–240

violence, 82, 123–4, 224, 227

virginity, 63, 102–3, 140, 164

Vlastos, G., 198

Weber, M., 20, 25

widows, 143, 168

wives, 46, 50, 68, 92, 96, 98, 103–4, 107–8, 127, 129–30, 141–2, 145, 147, 153, 157, 160–1, 164, 166–7

women, 41–7, 50–1, 58, 61–7, 73–5, 82–4, 87, 96, 98, 100, 102, 109, 130–70, 172–80, 184–7, 190–3, 196, 225, 227, 230, 233–4, 239–40

work, 45, 46, 48, 58, 151, 158, 161, 163, 166

Xenophon, 71, 81, 82, 96, 107, 137, 147, 149, 172, 174, 180, 183, 185, 187, 190, 194, 196, 197, 200, 201, 213, 214, 215, 226